Longitudinal Research
in the Study of
Behavior and Development

Longitudinal Research in the Study of Behavior and Development

Edited by

JOHN R. NESSELROADE
PAUL B. BALTES

College of Human Development
The Pennsylvania State University
University Park, Pennsylvania

ACADEMIC PRESS

A Subsidiary of Harcourt Brace Jovanovich, Publishers

New York   London   Toronto   Sydney   San Francisco

ACADEMIC PRESS, INC.
111 Fifth Avenue, New York, New York 10003

United Kingdom Edition published by
ACADEMIC PRESS, INC. (LONDON) LTD.
24/28 Oval Road, London NW1 7DX

Library of congress Cataloging in Publication Data

Main entry under title:

Longitudinal research in the study of behavior and
    development.

    Bibliography: p.
    Includes index.
    1. Psychological research––Longitudinal studies.
2. Developmental psychology––Longitudinal studies.
I. Nesselroade, John R. II. Baltes, Paul B.
BF76.5.L66   155'.07'2   79–23265
ISBN 0–12–515660–X

PRINTED IN THE UNITED STATES OF AMERICA

79 80 81 82   9 8 7 6 5 4 3 2 1

Contents

Chapter 8

Univariate and Multivariate Analysis of Variance of
Time-Structured Data   199
R. DARRELL BOCK

Chapter 9

The Analysis of Categorical Data in Longitudinal Studies of
Behavioral Development   233
J. RICHARD LANDIS AND GARY G. KOCH

Chapter 10

Causal Models in Longitudinal Research: Rationale,
Formulation, and Interpretation   263
DAVID ROGOSA

Chapter 11

Statistical Estimation of Structural Models in
Longitudinal–Developmental Investigations
KARL G. JÖRESKOG

List of Contributors

Numbers in parentheses indicate the pages on which the authors' contributions begin.

PAUL B. BALTES (1, 61), College of Human Development, The Pennsylvania State University, University Park, Pennsylvania 16802.

R. DARRELL BOCK (199), Departments of Behavioral Sciences and Education, The University of Chicago, Chicago, Illinois 60637

ALLAN R. BUSS (41), Department of Psychology, The University of Calgary, Calgary, T2N 1N4, Canada

STEVEN W. CORNELIUS (61), College of Human Development, The Pennsylvania State University, University Park, Pennsylvania 16802

CARL H. FREDERIKSEN (111), Department of Educational Psychology and Sociology, McGill University, Montreal, Quebec H3A 1Y2, Canada

PAUL A. GAMES (179), Department of Educational Psychology, The Pennsylvania State University, University Park, Pennsylvania 16802

KENNETH E. GUIRE (89), Center for Human Growth and Development, University of Michigan, Ann Arbor, Michigan 48104

KARL G. JÖRESKOG (303), Department of Statistics, Uppsala University, Uppsala, Sweden

GARY G. KOCH (233), Department of Biostatistics, School of Public Health, University of North Carolina, Chapel Hill, North Carolina 27514

CHARLES J. KOWALSKI (89), Dental Research Institute and Statistical Research Laboratory, University of Michigan, Ann Arbor, Michigan 48104

J. RICHARD LANDIS (233), Department of Biostatistics, School of Public Health, University of Michigan, Ann Arbor, Michigan 48109

JOHN R. NESSELROADE (1, 61), College of Human Development, The Penn-
    sylvania State University, University Park, Pennsylvania 16802
DAVID ROGOSA (263), Department of Education, The University of Chicago,
    Chicago, Illinois 60637
JOHN A. ROTONDO (111), Department of Psychology, University of Virginia,
    Charlottesville, Virginia 22903
BURTON SINGER (155), Department of Mathematical Statistics, Columbia
    University, New York, New York 10027
SEYMOUR SPILERMAN (155), Department of Sociology, Columbia University,
    New York, New York 10027

Preface

Longitudinal investigation, the repeated measurement of a given phenomenon over time, increasingly has become a focus of scientific activity. We believe longitudinal work to have great appeal because it is a tool for understanding change and process, both key ingredients in any theory about behavior.

The primary purpose of this book is to review selectively the major frontier areas in the advancement of longitudinal design and analysis. Longitudinal methodology has become a domain of expertise in its own right, and for this volume, experts in such areas as design, sampling, and mathematical and statistical modeling have refined their ideas concerning the proper use of longitudinal observations, particularly as they apply to the study of human development in the behavioral sciences. The intent is not to offer a methodological cookbook or an overview of substantive work. Rather, our aim is to stimulate the field by indicating novel developments and design concepts that we believe will help researchers to realize the unique potential of longitudinal data. Although the central theme is developmental-psychological, the contributors (and hence the book) represent such disciplines as psychology, sociology, education, and statistics.

In the introductory chapter we discuss the nature, purposes, and historical basis of longitudinal work, and take up some particular issues and problems not considered by the contributors. Of the five rationales of longitudinal research presented in the introductory chapter (*direct identification of intraindividual change; direct identification of interindividual differences in intraindividual change; analysis of interrelationships in behavioral change;*

analysis of causes [*determinants*] *of intraindividual change;* and *analysis of causes* [*determinants*] *of interindividual differences in intraindividual change*), the ones given the most attention in the succeeding chapters are those concerned with the identification of intraindividual change and interindividual differences in intraindividual change. In many ways, this disproportionate emphasis on description rather than explanation of developmental change reflects the state of the art in the field.

In Chapter 2 Buss initially focuses on the specific definition of the terms intraindividual change, intraindividual differences, and interindividual differences in relation to multivariate, multioccasion research designs. Within this general framework Buss examines two prototypical psychometric concepts—stability and regression toward the mean in relation to the conduct of longitudinal research.

Baltes, Cornelius, and Nesselroade (Chapter 3) further elaborate the distinction between intraindividual change and interindividual differences therein within a general examination of the role of cohort effects in behavioral development. Using Schaie's model as a sample case, they show it is important to be sensitive to the distinction between age changes, age differences, and cohort differences. Strategies for attaining both descriptive and explanatory objectives in cohort-sequential research are examined.

In Chapter 4, Guire and Kowalski provide methods for analyzing longitudinal data pertinent to both intraindividual change and interindividual difference models. Some strengths and weaknesses of the description and identification of intraindividual change and the interindividual differences therein are considered. Univariate and multivariate analysis of variance and polynomial growth curve models are presented for identifying interindividual differences in change.

Frederiksen and Rotondo, in Chapter 5, examine both research design and data analysis issues in the general context of studying change processes with the use of time series models. Their discussion cuts across all five rationales of longitudinal research. Time series models are organized around five dimensions (type of state space; nature of time representation; nature of probability structure; number of stochastic variables; presence or absence of measurement error) each of which provides a basis for either theoretical or practical decision making.

In Chapter 6, Singer and Spilerman focus mainly on intraindividual change. Compared to the models presented by other contributors, theirs emphasize the dynamic formulations that can be made accessible by using, for example, Markov models to represent stage linkages in developmental phenomena. Their approach does not rely on identifying antecedents or causal variables external to the system under study to account for change, but the relevant variables are indexed by some expression of time, such as the subject's age.

Games, in Chapter 7, focuses on the use of nonexperimental (organismic) variables in longitudinal research. He outlines a notational system for experimental design, considers the various roles of organismic variables in longitudinal studies, and systematically presents the use of analysis of covariance models and their application to longitudinal research.

In Chapter 8, Bock concentrates on various extensions of analysis of variance to represent developmental change functions. In addition to discussing the analysis of data pertinent to the study of development, he clarifies the nature of assumptions and implications pertaining to the use of univariate versus multivariate analysis of variance models. MANOVA applications for fitting change data are presented in detail.

Landis and Koch, in Chapter 9, examine how longitudinally gathered categorical data may be analyzed to answer questions about intraindividual change and interindividual differences in intraindividual change, and show how one can simultaneously examine several categorical variables in developmental research.

In Chapter 10, Rogosa focuses on the construction of causal models in longitudinal research, a procedure of considerable value in studying phenomena falling outside the domain of manipulative experimentation. Relationships between structural equation models and path analysis are discussed and the cross-lagged panel correlation approach to testing causal hypotheses is subjected to considerable scrutiny. The latter is seen to be less appropriate than the estimation of structural parameters.

In Chapter 11, Jöreskog examines various change models and the use of structural equations in longitudinal research. He elaborates on the important distinction between structural and measurement models, identification, specification, and estimation, and the use of three general computer programs in working out solutions. Growth-curve fitting and the structural analysis of data from various multiwave panel designs are featured.

One additional observation we want to make concerns how one can make one's way more effectively through the territory bounded by the covers of this book. Since it is not likely that the chapters will be read in sequence, we recommend that the reader begin with the introductory chapter and proceed to the abstracts of the remaining chapters. It is our hope that access to several inviting areas will thus be found. We have also prepared an extensive subject index to provide an alternate route to the volume's content.

ACKNOWLEDGMENTS

We would like to acknowledge a number of sources of support, without which this volume could not have been completed. A contract from the National Institute of Education (NIE-C-74-0127) provided the initial thrust. The ideas, suggestions, and efforts of many of our colleagues and students contributed to making this a more worthwhile enterprise than it would have been otherwise.

In granting the publisher the right to publish this material, The Pennsylvania State University waived its copyright rights.

In addition to those specifically mentioned elsewhere, we wish to thank Rosemary Blieszner, Steven W. Cornelius, Roger Dixon, Marjorie Lachman, Mike Rovine, Manfred Schmitt, Ellen Skinner, Avron Spiro, Catherine Stump, Linda Thompson, and Alison Okada Wollitzer, who, as graduate students and research assistants, were always available for critique, discussion, and collaboration. Ellen Skinner and Gwendolyn Sorell helped with the compiling and checking of references, and Rudolph Kafer was our main assistant in designing and preparing the subject index. Production and expert secretarial assistance was provided at various points by Sally Barber, Diane Bernd, Nellie Boyle, Kathie Hooven, Miriam Landsman, Joy Lose, Patty Senior, Ingrid Tarantelli, and Anna Tower.

Many others, of course, gave us a hand at various times. We cannot list them all, but we would be unforgivably negligent if we failed to recognize, with gratitude, the continued support of our spouses and colleagues, Carolyn Nesselroade and Margret Baltes. They, more than all others, know what it took to bring forth this volume.

Chapter 1

History and Rationale of Longitudinal Research[1]

PAUL B. BALTES
JOHN R. NESSELROADE

ABSTRACT

Within the context of developmental psychology, longitudinal research is defined and reviewed from a historical perspective. Longitudinal research is shown always to include repeated-measurement methodology as the defining attribute, with individuals being the entity under study in developmental psychology. Additional characterizations vary, depending on historical and theoretical contexts. The need for longitudinal research was recognized at least as early as the nineteenth century. Terminology and specification of rationale, however, did not appear until the second or third decade of the twentieth century. The term longitudinal was initially identified in the context of age-based definitions of development. Recent decades, however, have seen an expansion of developmental theory beyond monolithic views to include age-irrelevant and multidirectional conceptions of the nature of development, particularly if a life-span perspective is taken. Such a pluralistic conception of behavioral development implies a more generic definition of longitudinal methodology than is associated with the traditional age-developmental view. Finally, it is important to recognize that the objective of longitudinal methodology is not only the descriptive identification of change. The objective includes explanatory goals also. Only recently has the unique strength of longitudinal research for explanatory efforts been recognized.

In the second section of this chapter, a series of rationales for longitudinal research are outlined. These rationales are developed within the context of developmental psychology. They deal with (1) the direct identification of intraindividual change; (2) the identification of interindividual differences in intraindividual change; (3) the analysis of interrelationships in behavioral change; (4) the analysis of causes (determinants) of intraindividual change; and (5) the analysis of causes (determinants) of interindividual differences in intraindividual change. In a third section, selected issues in longitudinal designs and analysis are briefly reviewed. The need for complex longitudinal designs and control groups is emphasized to help counteract

[1] Writing of this chapter was supported by Grant BNS 76-22943 A02 from the National Science Foundation to the Center for Advanced Study in the Behavioral Sciences, Stanford, Calfiornia.

1

the rather widespread assumption that simple longitudinal studies are invariably sufficient for answering developmental questions. Furthermore, general limitations on aspects of developmental research associated with the study of assigned variables such as age, sex, or cohort are outlined. These limitations place constraints on design purity and mandate the use of and familiarity with alternative quasi-experimental designs. As an example, some of the problems associated with causal analysis involving distal (delayed, mediated) influences and the use of lagged paradigms and causal modeling are discussed.

I. Introduction

A variety of current issues relating to the use of longitudinal methods in developmental research are considered in this volume. The major portion of the book represents a collection of frontier discussions aimed at advancing the field in selected areas.

Though we feel confident that these frontier discussions are presented in sufficient depth and complexity to interest the most seasoned researcher, we also wish to reach readers less familiar with the area of longitudinal research. To do this, the book contains this introductory chapter to provide a brief overview of concepts and issues in longitudinal research as they apply to developmental psychology. In addition to an introductory statement, this chapter is an attempt to integrate and coordinate information by providing a perspective from which to view selected issues raised in subsequent chapters. In this way, the newcomer may be enticed to continue to the remainder of the book. We hope that through careful consideration of new developments in this area, readers may become familiar with the demanding and potentially rewarding task of developmental–longitudinal work.

II. Scope of Longitudinal Method

The study of phenomena in their time-related constancy and change is the aim of longitudinal methodology. Longitudinal methodology has been defined in a variety of ways by the disciplines and subspecialties that have used it. The spectrum of longitudinal methods ranges, for instance, from the panel or wave designs used in sociology (e.g., Campbell, 1978; Featherman, in press; Wall & Williams, 1970), to age-related repeated-measurement methodology in developmental psychology (e.g., Baltes, Reese, & Nesselroade, 1977; Wohlwill, 1973), to various forms of single-subject designs in operant psychology (e.g., Hersen & Barlow, 1976; Kratochwill, 1978; Shontz, 1976), and time-series arrangements in econometrics and political science (L'Insee, 1978). In each of these instances, the time-ordered study of processes is a focus of concern. The definition of process is difficult, and it varies by discipline and emphasis. One common denominator, however, is that process research centers on how and why a phenomenon exists in time in relationship to aspects of both constancy and change.

It is not our purpose in the present volume to provide exhaustive coverage of longitudinal methodology as it has evolved in practically all empirical sciences. Our aim is more limited in scope. The primary aim is to present, review, and evaluate longitudinal methodology in the study of the development of behavior. Careful attention, however, is paid to potential contributions from other change-oriented disciplines if they are judged to have fertility for application in developmental psychology or related specialties concerned with behavior and development.

As conceptualized by psychologists (e.g., Baltes, Reese, & Nesselroade, 1977; Lerner, 1976; Wohlwill, 1973), the study of behavioral development can be characterized by at least two features. First, the developmental study of behavior requires a concern with behavioral change and various subforms thereof. Developmental change in the framework of ontogeny is one such subform. In research design terminology, this concern can be translated into the study of *intraindividual change and interindividual patterns (differences as well as commonalities) of intraindividual change*. The use of the terms *intra-* and *interindividual* emphasizes that the primary unit of analysis for the psychologist is the individual. Buss (Chapter 2 of this volume) provides a detailed analysis of this approach while focusing on taxonomic considerations.

Second, the developmental study of behavior is oriented toward both *description* and *explanation* as necessary ingredients for knowledge about a given phenomenon. Thus, concern goes beyond examination of the questions what and when to considerations of how and why. The desired methodology, therefore, is one that involves both description (identification) and explanation (causal analysis) of development. In developmental psychology, the descriptive task is aimed at identifying the nature (form, sequence, patterning) of behavioral development; the explanatory task involves searching for underlying mechanisms and determining causes of development.

Given this general approach, longitudinal methodology is discussed in the present volume as it relates to both the descriptive and the explanatory study of ontogenetic change in behavior. It will become quite clear, however, that restricting longitudinal methodology to ontogenetic (developmental) psychology is not always useful and that it is occasionally desirable to branch out and consider cross-disciplinary perspectives and linkages. For example, there is a body of developmental research showing sizable interactions between ontogenetic development and historical change (e.g., Baltes, Cornelius, & Nesselroade, Chapter 3 of this volume; Bell & Hertz, 1976; Elder, 1975; Riegel, 1976a; Riegel & Meacham, 1976; Riley, 1976; Schaie, 1965; Schaie & Strother, 1968). This research suggests that longitudinal research should often be conducted with multiple cohorts rather than the traditional single-cohort designs. This example also makes clear that the unit or entity of analysis for the behavioral scientist is not always the individual. It may sometimes be groups of individuals, particularly when collaborative efforts with social scientists are instituted. As a consequence, as nonpsychologists evaluate the present book, they need to pay attention to the question of which entities are properly identified for their study, and to consider how such variations in the unit of analysis can affect the definition and application of longitudinal methodology.

III. Definition of Longitudinal Method

Any definition of the longitudinal method is cast in the framework of a particular disciplinary and theoretical orientation. Hindley (1972) expresses such a view in the following manner: "There is no hard and fast definition of what constitutes a longitudinal study [p. 23]" (see also NICHD Colloquium, 1965; Wall & Williams, 1970). In fact, because of the diversity of usages, Zazzo (1967) suggests that *longitudinal* is a blanket term and describes not a method but a wide variety of methods.

In our opinion there is, however, at least one definitional criterion. The one sine qua non of longitudinal research is that *the entity under investigation is observed repeatedly as it exists and evolves over time.* Thus, variation of time and repeated observation of a given entity are always part of longitudinal research. Which particular attributes of the entity are investigated is an aspect of problem definition in general; it is certainly not a decision peculiar to longitudinal investigation. How this minimum requirement is translated into concrete application varies by substantive area and conceptual framework. In the following sections, definitional aspects of the longitudinal method are discussed, in both historical and theoretical contexts.

A. Age-Developmental Definition

One of the main historical directions that researchers of behavioral development have taken (Baltes *et al.,* 1977; Birren, 1959; Kessen, 1960; Reinert, 1976, 1979; Thomae, 1959a; Wohlwill, 1973) has been to view the drama of developmental processes closely against the backdrop of chronological age. This view implies (in some cases assumes) that many ontogenetic processes are intrinsically linked to the age continuum. It should be recognized, however, that this particular approach to the study of development is only one of several views that could be adopted to identify and explain developmental phenomena (Baltes, 1979; Baltes & Willis, 1977, 1979a; Elder, 1975; Wohlwill, 1973). In fact, depending upon one's theoretical orientation (e.g., Baer, 1970 versus Sutton-Smith, 1970), a strategy focused on chronological age can be judged either useful, irrelevant, or, at worst, misleading.

Largely because of the historical preponderance of an age-oriented approach in the formative stages of developmental psychology (Reinert, 1979), the longitudinal method has often been defined in an age-developmental framework. An earlier definition proposed by Baltes (1968b) reflects an age-oriented approach: In a longitudinal study, "a sample of individuals is observed several times on the same dependent variable at different age levels, and therefore, by definition, at different times of measurement [pp. 146–147]." The object of this definition, which is similar to the one proposed by Kodlin and Thompson (1958), is to indicate that the longitudinal method is aimed at a direct identification of within-entity (individual) change, which in turn is conceived of as being age-related. Such a strategy follows the paradigm $B = f(A)$, where B refers to behavior, A to chronological age, and f to a functional relation between both (Kessen, 1960).

In this $B = f(A)$ paradigm, chronological age appears to be treated as an independent variable. It is evident to most researchers (e.g., Baer, 1970; Baltes & Goulet, 1971; Wohlwill, 1973), however, that the status of chronological age (as an assigned, subject variable) disqualifies it from being a full-fledged experimental–independent variable. Age functions "are inevitably in transition to being explained by other variables without recourse to the use of the term, age [Birren, 1959, p. 8]." This is one reason that Wohlwill (1973) has emphasized that it is not necessary to view chronological age as an independent variable in age-developmental approaches. His proposition is to view age as a dimension along which change is plotted. In that case, the identification and explanation of age functions (indexing change) becomes the critical objective.

Historically, it is also important to recognize that an age-developmental definition of the longitudinal method has been contrasted in the literature with its "shortcut" counterpart, the cross-sectional method, since the early twentieth century. For instance, Baltes (1968b) defined the cross-sectional method in the following manner: "*Samples of different ages are observed on the same dependent variable once at the same point in time* [pp. 146–147]." There are many assumptions to be met for the cross-sectional method to produce valid information about within-individual development. In Chapter 3, by Baltes *et al.* (see also Wohlwill, 1973) the relative merits of both methods will be discussed in detail; thus, no evaluative comparison is offered at this point.

B. Age-Irrelevant and Process-Oriented Definitions

Although chronological age is often an interesting marker, index, or search variable for the study of behavioral development, it is not the only design parameter that can be used for defining longitudinal research. Not all developmental change is equivalent to age change. In fact, historical precursors (e.g., Hollingworth, 1927; Stern, 1910) did not use chronological age as a primary criterion in defining longitudinal methodology but focused on such concepts as epochs or stages. Similarly, proponents of a "strong" developmental orientation argue that the main goal of longitudinal analysis is to "discard chronological age as a definition of a population and to replace it with the quest for developmental sequences and their interrelationships [Wall & Williams, 1970, p. 15]." In the literature on the longitudinal method, Zazzo (1967) has been a forceful proponent of such a view.

In many conceptions of development, then, chronological age is considered only indirectly relevant, or even irrelevant, in the process of identifying and explaining behavioral ontogeny. The concentration is upon alternative conceptions dealing with time-related trajectories of behavioral change such as developmental sequences, developmental progressions, epochs, stages, or general processes of acquisition, maintenance, and extinction. According to this theoretical position, relationships between such trajectories of behavioral change and chronological age are either coincidental or preliminary. They are observed because an extended time is needed for any process to occur, and therefore a spurious correlation between chronological age and behavioral change is established. Examples of developmental conceptions that do not assign a primary theoretical role to chronological age are Gagné's (1968) model of cumulative learning, Piaget's (1970) theory of cognitive development, and operant developmental psychology (Baer, 1970).

The approach that assigns little or no relevance to chronological age leads to a different generic definition of longitudinal methodology than that associated with an age-developmental position. For example, it is less important to relate the repeated observation to certain levels of age than to other time-ordered markers or events. From a historical perspective, however, it should be recognized that the juxtaposition of age-oriented and age-irrelevant conceptions of development is not an exclusive dichotomy. This juxtaposition is presented for didactic purposes in the present context, because it illustrates that any concrete definition of the longitudinal methods is implemented within a particular theoretical scheme. In fact, most research and theory in developmental psychology and human development attends to both age-related and age-irrelevant (or age-accidental) determinants and their interactive relationships in the production of behavioral development (see also Baltes, 1979).

C. Longitudinal Method versus Longitudinal (Developmental) Design Orientation

It follows from the preceding discussion that there is no single concrete definition of the longitudinal method. Depending on how development is conceptualized, different operational definitions ensue. Though there is a minimum definitional criterion (repeated observation of an entity), it is a

given theoretical and substantive context that suggests a particular reali-
zation of the different forms of implementing the longitudinal perspective.

Therefore, although the term *longitudinal method* will continue to be
used, it is important to recognize that this term actually refers to what one
might call a longitudinal–developmental design orientation rather than to a
specific method. The longitudinal–developmental orientation is aimed at the
descriptive and explanatory study of constancy and change in behavior.
Thus, in the context of developmental psychology, a working definition of
the longitudinal–developmental orientation becomes largely synonymous
with the goal of the field as a whole. The following working definition is
offered for the field of developmental psychology in relation to the purpose
and content of this book:

*Longitudinal methodology involves repeated time-ordered observation
of an individual or individuals with the goal of identifying processes and
causes of intraindividual change and of interindividual patterns of intraindividual change in behavioral development.*

As mentioned before and further discussed by Buss in Chapter 2, intraindividual change refers to within-entity change (e.g. within-individual
change). Interindividual differences of patterns refer to between-entity comparisons. This definition of longitudinal methodology permits the inclusion
of age-developmental definitions of the longitudinal methods as one special
case. It also states that longitudinal methodology is not necessarily descriptive. On the contrary, longitudinal methodology can contain almost any
ingredient of descriptive and interventive–experimental design.

The working definition of longitudinal methodology suggested above does
not specify the span of the time dimension. The span of time, of course,
varies considerably according to the subject matter considered. For example, the term *longitudinal* is usually not applied in developmental psychology to short-time intervals such as a day or a week. Hindley (1972), for
example, suggested that a repeated-measurement study qualifies as longitudinal in developmental psychology only if it involves the study of an
ontogenetic process that typically extends over months and years. The only
logic justifying such restrictions stems from assumptions of the "latent"
theory of the phenomenon under investigation—in this case, development.
In principle, from a strict design perspective, any repeated observation of
the same entity qualifies as being longitudinal. In fact, investigation of some
developmental phenomena (e.g., critical periods) may require longitudinal
research involving relatively short intervals between observations.

IV. A Brief History of the Longitudinal Method

A comprehensive history of longitudinal research, as both a method and
a data base, is unavailable. Yet, to appreciate more fully its value, it is

helpful to review at least some of the historical events that resulted in our current conceptions (and misconceptions) of the longitudinal method and longitudinal methodology.

A. Field of Developmental Psychology

Longitudinal studies abound in the literature of the social, biological, and medical sciences.[2] The formative period of developmental psychology is often dated in the late nineteenth century. Following the classic precursor of Tiedemann (1787), a series of "longitudinal" biographies of infants and children (e.g., Darwin, 1877; Preyer, 1882, Taine, 1876) is usually quoted as evidence for identifying that era as the time of origin. European historical reviews (Groffmann, 1970, Hofstätter, 1938; Höhn, 1959; especially Reinert, 1976, 1979), however, have been successful in enriching this picture and delineating a more complex set of historical trends.

Of particular significance in this reassessment of the history of developmental psychology is the emergence of information indicating that the origins of developmental psychology involved a much greater interest in life-span views of human development and associated methodological issues than had been recognized before. Two significant life-span-oriented publications—one by J. N. Tetens (1777) and the other by F. A. Carus (1808)—deserve particular credit. As is carefully documented by Reinert (1976, 1979; see also Baltes, 1979), both Tetens and Carus were successful in anticipating much of the generic conceptual framework associated with the field of human developmental psychology.

B. Emergence of Issues in Methodology

A review of the history of the study of development and behavior reveals much concern with and insight into methodological issues (Baltes, 1979). Because of the strong focus on age-developmental work, many of these methodological issues were identified by comparing longitudinal with cross-

---

[2] For informative historical writing on longitudinal growth studies in child development, an article by Scammon (1927) and a monograph on physical growth by Baldwin (1921; see also Dearborn & Rothney, 1941) are recommended. In Scammon's article, a longitudinal study on height conducted by Montbeillard on his son from 1759 until 1777 is identified as a historical marker. This study was published in French by Buffon in 1799. Good historical summaries of major twentieth-century longitudinal studies in the behavioral sciences, largely from the Anglo-American literature, are contained in Kagan (1964) and Wall and Williams (1970). For information on early European longitudinal research, the handbook on developmental psychology edited by Thomae (1959a) is a good beginning source. A recent historical chapter on life-span developmental psychology by Reinert (1979) is also recommended for a review of eighteenth- and nineteenth-century beginnings of longitudinal work in psychology.

sectional designs (although such terminology was not used) or by elucidating some of the weaknesses inherent in simple cross-sectional studies.

Consider, for example, the domain of external validity of age-developmental work. As early as 1741, Süssmilch made some incisive statements about problems of generalizability in cross-sectional data collected at one point in time. He wrote: "One needs a series of good and average years, if one is interested in obtaining something reliable in terms of age relationships [p. 226]" (translation by authors). As will be shown later, it was not until the 1960s that this recognition of the need for repeated cross sections or cross-sectional sequences was generally heeded in psychological and sociological research on the development of behavior.

Similarly, by 1835 Quetelet had already discussed at great length methodological pitfalls when studying development across the life-span. He presented a large array of cross-sectional developmental data on demographic (birth, fecundity, mortality), physical growth (stature, weight, height, strength, swiftness, respiration), and psychological variables (crime, morality, intellectual qualities). Data were presented in many cases for the entire life-span. In discussing the interpretation of his empirical findings, Quetelet (1842) painstakingly enumerated a host of possible design issues. For instance, he pointed out that any observed age differences and variations therein can be a function of a multitude of influences. He also identified the notion of critical periods (pp. 31, 57) in the life-span, pointed to the effect of period-specific historical events such as wars and epidemics (p. 33), elaborated at length on the possible impact of social change (civilization) on the nature of age development and the need for multiple-period census data (pp. 43, 49, 97–100), outlined some salient issues in measurement validity and equivalence (pp. 72–74), and drew attention to selection (p. 59) and selective survival effects (pp. 62–63). Selective survival effects may be the best concrete illustration of Quetelet's awareness of design problems. He discussed selective survival effects in connection with the establishment of physical height changes in individuals during adulthood (40–90 years of age). Finding negative age differences in height, he stated: "It may be asked if the diminution of stature towards the end of life is not rather apparent than real, and if it be not owing to the circumstance that longevity is generally shorter for individuals of great stature [Quetelet, 1842, p. 63]."

The theoretical contributions by Carus (1808) and Tetens (1777), as well as the more empirical–methodological work by Süssmilch (1741) and Quetelet (1842), are highlighted here because they are historical markers for the study of development and behavior, both conceptually and methodologically. Much of what has been systematized in current research design on age-developmental work was identified with remarkable insight and precision quite some time ago. In many ways, it is surprising that it has taken until the second part of the twentieth century for some of the core methodological issues related to the study of development to become generally crystallized and articulated for the practicing researcher.

C. Evolution of Terminology

1. Overview

The precise historical origin of the term *longitudinal method* in developmental psychology is unknown. However, the term was introduced most likely as a contrast to its strategic counterpart, the *cross-sectional method.* Thus, the crystallization of the term *longitudinal* occurred in the context of age-developmental research, which was a dominant approach to the study of ontogeny in the early stages of the field. This fact limited the initial definition of the term *longitudinal.* Actual longitudinal research, however, was conducted in the late nineteenth century and labeled with terms such as *follow-up* or *individualizing studies*.

The earliest direct references to the terms *longitudinal* or *cross-sectional* (not to the procedural identification of different strategies, as Quetelet had done) known to us are found in the early twentieth century. However, it was not until the late 1920s that the terms were employed in the same manner now used by developmental psychologists. It is important to note that the choice of the term *longitudinal* was not greeted with unanimous enthusiasm. For example, Dearborn and Rothney (1941) regretted the then recent introduction of the term to denote "the repeated measurements of the same children at stated intervals in contrast to 'cross-sectional' studies of different groups of children [p. 59]." Dearborn and Rothney's own preference would have been the word *vertical.*

We tend to agree that *longitudinal* and *cross-sectional* are not necessarily the best terms for characterizing two disparate lines of activity. Possible confusion arises because the words are tied to an age-developmental framework and neither one specifies the entity or the dimension along which a longitudinal or a cross section is taken. Thus, *cross section* is often used to indicate either or all of the following: sampling from different age groups at one point in time, sampling more than one behavior, and averaging across individuals. Because of such ambiguities (and others), the terms are not ideal. However, their widespread use is not likely to be halted by the introduction of new and more precise terminology.

2. Historical Notes

Presented here are a few examples of historical interest that indicate the evolution of terminology. Camerer (1910; see also Baldwin, 1921), who studied physical growth in Germany, described explicitly "generalizing" (*generalisierende*) and "individualizing" (*individualisierende*) methods of studying age relationships. The operations underlying these two methods are identical to age-oriented definitions of cross-sectional and longitudinal methods.

The first explicit use of the terms *longitudinal (Längsschnitt)* and *cross-*

sectional (Querschnitt) is ascribed by Groffmann (1970) to William Stern (1910, p. 177). Stern's use of these terms, however, only roughly approximates what later became their standard age-referenced definitions in developmental psychology. Specifically, Stern identified a chronological longitude (*Längsschnitt*) approach and a synchronistic cross-section (*Querschnitt*) approach for studying development. In Stern's explanation of these terms, it is evident that *longitudinal* refers to follow-up (longitudinal) work, as is true for current usage of the term. However, Stern used the term *cross section* to identify a methodological approach with two distinct aspects: first, to refer to a method oriented to one point in time (equivalent to the current use of cross-sectional method); second, to signify the measurement of several distinct behaviors. It is clear, therefore, that Stern did not have a single conception of cross-sectional study; that is, involving a developmental (age) comparison conducted at one point in time.

Whatever the precise historical origin, the terms *cross-sectional* and *longitudinal* had acquired their currently predominant definition by the late 1920s. Whereas Baldwin (1921), for example, in a classic book on physical growth in children, continued to use Camerer's terms, *individualizing* versus *generalizing,* to identify longitudinal and cross-sectional research, a few years later, both Hollingworth (1927, pp. 34–35) and Anderson (1931, p. 17), in the first American review of research methods in child psychology, used "cross-sectional" and "longitudinal" methodology. Hollingworth (1927) credited Müller-Lyer (1921, pp. 62–64) with giving precursor definitions when he used the terms *cross-sectional* and *longitudinal methods.*[3]

Because of the historical significance, it is worthwhile to cite some of the original sources. Hollingworth (1927), for example, applied Müller-Lyer's (1921) proposals to the study of developmental psychology using the terms *longitudinal* and *cross-sectional* in the following manner: "Thus in developmental psychology we might take the longitudinal approach . . . tracing out the growth . . . moving through the course of human life for each topic studied. This would have the advantage of observing the continuity inherently characteristic of development, and of contributing a distinct sense of movement and process [p. 35]." Contrasting the longitudinal method with the cross-sectional method, Hollingworth continues: "Instead . . . it seems wise, for the purpose of our general survey, to adopt the horizontal or cross-sectional method. We shall attempt to mark off certain convenient developmental stages or epochs, and to get as clear a picture in each of these of the progress of the most important and interesting characteristics, and to discern their interrelations [p. 35]."

These definitions by Hollingworth resemble Stern's (1910) earlier suggestions. Whereas longitudinal is defined as follow-up of the same behav-

---

[3] Of conceptual interest is that Müller-Lyer (1921) used social institutions rather than individuals as entities of analysis. This fact illustrates historically the important role of the unit of analysis (entity) for the definition and analysis of longitudinal research.

ioral class in the same observational units, the term *cross section* involves again two implicit dimensions: static observations and multiple behavioral categories. Thus, the key distinction between repeated observations and independent observations had not yet been made unequivocally.

Anderson's (1931) later definition, in Murchison's first handbook on child psychology, is the first known to us that bears unequivocal resemblance to current use. Anderson makes reference (without citation) to earlier texts on child psychology and offers the following definitions of the cross-sectional and longitudinal methods: "Briefly, the distinction between them may be made in terms of whether norms are secured by the study of different groups of subjects at different stages of development (cross section) or by the study of one and the same group at different stages (longitudinal) [p. 17]."

To conclude these historical observations on the evolution of terminology in developmental psychology, we note that many of the key methodological issues related to the longitudinal-versus-cross-sectional study of development and behavior were identified as early as the nineteenth century, though in a preliminary form. Furthermore, discussions of specific deliberations on research methodology requisite for the study of development, such as the distinction between cross-sectional and longitudinal methodology, were offered in the early twentieth century, although the discussion did not use the terms in ways identical to current use. Thus, the exact date for the crystallization of the term *longitudinal method* in its current usage is not clear. It is documented, however, that the terms were used as early as 1910 by W. Stern and, in their current formulation, as early as 1931 by John E. Anderson.

By the late 1930s, it appears that a consensus was reached among developmental psychologists to use the terms *longitudinal* and *cross-sectional* in their age-based definition. A corollary of this historical observation is that actual longitudinal work conducted before the 1930s was not likely to be called longitudinal. The preferred terminology before that time period included such words as *repeated observation, individual growth study, individualizing method, or follow-up study.* Readers interested in further tracing this historical development may want to begin their search with a careful study of Baldwin (1914, 1921). Baldwin's work on physical growth contains an extensive annotated bibliography of many earlier studies conducted both in Europe and in the United States. Baldwin also distinguished explicitly between cross-sectional versus longitudinal research, although the terms he used, of course, were not those. His terminology, instead, centered on Camerer's terms, *individualizing* and *generalizing* (averaging) methods.

A final note to this review of terminology development concerns the importance of context. The evolution of a term has, of course, its own historical context involving the theory in which the term is embedded. It is apparent that the terms *longitudinal* and *cross-sectional* changed meaning as the field developed as a whole. Much of the developmental work in the

early part of the twentieth century was tied to age-developmental conceptions. Thus, it is not surprising that age-developmental definitions of the
longitudinal method became widely accepted. Because many researchers
currently embrace a conception of development that is based less on age,
it is likely that the terminology will undergo further modification. In our
view, a focus on direct assessment of change via repeated-measurement
design is likely to be the only criterion exhibiting invariance for the definition of longitudinal methodology.

V. On the Relationship between Developmental Theory and Research

Before we discuss specific rationales for longitudinal methodology in later
sections of this chapter, some further observations on the relationship between developmental theory and design are offered. One conclusion drawn
from the literature is that there should be convergence between theory and
methodology in the study of behavioral development. Distinct theoretical
conceptions of development require distinct methodologies and vice versa
if the outcome of research is expected to advance the field in a concerted
manner and if communication among researchers with distinct orientations
is to be possible. The nature of longitudinal methodology is defined to a
large extent by the nature of developmental theory.

The issue of theory–methodology match has received much attention in
the developmental literature in recent years (e.g., Datan & Reese, 1977;
Kuhn, 1974; Overton & Reese, 1973; Reese & Overton, 1970). Similarly,
understanding the rationale for longitudinal methodology is helped if attention is given to the basic foundation of a developmental orientation in the
study of behavior. The following observations related to this issue draw
heavily from our previous writings and those of our colleagues in both
psychology (Baltes, 1979; Baltes, Cornelius, & Nesselroade, 1978; Baltes
et al., 1977; Labouvie, 1976) and sociology (e.g., Bengtson & Cutler, 1976;
Elder, 1975, 1979; Riley, 1976).

A. Strong versus Weak Conceptions of Development

Much of the earlier writing on the longitudinal method has appeared in
the field of child development, where the dominant conception of development has been one of linearity and unidirectional sequentiality (Baltes,
1979; Baltes & Willis, 1979a; Labouvie-Vief & Chandler, 1978). This conception was responsible for the strong concern with an age-developmental
definition of the longitudinal method. It also poses fewer requirements on
the design of longitudinal research than do conceptions that encompass

alternative and often more complex forms of change. This becomes very evident when one contrasts several models of change and their requirements for alternative strategies in time-series analysis (e.g., Frederiksen & Rotondo, Chapter 5 of this volume; Glass, Willson, & Gottman, 1972).

What is the current situation in developmental psychology regarding the nature of change? The forms of change, which are defined as developmental, cannot be specified in an absolute manner. The answer depends on meta-models of behavior and development and the properties that a given class of behavior suggests as useful organizing principles (Baer, 1970; Reese & Overton, 1970; Sutton-Smith, 1970). Historically, a continuum (strong–weak) has evolved that is helpful in organizing distinct conceptions of developmental change. The continuum reflects the number and type of properties that researchers use to classify which forms of behavioral change deserve to be labeled *developmental* change.

At one end of the continuum there are conceptions that require the presence of many properties for change to be classified as development; these are so-called *strong* conceptions of development. In the developmental psychological literature, organismic models of development (Reese & Overton, 1970), such as Piaget's conceptions of cognitive development or traditional models of biological growth (Harris, 1957b), are usually identified as examples of strong conceptions of development. Organismic models of development suggest that behavioral change may be characterized as developmental change only if it exhibits all or most of the following features: universality, fixed sequentiality, irreversibility, qualitativeness, structuralism, and orientation toward an end-state. The organismic model of development, according to some of its proponents (e.g., Overton, 1973, 1976), requires also the presence of several additional features when it comes to proper explanation of developmental change, such as principles of formal and final (teleological) causation. Researchers such as Sutton-Smith (1970), Wohlwill (1973), and McCall (1977) are representatives of a strong conception of development, although they express less strong conceptions than Overton's position.

The other end of the continuum is identified by the so-called *weak* conceptions of development. Developmental scholars working in the weak-conception tradition require fewer properties of behavioral change for it to be labeled developmental change. Operant developmental psychologists (e.g., Baer, 1970) are often identified with this position, as are researchers of the social learning paradigm (Bandura, 1971). An extreme, though infrequently found, position of the weak type would be to label any reliably identified behavior change as development. Most developmental researchers would reject such an extreme position and insist that at least some of the properties associated with the strong conception (in terms of either description or explanation) are necessary for a developmental orientation to be a fruitful one.

Our own attitude is to accept a pluralistic taxonomy of developmental behavior-change processes that incorporates a variety of conceptions along the strong–weak continuum (Baltes et al., 1977). However, there are two minimal criteria for labeling change as developmental. First, one needs a theory-based or empirically derived behavior-change process on the descriptive level. Second, a developmental orientation requires the use of historical time-ordered paradigms of influences for the explanation of developmental change. Beyond these two properties, it is important to formulate and acknowledge variations in the nature of developmental change rather than to take an absolute position (see also Loevinger, 1966b). Recent review chapters (Baltes, 1979; Baltes, Reese, & Lipsitt, 1980) illustrate variations in developmental analysis in greater detail.

B. Descriptive Features of Developmental Change

The search for pluralistic conceptions of development is largely the result of two trends. First, the emergence of a behavioristic learning approach to the study of development, as exemplified by such writers as Bandura (1969, 1977) and Baer (1970, 1973, 1976), has emphasized the importance of environmental contingencies and the kind of behavior-change processes that are not necessarily programmed by chronological age. Second, the advent of a life-span orientation to the study of development (Baltes, 1979; Baltes et al., 1980; Neugarten, 1969; Thomae, 1979) has produced data on developmental-change functions that depart in marked ways from the form suggested by biological-growth models of development. Unidirectionality and irreversibility, for example, do not appear to be generally good descriptors of life-span developmental changes, and chronological age is not always an important search or organizing variable when investigating behavioral changes in a life-span framework. The following observations, however, are not restricted to life-span considerations. In the infancy literature, for example, Clarke and Clarke (1976), as well as Kagan (1976), have expressed similar positions by deemphasizing the dominant themes of continuity and irreversibility in infant development.

Figure 1.1 (after Baltes, 1979; Baltes & Willis, 1977) represents a summary of some considerations that a life-span approach has stressed in the study of development. While acknowledging strong conceptions of development as one viable alternative, a life-span approach emphasizes the existence of additional forms of developmental change. Note first that Figure 1.1 deals with descriptive aspects of life-span change. A later figure will summarize counterpart information representing explanatory approaches.

Figure 1.1 has two parts, labeled (a) and (b). Together they present a view of development that is more complex and pluralistic than that represented by simple cumulative and unidirectional change principles as contained in traditional concepts of biological growth. The upper portion of

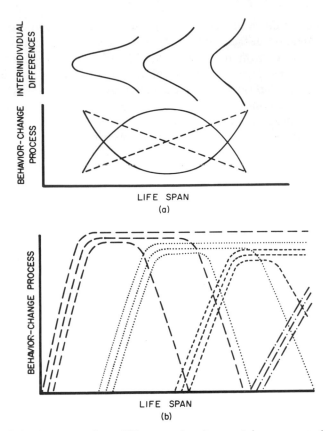

FIGURE 1.1. **Selective examples of life-span developmental processes. (a) Age-correlated increases in interindividual variability in the upper part and multidimensionality and multidirectionality in the lower part are illustrated. (b) Notions of life-course grading and discontinuity are summarized. It illustrates that developmental functions (behavior-change processes) differ in terms of onset, duration, and termination when charted in the framework of the life course (see also Baltes, 1979; Baltes, Cornelius, & Nesselroade, Chapter 3, this volume).**

Figure 1.1a depicts the notion that between-person differences, or *interindividual variability* in behavior, by and large increase with age as the life course unfolds. Individuals become less and less similar to one another. The lower portion of Figure 1.1a further suggests that life-span changes can be rather diverse in form when different classes of behavior are compared. Unitary, linear, and monotonic developmental changes are possible. In addition, however, *multidirectionality* and *multidimensionality* of behavior-change processes are also frequent outcomes. Multidirectionality means that behavior-change processes can exhibit nonlinear and nonmonotonic trajectories; multidimensionality suggests that the form of change patterns can differ markedly for distinct behaviors, even for behaviors identified as part of the same general construct (e.g., intelligence). The characteristics of multidimensionality and multidirectionality are not compatible with a model of developmental change positing features such as linearity, end-state orientation, universality, or irreversibility, as sine qua nons. The nature of developmental change is more diversified in outcome than a "strong" model of development would suggest.

Figure 1.1b provides further information on the complexity of life-span development. In addition to characteristics of multidimensionality and multidirectionality, it shows that not all behavior-change processes necessarily extend through the entire life-span. Thus, behavior-change processes such as those associated with age gradation or developmental tasks can differ in terms of onset, duration, and termination when charted in the framework of the life course. Novel behavior-change processes with little connection (or continuity) to earlier developments can emerge at many points in the life-span, including old age. An example of such discontinuous change concepts is Neugarten's (1969; based on Havighurst's developmental task model) concept of life-course grading; another one is the role that nonnormative life events (Baltes, 1979; Hultsch & Plemons, 1979) might play in regulating the onset and duration of certain behavior-change processes. The particular prototypical functions depicted in Figure 1.1b are not exhaustive but only illustrative.

It is not the goal of this book to present a review of empirical research supporting a pluralistic conception of developmental change summarized herein or to express a preference for one or the other. Which form or forms of developmental change are useful will depend upon the class of behavior under investigation. For the reader interested in concrete research examples, publications by Lerner and Ryff (1978) on attachment, Elder (1979) and Nesselroade and Baltes (1974) on the interaction between history and personality development, and Schaie (1979), Labouvie-Vief (1977), and Baltes and Willis (1979a, 1979b) on life-span intelligence contain summaries of empirical work relevant to the question of which form of developmental change is appropriate in a specific research area. Clarke and Clarke's (1976) recent critical review of evidence on the effect of early experience on adulthood is another example pointing to much more diversity and discontinuity in development, even in early childhood, than has been traditionally assumed.

On a conceptual level, articles by Bell and Hertz (1976), Weisz (1978), Riegel (1976a), and Gergen (1977) include discussions of variations in development due to cultural and historical differences (see also Baltes *et al.,* Chapter 3 of this volume). However, no clear conclusion results from an examination of this work except that there currently appears to be less agreement about what constitutes development than at any other time in the history of developmental psychology. In any case, the other side of that same coin is a growing recognition (see also Loevinger, 1966a) that the term *development* covers processes that differ markedly in their formal aspects.

C. Explanation of Development

A second issue pertinent to the discussion of the rationale of longitudinal research is the task of explanation, or causal analysis, of development. If there is variation in definitions of development on the descriptive level, there is at least equal diversity in proposed explanations for it. Some of these variations result, of course, from differences in descriptive identification of what constitutes developmental change. Other variations result from paradigmatic differences in explanatory postures (e.g., Overton, 1976; Overton & Reese, 1973; Wohlwill, 1973). There are marked differences in the sources (agents) of influence on and mechanisms of development that are judged to be important in a given research area by a given researcher.

The purpose of this chapter is not to provide a comprehensive overview of explanatory theoretical positions in developmental psychology. The more modest goal is to illustrate the kind of interaction between explanatory theory and longitudinal methodology one can expect. In line with our own research interests, the example chosen to illustrate the influences of multiple causal sources on development is derived from recent discussions in life-span developmental psychology. In principle, however, similar perspectives apply to most areas in developmental psychology. The following presentation is based primarily on earlier writings by us and our colleagues (e.g., Baltes *et al.*, Chapter 3; Baltes & Willis, 1979b). However, work by Neugarten, Riley, Elder, and their co-workers is equally relevant (e.g., Elder, 1979; Neugarten & Datan, 1973; Neugarten & Hagestad, 1976; Riley, 1976, 1979).

Figure 1.2 summarizes the kind of multiple interactive causal system that appears to be necessary to account for the complexity of life-span development illustrated in Figure 1.1. It should be recognized that there is convergence between the two figures. Figure 1.1 dealt with descriptive identification of developmental change and focused on the complexity of the change process (multidirectionality, multidimensionality, large interindividual differences, discontinuity, etc.). Figure 1.2 presents counterpart information on the complexity of explanatory principles. Multicausal systems of influences on development are postulated to be likely because multicausality is a reasonable prerequisite for diversity in developmental outcomes on the descriptive level.

Specifically, Figure 1.2 suggests three sets of influences on development: *normative age-graded* influences, *normative history-graded* influences, and *nonnormative* influences. These three classes of influences interact and result in the kind of developmental-change processes depicted earlier in Figure 1.1. The definition of these three sets of influences is not absolute and totally exclusive because it potentially varies by research emphasis. Moreover, it should be recognized that it is the developing organism that functions as the carrier, as both a recipient and a processer of the outcomes

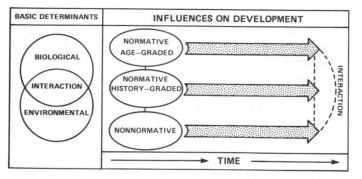

FIGURE 1.2. **Illustration of three major influence systems on development: normative age-graded, normative history-graded, and nonnormative (see also Baltes, 1979; Baltes, Cornelius, & Nesselroade, Chapter 3).**

produced by these influences. For the present purpose, suffice it to define the three sets of influences in the following manner.

Normative age-graded influences refer to biological and environmental determinants that exhibit a high correlation with chronological age across a wide variety of subpopulations and historical epochs. They are normative if their occurrence and sequencing are highly similar for different individuals. Examples of such influences include variables and processes related to biological maturation and socialization processes associated with the acquisition of age-graded competencies and roles. Such age-graded influences on development are similar to what Wohlwill (1973) has defined and accepted as truly developmental factors and processes.

Normative history-graded influences consist of biological and environmental events and event patterns that are associated with biosocial (cultural) change. A concrete example is cohort effects (Baltes *et al.,* Chapter 3; Riley, 1976; Schaie, 1979). In the present scheme, these history-graded influences are assumed to include only those effects of historical change that are fairly general. *Normative* is used here to denote those history-graded events that affect most of the members of a given set of cohorts in similar ways, although the effects do not need to be identical for different age cohorts living at the same point in time. Elder's (1974, 1979) work on the effect of economic depression on child and family development is another example of what we consider to be normative history-graded influences.

Nonnormative influences involve biological and environmental determinants of development that do not occur for everyone or that, if they do occur, do not do so in easily discernible invariant sequences or constellations. Events or event patterns related to periods of temporary unemployment, some family-life events (divorce, death of a significant other), institutionalization, or health trauma (serious illnesses) are examples. In all these instances, it is assumed that such events are potentially powerful influences on development. Their impact on development depends on the timing, constellation, and sequence of their occurrence (if they occur at all), and these characteristics can be rather diverse. Hultsch and Plemons (1979) have recently reviewed relevant theory and research under the heading of life events.

At present, very little is known about how the three sets of influences interact, whether there are unique mechanisms or processes mediating their outcomes, and how individuals, as developing organisms, process and act on information derived from these sources of influence. In addition, relatively little is known about possible profiles of combinations of influences throughout the life-span, especially if we conceptualize organisms as "active" organisms. For instance, if one were to plot the frequency and timing of influences across the life-span, prototypical profiles of the relative importance of age-graded, history-graded, and nonnormative influences might result. In fact, Baltes et al. (1980) have speculated that: (1) normative age-graded influences are dominant in the control of development and developmental differences in early and late life; (2) normative history-graded influences operate most strongly in adolescence and early adulthood; and (3) nonnormative influences gain in importance in adulthood and old age. Such a differential life profile of these three sources of influence would help to explain why much work in child development has been focused on age-graded influences and, conversely, why adult-developmental work has contributed much to the identification of history-graded and nonnormative influences.

D. Implications for Longitudinal Method

The previous sections were aimed at illustrating variations of developmental theory and analysis. It was shown that the nature of developmental theories or models varies considerably, as do the forms of behavior-change processes characterizing development. On a descriptive level, behavior-change processes differ, for example, in directionality, degree of interindividual homogeneity, time of onset and termination, and extent and number of sequential units or steps. Other features can be added such as the relationship among distinct behaviors (e.g., perception and cognition) during development. On an explanatory level, there are differences due to distinct metamodels of development that regulate how change phenomena are represented and which forms of explanation are judged to be appropriate. Besides the issue of metamodels, there are differences in the nature and locus of influences on development that researchers judge to be salient, and in how influences are conceptualized and combined to determine the course of development. The role of the developing organism in receiving and acting on these influences is an equally important source of differences in explanatory postures.

Why is it important to be aware of these differences in the description and explanation of developmental phenomena? In our view, this knowledge is crucial because the nature of theory helps to define what constitutes longitudinal methodology. Unless one is aware of the fact that developmental theory is currently in a state of conceptual expansion and pluralism, one runs the risk of miscommunication and inappropriate rigidity in definition.

An age-developmental definition of longitudinal methodology, for example, is appropriate only if the correlated substantive interest and developmental theory deals with relatively normative age-graded determinants and processes. In addition, whether longitudinal methodology necessarily involves extended time periods depends on which theoretical conception of a developmental process and substantive question is at stake. Furthermore, how many repeated observations are necessary for a useful longitudinal design is a function of the developmental process under consideration (e.g., see Chapters 5, 6, and 8 for more extensive discussion). If the behavior-change process is judged or expected to be linear, fewer observations are necessary than if it is judged to involve nonlinear, multidirectional change functions or states that are sensitive to particular input (e.g., critical periods). To give one final illustration, whether the longitudinal method is primarily descriptive or explanatory is related to the relative emphasis given to each type of question. Furthermore, in explanatory research, the frequency and sequence of observations and whether the time is homogeneous or heterogeneous across individuals depend on a given researcher's causal perspective. The operation of nonnormative life events, for example, suggests the use of subject-specific time schedules because the onset, duration, and sequence of significant nonnormative life events can show large interindividual differences. It is important as we move toward discussing the rationale of the longitudinal method to be aware of marked differences in how and why longitudinal research is judged to be salient in a given area of interest. The theoretical nature of the process under investigation modifies the form of longitudinal design and analysis deemed appropriate.

VI. Objectives of Longitudinal Methodology

In the following sections, an effort is made to specify, in design terminology and within the framework of the developmental study of behavior, the rationales for longitudinal research. Concrete examples are used to illustrate the rationales. Again, our primary emphasis is on showing the importance of linking theory with methodology and on demonstrating variations in longitudinal methodology associated with distinct conceptions of developmental change—in both its descriptive and its causal–analytic aspects.

A. Summary of Rationales

In developmental psychology, the rationale for longitudinal research has evolved piecemeal in conjunction with ongoing research programs rather than as the product of a deliberate, well-articulated conceptual framework. Although most researchers extol the design virtues of longitudinal methodology (though often emphasizing at the same time its pitfalls), it is not easy to extract from the historical literature a systematic, precise statement on the rationale for longitudinal research.

For the reader interested in publications representing historical milestones, those by Dearborn and Rothney (1941), Hindley (1972), Kodlin and Thompson (1958), Thomae (1959b), Zazzo (1967), and two committee reports (NICHD, 1965; Wall & Williams, 1970) are particularly helpful. In addition, a number of discussions of longitudinal method have been written in conjunction with presentations of ongoing longitudinal studies (e.g., Bayley, 1965; Jones, 1958). These articles, though not primarily focused on rationale, contain valuable perspectives and many insightful and important practical suggestions for the design and conduct of longitudinal work. In addition to these historically and conceptually important papers, our discussion draws heavily from our own previous writings (e.g., Baltes, 1968b; Baltes et al., 1977) and those of our close colleagues (e.g., Labouvie, 1976; Schaie, 1965, 1977). Wohlwill's (1973) book, written primarily from the viewpoint of an organismic developmentalist, is another important source of ideas and information.

The rationale of longitudinal research not only is intrinsic to the methods but also follows from the objectives of a given research program. This is the reason that, with the exception of the common denominator of repeated observation of an entity, there are rather diverse specifications of what constitutes a longitudinal study. Furthermore, in reviewing the rationales for the longitudinal method given here, the reader should note that they are statements of principle with regard to design and analysis.

The degree to which the desired research goal can be accomplished is a function of design implementation. For example, from a traditional ANOVA perspective it is seldom sufficient to conduct a longitudinal study without including additional control arrangements for such contaminants as testing and selective drop-out effects. Moreover, in the typical research study only some of the rationales outlined are directly pertinent. In addition, the objectives and rationale(s) can change during the conduct of a longitudinal research program. Often, such alterations in objectives cannot be accomplished without substantial costs in design validity. In fact, the overt and covert changes in rationale(s) of a given longitudinal project may impose a host of design and interpretation costs rarely anticipated when those decisions are made.

Five main rationales for longitudinal research in the study of behavioral development are identified. Three of these rationales relate to description of development, and the remaining two concern its explanation.[4]

1. Direct Identification of Intraindividual Change

The first general rationale of the longitudinal method pertains primarily to the identification of intraindividual change (or constancy as a special case). The rationale stipulates that the only direct method for identifying intraindividual change is to observe the same entity (e.g., individual) repeatedly. Change, constancy, and process extend through time; thus, static observations do not provide the data base necessary for development of representations of the phenomena of interest.

As Buss points out (Chapter 2), the term *intraindividual change* can involve two major components. First, it can include change in the level or frequency (rate) of the same class of behaviors across time within an individual. Second, intraindividual change can refer to interbehavior change, such as a change from aggression to anxiety, or from one class of cognition to another, as in Piagetian theory involving sequential–hierarchical levels of cognitive operations.

The first rationale of the longitudinal method identifies an entity-specific analysis of change as *the* foundation of developmental research. The only fully appropriate departure from the use of direct repeated measurement of the same entity would involve having available a sample of perfectly identical entities (e.g., individuals) who had been exposed to identical conditions across developmental time and drawing an independent sample of these entities at each of the several measurement occasions. The assumption of perfect equivalency of the entities and of their developmental histories would permit the charting of intraindividual change or constancy. Such a logically possible arrangement, however, does not appear to be available in human developmental psychology.

Thus, when it comes to the identification of intraindividual change, there are only imperfect approximations to the use of longitudinal design. For example, in age-developmental work, a frequent but rarely defensible approximation (or shortcut) is the use of cross-sectional methodology. The validity of a cross-sectional method hinges on the assumption of between-age equivalency of subjects. In other words, for cross-sectional research to produce valid identification of intraindividual change, the following condi-

---

[4] Throughout, we emphasize change rather than constancy. The study of constancy requires longitudinal methodology as well. We use the term *change* because we treat constancy as a special case of change, (i.e., no change). Alternative conceptions are possible.

tions must hold: (1) Different-aged subjects must come from the same parent population at birth; (2) it must be possible to match subjects across age levels; and (3) the different-aged subjects must have experienced identical life histories. In human developmental psychology, these conditions are never strictly met. As a consequence, cross-sectional methodology is not a direct approach to the study of intraindividual change. There are limiting conditions, however, where cross-sectional methodology can be used to examine *average* (but not entity-specific) intraindividual change functions.

2. Direct Identification of Interindividual Differences (Similarity) in Intraindividual Change

The second rationale of longitudinal research requires the comparison of change processes for the different entities (e.g., individuals) under developmental investigation. The central question concerns the degree of homogeneity displayed by units as they develop; that is, the degree of similarity in the course of intraindividual change shown by different individuals.

Unless longitudinal observations are available for all entities, differences or similarities in intraindividual change cannot be examined. This rationale, then, asserts that the assessment of differences or similarities in change between entities (individuals) has as a prerequisite the valid quantification of longitudinal change at the individual (entity) level of analysis. After obtaining intraindividual change data, it is possible to examine interindividual differences therein by comparing growth functions or change trajectories (rate, form, timing) among individuals.

The conditions under which group-level (or multiple-entity) data adequately represent the individual units has been discussed frequently in the literature. Usually this question is raised in the absence of single-entity longitudinal data. In principle, however, from an inductive standpoint this question should be reversed. Only if single-entity longitudinal data are available can precise statements about differences or similarities between entities (individuals) be made. Without such entity-specific data, or good estimates thereof, the appropriateness of generalizing averages, for example, cannot be assessed. Nor can the reasons for lack of generality be identified.

In the history of longitudinal research, single-subject researchers (e.g., Shontz, 1976; Sidman, 1960) have been, perhaps, the most explicit concerning both the need for unit-specific data and the dangers involved in generalizing from group data to individual entities. The more behavior-change processes differ between entities (in level, onset, rate, etc.), the more critical it is to base statements about differences in change on a careful analysis at the single-entity level. Awareness of the existence of diversity, multidirectionality, and large interindividual differences in developmental outcomes as illustrated in Figure 1.1 suggests why it is imperative to build and evaluate group data on the basis of single-entity longitudinal observations rather than the reverse.[5]

3. Analysis of Interrelationships in Behavioral Change

The third rationale for longitudinal research is related to the identification of interrelationships among classes of behavior during development. The goal is to represent constancy and change of the entity under investigation in more than one attribute; that is, from a multivariate perspective. The rationale of assessing interrelationships among behavioral variables as they change, again, has as a prerequisite the precise analysis of each of the behaviors involved over time at the individual (entity) level of representation.

The examination of interrelationships in change among distinct behavioral classes is particularly important if a structural, holistic approach to development is taken. In the study of human development, structuralism (e.g., Gardner, 1972: Riegel & Rosenwald, 1975) has been a prominent concern. This is also true for counterpart historical trends in developmental biology where concepts such as systems and differentiation are key components of growth (e.g., Lund, 1978; Urban, 1978) and always involve relationships among several elements or attributes. Even aside from the metatheoretical posture suggested by structuralism or other systems views of growth, however, it is useful to examine the relative degree of similarity in intraindividual change processes in different behavioral domains as part of an inductive process. Historically, for example, it has been of interest to study the conjoint development of physical growth and cognition, or the conjoint development of the neurophysiological system and of sensory or perceptual behavior in infants. Only longitudinal research, involving repeated observation of multiple behaviors, can provide a direct data base for elaborating such multivariate (structural) representations of the interrelationships in changes among behaviors. In principle, static (cross-sectional) observations do not contain direct evidence on interrelationships in behavioral change. Multivariate observations obtained in cross-sectional design formats provide structural information on static patterns of interindividual differences but not on changes in such patterns.

Often a conjoint focus on multiple behaviors is seen as the foundation for causal analysis of change, provided such multiple behaviors are ordered in time. Sequential and systematic changes in distinct behaviors (e.g., from academic achievement to occupational success) are identified as initial ev-

[5] The perhaps classical example in the developmental literature illustrating differences in group versus individual trends is that on physical growth spurts in adolescence (Dearborn & Rothney, 1941). Since the timing of onset and subsequent rate of physical growth vary considerably between individuals, group-based (whether cross-sectional or longitudinal) age curves do not represent a useful approach to the identification of change at the individual level.

idence of precursor behaviors or of causal linkages among behaviors. This perspective leads to the next rationale for longitudinal research.

4. Analysis of Causes (Determinants) of Intraindividual Change

Intraindividual development extends over time. Explanation of a phenomenon that extends over time requires establishing linkages between outcome variables (consequents) and determining factors, which also extend over time and which, as antecedents, precede the phenomenon. Thus, a time-ordered approach to the descriptive study of change needs to be supplemented by a time-ordered study of explanatory determinants.

The need to supplement descriptive study with an examination of causal determinants is pertinent for constancy as well as change. Constancy of a phenomenon extends in time and, in a determinist framework, at least one determining condition (or its consequents) must be in temporal (antecedent) proximity with the constant phenomenon. Both constancy and change, then, require the operation of time-ordered antecedents (Baltes *et al.*, 1977), whether these antecedents are internal or external to the entity considered. In principle, this call for time-ordered antecedent factors is simply a reflection of the notion that temporal antecedence is a necessary but not sufficient condition for making causal inferences.

A longitudinal approach to identifying antecedent factors becomes more important the more, in a specific theoretical conception about the determinants of a behavior-change process, these antecedents are viewed as (1) processes of influence and (2) involving not only proximal but also distal (delayed) action. For example, a conceptualization of learning as a process of acquisition associated with experience requires a longitudinal approach, as the learning "treatments" extend over time and interact with behavior. Moreover, if antecedent factors result in protracted consequences (such as is postulated in various theories of generalization, in the case of sleeper effects, or in the case of extended processes such as lung cancer), a historical–longitudinal approach to causal analysis, also called a causal lag approach, is necessary (Baltes *et al.*, 1977; NICHD, 1965).

The longitudinal analysis of determining factors becomes increasingly complex the more it is appropriate to depart from simple, cumulative unidirectional, and unifactorial paradigms. Thus, extensive longitudinal analysis of determinants is necessary, if, for example, the process of causation involves multidirectionality, discontinuity, or multivariate patterning of influences. Figure 1.2 illustrated such situations in developmental psychology. Multivariate causality poses additional problems requiring special forms of longitudinal analysis. Multiple causes do not necessarily simply augment one another in directionality and timing but can operate in synergism or even in a counteracting manner (see also Heise, 1975). Recognition of such pluralistic models of causality makes it clear why decisions on the nature of a given longitudinal design need to be made with consideration given to the theory of and knowledge about the developmental phenomenon under investigation.

5. Analyses of Causes (Determinants) of Interindividual Differences in Intraindividual Change

A fifth rationale for longitudinal analysis follows from the possibility that causes for intraindividual change differ for entities (individuals). In principle, this rationale parallels the second rationale presented. In order to understand the cause of interindividual differences, a precise account of the causal situation for each comparison entity must be available. The need to recognize differential patterns of causation applies both to the extreme situation, where identical intraindividual-change processes are observed for two individuals, and to the more usual situation; that is, the causal analysis of interindividual differences in change.

Although a given intraindividual behavior-change process, such as an age-correlated increase in a personality trait (e.g., independence), may show identical patterns on the level of observation for several individuals, the change process is not necessarily the result of identical patterning of determinants. In order to detect interindividual differences in the nature of causal linkages, it is necessary to have information about antecedent–consequent relationships for all individuals considered. That, in turn, requires longitudinal analysis for each individual. Furthermore, with respect to interindividual differences in intraindividual change, it is reasonable to assume that interindividual differences in change result because of differences in causal influences. Such differences in causal influences can involve variations in the intensity, timing, or patterning of the same basic causal factors, or they may result from variations in the actual substance or content of influences.

Reference again to Figure 1.2 may be helpful in illustrating a position of differential causality in development. This figure suggested that ontogenetic changes and differences in a given behavior, such as intellectual performance with age in adulthood, can result from a variety of influences. Some of these influences are fairly normative, such as age-graded and history-graded ones. Other influences show large interindividual variation; they are nonnormative. Examples of nonnormative influences are episodes of psychopathology, physical illness, other forms of bodily injury (accidents), migration, or the death of a significant other. The detection of individual patterns of such diverse influences requires the use of intraindividually based longitudinal data. Sensitivity to differential causality becomes increasingly important the more that influences are assumed to be discontinuous and nonnormative (in their occurrence, sequence, and combination) as the development of the individual proceeds over the life-span.

B. Cohort-sequential Strategies and Longitudinal
Analysis: A Separate Rationale?

In the last 25 years, there has been considerable interest in the development of so-called sequential strategies involving successions of longitudinal and cross-sectional studies, each covering different birth cohorts (Baltes, 1968b; Bell, 1953; Kodlin & Thompson, 1958; Schaie, 1965; Welford, 1961). In Chapter 3 of this volume, the development of sequential strategies is summarized in relation to descriptive and explanatory research in life-span development.

The central theme of cohort-sequential longitudinal research is that there are two streams of change involved in the study of development—individual change and evolutionary–historical change. From this viewpoint, the question arises whether single-cohort longitudinal studies can provide adequate information on the nature of intraindividual change and interindividual differences in such change for both descriptive and explanatory purposes. It is argued, for instance, that birth cohorts (individuals born at different points in time in a given cultural unit) may differ markedly in the form of their ontogenetic change and in the causes (or patterns of causes) of their life-span development (Gergen, 1977). Accordingly, expansion of the method of single-cohort longitudinal studies to include the sequential–longitudinal study of multiple cohorts was proposed. The terms *cross-sectional sequences* and *longitudinal sequences* (both variations of cohort sequences) were introduced to describe these expanded longitudinal designs.

For the present discussion, the central question is whether sequential designs are based on a separate rationale for the longitudinal method or whether they can be properly justified with existing rationales. In our view, the most expedient solution treats the rationale for cohort-sequential methodology as a special case of two previously mentioned rationales: (1) the identification of interindividual differences in intraindividual change; and (2) the causal analysis of interindividual differences in intraindividual change. If one answers the question in this manner, cohort-sequential methodology simply requires the specification of two components of interindividual differences—within-cohort differences and between-cohort differences, on both the descriptive and explanatory level (see Chapter 3). In other words, cohort differences are a special case of interindividual differences.

The parsimonious solution of treating the rationale for cohort-sequential methodology as a particular combination of two aforementioned ones, however, has an alternative that may be desirable in some circumstances. The reason is that between-cohort comparisons, in contrast to within-cohort interindividual differences, involve distinct segments of historical time. Eighty years of one cohort's life-span development, for example, might occur from 1800 to 1880; another cohort's 80-year development might occur between 1900 and 1980. Because of differences in historical time when cohorts develop, some researchers prefer to consider the operation of distinct processes and influences on development for different cohorts (e.g., Elder, 1975; Gergen, 1977). This could be because it is assumed that conditions in different historical times (compared with different conditions within a given historical period for different members of the same cohort) may be sufficiently dissimilar to warrant separate conceptualizations. Given such an assumption, the cohort variable attains a logical status that requires, at least in part, separate analysis from that performed for the lifetime of individual cohorts. This issue is discussed further by Baltes *et al.* (Chapter 3), who distinguish among four different ways of treating the cohort variable in developmental psychology (as error, temporary disturbance, dimension of quantitative generalization, or theoretical–process variable). Incidentally, the likelihood of treating the cohort variable as an indicator of a unique process is higher if one adopts a unit of analysis other than the individual, as is often the case in sociology (e.g., Riley, 1976; Ryder, 1965).

In summary, our general preference is to subsume the rationale for cohort-sequential longitudinal methodology under the general ones stated for longitudinal research; that is, to conceptualize cohort differences as a special case of interindividual differences in intraindividual change. From this perspective single-cohort longitudinal studies can provide comprehensive information on the nature and causes of intraindividual and differential development, but cohort-sequential longitudinal work is necessary whenever generalization beyond one cohort is attempted. However, a view of the cohort variable as a dimension of quantitative generalization is not the only option. If one attempts to create a body of knowledge about the form and causes of development that recognizes structural–qualitative differences in the nature of behavioral development, cohort-sequential and cohort-comparative research becomes critical for theory construction and must be a part of the research scenario. In other words, cohort-sequential longitudinal research is considered important in certain areas of developmental inquiry, but it is not viewed as a sine qua non of any longitudinal study. As is the case for longitudinal research in general, cohort-sequential designs occupy different roles depending upon one's research objectives and theoretical position.

VII. Perspectives on Selected Issues in Longitudinal Design and Analysis

In recent years, a number of books (e.g., Achenbach, 1978; Baltes *et al.*, 1977; Bentler, Lettieri, & Austin, 1976; Hoppe, Schmid-Schönbein, & Seiler, 1977; Petermann, 1978; Wohlwill, 1973) and chapters (e.g., Bentler, 1978; Labouvie, 1976; Rudinger, 1972, 1975; Schaie, 1977) have appeared that provide general summaries of longitudinal design and analysis in the context of developmental research. Therefore, it would be unnecessarily redundant to attempt a similar enterprise. However, selected issues, which have produced much confusion and require additional clarification, are addressed. Some familiarity with the reviews cited above and similar ones is an essential background for the following observation.

The perspectives offered usually involve more than one of the aforementioned rationales for longitudinal research because longitudinal work is typically oriented toward a cluster of questions. Also, because of the desirable convergence between substantive theory and longitudinal methodology and because of marked differences in the nature of developmental models, there is probably never an absolutely best design for the longitudinal study. Each longitudinal study can be oriented only toward achieving a good balance between a variety of intentions, such as between internal and external validity and between substantive theory and procedural adequacy. In other words, each longitudinal study is an approximation to an implicit or explicit ideal from the viewpoint of both substantive theory and experimental design.

A. Need for Control and Complex
Longitudinal Design

Repeated-measurement methodology is necessary for certain research questions. However, despite this sine qua non feature, conducting a longitudinal study per se is not enough. Historically, there has been a general tendency to assign to longitudinal research a status of immediate superiority simply because repeated measurement was seen as the critical prerequisite for assessing change. However, it has become apparent over the years that repeated measurement, though essential, creates problems involving a variety of sources of error that are not encountered with cross-sectional design formats.

As elaborated in several sources (e.g., Baltes, 1968b; Campbell & Stanley, 1963; Hoppe *et al.,* 1977; Labouvie, 1976; Petermann, 1978; Rudinger, 1975; Schaie, 1977), the basic design of a simple longitudinal study involves a pretest–posttest arrangement with a minimum of two occasions of measurement. In a nonexperimental situation, some specific interval of time would be the intervening "treatment" variable, such as a difference in chronological age. This simple longitudinal scheme is included in what Campbell and Stanley (1963) labeled *pre-experimental designs.* Such designs are afflicted with many confounds and potential sources of error that severely jeopardize both internal and external validity. A simple inspection of Campbell and Stanley's (1963) design framework (see also Baltes, 1968; Campbell, 1978; Cook & Campbell, 1975) shows the extent of the problem, involving such sources of error as sampling, history, maturation, testing, instrumentation, statistical regression, experimental mortality, and so forth.

An examination of longitudinal designs by the Campbell and Stanley criteria (Baltes *et al.*, 1977; Schaie, 1977) makes it readily apparent that longitudinal research needs to move from the status of preexperimental designs as much as possible in the direction of quasi-experimental and experimental designs. This may be accomplished by (1) including control groups; (2) including treatment groups via random assignment involving variation beyond that associated with time; and (3) extending the number of occasions making up the sequence of longitudinal observations. Campbell's (1969) discussion of the use of reforms as experiments illustrates well such an approach. Likewise, Labouvie (1978) has discussed the use of experimental subgroups in cohort-sequential methodology as a vehicle by which outcome patterns associated with cohort and age effects can be further explicated.

If longitudinal research is not properly designed and the resulting data not carefully analyzed, it has the disturbing characteristic of appearing to be a design panacea but a Pandora's box for the interpreter. In fact, once longitudinal research on behavioral development has been conducted, the difficulties of interpretation occasionally become substantially more apparent than its curative properties. This appears to be true particularly for early longitudinal research in developmental psychology. For example, consider the situation where subjects were repeatedly observed for tens of times over a 30-year period without proper controls for retest effects. It is important, then, to recognize that simple longitudinal designs per se are not the royal road to understanding development.

B. Design Limitations in Developmental Research

As one attempts to elevate simple longitudinal research to the level of quasi-experimental and experimental designs, it becomes apparent that this is not always desirable or possible in the study of development. There are two primary reasons for this. First, as persuasively shown by Wohlwill (1973; see also Hoppe *et al.*, 1977), some aspects of development are not fully manipulable, partly because of theoretical fiat. The classical illustration is the role of chronological age, which is an assigned rather than an experimental variable. Thus, if chronological age is an important component of developmental theory or a defining characteristic of developmental-change functions (Wohlwill, 1973), full experimentation is not possible. Because of the preponderance of such situations in developmental research, and in order to emphasize the notion of approximation, the strategy of simulation of developmental processes (Baltes & Goulet, 1971; Baltes *et al.*, 1977) was introduced.

Second, another limitation in available developmental-research designs is due to the fact that some of the sources of error listed in the design framework of Campbell and Stanley (1963) are important theoretical or process variables in developmental research. For example, history and maturation are both sources of error in classical nondevelopmental-research design. For developmentalists, however, at least some processes associated with history (e.g., cohort) and maturation become important ingredients for a theory of development and thereby attain the status of treatment rather than error variables. Another example is that of mortality (see also Baltes *et al.*, 1977). Experimental or biological mortality is a source of error in nondevelopmental research. But in the study of life-span development, changes in the composition of a given birth cohort associated with increasing age and reflecting differences in length of life provide important information about life-span development.

Not all variables of developmental models are nonexperimental (i.e., not under full control of the experimenter in terms of variability, manipulability, and replicability), as is true for chronological age or cohort. However, there are enough such variables that some researchers have suggested that certain features of longitudinal research in developmental psychology suffer from the limitations usually associated with the establishment of causality in the historical sciences. This is the reason that quasi-experimental designs and causal-modeling procedures (Bentler, 1978; Duncan, 1975; Heise, 1975; Jöreskog, Chapter 11 of this volume; Rogosa, Chapter 10 of this volume) are becoming more prominent in the design repertoire of developmental researchers. Causal modeling, for example, uses nonexperimental data to examine alternative conceptions of causal relationships suggested by specific theoretical statements. Thus, although causal-modeling procedures do not verify unequivocally the existence of a causal chain, they permit the rejection of inadequate theories about causal relationships in light of nonexperimental data.

Because of the nature of developmental theory, a judicious combination of experimental, quasi-experimental, and correlational approaches becomes an important part of longitudinal research. Attainment of Cronbach's (1957, 1975) 2-decades-old quest for integration of correlational and experimental strategies remains a necessity for much longitudinal work in developmental psychology. The insistence on classical experimentation as the only strategy for generating knowledge about development is too restrictive. This demand would produce a situation in which some researchers—for example, those with an organismic world view (Hoppe *et al.*, 1977; Overton & Reese, 1973; Wohlwill, 1973)—would be unable to study what they consider the important factors and processes in development. For purists, then, the convergence between theory and methodology has both strengths and weaknesses. Although one might be committed fundamentally to classical experimentation as the ideal base for statements about explanatory–causal relationships, strong commitment to the substance of a theory can require departures from a strict methodological ideal.

It follows from the foregoing observations that the design of longitudinal research in developmental psychology and human development requires much insight into conflicts between theoretical positions and methodological ideals. The foregoing observations also suggest the need for considerable sensitivity to the use of unique constellations provided by nature or naturalistic human behavior, especially if it is combined with careful a posteriori controls. In addition to Campbell's (1969) ground-breaking contribution, another excellent example of such an approach is a study by Scarr and Weinberg (1978). They contrasted the longitudinal development of samples of children from adoptive and biologically related families and their respective similarity to their biological mother and adoptive parents on measures of intelligence. Using a variety of a posteriori controls, it was possible for Scarr and Weinberg to arrive at fairly precise causal inferences about the relative contribution of genetic and environmental variance to intellectual performance.

C. Measurement of Change

The examination of intraindividual change and interindividual differences therein must be realized at some point in actual data manipulations. Proposals concerning how change should be represented and measured (or whether it should at all) exist in generous number—some being the products of considerable thought and sophisticated development and others basically ad hoc. Nevertheless, the need for ways to represent change, real or apparent, remains very much a part of the thinking of the social and behavioral scientists and is especially pertinent to developmental research of a longitudinal type.

The change-measurement literature in the social and behavioral sciences dates from the 1930s and earlier. A sampling of insightful papers includes those by Bereiter (1963), Bohrnstedt (1969), Cattell (1963), Coleman (1968), Cronbach and Furby (1970), Fiske and Rice (1955), Lord (1963), Petermann (1978), Wheaton, Muthén, Alwin, and Summers (1977a), and Woodrow (1932). The problems so often cited within the context of measuring change seem to arise from uncertainty concerning how change should be defined and from the use of measurement and scaling procedures whose properties prompt little faith in the validity of any derived measures, such as change scores. Even the use of psychological-measurement instruments that possess "good" psychometric properties is viewed with considerable suspicion when they are used to construct change scores. Probably the strongest criticism of change measurement was leveled by Cronbach and Furby (1970). They argued against the construction of change scores and suggested instead the use of indirect methods for inferring changes. Their recommendations included, for example, the posttreatment comparison of experimental and control groups who initially scored at the same level on the dependent variable.

Hummel-Rossi and Weinberg (1975) pointed out that interest in and concern for measuring change remain pertinent because of the insistence on program assessment or evaluation that often involves simple pre- and post-test comparisons for a treatment group. Likewise, even descriptive longitudinal studies often involve so few occasions of measurement that more or less direct change measures seem to be the appropriate vehicle for conveying aspects of development.

The perspective taken here is that the study of developmental change generally ought to encompass more than two occasions of measurement, and descriptive accounts should involve more than just the differences between two scores. This perspective is exemplified, for instance, in discussions of the characteristics of the regression-toward-the-mean phenomenon, especially in developmental research (Nesselroade, Stigler, & Baltes, 1979; Buss, Chapter 2; Rogosa, Chapter 10). Moreover, multiple occasions of measurement in longitudinal research permit the specification of change functions as illustrated in the various chapters to follow.

From an instrumentation viewpoint, much is gained if sufficient attention is given to the use of measurement instruments and procedures that are appropriate for measuring attributes that are expected to change. As substantive theory develops, concepts of change dimensions need to be given explicit consideration, and the application of somewhat different principles to the development of measurement instruments becomes important (Nesselroade, 1977). Some attributes are inherently more changeable in an intraindividual sense, and this recognition should be explicitly considered in the development and refinement of measurement instruments.

In relation to the rationales presented for longitudinal research, there are good reasons for adopting a multivariate orientation to the study of substantive change, as noted earlier. Multivariate approaches permit one to focus directly on a more abstract type of change concept—changes in patterns of interrelationships among variables. This not only allows one to identify qualitative changes within a network of empirical relationships, but also permits one to search for stable patterns of intervariable relationships. Such stable patterns provide one basis for justifying quantitative comparisons (e.g., comparison of means) in the study of change (Baltes & Nesselroade, 1970).

D. Causal Analysis of Development

As already alluded to, the design characteristics of longitudinal research in the study of development have parallels in certain features of causal analysis. The explanatory–causal study of development is not a freewheeling enterprise. It is guided by developmental theory and by the limitations associated with some nonexperimental variables such as chronological age. The specificity of such guidelines varies depending on the class of behavior and developmental theory or model involved. For example, the world view of organismic models has particularly strong implications for the appropriate type of causal analysis (Overton & Reese, 1973; Reese & Overton, 1970; Wohlwill, 1973).

1. Concurrent (Proximal) versus Historical (Distal) Explanation

One perspective on the explanatory–causal analysis of development involves recognition of the distinction between concurrent explanation and historical or developmental explanation (see Baltes *et al.*, 1977, for further discussion). This is a heuristic distinction based on the length of the interval between the occurrence of a causal agent and its consequent outcome.

Most empirical researchers agree that the process of establishing causal relationships involves sequential approximation. That is, the process involves a number of observations and analyses pointing with some consistency to a putatively causal relationship between at least two variables. The first key condition is that two variables evidence reliable *covariation*. One variable is designated as the causal agent (broadly defined) and the other as the outcome. The second key condition for making causal inferences is *temporal order*. The assumption is that a cause must occur prior to the outcome and requires some minimum length of time for its operation to be effective. In strict models of causation, there is a third key condition that the causal agent be capable of *controlled manipulation*. This feature is seen to be necessary in order to ensure that both the causal agent and the outcome are not jointly dependent upon some third determinant(s). There is much discussion and disagreement about this third requirement.

Explanation is concurrent if the causal agent is *proximal* to the outcome. It is historical if it occurs in *distal* antecedence. There are two reasons that historical forms of explanation are important in developmental research. First, on the descriptive level, development involves a series of behavior-change events, such as the movement from sensorimotor to preoperational to concrete-operational to formal-operational intelligence in Piaget's theory of cognitive development. It is usually assumed that any event in such a behavior-change sequence is defined not only by the immediately preceding event but also by earlier ones in the sequence. Concern with developmental prediction even at the level of description of development involves multiple-occasion data and therefore historical representation.

Second, a historical perspective becomes most important if one goes beyond representation of a unidimensional behavior-change sequence to the identification of causes external to the target behavior. The argument is that not all causal determinants of development are proximal, but that some are located in earlier segments of the event sequence resulting in the outcome of developmental change. Thus, both concurrent (proximal) and historical (distal) causal agents influence the outcome at any point in the behavior-change process. In fact, it is occasionally argued that the developmental orientation to the study of behavior becomes increasingly salient the more "historical" the phenomenon (in terms of both description and explanation), the longer the causal chain, and the more distant its causal origin.

2. Models of Developmental Causation

Without claiming originality or inclusiveness, we offer some perspectives on specific issues related to developmental causation. We address two in particular: the role of metamodels of development and the conception of causal lag.

A. METAMODELS OF DEVELOPMENT AND EXPLANATION.

Historical or distal explanation is essential to a developmental orientation. However, there are variations in how explicitly the recognition of distal causality influences the course of research. One important factor is the role of metamodels (Overton & Reese, 1973; Reese & Overton, 1970) in specifying the nature of causal analysis. On the one hand, mechanistic models of developmental change are fairly broad in defining developmental change and specifying what explanation is sufficient to account for the origin(s) of development. On the other hand, organismic models impose fairly stringent limits on the specification of developmental phenomena (structural, sequential, irreversible, etc.) at the descriptive level and on the acceptable nature of explanation.

Specifically, in Aristotelian terms, organismic models do not rely solely on principles of material and efficient cause. In addition to, or instead of, these principles, they incorporate the concepts of formal and final cause. Formal cause is perhaps best understood as a type of structural or multivariate causation: Several determining factors, in their structure, are related to developmental outcomes. Final cause is often associated with teleological principles, although this is not necessarily so. A more permissive form of final causation views it as denoting that the course of development is set in a particular direction as soon as its unfolding begins. An example would be the kind of general directionality exerted by a gene pool on development. A specific directionality (e.g., physical growth, cognitive development à la Piaget) would be pursued, despite even major variations in environmental input.

The earlier discussion of pluralism and diversity in extant models of development and the role of distinct sources of influence (age-graded, history-graded, nonnormative) makes it apparent why developmental research must vary according to contextual factors of metatheory and the substantive theory in a given domain of research. It is also reasonable to assume that a comprehensive theory of development may need to attend conjointly to multiple forms of causation. For instance, Kohlberg (1973) could be interpreted as arguing that childhood moral development follows principles of an organismic model, whereas adulthood moral development may be more appropriately represented by a mechanistic model. Similar views apply to the area of cognitive development considered from a life-span developmental perspective (Baltes & Willis, 1979b).

B. CAUSAL LAG.

Historical causation, because of its emphasis on distal causes, requires explanatory constructions with conceptions of causal lag. The effect of a causal agent is not completely apparent until the causal process has run its course or until it has been enhanced by other contingencies. In the child-development literature an example of causal lag is discussed under the label of *sleeper effect*. Concrete examples can easily be noted in the medical sciences, where several diseases have been described that involve the occurrence of symptomatology at points in time many years removed from the occurrence of the initial causal event.

Consider the following illustration. It is possible at least for heuristic purposes to distinguish between two types of lagged or historical causation. In one type, antecedent events, through what may be a lengthy process of causation, lead inexorably to a certain outcome. Well-known medical examples are disease processes associated with slow viruses (e.g., kuru) or with presumed lung-cancer-producing antecedents such as cigarette smoking or asbestos inhalation. Another instance from the medical literature includes the long-term, delayed effects of atomic radiation in Japan on the occurrence of leukemia some 20 years later. Another is the negative side effects produced by extensive medication of cortical steroids aimed at reducing certain allergies and inflammatory symptoms such as are evident in arthritis. These steroids, if consumed for longer time periods, are associated with a slow but continuous degeneration of bone structures that does not appear, however, until a threshold of bone deterioration is reached. In the psychological literature, examples of lagged causation of this type (process of causation extends in time) include the cumulative effects of early childhood socialization in females on their professional attainment during adulthood. Another example is the slow but systematic acquisition of learning sets or of other cognitive styles.

The second major model of lagged causation represents a time-lagged multicausality–contingency relationship. In this scheme, it is assumed that a given causal agent operated at an earlier time. However, its effect does not become apparent until at least one additional precipitating factor (contingency) becomes part of the developmental history of the individual. Thus, the initial causal agent is a necessary but not sufficient condition for the criterion outcome to appear. Examples of this model of lagged causation are numerous in the medical literature, if not as facts, then at least as reasonable hypotheses. For example, tuberculosis is thought to involve an initial genetic predisposition. However, the outcome results only if the genetically predisposed individual is exposed to excessive amounts of tubercle bacillus, particularly in certain sensitive time periods. Developmental theories of schizophrenia are based on similar arguments that involve various combinations of genetic disposition (a primary causal agent) and later ontogenetic events related to psychosocial family backgrounds, birth injury, or as yet unspecified infectious processes, perhaps including the effect of slow viruses.

In the developmental-psychology literature, examples of lagged-causation models of the contingency type are perhaps more difficult to identify, although it appears that many etiological schemes of psychopathology (e.g., Urban & Lago, 1973) represent such a framework. Another psychological example of lagged or distal relationships comes from research on social interaction and the application of sequential analyses (e.g., Gottman, 1979; Lamb, Soumi, & Stephenson, in press; Sackett, 1977). In this area of investigation, the focus is explicitly on the use of lagged correlations or alternative measures of time-ordered association, such as conditional probability (see also Singer & Spilerman, Chapter 6, this volume), as strategies by which a process of sequential connectedness or distal causation, broadly defined, can be represented and examined. In this instance, antecedent and consequent variables are indexed by various classes of social interaction, and lagged correlations or lagged conditional probabilities are used to describe causal trajectories over time. In such an approach, particularly if it involves experimental treatments, the time-extension-of-effect patterns associated with antecedent events on subsequent social interaction can be studied. It is also possible to depart from linear models to conceptualize the nature of lagged or distal causation (connectedness) in nonlinear (e.g., cyclical) and interactive ways.

The possibility of causal lag requires special considerations in the design of longitudinal research. Heise (1975), for example, has argued that a theory of causal lag is necessary in order to decide on the duration and spacing of longitudinal observations (also see Singer & Spilerman, Chapter 6). Such a theory of causal lag is likely to be highly specific to the class of behavior under consideration. The unfortunate byproduct is that good decisions about the timing of observations (frequency, duration, spacing) can be made only if a sound theory concerning the relevant processes is already available. Since this is rarely the case, initial longitudinal forays need to be rather generous in the duration and spacing of observations, in terms of both antecedents and consequents. It may also be necessary to vary aspects of timing and duration for subgroups of experimental subjects, in order to maximize the likelihood of identifying not only developmental processes but also explanatory mechanisms.

The examples of historical causation presented here are perhaps not yet sufficiently precise or empirically supported to command acceptance of the concept. Nevertheless, it is important to recognize that the design of longitudinal work should be modified according to one's conception of historical causation in a given domain of research. As mentioned before, such specification applies to the spacing of observations (length, frequency, duration) and also to the number of treatment levels and control groups required. For example, equal-interval spacing of observations is not necessarily an optimal solution, although it appears to be routinely practiced. Departure from equal-interval spacing is likely to become more frequent as the understanding of a causal process increases. The same applies to the application of intervening treatment conditions. As a causal theory of a specific developmental process is articulated, the design of treatments will be guided more by theoretical criteria than by an intuitive segmentation of the time continuum. Finally, the judicious use of quasi-experimental designs and causal-modeling procedures is a critical ingredient in the study of relevant developmental phenomena. Otherwise, longitudinal work is less sensitive than it should be to developmental theory and more constrained than is desirable to what is merely expedient from a methodological or design perspective.

ACKNOWLEDGMENTS

The authors are grateful for the support of the staff of the Center for Advanced Study in the Behavioral Sciences at Stanford, California, and for the helpful comments of David L. Featherman and Steven Cornelius.

Chapter 2

Toward a Unified Framework for Psychometric Concepts in the Multivariate Developmental Situation: Intraindividual Change and Inter- and Intraindividual Differences

ALLAN R. BUSS

ABSTRACT

A general developmental model for considering interindividual differences, intraindividual differences, and intraindividual change is presented. The model consists of defining each of the latter concepts in terms of Person × Variable × Occasion data and considering their interrelationships. Two major psychometric concepts, stability and regression, are then singled out for special consideration within the model. The latter tack provides for some useful conceptual distinctions, in which several different kinds or aspects of both stability and regression become readily apparent. In this way, the developmental researcher can become more self-conscious of, and achieve greater clarity of, some key psychometric issues that will undoubtedly intrude upon his or her theory and practice.

I. Introduction

The mission of this brief chapter is to present the beginnings of a unified conceptual framework which to view traditional psychometric concepts such as stability, regression, reliability, and measurement error within a developmental context. In addition, the emphasis will be upon the multivariate situation—accommodating the notion of repeated measures through time on multiple variables for several individuals. Critical in the model to be presented are the concepts of interindividual differences, intraindividual differences, intraindividual changes, and their interrelationships. To the extent that developmental psychologists should focus on intraindividual

41

LONGITUDINAL RESEARCH IN THE
STUDY OF BEHAVIOR AND DEVELOPMENT

change and interindividual differences in intraindividual change (Baltes, 1973; Wohlwill, 1970b, 1973), then there is a real need to consider within developmental methodology the interface between such concepts as intraindividual change and inter- and intraindividual differences, and traditional psychometric issues. Thus what follows is an exercise in concept methodology rather than in formal methodology. In this way, the practicing developmental psychologist may acquire a firmer grasp of some of the psychometric concepts necessary for carrying out valid developmental research in the multivariate situation.

II. Overview of the General Developmental Model

In 1974 I proposed a general developmental model (Buss, 1974a) that attempted to integrate the concepts of interindividual differences, intraindividual differences, and intraindividual change within a multivariate developmental perspective. The major focus at that time was upon data-gathering strategies and data analyses rather than on traditional psychometric issues. In order to prepare the ground for a consideration of the latter, a brief overview of the 1974 model will be undertaken at this time. Note at the outset that the general developmental model proposed by Buss (1974a) is not identical with the one advanced by Schaie (1965) in the context of age-cohort research.

A. Multiple Values on One Dimension

The 1974 version of the basic general developmental model involved taking Cattell's (1946, 1952) three-dimensional Person × Variable × Occasion covariation chart as a basis for defining the concepts of interindividual differences, intraindividual differences, and intraindividual change and their interrelationships. Figure 2.1 presents the simple case, where the datum in each cell is an individual's score on a variable at a particular occasion. In this model, interindividual differences are defined by sampling across individuals for each variable at one occasion; intraindividual differences are defined by sampling across variables for each individual at one occasion; and finally, intraindividual changes are specified by sampling across occasions for each variable for one individual.

B. Multiple Values on Two Dimensions

Figure 2.2 extends the concepts of interindividual differences, intraindividual differences, and intraindividual changes by considering the six possible ways of comparative sampling across each of the three dimensions. That is to say, for each of the three dimensions, the simple case is indicated

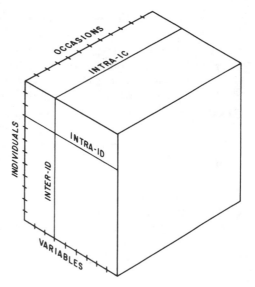

FIGURE 2.1. **The three cases generated by sampling across each of the three dimensions of individuals, variables, and occasions are interindividual differences (Inter-ID), intraindividual differences (Intra-ID), and intraindividual changes (Intra-IC), respectively. [From Buss, 1974a.]**

in which at least two values, components, or *ids* (Cattell, 1966) are sampled across each of the remaining two dimensions or sets. The six cases thus generated are:

CASE 1. Interindividual differences in intraindividual differences, in which individuals are compared in terms of sampling across variables at one occasion.

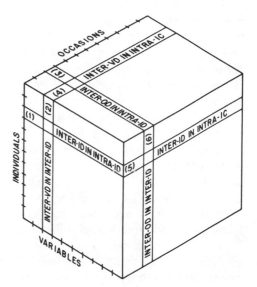

FIGURE 2.2. **The six cases generated by comparative cross-sampling for the simple case in which only two components from one dimension are compared in terms of sampling across a second dimension are shown. (Abbreviations for terms are as follows: ID=individual differences, IC=individual changes, VD=variable differences, and OD=occasion differences.) [From Buss, 1974a.]**

CASE 2. Intervariable differences in interindividual differences, in which variables are compared in terms of sampling across individuals at one occasion.

CASE 3. Interoccasion differences (changes) in intraindividual differences, in which occasions are compared in terms of sampling across variables for one individual.

CASE 4. Intervariable differences (or intraindividual differences) in intraindividual changes, in which variables are compared in terms of sampling across occasions for one individual.

CASE 5. Interindividual differences in intraindividual changes, in which individuals are compared in terms of sampling across occasions for one variable; and finally.

CASE 6. Interoccasion differences (changes) in interindividual differences, in which occasions are compared in terms of sampling across individuals for one variable.

Each of the above six data-gathering strategies is defined by what is compared (which gives the first aspect or the interindividual differences, intervariable differences, or interoccasion differences part), and in terms of what set is sampled across (which gives the second part of interindividual differences, intraindividual differences, or intraindividual changes aspect). The two interoccasion comparison cases (see Cases 3 and 6 above) may be considered as changes through time. It may be appropriate to consider Case 4 as intraindividual differences in intraindividual changes, since different variables are compared in terms of intraindividual changes. This observation reveals that there are two distinct ways of operationalizing the concept of intraindividual differences in Figure 2.2: by sampling across variables for one individual at one occasion (Cases 1 and 3) and by comparing variables in terms of sampling across occasions for one individual (Case 4). Similarly, there are two distinct views of interindividual differences: by sampling across individuals for each variable at one occasion (Cases 2 and 6), and by comparing individuals in terms of either sampling across variables at one occasion (Case 1), or sampling across occasions for one variable (Case 5).

Each of the six cases in Figure 2.2 is illustrated by comparative sampling for two ids, although the more general case would involve an entire two-dimensional matrix. The latter situation would make use of the exact same data from an Individual × Variable matrix at one occasion, but in Case 1 one would first get an overall measure (e.g., a variance measure) of variable differences within each individual (intraindividual differences) and compare individuals (interindividual differences in intraindividual differences) in terms of variances, whereas in Case 2 one would first get a variance measure of differences between individuals for each variable (interindividual differences) and compare variable variances (intervariable differences in interindividual differences). Allowing for necessary changes, a similar situation exists for the remaining four cases in Figure 2.2.

Since Case 1 and 2 data-gathering strategies are carried out at one occasion, they are not particularly useful for addressing developmental aspects of changes in variable scores, unless one simultaneously considers the third dimension of occasions (see below). In contrast, the remaining four data-gathering strategies, which involve, in part, sequential dependent measures or changes in variable scores through time, would be especially useful developmental paradigms. In considering Cases 4 and 5, which are samples across the occasion dimension and are thus concerned with intraindividual changes, one must compare either variables (Case 4) or individuals (Case 5), and this requires that the unit for analysis be the plotting of the entire set of variable scores through time. A useful statistical technique that could be employed here would be testing for trends. This focus on the pattern of changes in variable scores may be contrasted with the other four cases, in which the unit of analysis for making comparisons would be variances. In Case 1, for example, where interindividual differences or comparisons are made with respect to intraindividual differences, the appropriate index for the latter is a measure of the within-person variance of variable scores at one occasion. In order to compare variables at one occasion in terms of interindividual differences (Case 2), again it is a variance measure that captures the extent of the interindividual differences. A similar situation holds for Cases 3 and 6.

Variable scores are typically standardized across individuals for each variable at one occasion. This common practice needs to be avoided in the present scheme, since it would result in identical variances for each variable at each occasion (the variance of a standardized variable is equal to unity). If such a standardizing procedure were adopted, it would be impossible to detect intervariable differences in interindividual differences (Case 2). By a similar argument, it would be undesirable to standardize each variable across occasions for each person, each occasion across variables for each individual, etc. What is necessary for meaningful comparisons for all six cases is to standardize each variable in terms of both individuals and occasions; that is, across each rectangular "slab" or matrix for each variable. In this way, spurious, identical interindividual-differences variances for each variable at each occasion, which are brought about by rescaling procedures, are avoided. One of the advantages of standardizing in the manner being recommended here is that absolute changes in variable scores result in correspondingly higher or lower standard scores, since variables are not restandardized within each occasion.

C. Multiple Values on Three Dimensions

It is possible to extend each of the six data-gathering strategies outlined above to that situation in which one also samples through the third dimension. In other words, there is a three-step process here, in which one first samples across the first dimension, compares such sampling in terms of the ids, or components, on the second dimensions (the six cases just outlined above), and then proceeds to sample the comparisons of cross-sampling through the third dimension. In the complete three-step procedure, two dimensional "slabs", or matrices, are compared. This process generates six cases, in which those data-gathering strategies in Figure 2.2 are now moderated by a term referring to the third dimension that is sampled through.

Figure 2.3 illustrates the complete three-step procedure for the simple case in which two ids (which have been sampled across on one dimension) are successively compared across the third dimension. The more general case would involve successive sampling of entire matrices through the third dimension. As before, the latter procedure could involve the same data for various cases, but it is the operational sequence of the three sampling steps that determines the six separate relational systems.

The six three-step cases in Figure 2.3 are the following:

CASE 1. Interoccasion differences (changes) in interindividual differences in intraindividual differences, in which the variances reflecting the extent of intraindividual differences for each individual at an occasion are compared for individuals through time or the occasion dimension.

CASE 2. Interoccasion differences (changes) in intervariable differences in interindividual differences, in which the variances reflecting the extent of interindividual differences for each variable at an occa-

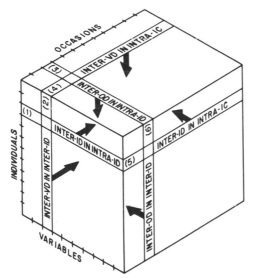

FIGURE 2.3. **The six cases generated by sampling the labeled comparative cross-samplings through the third dimension are shown. (The simple case is indicated in which only two cross-samplings are successively compared through the third dimension. Abbreviations for terms are as follows: ID = individual differences, IC = individual changes, VD=variable differences, and OD = occasion differences.)** [From Buss, 1974.]

sion are compared for variables through time or the occasion dimension.

CASE 3. Interindividual differences in interoccasion differences (changes) in intraindividual differences, in which the variances reflecting the extent of intraindividual differences for each occasion for an individual are compared for occasions through the individual dimension.

CASE 4. Interindividual differences in intervariable differences (intraindividual differences) in intraindividual changes, in which the plots of variable scores across occasions at an individual are compared for variables through the individual dimension.

CASE 5. Intervariable differences in interindividual differences in intraindividual changes, in which the plots of variable scores across occasions at a variable are compared for individuals through the variable dimension; and finally.

CASE 6. Intervariable differences in interoccasion differences (changes) in interindividual differences, in which the variances reflecting the extent of interindividual differences for each occasion at a variable are compared for occasions through the variable dimension.

Although these extended six data-gathering strategies may appear quite complex prima facie, acquiring a firm conceptual understanding of them

TABLE 1

Data-Gathering Strategies for Interindividual Differences, Intraindividual Differences, and Intraindividual Changes[a]

Dimension 1: sample across	Dimension 2: compare on	Dimension 3: sample through	Type[b]
Individuals	No	No	Inter-ID
Variables	No	No	Intra-ID
Occasions	No	No	Intra-IC
Variables	Individuals	No	Inter-ID in intra-ID
Individuals	Variables	No	Inter-VD in inter-ID
Variables	Occasions	No	Inter-OD in intra-ID
Occasions	Variables	No	Inter-VD intra-IC
Occasions	Individuals	No	Inter-ID in intra-IC
Individuals	Occasions	No	Inter-OD in inter-ID
Variables	Individuals	Occasions	Inter-OD in inter-ID in intra-ID
Individuals	Variables	Occasions	Inter-OD in inter-VD in inter-ID
Variables	Occasions	Individuals	Inter-ID in inter-OD in intra-ID
Occasions	Variables	Individuals	Inter-ID in inter-VD in intra-IC
Occasions	Individuals	Variables	Inter-VD in inter-ID in intra-IC
Individuals	Occasions	Variables	Inter-VD in inter-OD in inter-ID

[a] From Buss, 1974a.

[b] ID = individual differences, IC = individual changes, VD = variable differences, and OD = occasion differences.

may be facilitated by working backward through the three steps and consequently their verbal designations. For example, in the case of interoccasion differences in interindividual differences in intraindividual differences, the focus is initially on the extent of intraindividual differences in variable scores at one occasion and for one individual as reflected by a variance measure. If one were then to proceed to compare such variances for two individuals at one occasion, we would arrive at the two-step concept of interindividual differences in intraindividual differences. Considering now the third dimension of occasions, in which individuals are now compared through time (occasions) in terms of the extent of intraindividual differences in variable scores, we arrive at the three-step concept of interoccasion differences in interindividual differences in intraindividual differences. One may work backward in a similar fashion for each of the six extended cases in order to grasp fully their conceptual significance.

The 15 data-gathering strategies for interindividual differences, intraindividual differences, and intraindividual changes are summarized in Table 2.1 in the order presented above, in which the first three cases consider multiids on only one dimension, the next six cases on two dimensions, and the last six cases on all three dimensions.

D. Limitations of the Model

Before leaving the general developmental model per se for a consideration of some key psychometric concepts within its framework, a few cautionary comments are in order. First, the model makes the assumption that the meanings of the constructs that the variables are measuring remain invariant across time. In other words, it is quantitative rather than qualitative or structural change (e.g., see Baltes & Nesselroade, 1973; Buss, 1974c; Nesselroade, 1970) that the model is capable of addressing, and it is therefore confined to slices of the life-span where the invariance of one's constructs has been demonstrated.

A second limitation related to the above is that the present model is not focused upon an analytic treatment of interbehavioral change. That is to say, the strength of the model lies in those situations where change is monitored within a given variable or variables rather than where interbehavioral changes involving cross-variable paths through time are marked out. The latter would also require techniques capable of analyzing qualitative change. A third, and once again related, limitation serves to place the entire model in proper perspective. This point can be best appreciated by contrasting the model and its intent with related notions.

Mention has already been made of Cattell's (1946, 1952) original three-dimensional covariation chart. The purpose of that model was to set out the six different factor-analytic techniques defined by what was correlated (persons, variables, or occasions) over what (one of the two remaining options after the initial selection). In the expanded version of the covariation chart into a generic data box Cattell (1966) has gone beyond his initial desire to set out various methods of factor analyzing Person × Variable × Occasion data and has employed a full 10 dimensions for indexing a datum. Important to note in the present context is that Cattell's more recent treatment of data relations is not confined to specific data-analysis techniques. Implicit in his data box is the notion that different data analyses are appropriate for different aspects or relational systems. In the context of longitudinal data-analysis techniques, Kowalski and Guire (1974) (see also Chapter 4, this volume) have explicitly linked specific analytic techniques[1] to various relational aspects of Person × Variable × Occasion data. In contrast to Cattell's (1966) comprehensive treatment of how one can conceptualize data in general, and in contrast to Kowalski and Guire's (1974) general account of the various analytic techniques available for longitudinal data, the present model is restricted to conceptualizing specific concepts (inter- and intraindividual differences, intraindividual change) within the three-dimensional data frame. Its intent, therefore, is to focus upon a specific set of concepts as these are related to longitudinal data. The present model makes no attempt to explore terrain previously charted out by others.

III. Psychometric Concepts and the General Developmental Model: Stability

The two psychometric concepts singled out for specific treatment in terms of the multivariate developmental situation and the preceding model are stability and regression to the mean. Other concepts, such as reliability, measurement error, and true scores, are introduced as needed and as they are related specifically to stability and regression.

A. Stability in Two Dimensions

By stability in the multivariate developmental situation, one can mean the stability of differences either between or within persons through time. In considering Figure 2.2, these two cases translate respectively into noting either the degree of stability of interindividual-differences scores on a single variable through time (Case 6), or the stability of intraindividual-differences scores on a single person through time (Case 3).

In each of these simple cases, multiple values on one dimension (either individuals or variables) for one id (either a variable or individual) are obtained on two successive occasions. The simple two-occasion situation

---

[1] Some of those considered are the following: curve fitting, factor analysis, multivariate analysis of variance, polynomial growth-curve models, regression, and time series.

would involve calculating a correlation coefficient as the stability coefficient, whereas the multiple-occasion situation would involve calculating successive stability coefficients (see page 51). Since the Pearson product-moment correlation restandardizes scores at each occasion—that is, it cancels out means and variances—this statistic would permit inferences concerning the degree of stability of the pattern or shape of the multiple scores through time. Thus, it would be possible to have absolute changes in scores yet obtain a high stability coefficient so long as there was relatively high invariance of the pattern of interindividual differences through time. It can be noted in passing that the ceiling of a two-occasion product-moment stability coefficient would be the lower reliability coefficient as determined by assessing reliability at each occasion.

An alternative index of stability that takes more than just the consistency of shape into account would involve one of the measures of similarity based upon distance (see Bolz, 1972, for a review of such indices of similarity). Cattell's (Cattell Coulter, & Tsujioka, 1966) pattern-similarity coefficient is probably the superior statistic in that it simultaneously considers differences between two patterns of variable scores due to elevation (the mean of all scores in a profile), scatter (the square root of the sum of squares of the deviation scores about the mean), and shape (the residual information after equating two patterns for both elevation and scatter). In addition, the pattern-similarity coefficient is readily meaningful—varying between 0 (no pattern similarity) and +1 (perfect pattern similarity)—and it has known distribution and a test for significance (Horn, 1961).

If one were to employ the pattern-similarity coefficient as a two-occasion index of stability of either interindividual differences or intraindividual differences, it would be necessary to standardize across each rectangular slab, or matrix, for each variable, as previously outlined. In this way, one can make the best use of the additional measurement properties of the pattern-similarity coefficient; that is, its sensitivity to differences in both the means and variances of two patterns. Thus, the pattern-similarity coefficient should be used as an index of the stability of inter- or intraindividual differences when the concern is for absolute rather than relative pattern invariance over two occasions.

B. Stability in Three Dimensions

The above notions of stability can be readily generalized to the three-dimensional situation; that is, where it is desirable to make variable comparisons in the stability of interindividual differences or person comparisons in the stability of intraindividual differences. Each of these cases in the two-occasion situation can be visualized by reference to Figure 2.3. Variable comparisons in the stability of interindividual differences involve Case 5—where that case is extended through the third dimension of Variables such that variable differences in stability coefficients are observed. The same rationale follows in making person comparisons in the stability of intraindividual differences, which involves extending Case 3 in Figure 2.3 through the third dimension of Individuals. In either of these two cases, the product-moment or pattern-similarity coefficient may be used, depending upon the question being asked in light of the unique properties of each of these statistics as previously discussed.

Thus far the concept of stability has been extended to both inter- and intraindividual differences in the multiple-variable and person situation. However, a truly adequate treatment of stability in a multivariate developmental context must provide for more than the restrictive two-occasion model. Extending Cases 5 and 3 in Figure 2.2 right across occasions to involve an entire matrix, or slab, illustrates successive or multiple-occasion data gathering. Thus, in Case 5 successive stability coefficients for a single variable could be obtained, where each stability coefficient is calculated from adjacent occasions. The values of the stability coefficients could then be plotted for purposes of variable comparisons in trends over time, and Figure 2.4 illustrates three prototype cases: increasing stability (IS), stable stability (SS), and decreasing stability (DS). By using curve-fitting techniques, one may then determine variable differences in stability trends through time. The same logic may be applied to Case 3 in Figure 2.2, where Figure 2.4 may now be regarded as illustrating three prototype stability functions for intraindividual differences. Each function, then, characterizes a particular individual rather than a particular variable. The term *prototype* in the latter situation is more than a casual label, since it may indeed be possible to distinguish "types," or clusters, of persons on the basis of stability functions for intraindividual differences.

What about the interrelationship between the degree of stability of inter-

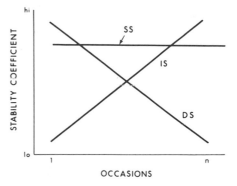

FIGURE 2.4. **Three prototype cases of increasing stability (IS), stable stability (SS), and decreasing stability (DS).**

individual differences and the degree of stability of intraindividual differences, where the same data are analyzed in the appropriate manner? High stability of interindividual differences on each of the variables is a prerequisite for high stability of intraindividual differences for each person, and vice versa. In other words, in the extreme case (i.e., considering the stability of the entire Variable × Individual matrix through time), the stability of inter- and that of intraindividual differences are two different ways of looking at the same phenomenon. However, the direct translation between the degree of stability of inter- and intraindividual differences evaporates as soon as one selectively focuses upon a subsample of variables or persons through a limited number of occasions. The latter statement, of course, does not deny the ever-present nonindependence of the stability of inter- and intraindividual differences when calculated from the same data.

C. Stability of Population Parameters

Having distinguished between inter- and intraindividual differences according to their stability, there remains another important sense of the term *stability* applicable to the multivariate developmental situation. Thus, one may speak of the stability of various variable properties of a population through time, where the focus is now upon the degree of stability of certain descriptive statistics such as the mean or variance. Clearly, in this case, one would not restandardize the variable scores at each occasion, since this would mask changes in absolute value of the mean and variance. In mapping out various statistical properties of variables over time, it is quite possible to have stability of, say, the mean and variance, yet at the same time have radical instability of inter- and/or intraindividual differences.

The distinction being made here is conceptually quite important, since the stability, or "dynamic equilibrium," of a population on a particular variable does not entail stability and/or systematic change at the individual level. To the extent that in multivariate developmental psychology there should be an emphasis upon intraindividual change and interindividual differences in intraindividual change (e.g., in the present context, the degree of stability of intraindividual differences and person differences or interindividual differences in the stability of intraindividual differences), then it is important to make the kind of distinction presently being made. This is not to say that questions concerning the stability of properties of a population on a particular variable, or the stability of interindividual differences through time, may not be extremely interesting or important. Rather—and this is the basic point—there are several ways one can frame questions concerning stability in the multivariate developmental situation, and the practicing researcher should be quite conscious of the various alternatives available and effect an adequate match between the research question and the concept of stability employed.

IV. Psychometric Concepts and the General Developmental Model: Regression

A. Regression as a Prediction Model versus Type of Change

Regression toward the mean is a thorny issue in developmental psychology, and, although it has been discussed within a developmental context (e.g., Baltes & Nesselroade, 1976; Baltes, Nesselroade, Schaie, & Labouvie, 1972; Clarke, Clarke, and Brown, 1960; Furby, 1973), there remains a need for further clarification. Any discussion of regression must, of necessity, consider such psychometric concepts as measurement error, reliability, and true scores. In discussing regression within a developmental context, it is advantageous, as suggested by Baltes & Nesselroade (1976), to separate the typical psychometric issue associated with this term—namely, regression as a prediction model—from observed regression in the data.

The previously outlined developmental model of Buss (1974a) can be fruitfully consulted in attempting to keep separate regression as a prediction model and observed regression in the data. Thus, in Figure 2.2 regression as a prediction model can be best located in terms of Case 2, where one would employ regression techniques for predicting scores on one variable from scores on another variable. Regression in this instance is not "in" the data, or in other words, is not a "real" phenomenon.

In order to understand better the point I am trying to make here, consider Case 6 in Figure 2.2, where measures are obtained on the same variable on two separate occasions. In the latter instance, there is continuity over time, and if there is regression from occasion to occasion, it is a phenomenon intrinsic to these data. In other words—and this is the basic point—when regressing one variable against another, different variable, we are using regression as a prediction model. When we obtain repeated measures for two occasions on the same variable, regression toward the mean, if it occurs, is a phenomenon to be explained. In the latter situation, regression toward the mean is a special kind of change in one's data. Should one desire, variable differences in regression as a type of change can be located in the general model by considering Case 6 through the third dimension; that is, as illustrated in Figure 2.3.

In the following discussion, regression as a prediction model is bracketed. The focus of attention is exclusively upon that situation where observed regression is in the data (regression as a type of change) in order to try to clarify some of the developmental issues in this area.

B. Regression of Extreme Samples

Observed regression to the mean may be associated with either changes in true scores or changes in error scores in the classical measurement model of $x = t + e$; that is, the observed score is the sum of a true-score component and an error-score component. Important to note, then, is that observed regression, which is in the data, may or may not reflect true changes in the underlying trait or variable of a particular sample.

The developmental psychologist must, in certain situations to be explicated, take account of observed regression associated with the error part of scores in order to make valid inferences concerning real, or true-score, change over time. The classical case where the developmental psychologist simply must consider the extent to which observed regression toward the mean is associated with true changes in the variable is illustrated in Figure 2.5 (see also Baltes & Nesselroade, 1976; Furby, 1973).

In Figure 2.5, the sample of individuals is initially selected from the extreme range of the normal distribution of the population. We can make the assumption in Figure 2.5 that measurement error exists and is constant across occasions; that is, reliability is invariant. As the second occasion, the entire sample has shifted closer to the population mean μ. To the extent that the reliability of variable X is less than unity—that is, there is some measurement error—then there will be observed regression associated with changes in error scores. This follows from the classical measurement model—a model that forms the bedrock of measurement theory—and a model that must be accommodated until displaced by something shown to be superior.

The classical measurement model states that (because errors of measurement are assumed to be uncorrelated over time) extreme scores in a distribution are biased in that same extreme direction, and that on a second occasion, the error associated with these individuals' scores will, on the average, be less—thereby effecting observed regression toward the population mean. Another way of saying this is that in nonerror-free measures, observed scores are biased estimates of true scores, where observed scores above the population mean are biased upward, and vice versa for observed scores below the population mean.

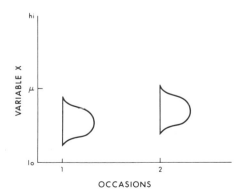

FIGURE 2.5. **The classical situation of regression toward the population mean, where the sample is initially selected from the extreme range of the normal distribution of the population.**

For the developmental psychologist who is working with a select sample of nonerror-free extreme scores, regression toward the mean associated with changes in error scores will occur. It will show up as observed regression, all other things being equal. To the extent that there are true changes in the underlying trait or construct that a variable is tapping, this may effect no observed change in the sample distribution if the true-score and error-score changes, on the average, cancel each other out. Thus, the developmental researcher, when working with a sample under conditions described above, must know from where the sample came, as well as the reliability of measures, in order to make valid conclusions as to the extent of true-score, or real, changes in the underlying construct over time. The latter conclusion is not the consequence of a specific prediction model, but is the consequence of a very general measurement model underlying all measurement—psychological or otherwise.

In regard to intergrating the concept of regression within the present methodological model, we can note that, in that ideal case of error-free measures and where regression is associated with changes in true scores and, for argument's sake, the Pearson product-moment stability coefficient is unity, then in the shift toward the population mean in Figure 2.5 there will be no interindividual differences in intraindividual change. The latter would be a very unlikely situation in any actual research outcome. More probable would be observed interindividual differences in intraindividual change toward the population mean associated with real and / or spurious factors, respectively paralleling true-score and error-score changes.

C. Regression of Representative Samples

There is another, quite different, situation involving regression toward the mean, and previous discussions have failed to place it in sharp contrast with what is most typically meant by regression (but see Baltes & Nesselroade, 1976). On occasion there has even been a tendency to confuse the two situations of regression, or at least switch from one to the other without adequate awareness.

The second major case of regression toward the mean is illustrated in Figure 2.6, where, in this instance, the sample distribution can be considered as representative of a population rather than coming from a selective region of the population distribution as was previously the case. In Figure 2.6 there is observed regression toward the mean, but in this instance regression is defined by a reduction in the sample variance rather than a shift in the sample mean (and thus the sample) toward the population mean. Thus, in Figure 2.6 the means at each occasion are identical, yet there is within-sample regression toward the mean, and within-population regression to the mean to the extent the sample is representative of a population. As before, such observed regression may be associated with changes in either true

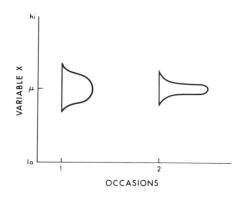

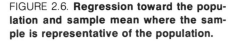

FIGURE 2.6. **Regression toward the population and sample mean where the sample is representative of the population.**

scores or error scores. However, in this second case of regression, any regression associated with changes in error scores is due to increased reliability across occasions and a reduction of the error variance—which was not the case in the first instance of regression, where it was assumed reliability was constant over time. Of course, in considering only changes in error scores, both within-sample regression to the sample mean and regression of the sample to the population mean could occur simultaneously in Figure 2.5 if there were an increase in reliability over time.

In Figure 2.7 it can be seen that mean sample changes in either an upward or downward direction are independent of within-sample regression to the mean. Thus, the entire distribution of scores may shift in either direction—regression still being defined as a reduction in variance. The latter observation brings us to the point that, in the multiple-occasion situation, changes in regression to the mean may be mapped via noting changes in variance through time. However, this conclusion reveals that observed regression is "merely" observed change in a specified direction, although there is more to it than that. The observed change may be associated with changes in error scores (reliability) and / or true scores, and valid developmental conclusions require separating these two sources in both types of regression discussed in this section.

D. Concluding Comments on Regression

Although it is true that within-sample regression may or may not occur—depending upon whether there is a reduction in error variance and / or real changes in true scores toward the mean—regression of observed scores, as discussed in the first instance and illustrated in Figure 2.5, will occur, assuming that nonerror-free measures and all other things are equal. Developmental psychologists will need to assess any true-score change in the

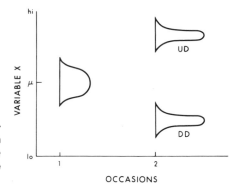

FIGURE 2.7. **Regression toward the sample mean but not toward the population mean in two different situations: change in an upward direction (UD) and change in a downward direction (DD).**

sample mean either toward or away from the population mean in light of error-score change.

Baltes and Nesselroade (1976) have concluded that regression toward the mean is often an irrelevant issue in developmental research to the extent that we should focus upon change and multiple-occasion data beyond the two-occasion case. According to them, regression is only one form of change rather than some immutable law, and in multiple-occasion data it can be assessed via error-centered baseline comparisons. This view has much to recommend it, since it places the typical two-occasion regression situation within a broader framework for multivariate developmental researchers. Such being the case, the spirit of their effort is consistent with perspectives developed here.

V. Summary

The concepts of interindividual differences, intraindividual differences, and intraindividual change were defined in terms of sampling across one of the three dimensions of individuals, variables, and occasions, respectively. Each of these concepts was then considered in comparative sampling by introducing a second dimension, thus generating six data-gathering strategies. Each of the latter six cases was extended to include the third dimension through which the comparative sampling is sampled. Out of the total 15 data-gathering strategies considered, 11 were defined in part by the occasion dimension and are therefore capable of dealing with change data.

Limitations of the general developmental model were discussed. These included the following:

1. The model rests upon the assumption that the meaning of the constructs that the variables are measuring remains invariant.

2. The model is not equipped to deal in an analytic way with interbehavioral change.
3. The model is to be used for focusing upon a specific set of concepts as these are related to longitudinal data, rather than for attempting a general and comprehensive delineation of various developmental data-analysis techniques.

After the general developmental model and its limitations were outlined, two important psychometric concepts were considered within the developed framework: stability and regression. Two kinds of stability were outlined that were defined by two of the three dimensions of persons, variables, and occasions: the stability of interindividual differences on a single variable through time; and the stability of intraindividual differences on a single person through time. Stability in three dimensions involves extending each of these types of comparing stability coefficients across variables or persons, respectively.

Stability can also involve multiple-occasion data, where successive stability coefficients are calculated at each occasion for determining changes in stability of either interindividual differences on one variable or intraindividual differences for one person. One can then make variable or person comparisons, respectively, of trends in stability functions. Finally, stability of population parameters was another aspect considered, where it was pointed out that one can plot the values of certain descriptive statistics over occasions. This meaning of stability reveals the important conceptual point that it is quite possible to have stability of, say, the mean and variance of a population yet at the same time have radical instability of inter- and/or intraindividual differences.

In considering regression toward the mean, two fundamental types were defined within the general developmental model: regression as a prediction model; and regression as a kind of change. The former was seen as essentially nondevelopmental, and thus discussion was confined to regression as a special kind of change over time.

Two kinds of regression toward the mean as change were considered for the two-occasion case only: regression of extreme samples; and regression of representative samples. Regression of extreme sample means to population means was seen to occur given the assumptions of the classical measurement model and all other things being equal. To the extent that there are changes in the true-score component of observed scores, this will effect the amount of observed regression that would otherwise be due solely to changes in measurement error over occasions. Regression of representative samples of particular populations was seen to involve a decrease in variance over time rather than changes in sample means. Thus there can be a decrease in sample variance (and thus regression toward the mean) brought about by changes in the true scores and/or the error scores. The mean may or may not change over time—regression in this case being independent of such change.

In conclusion it should be noted that greater clarity of psychometric concepts in the developmental situation is possible and necessary for those practicing the craft of developmental research. The proposed formulation of a general developmental model involving interindividual differences, intraindividual differences, and intraindividual change is helpful in this regard.

Chapter 3

Cohort Effects in Developmental Psychology[1]

PAUL B. BALTES
STEVEN W. CORNELIUS
JOHN R. NESSELROADE

ABSTRACT

After offering definitions of developmental psychology and the cohort variable, a brief historical review of cohort research is provided. In addition, some observations are offered on Schaie's General Developmental Model and the design of cohort-sequential studies. Particular attention is paid to the distinction between descriptive identification of change versus its explanation. Baltes' earlier position, espousing an age–cohort matrix as the preferred scheme of descriptive analysis for sequential data in the context of developmental psychology, is elaborated. After a selective review of research on cohort effects in behavioral development, discussion concerning the nature of cohort effects is presented. The logical status of cohort as a design variable is considered, various alternative conceptions of the cohort variable are outlined, and some methodological approaches are reviewed. In a concluding section, a number of implications of cohort effects for research and theory in developmental psychology are summarized. With a focus on methodological implications, the study of cohort effects points to multiple components of variability between and within individuals and cohorts, and to potential problems in the explanation of development when cohort effects are not considered. With respect to general theoretical issues, cohort effects suggest that patterns of change in behavioral development do not always evidence simple age-related nomothetic and universal characteristics, that intraorganismic models of development are insufficient, and the need for multidisciplinary analyses of the impact of both ontogenetic and historical-evolutionary change components.

[1] Preparation of this chapter was facilitated by a contract from the National Institute of Education (Grant No. NIE-C-74-0127) to John R. Nesselroade and Paul B. Baltes. The second author was supported by a National Science Foundation Graduate Fellowship during the preparation of this chapter. The present chapter is an abridged and modified version of an earlier chapter (Baltes, Cornelius, & Nesselroade, 1978).

61

I. Introduction

The cohort variable has achieved prominence in many disciplines, including sociology (e.g., Elder, 1975; Riley, 1976; Ryder, 1965), psychology (e.g., Baltes, 1968b; Schaie, 1965, 1970), and education (Goulet, 1975). Thus, the definition and explanation of cohort effects varies widely among disciplinary emphases, but there have been recent attempts to clarify the similarities and differences in the use and treatment of the cohort variable by various disciplines (e.g., Rosow, 1978).

In the present chapter, the role of the cohort variable in research and theory of developmental psychology is discussed. *Developmental psychology* is defined here with an emphasis on methodology: "Developmental psychology deals with the description, explanation, and modification (optimization) of intraindividual change in behavior across the life span, and with interindividual differences (and similarities) in intraindividual change [Baltes, Reese, & Nesselroade, 1977, p. 4]." This definition emphasizes both changes within an individual and differences between individuals in change patterns.

Cohort is generically defined as "the aggregate of individuals (within some population definition) who experienced the same event within the same time interval [Ryder, 1965, p. 845]." The cohort variable is specifically defined in the present chapter as birth cohort using Schaie's (1965) definition. That is, individuals are members of a given cohort if they are born within a defined time interval (e.g., month, year, decade). Other definitions of the cohort variable can be important, particularly if an explanatory posture on the nature of cohort effects is taken. In the present context, we treat the birth-cohort definition of cohort as an illustrative indicator of biocultural change leading to interindividual differences in ontogeny. We are comfortable with this restriction because the present chapter is intended to be illustrative rather than comprehensive.

Consideration of the cohort variable by developmental psychologists reflects an increasing awareness that sociobiological history (change) can influence behavioral development. The relative neglect of cohort effects in the formative decades of developmental psychology may have resulted from (1) a lack of disciplinary communication among social and behavioral scientists interested in biocultural and ontogenetic change; and/or (2) the predominance of intraorganismic, personological models of development such as biological growth-oriented conceptions of development (see Harris, 1957a, for review). Conversely, the relatively recent interest among developmentalists in analyzing individual (ontogenetic) and generational (historical) development may be due to an acknowledgment that much theory and research in developmental psychology are parochial from a historical perspective (e.g., Keniston, 1971; Riegel, 1976a, 1976b), that a rapprochement between psychological, biological, and sociological approaches is desirable (e.g., Nesselroade & Baltes, 1974), and that the design validity of research on ontogenetic change and development may be seriously hampered if questions of evolutionary or biocultural stability versus change are not considered.

A number of substantive orientations in developmental psychology have suggested the important role of historical context for human development. However, it seems fair to state that life-span developmental research has contributed most significantly to an understanding of the importance of biocultural change and cohort effects (e.g., Baltes & Schaie, 1976). This is true because life-span research focuses on long-term processes and change. Long-term processes, however, cannot be easily studied without considering them in the context of a changing society or biocultural system. In fact, a review paper by Baltes (1979) shows that throughout the history of life-span developmental psychology biocultural change has been a central issue for researchers committed to a life-span orientation.

II. Identification of Cohort Effects

The definition of developmental psychology offered in the previous section emphasized a methodological focus because it was largely a methodological concern that led to the identification of the role of cohort effects in developmental psychology. In the present section, some methodological issues are summarized regarding sequential designs in developmental research vis-à-vis the definition of developmental psychology. Thereafter, three applications of sequential strategies in developmental research are discussed. Sequential research strategies are intrinsically linked to research on cohort effects because they involve conjoint variation of age and cohort.

A. Sequential Research Design: Cross-Sectional and Longitudinal Sequences

Schaie (1965) presented a General Developmental Model describing the relationship among the components of *age, cohort,* and *time of measurement* in developmental functions (for earlier attempts see Bell, 1953, 1954; Kuhlen, 1940, 1963; Welford, 1961). In Figure 3.1, the components of Schaie's model are illustrated, and data-collection strategies are depicted. It is important to recognize that the methods depicted are methods for data collection. Schaie (1965) has also presented methods for data analysis (cohort-sequential, cross-sequential, time-sequential). Schaie's (1965, 1970) methods for data analysis, however, are special cases of analysis and have come under critical review (e.g., Baltes, 1967, 1968b).

The figure shows an arrangement involving birth cohorts 1880 to 2000, ages 0 to 80 years, and times of measurement 1880 to 2080. Three simple

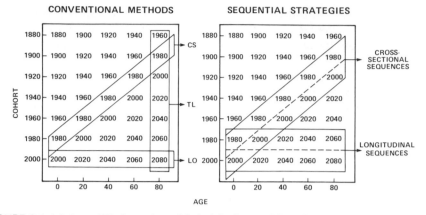

FIGURE 3.1. **(a) A modified version of Schaie's General Developmental Model illustrating conventional (CS = cross-sectional, LO = longitudinal, TL = time-lag) and (b) sequential (CSS = cross-sectional sequences, LOS = longitudinal sequences) data-collection strategies. Cell entries refer to time of measurement. [Based on Baltes, 1968b, and Nesselroade and Baltes, 1974.]**

one-factor designs (i.e., cross-sectional, longitudinal, and time-lag methods) are shown in Figure 3.1a. Each of these descriptive designs is a special case of Schaie's general model. Cross-sectional designs involve comparisons of different age-cohort groups at one time of measurement; longitudinal designs involve the repeated observations of one cohort at different age levels and thus at different times of measurement; time-lag designs involve comparisons of different cohorts at the same age level measured at different times.

It should be noted that two types of subject sampling may be used in cohort-specific ''longitudinal'' designs: One involves *repeated observations* of the same subject sample at different age levels and times of measurement (the traditional longitudinal method), whereas the other involves the *independent observations* of different subject samples (drawn randomly from one specific cohort) at different age levels and times of measurement. This distinction is the primary reason that it is useful to identify the following two kinds of sequential data-collection strategies.

These two kinds of sequential data-collection strategies are depicted in Figure 3.1b. Cohort variation always involves different individuals because an individual has only one date of birth. However, age variation within a cohort can be implemented via independent and/or repeated measurements. Thus, the independent and repeated-measurement approaches may be labeled *cross-sectional sequences* and *longitudinal sequences,* respectively (Baltes, 1968b). Cross-sectional sequences involve successions of cross-sectional studies, whereas longitudinal sequences involve successions of longitudinal studies. The primary difference between cross-sectional and longitudinal sequences is that the former produces independent observations for both age and cohort levels, and the latter results in repeated observations for the age variable.

Each sequential strategy leads to observations in all cells of Schaie's General Developmental matrix. Moreover, control groups for examining testing and instrumentation effects in longitudinal data can be included through simultaneous planned applications of cross-sectional and longitudinal sequences (Baltes *et al.*, 1977). Data obtained from cross-sectional or longitudinal sequences may be analyzed by a number of statistical techniques ranging from tests for mean differences (e.g., analysis of variance) to multivariate regression, time-series analyses, curve fitting, structural-equation analysis, and so forth (see Chapters 4-11, this volume). Further discussions of selected issues inherent in the use of sequential strategies in developmental research may be found in a series of publications (e.g., Baltes, 1967, 1968b; Baltes & Schaie, 1976; Buss, 1973; Cattell, 1970; Goulet, 1975; Labouvie, 1975a; Nesselroade & Baltes, 1974; Schaie, 1965, 1970, 1973, 1977; Schaie & Baltes, 1975; Wohlwill, 1973). Our own position has been most explicitly summarized in Baltes, Cornelius, and Nesselroade (1978), and Schaie and Baltes (1975).

B. Sequential Data: Description versus Explanation

Schaie (1965) formulated his General Developmental Model in an attempt to provide a format for both descriptive data collection and explanatory data analysis. Three separate but related sequential methods of data analysis were proposed for this dual purpose: cohort-sequential (age by cohort), time-sequential (age by time), and cross-sequential (cohort by time). The third component is confounded in each of the three methods.

According to Schaie (1965), developmental explanation was possible and interesting because the three developmental parameters (age, cohort, time of measurement) could be linked to distinct sources of developmental change by means of various data manipulations: age effects to maturational antecedents, cohort effects to genetic and/or environmental antecedents, and time of measurement to cultural factors. Schaie's argument involves strong paradigmatic assumptions about the nature of behavioral development. Moreover, the model is subject to technical difficulties in testing because the three parameters are not independent of one another; this situation prevents a precise estimation of their separate effects (Baltes, 1967, 1968b; Buss, 1973; Glenn, 1976).

Thus, Schaie's (1965) dual concern for *descriptive data collection* and *explanatory data analysis* was the source of dissatisfaction that other researchers (e.g., Baltes, 1968b) expressed concerning sequential strategies in developmental research. Schaie and Baltes (1975) have clarified their positions in a joint paper. They agree now that it is important to distinguish between the use of sequential strategies (1) as data-collection methods for the descriptive identification of developmental change; and (2) in explanatory data analysis aimed at the construction of theoretical models of the origins of observed behavioral changes.

When the objective is the *descriptive identification of developmental change,* Schaie and Baltes (1975) now jointly propose to use (1) the terms *cross-sectional* and *longitudinal sequences;* and (2) a bifactorial age-by-cohort model as the ideal data matrix. An age-by-cohort data matrix is the only two-factor scheme that permits a direct and complete assessment of intraindividual change both within and between cohorts—directly corresponding to the definition of developmental psychology offered above. If one accepts the use of Schaie's model for descriptive purposes only, the issue of component confounding (age, cohort, time of measurement) is not only secondary but, strictly speaking, even irrelevant. The primary task is simply to identify certain components of change (intraindividual change, within-cohort interindividual differences, between-cohort interindividual differences) on a descriptive level. In that case, time of measurement loses its conceptual status as age and cohort variation alone lead to all incidents of change and differences in change. Here is where there is much misinterpretation in the literature. It needs to be recognized that as soon as one departs from the use of Schaie's (1965) model for explanatory purposes and uses it for descriptive purposes only, two conclusions follow. First, the terms *time-sequential, cross-sequential,* and *cohort-sequential* are not appropriate because they are not data-collection strategies but schemes for explanatory, causal analysis of a particular ilk. Second, the question of parameter confounds is altered because time of measurement has lost its status as an independent design component. In short, there is no confound if one decides to accept an age-by-cohort matrix as the ideal scheme for descriptive identification of change. In fact, the latter is the procedure usually espoused by the authors.

When *developmental explanation* is the objective, Schaie and Baltes (1975) recognize that a number of explanatory strategies may be adopted that are largely independent of the data-collection methods used to identify descriptive age changes and cohort effects. Explanatory strategies are a function of the behavioral class studied and the metatheoretical assumptions a researcher embraces. Schaie's (1965) sequential methods of data analysis (i.e., cohort-sequential, time-sequential, cross-sequential) represent *one* particular model of developmental explanation or causal analysis. Baltes himself (e.g., Schaie & Baltes, 1975) prefers explanatory models that are distinct from Schaie's model. Examples would be age or cohort simulation strategies (Baltes *et al.,* 1977) or within-cohort contrasts (Elder, 1974, 1977).

C. Alternative Schemes for Data Analysis

We have proposed here, in line with earlier arguments by Baltes (1968b; Schaie & Baltes, 1975), that in developmental psychology Schaie's age–

cohort-time-of-measurement matrix is best approached via an age-by-cohort scheme of analysis, especially if the aim is one of descriptive identification. This line of reasoning follows from the conceptual framework espoused by developmental psychology that focuses on behavior, the individual as the unit of analysis, and the correlated definition of developmental psychology as dealing with the study of intraindividual change and interindividual differences in such change. Incidentally, as to description, the age-by-cohort arrangement also includes information about time of measurement in the age-by-cohort interaction term.

When it comes to explanation, our primary position is that neither age, cohort, nor time of measurement carries with it any unique information about distinct influences on development. Thus, with regard to time of measurement, for example (even if one were to use it as a design parameter), all that would be defensible to state is that certain (otherwise unspecified) influences operated during the period specified by the time of measurement involved. The same argument would apply to age and cohort effects. However, we have argued that for the developmental psychologist, age and cohort are the parameters that delineate in a direct manner the boundaries for change and differences in change.

What is recommended, then, is only that the explanatory search for the developmental psychologist should begin with developmental variability as indexed by age and cohort. However, this view is epoused primarily for the field of developmental psychology and is not necessarily the most useful one when other disciplines are considered.[2] Indeed, the explicit recognition of all three components and the evaluation of the influence of age, time of measurement, and cohort-related influences on measurement variables has attracted the attention of researchers in a number of the social sciences not only for methodological but also for substantive reasons. In sociology, for example, Riley (1976), among others, has suggested that time-bound period effects (a counterpart of time-of-measurement effects) may be potentially meaningful. Identifying them as phenomena distinct from cohort and age effects might be useful for descriptive *and* explanatory purposes. In that case, the third potential design component—time of measurement—would be added to age and birth cohort as a mode of classification. Then the question of separating age, cohort, and time of measurement influences becomes an important one, and issues related to inherent confounding and estimation of effects must be faced.

[2] To clarify this further, there are also cases in developmental psychology where time of measurement could attain theoretically meaningful status as an indicator for time-specific influences on the nature of developmental functions. However, we need to be careful not to assume that such a situation would permit the researcher to identify time-of-measurement effects on the explanatory level as aligned with environmental factors as suggested by Schaie (1965). In our view, developmental psychologists need to search for mechanisms of explanation that are intrinsically interactive with regard to genetic and experiential determination. Schaie's (1965) model, in principle, does not espouse such an interactive approach.

In such a circumstance, because values of any two of the three design components (age, cohort, time of measurement) define the third one (e.g., age equals time of measurement minus birth year), the effects associated with these classifications are inherently confounded. Thus, desirable as they may be in some cases, three-way analyses are, strictly speaking, impossible (Baltes, 1968b; Glenn, 1976. Mason, Mason, Winsborough, & Poole, 1973). Moreover, two-way analyses such as in age-by-cohort data arrangements do not avoid the basic problem of confounding if one assigns time of measurement the status of an independent, theoretically meaningful design parameter. Rather, two-factor analyses include the effect of the third factor, since the third component in a two-way analysis manifests its effect through the interaction term (Baltes, 1968b).

Developmental psychologists have been aware of these problems for some time (Baltes, 1968b; Schaie, 1965). In his seminal paper on the General Developmental Model, Schaie (1965) explicitly recognized the difficulty and proposed one set of procedures to allow estimation of age, cohort, and time-of-measurement effects. Researchers in other disciplines (e.g., Converse, 1976; Fienberg & Mason, 1979; Jackson, 1975; Mason et al., 1973; Price, 1976) have approached the identification and estimation problems with alternative schemes of analysis. They have proposed the use of sophisticated statistical procedures and have shown how, with various assumptions, respecifications, and other devices, certain effects and combination of effects (age, cohort, time of measurement) can be estimated. The confounding of age, cohort, and time-of-measurement effects (if one assigns significance to all three for theoretical reasons) has not yet been solved in any general manner. In fact, Glenn (1976), in a brief but cogent review of some of the analysis alternatives, concludes that purely statistical approaches to analyzing age, cohort, and time-of-measurement effects will be unsuccessful. Rather, he argues that successful analysis of such multiply classified data is heavily dependent on knowledge about theories of aging and development, history, and other substantive domains, since model assumptions and outcomes must also be evaluated by nonstatistical criteria.

Glenn's (1976) position is in accord with our own, particularly as it applies to developmental psychology. We predict that in future work the salient issues related to sequential strategies in developmental psychology (but not necessarily in other disciplines, such as sociology) will not involve solving the compounded effect question by alternative schemes of data analysis. Rather, the salient issues will focus on how to use sequential strategies in a way that makes them an important ingredient to theory construction. In our view, the use of sequential strategies and subsequent data analysis should be guided more by theoretical considerations about the developmental phenomena and much less by mathematical–statistical decisions inherent to the matrix provided by age, cohort, and time of measurement. This is particularly true in applications to developmental psychology, where the immediate task is one of accurate identification of intraindividual change, which, we maintain, can best be done via an age-by-cohort matrix. In such an instance, the discussion surrounding the unconfounding of age, cohort, and time of measurement is largely an irrelevant issue. Moreover, as argued previously (Schaie & Baltes, 1975), whenever a complete age-by-cohort matrix is not available, the solution chosen should be one of approximating that ideal.

D. Mixed Strategies

Often, for practical reasons, a complete data matrix involving all levels of age and cohort is not available. Depending upon one's area of research and one's views on the role of age and cohort (see later section), different approximations have been espoused. They are usually labeled as *mixed models,* a term denoting the fact that incomplete arrangements involving longitudinal and cross-sectional designs are used in combination.

Historically, Bell (1953, 1954; see also Welford, 1961) espoused such a mixed approach under the label *convergence* as an accelerated longitudinal strategy. His emphasis was on approximating a longitudinal assessment of long-term age change via a series of shorter longitudinal studies than the entire age range under investigation would require. Since Bell's primary focus was on age development (and not cohort effects), his suggestion was to check for convergence of findings at critical age levels. Critical age levels were those where data from at least two short-term longitudinal designs would be available. Bell's proposition was to treat the series of short-term longitudinal studies as representative for the entire age range if convergence at selected age levels was existent. His proposal is practical, however, only in restricted circumstances. First, incidents of convergence may not be frequent. Second, Bell's model assigns primary weight to age effects while neglecting the potential significance of the cohort variable. Third, convergence applies to level only; it does not include information on stability of interindividual differences across the points where convergence is assessed.

Van't Hof, Roede, and Kowalski (1977) have reexamined the need for mixed models. Contrary to that of Bell, their interest is in a joint analysis of age and cohort effects using what they label a *mixed-longitudinal design.* A mixed-longitudinal design, similar to Bell's 1953 proposal, involves a series of longitudinal studies covering segments of the age span under investigation. Van't Hof *et al.* (1977) argue that, for theoretical reasons, such a mixed-longitudinal design in conjunction with appropriate analytic techniques can provide for adequate data on change and cohort (and time-of-measurement)-related differences in change. This appears to be correct, if the goal is only a reasonably good estimation of cohort (or time-of-measurement) effects as modifiers of age functions.

Mixed-longitudinal designs, therefore, are useful as approximations. This is particularly true if one's interest is in conceptualizing the cohort parameter as a dimension of quantitative generalization; that is, as a determinant for variation around a "true" age function. Such a perspective is discussed further in a later section of this chapter when distinct conceptions of the cohort variable are identified and contrasted.

III. Three Applications of Sequential Strategies

Three cohort-sequential (cross-sectional and/or longitudinal data sequences) studies are discussed in the present section to illustrate the application of sequential strategies and demonstrate the significance of cohort effects in developmental psychology. The first study (Baltes, Baltes, & Reinert, 1970; Baltes & Reinert, 1969) examined intellectual development of children; the second study involved a cohort-sequential analysis of adolescent personality development (Nesselroade & Baltes, 1974); and the third study is Schaie's work on adult intellectual development (e.g., Nesselroade, Schaie, & Baltes, 1972; Schaie, Labouvie, & Buech, 1973). The descriptions given here are highly condensed. Original articles should be consulted for technicalities, refined aspects of interpretation, and discussions of control analyses for examining testing and experimental mortality effects.

A. Intellectual Development in Children

The study presented in Baltes *et al.* (1970; see also Baltes & Reinert, 1969) was conducted in Saarbrücken, Germany, with 315 male and 315 female children, using cross-sectional sequences as the data-collection strategy. Independent samples of 8-, 9-, 10-year-old children were tested on three occasions at 4-month intervals in 1964 and 1965 (November 1964, March 1965, July 1965) on four intellectual measures similar to Thurstone and Thurstone's (1962) Primary Mental Abilities (i.e., Induction, Verbal Comprehension, Number, Perceptual Speed). The objective was to determine the significance of cohort effects in children born within a given calendar year. In some respects, this study represents an extreme case of cohort effects because cohort variation involved birth cohort differences of 8 months or less.

In Figure 3.2 the findings for two measures of intellectual performance (Letter Counting, Basic Arithmetic) are presented. Vertical contrasts indicate cross-sectional age differences between 8-, 9-, and 10-year-olds at three time points during one academic year (i.e., November 1964, March 1965, July 1965). Horizontal comparisons indicate time-lag differences between same-aged children (8-, 9-, or 10-year-olds) belonging to different birth cohorts.

Data in Figure 3.2 demonstrate that cross-sectional age differences in

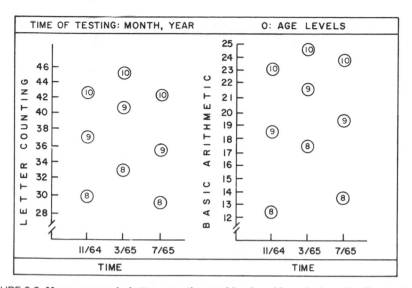

FIGURE 3.2. **Mean scores in letter counting and basic arithmetic from the Saarbrücken Cohort Study (after Baltes, Baltes, & Reinert, 1970). Using cross-sectional sequences as data-collection strategy, children of the same age levels (8:0, 9:0, 10:0) are shown to differ in performance at different times of the year (November, March, July). Differences are likely to be due to differences in length of schooling, with the same-aged children born and tested in March having at least 4 months more school experience than the other same-aged children (see Table 4.1 for further explanation).**

children's intellectual performance are not invariant across cohorts within a given year. Note that children at the second time of measurement (March 1965) perform significantly higher than their same-aged counterparts at either the earlier (November 1964) or later (July 1965) times of measurement. For example, performance of 8-year-olds in March on Basic Arithmetic is closer to the performance level of 9-year-olds than that of 8-year-olds measured either in November 1964 or July 1965. This pattern of superior performance for children born and tested in March held for all intelligence measures collected (see Baltes et al., 1970).

There are a number of potential explanations for these findings. For instance, several studies in the British literature deal with the establishment of so-called season-of-birth effects in intelligence (see Baltes et al., 1970, for review). The Baltes et al. (1970) study investigated the cohort-related variable—length of schooling. During the period of investigation, school entry in the state of Saarland, Germany, was set at April 1 with a minimum age of 6 by that date. Therefore, the initial age distribution of children entering first grade was 6:00 to 6:11, and at the end of the academic year (i.e., after 10 months of schooling) the age distribution was 6:10 to 7:9 for first-graders. Thus, when same-aged children were observed at different times in an academic year they had experienced differential amounts of schooling because of the shifting age distribution and definite age cutoff for school entry.

Thus, it is possible to identify children differing in "educational age" but not in chronological age (see also Goulet, 1975; Goulet, Hay, & Barclay, 1974). The relationship between age, time of measurement, and length of schooling is summarized in Table 3.1 for the Saarbrücken cohort study. There is a direct correlation between length of schooling and the level of intellectual performance reported in Figure 3.2: Children born and tested in March experienced more schooling and showed a higher test performance than same-aged children born and tested either in November or July.

Thus, it appears likely that the cohort effects in the Baltes *et al.* (1970) study are due to differential lengths of schooling. The notion of systematic within-year cohort effects makes the validity of simple cross-sectional or longitudinal designs questionable for investigating age changes. Furthermore, this study demonstrates how it is possible, in special circumstances, to use cohort-sequential designs that address questions of both descriptive identification of cohort effects and their explanatory analysis. Cohort effects were explained by linking cohort variation with differences in length of schooling.

B. Adolescent Personality Development

Nesselroade and Baltes (1974) investigated the age development of personality from 1970 to 1972 based on a sample of approximately 1900 male and female adolescents residing in northwestern West Virginia. Subjects were administered a battery of personality tests from Cattell's (1964) High School Personality Questionnaire and Jackson's (1968) Personality Research Form, as well as a battery of ability tests from the Primary Mental Abilities (Thurstone & Thurstone, 1962). Four birth cohorts (1955, 1956, 1957, and

TABLE 3.1
Length of Schooling in Years and Months for Children in the Saarbrücken Cohort Study[a]

	Time of testing		
Age	November 1964	March 1965	July 1965
8:0	1:7	1:11	1:3
9:0	2:7	2:11	2:3
10:0	3:7	3:11	2:3

[a] Differences in length of schooling (educational age) for same-aged children are a function of differences in chronological age at time of school entry. Children born in November entered school at 6:5, in March at age 6:1, and in July at age 6:9. (After Baltes, Baltes, & Reinert, 1970).

1958) were examined at three times of measurement (1970, 1971, and 1972) for age ranges of about 12–14, 13–15, 14–16, and 15–17 years.

Results for 2 of 10 personality dimensions—Independence and Achievement—are summarized in the upper part of Figure 3.3. Vertical comparisons in 1970, 1971, and 1972 represent cross-sectional age differences; horizontal comparisons across 1970, 1971, and 1972 represent longitudinal age changes for each of the four birth cohorts. The data on Independence suggest that all adolescents (as an entity) "developed" in the direction of more Independence during the 1970–1972 historical period in West Virginia. The finding of marked cohort effects may be illustrated by comparing the performance of 14-year-olds on Independence at three points in time. In 1972, 14-year-olds were significantly higher in Independence than their same-aged counterparts were in 1970 or 1971 and were even higher than 15-year-olds were in 1971 or 1972. The 1970–1972 cohort phenomenon is more pronounced than any discernible normative (ontogenetic) age trend for the adolescent period. The import of cohort differences is more dramatically illustrated in the performances of 14-years-olds on Achievement in 1970, 1971, and 1972. Fourteen-year-olds in 1970 exhibit the highest score on Achievement, whereas their same-aged peers in 1972 present the lowest score of all age groups.

In general, the outcomes for many of the 10 personality dimensions reported by Nesselroade and Baltes (1974) are very consistent and in line with the data reported here on Independence and Achievement. First, a very large share of variance in cross-sectional age differences is related to cohort membership rather than chronological age. Indeed, the three cross-sectional age differences (at each time of measurement) for the different dimensions of personality do not exhibit similar age-difference outcomes in either level or shape. Second, intercohort differences in longitudinal age changes are rather substantial. The results support the position that the average quantitative standing and the ontogenetic age trends of adolescents on dimensions of personality are less dependent upon chronological age than upon the historical time (cultural moment) to which the adolescents have been exposed. The age development of adolescents on the personality dimensions is neither normative nor invariant; cohort differences in the level and shape of adolescent developmental functions are marked and consistent.

The pattern of cohort effects reported by Nesselroade and Baltes (1974) cannot be linked to a specific set of antecedent or concomitant factors because the study did not incorporate variables aimed at cohort explanation (such as length of schooling in the Saarbrücken study). However, the consistency in outcome—all age-cohorts changed toward more Independence, less Achievement, and less Superego Strength from 1970 to 1972—suggested that the age-change functions might be linked to cultural experiences from 1970 to 1972 that were common to American adolescents (e.g., the impact

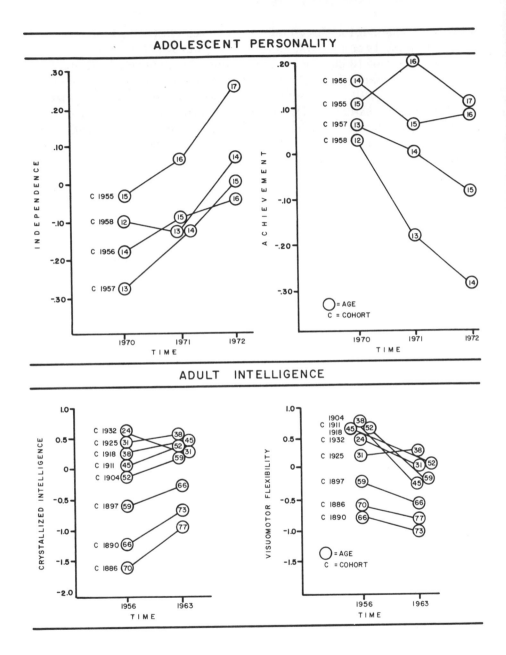

of influences in the United States associated with the Vietnam War). However, efforts at specifying antecedents of the age functions of adolescent cohorts observed by Nesselroade and Baltes (1974) are speculative, tentative, and of a post hoc nature because sequential strategies are, in principle, descriptive and not explanatory.

C. Intellectual Development in Adulthood

Schaie's (e.g., 1970) study of intelligence in adulthood and old age is presented here based on 7-year longitudinal observations (from 1956 to 1963) of eight cohorts (birth dates: 1886, 1890, 1897, 1904, 1911, 1918, 1925, 1932) covering the adult age range from 21 to 77 years in 7-year intervals (Nesselroade *et al.*, 1972). In the meantime, Schaie's work spans a 14-year longitudinal period (e.g., Schaie, Labouvie, & Buech, 1973; Schaie & Parham, 1977) and has attracted much attention and heated debate (e.g., Horn & Donaldson, 1976 versus Baltes & Schaie, 1976). Schaie's study began with a stratified random sample ($N = 500$) selected from a medical insurance plan in Seattle, Washington. The original sample has been reduced through attrition, and it has been supplemented with various follow-up and control samples (Schaie, 1979). The dependent variables include tests from both Thurstone and Thurstone's (1949) Primary Mental Abilities and Schaie's (1960) Test of Behavioral Rigidity.

Data from two of four second-order dimensions of intellectual performance (i.e., Crystallized Intelligence, Visuo-Motor Flexibility) taken from the Nesselroade *et al.* (1972) analysis are presented in the lower portion of Figure 3.3. The figure contains results of two "cross-sectional" studies based on longitudinal sequences conducted in 1956 and 1963. Cohort-specific age changes are plotted in 7-year longitudinal gradients for each of the eight cohorts.

The key findings are the following (also see Baltes & Schaie, 1976). First, the amount of cohort-related variance is at least as sizable as longitudinal age-change variance for most intellectual dimensions. The import of cohort differences can be most easily discerned in Figure 3.3 by comparing same-aged persons in 1956 versus 1963 on Crystallized Intelligence. For example, 66-year-olds in 1963 were significantly higher in performance than 66-year-olds in 1956 or even 59-year-olds in 1956.

Second, Schaie's data demonstrate multidimensionality, multidirectionality, and variability in intellectual performance during adulthood (Baltes & Schaie, 1976). Multidimensionality is evidenced in distinct change patterns for distinct ability dimensions (e.g., Crystallized Intelligence versus Visuo-Motor Flexibility), and multidirectionality is shown in the distinctive cohort-specific change patterns (see, e.g., Schaie *et al.*, 1973). Contrary to widely held stereotypes about aging decline, intellectual performance does not universally (i.e., for all persons and all ability dimensions) and necessarily decline. Large variability is manifest not only in intercohort differences but also in within-cohort variability. For example, the older age/cohorts (ages: 59–66, 66–73, 70–77) increased in Crystallized Intelligence, at least from 1956 to 1963, whereas younger age/cohorts maintained their performance levels during this period. In addition, many older adults performed at levels well above the average younger adult even though the age peers of some of the elderly may have performed on the average at a lower level than younger adults (see Schaie & Parham, 1977, for further documentation).

Researchers interested in the theoretical meaning and origin of these cohort effects may be somewhat disappointed about our position, contrary to Schaie's, that sequential research designs do not permit an appropriate causal analysis unless they include special circumstances. Strictly speaking, all one can state is that from 1956 to 1963 the biocultural context and contingencies for distinct cohorts were such that a complex pattern of change functions (i.e., multidimensional, multidirectional) resulted that did not exhibit a simple picture of normative age trends in intelligence during adulthood and old age. Moreover, it is necessary to be careful (see Baltes & Baltes, 1977; Baltes & Schaie, 1976) that we do not make an assumption that the intellectual change patterns observed in a given historical period will generalize to other cohorts and time periods. In fact, the nature of cohort effects implies a notion of uncertainty and historical relativity.

D. Corroborative Evidence for Cohort Effects

In addition to the three research projects described above, a number of other research investigations in developmental psychology emphasize the impact of cohort membership on behavioral development. Much of this evidence can be found in research specifically using cohort sequential designs as well as in research employing simple time-lag designs. A review of such research in developmental psychology is reported in Baltes *et al.* (1978). A partial review and good usage of sociological research on age-cohort issues is contained in Elder (1979).

In general, it is notable that most of the research conducted thus far, covering a wide spectrum of developmental psychology, has indeed supported the notion of birth-cohort-related differences in ontogenetic development. These differences, though not always striking or indicative of structural cohort-related effects, point to the conclusion that cohort effects are a relatively likely and pervasive phenomenon. However, we need to recognize that much of the existing literature on cohort effects has been provided by researchers interested in the existence of cohort effects. It may very well be that researchers with different interests will produce outcomes exhibiting less dramatic evidence for cohort variation (e.g., Weisz, 1978).

IV. Toward Explanations of Cohort Effects

It is not the aim of this chapter to propose a single model of the explanatory–causal analysis of cohort effects and their role in conceptions of individual development. Rather, a number of general issues and criteria pertinent to the construction of explanatory models of cohort effects are discussed. Indeed, our assumption is that explanatory work on cohort effects will lead to neither a single monolithic conception of the cohort variable nor any specific research paradigm. On the contrary, it is our contention that the explanatory search for the meaning and mechanisms of cohort effects will best be implemented by diverse conceptual and paradigmatic approaches. The presentation is divided into three subsections. First, the logical status of the cohort variable is analyzed, and second, various treatments of its role in design and theory are outlined. Third, a couple of generic methodological approaches to cohort explanation are discussed in the final subsection.

A. The Logical Status of the Cohort Variable

The logical status of cohort is similar to that of chronological age (e.g., Baer, 1970; Baltes, 1968a; Baltes & Goulet, 1971; Wohlwill, 1970a, 1973). Cohort, if defined as birth cohort, is a person or assigned variable (Kerlinger, 1964) that does not have the characteristics of a full-fledged experimental variable. The design status, which is allocated to the cohort variable, has many implications for theory building.

On the one hand, some researchers argue that cohort-related change and cohort-related determinants are "primary" and key elements for developmental theory (e.g., Baltes & Willis, 1977; Bengtson & Black, 1973; Bengtson & Laufer, 1974; Buss, 1974a; Elder, 1975; Riley, 1976). Similar to Wohlwill's (1970a) position, which states that the regularities and robustness of age functions are an important sine qua non for explanatory developmental research, such cohort researchers view the nature of cohort functions and cohort-related indicators as a powerful avenue toward developmental explanation. In their opinion it is necessary to capitalize on the opportunity provided by cohort effects to design research leading to a more refined theoretical explanation of cohort effects. To paraphrase Birren (1959, p. 8), cohort relations "are inevitably in transition to being explained by other variables" without recourse to the use of the term *cohort*.

On the other hand, some researchers will be less than enthusiastic about the cohort variable because of its deficiencies as a manipulable variable in experimentation and its associated lack of explanatory power. Similar to Baer's (1970) view that the age variable is largely irrelevant for the study of behavioral development, their argument would be that the study of cohort effects does not focus sufficiently on a theory of behavioral or social change. Therefore, they would advocate moving as quickly as possible toward a "cohort-irrelevant" conception and strategy of studying the interaction between ontogenetic and biocultural components of change. Such an approach, in its extreme form, represents the cohort variable at its worst.

Because of its status as a person variable, the cohort variable is considered theoretically impotent with the risk of misleading the field. As Underwood (1975) stated in another context: "We cannot deal constructively with individual differences when we identify the important variables as age, sex, grade, IQ, social status, and so on [p. 134]." (We add cohort.) The critical variables are process variables. In the history of life-span developmental psychology, it was Quetelet (see Baltes, 1979) who in 1835 already viewed the cohort variable in such a manner. For Quetelet, it was important to "see through" the disturbances created by historical moments in order to ascertain the true nature of age-developmental functions.

B. Cohort Variable in Design and Theory

The cohort variable will be treated differently depending on the conceptual beliefs that researchers share regarding the significance of (1) the role of biocultural change; (2) the role of experimental design; and (3) the need for process approaches. These differences will be reflected in the way cohort is treated in research and theory.

1. Cohort as Error or Disturbance

Cohort variability might be treated as error or nondevelopmental (though systematic) variance. Similar to other individual-differences conceptions, the position is that any behavioral principle or law is formulated and examined within a context of contingencies that are irrelevant for the behavioral principle or theory under consideration. Cohort effects and the nature of biocultural history are seen as providing for such a framework of irrelevant contingencies. The objective of developmental research in this case would be the search for and isolation of basic developmental–onotogenetic processes in the face of the "disturbances" created by irrelevant cohort effects (similar to the 1835 Quetelet position).

This view of cohort-related phenomena as error or disturbance will be accepted most likely among developmental psychologists who are primarily child- rather than life-span–oriented and at the same time interested in either so-called basic processes (learning, cognition, memory, etc.) or organismic growth-oriented conceptions of development (such as Piagetian approaches to cognitive development). We recognize that any conceptual position will necessarily include some aspects of uncertainty (Labouvie, 1975b), and the cohort variable might most easily be justified as part of the realm of assumptive uncertainty in the area of basic cognitive development in children. Nevertheless, relegating cohort effects to the level of assumptive uncertainty will restrict the precision and scope of developmental theory in the domains involved. Moreover, a cohort-irrelevant posture vis-à-vis the field of child development necessarily leads to conceptions that are impoverished when it comes to understanding social change, the changing role of children in society, and the design of intervention programs for childhood development (e.g., Montada & Filipp, 1976).

2. Cohort as Dimension of Generalization

A general position that is more favorable to treating the cohort variable as a viable element for theory construction is one that views cohort as a dimension of generalization. This approach can be illustrated by reference to Campbell and Stanley's (1963) conceptualization of external validity (also see Baltes *et al.*, 1977; Bell & Hertz, 1976). External validity involves a scheme of generalization across the following five facets, or dimensions: experimental units (persons), setting, time, treatment conditions, and measurement variables. The external-validity question is whether a given relationship, such as a developmental finding, observed in one set of data (with specific persons, setting, time, treatment, and measurement properties) can be generalized to other potential data sets. In all instances, cohort effects represent interindividual differences (across time, persons, and settings). Therefore, conceptualizing the cohort variable as a dimension of generalizability is one viable tack that goes beyond its use as error or nondevelopmental variance.

Identifying cohort as a facet of generalizability, however, does not yet elevate it to the status of a full-fledged theoretical variable. But characterizing it as such does suggest that cohort-sequential research is important in the study of behavioral development for the purpose of examining the quantitative boundaries of "basic" developmental findings. Thus, the primary goal would be to examine the range within which developmental–ontogenetic change and processes could occur. In some ways, viewing cohort effects as part of external validity is comparable either to the treatment of chronological age in developmental research as a parameter of quantitative rather than structural variation (also see Hultsch & Hickey, 1978), or to a definition of the field of developmental psychology as a straightforward application of basic general learning principles to nonadult age groups such as children.

In any case, accepting cohort as a dimension of generalization, which is apt to identify interindividual differences in ontogenetic development, makes it mandatory to conduct cohort-sequential research. Such research permits a direct assessment of the relative degree of invariance or stability (across historical time) for distinct classes of developmental behavior. It protects the researcher from falsely treating cohort-specific (simple longitudinal) or cross-sectional information on age development as a representative or normative indicator of ontogenetic development.

3. Cohort as Theoretical and Process Variable

An approach that views the cohort variable as a potentially major ingredient in developmental theory treats cohort as (1) an indicator of a hypothetical construct that has not yet been fully delineated; and (2) a construct that contains information about sources of and mechanisms in behavioral development. Such an approach is the most difficult (Rosow, 1978). It explicitly recognizes that, depending on the particular research question, cohort can be linked to a system of antecedent, process, and consequent events in ways that are useful for the description, explanation, and modification of developmental change. The treatment of cohort as a theoretical process variable parallels Wohlwill's (1970a, 1973) approach to the age variable where age is considered part of the dependent variable (i.e., the dependent variable is conceptualized as an age-change function).

If one views the cohort variable as a viable theoretical variable, it will be necessary to delineate the nature of dimensions involved in cohort explication: the form and nature of cohort change that is judged to be developmental, the need for such concepts as stages or transitions in representing cohort change, and the types of explanatory mechanisms involved in producing cohort change. Such efforts will in the final analysis permit conclusions about the viability of the cohort construct in the study of behavioral development. Perhaps the best way to illustrate the issues involved in the explication of the cohort variable is to consult Wohlwill's (1970a) excellent discussion of the age variable in developmental research and to apply similar perspectives to the cohort variable.

Figure 3.4 is designed to illustrate the cohort variable as an important theoretical search variable in developmental theory construction. As discussed in Chapter 1, the upper part of Figure 3.4 indicates three major influence systems that control behavioral development: (1) *ontogenetic age-graded influences,* (2) *evolutionary history-graded influences,* and (3) *non-normative influences.* The assertion expressed in Figure 3.4 is that a major share of the influences on or determinants of behavioral development can be organized into two classes that covary with temporal indices: those that exhibit a high correlation with chronological age (ontogenetic, age-graded) and those that exhibit a high correlation with biocultural history (evolutionary, history-graded). This distinction is similar to the one made by Neugarten and Datan (1973), who contrast life time with historical time, and to the two major components contained in Riley's (1976) age–cohort stratification model (see also Elder, 1975). Influences from both ontogenetic and evolutionary systems can include biological as well as environmental variables. Moreover, the systems of influence can change across time and may interact with each other. In the upper part of Figure 3.4, basic conceptions of

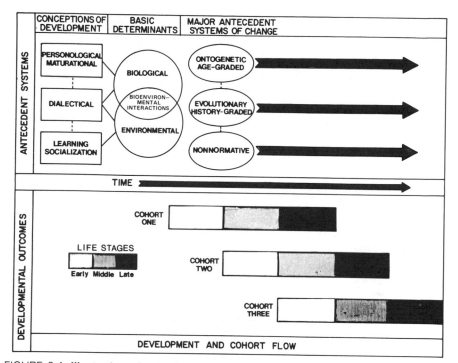

FIGURE 3.4. **Illustration of relationship between life-span development, cohorts, and three major influence systems: ontogenetic, evolutionary, and nonnormative sources of development. The lower part of the figure is a modification of the age–cohort stratification model presented in Riley, Johnson, and Foner (1972).**

development (personological, maturational, etc.) corresponding to each of these origins of change are indicated.

Figure 3.4 depicts a third set of influences on behavioral development that is graded by neither age nor history in any systematic fashion. This set of influences is labeled nonnormative to emphasize that these influences (biological and environmental) do not occur universally for all people, nor, if they occur, are they universal in terms of such parameters as timing, sequencing, duration, or event constellation. Examples of nonnormative influences would be area- and period-specific events (e.g., floods, droughts, earthquakes, wars, depressions, epidemic health hazards) or some forms of life events (e.g., career change, illness, loss of employment, institutionalization, divorce, deaths of parents, spouse, or children) as described by Dohrenwend and Dohrenwend (1974) and Hultsch and Plemons (1979). Although nonnormative influences do not occur in a temporally systematic fashion, their impact on the nature of life-span development can be important and, as argued in Chapter 1, they may increase in relative importance with increasing age.

An important task for the immediate future is to construct taxonomies dealing with the likely form of the three influence systems. For example, it could be argued that the traditional concept of development (with its focus on age-normative, unidirectional, irreversible attributes, etc.) might be applicable primarily to age-graded influence systems and to distinct age periods in the life span (e.g., childhood). History-graded and nonnormative influence systems, on the other hand, would tend to produce developmental change sequences that exhibit characteristics of multidimensionality and plasticity. That is, behavior-change processes resulting from history-graded and nonnormative influences would demonstrate properties that depart markedly from a traditional concept for development. Baltes and his colleagues (Baltes, 1979) have taken such an approach when discussing the formal nature of life-span change, for instance in the area of intellectual development (Baltes & Willis, 1979b).

The lower part of Figure 3.4 illustrates how these sources of influence combine in generating ontogenetic development. That part of Figure 3.4 depicts the life-course development of several cohorts, which, of course, occurs at different historical points in time. Thus, the juxtaposition of the upper and lower parts of Figure 3.4 represents the notion that ontogenetic (age-graded), evolutionary (history-graded), and nonnormative influence systems operate simultaneously over time in the production of life-course outcomes (i.e., behavioral development). Moreover, the lower part of Figure 3.4 is designed to illustrate that similar age groups existing at different points in time may be influenced by *distinct* ontogenetic and historical systems of antecedents that thereby produce *different* patterns of changes in the life course and cohort flow. In addition, the life courses of individuals may be affected by nonnormative events. Within cohorts such nonnormative influences would tend to be the primary agents for producing interindividual differences in developmental change.

One final observation on Figure 3.4 is that the prototheoretical conception of development postulating that ontogenetic and evolutionary influences operate conjointly and interactively has come to be labeled the *dialectical conception of development*. Proponents of a dialectical orientation (e.g., Baltes & Willis, 1977; Riegel, 1972, 1973, 1976a, 1976b; Rychlak, 1976) imply that other major prototheoretical conceptions of development (such as maturational and learning) have for the most part not given an adequate and balanced treatment to both ontogenetic and evolutionary perspectives. Although a dialectical conception of development is far from being articulated with sufficient clarity (see Baltes & Cornelius, 1977), the key attributes of dialectics form a fairly coherent and novel pattern of assumptions and prescriptions for research and theory in the field of developmental psychology. Thus, in our view (Baltes & Cornelius, 1977), it is becoming apparent that dialectics—because of its intrinsic focus on both historical and individual change as a primary condition;   on interactive relationships, transitions, structure, and qualitative structural transformations; and on less than absolute predictive determinancy—exhibits a pattern of theoretical characteristics that show a high degree of convergence with the basic tenets of developmental research and theory.

C. Methodology and the Explication of Cohort Effects

Attempts to describe and structure the nature of cohort as a variable and to incorporate it into explanatory accounts of long-term developmental change must rely, at least in part, on alternatives to conventional manipulative experimentation. We shall briefly mention two approaches that seem especially pertinent (see Baltes *et al.*, 1977, and the remaining chapters in this volume).

One general approach is the construction of plausible causal explanations by *simulation studies* (Baltes & Goulet, 1971). A simulation study involves the arrangement of experimental conditions in the laboratory to produce, in a short time span, a target change function (in this instance a cohort-change function) that would ordinarily be observed in vivo as a long-term change phenomenon. The knowledge generated experimentally may, with obvious risks, be used to construct explanatory accounts that in turn lead to even more pertinent simulated as well as naturalistic data for further refinement and testing. Eckensberger (1973) and Labouvie (1975a) emphasized the need to initiate simulation research representing the mechanisms of long-term cohort-related cultural changes, if further progress in detailing the nature of cohort effects is to be realized. Similarly, Elder's (1974, 1977) work, involving a comparative analysis of intracohort processes, can be conceptualized as a form of cohort-simulation research.

A second general approach to the development of explanatory accounts of the relationship between cohort and developmental change is the use of extended time-series analyses (Campbell, 1969, 1975; Frederiksen & Rotondo, Chapter 15, this volume) and especially the application of causal modeling techniques and strategies. Causal modeling, or structural-equation analysis, is being developed rapidly by sociologists, economists, psychologists, and statisticians (Baltes *et al.*, 1977; Duncan, 1975a; Goldberger & Duncan, 1973; Jöreskog, Chapter 11; Labouvie, 1974; Rogosa, Chapter 10). The purpose of such techniques is to build and test causal representations of phenomena that are not experimentally tractable. The techniques generally involve an explicit mathematical specification of the network of hypothesized causal relationships among concepts and variables. Statistical procedures are then employed to estimate the parameters of the causal system and to evaluate its fit to data. Refinements allow the use of multiple indicators of theoretical constructs and the representation of complex chains of causation, including reciprocal causation.

V. Summary Implications for Theory and Research in Human Development

In concluding, we will summarize some of the implications of cohort effects with a particular concern for methodological strategies, theoretical paradigms, and the role of multi- and interdisciplinary approaches to the study of human development.

The empirical power of the cohort variable in the twentieth century in the Western world appears to be of such a magnitude that it is not justified to formulate categorically an assumptive framework about behavioral development that denies the potential existence of cohort-related influence patterns. In general, however, the available evidence on the role of cohort effects in behavioral development is largely descriptive. Efforts at theoretical–explanatory analysis are rare and at best prototheoretical. Therefore, in principle, it is possible to treat the cohort variable in any of three major ways: as error or disturbance, as a dimension of generalization, or as a theoretical process variable.

The following methodological and theoretical propositions are advanced to delineate a framework within and from which distinct lines of march for further investigation can be deduced. These perspectives are not mandatory but rather reflect our metatheoretical position on the role of cohort effects in developmental psychology. Similar propositions have been advanced recently in a number of research quarters in developmental psychology not necessarily for the same reasons (e.g., Baltes & Willis, 1977; Bronfenbrenner, 1974, 1977; Chandler, 1976; Elder, 1975; Hartup, 1976; Hartup & Lempers, 1973; Riegel, 1976a, 1976b; Willems, 1973). In fact, in our view the convergence of the propositions derived from cohort research, other areas of emphasis in developmental psychology, and a historical review of the field of life-span development (Baltes, 1979) is indeed remarkable.

A. Methodology

The definitional assumption is that developmental psychology deals with multiple components of variability.

In behavioral development, there are intraindividual change and interindividual differences therein. Interindividual differences in intraindividual change, however, exist not only within a given cohort, but also between cohorts. Both kinds of interindividual differences need to be separated from each other and from true intraindividual change in order to provide valid targets for subsequent explanatory analysis. Specifically, there are four core components of variability: within-cohort developmental (intraindividual) changes, within-cohort interindividual differences in developmental change, between-cohort differences in developmental change, and between-cohort differences in interindividual differences in developmental change.

Developmental research designs are more powerful to the degree that they are able to identify these separate components of variability. The unequivocal conclusion is that descriptive identification of these components of developmental variability and change needs to go beyond the use of simple cross-sectional or longitudinal methodology. The application of cohort-sequential methodology is suggested for that purpose. Simple cross-sectional age differences are most likely hopelessly confounded and, at the very least, the joint product of age changes and cohort differences. Simple longitudinal age-change gradients have limited generalizability and do not provide evidence for the relative degree of invariance or stability of developmental phenomena across historical time. Some mixed designs involving combinations of partial cross-sectional and longitudinal studies are useful approximations when resources are limited.

The appropriate search for explanation of developmental (ontogenetic) change is easily misled if the target phenomena are not indicative of valid ontogenetic change.

The likelihood of successful explanatory developmental research is increased if it is addressed to a validly identified developmental phenomenon. The pervasiveness of cohort effects is either a major threat to valid identification of developmental change or an indicator of the need for identifying multiple components of change (variability), each existing in its own right and requiring separate formats of causal analysis.

For example, if much of the cross-sectional age variance is not identical with or representative of age-developmental change, then searching for age-related explanations or origins of change is a misguided task, since there will always be a conceptual mismatch between product and process. Similarly, if cohort-specific longitudinal gradients do not generalize across historical periods, then subsequent explanatory efforts (often conducted at later historical points) are equally bound to be misdirected and likely to result in either discrepant and confusing outcomes or a lack of precision and predictive utility.

The issue of trifactorial age–cohort–time of measurement confounds is only relevant if one assigns theoretical status to all factors.

Schaie's (1965) original General Developmental Model provided for three distinct analytic schemes because the intent was both to describe and to explain development using age, cohort, and time of measurement as independent explanatory factors. In the meantime, it is recognized that this approach represents a special case of causal analysis and that alternative strategies might be more useful. As a consequence, the preferred use of sequential strategies is for descriptive identification of developmental variability. Moreover, for developmental psychology, use of age and cohort variation provides for direct estimates of all components of developmental variability: intraindividual change and within- as well as between-cohort interindividual differences in change. Therefore, for both substantive and statistical reasons, there is no problem of trifactorial confounding in most situations. Age and cohort represent adequate and comprehensive descriptive indicators of developmental change and variation.

Theory

In general, cohort effects point to a lack of simple age-graded nomothetic and universal patterns in behavioral development.

Findings on cohort effects suggest plasticity, variability, and often multidirectionality, on the level of both individual and group analysis, at least at the "phenotypic" performance level. Whether these phenotypic cohort differences reflect changes in basic processes is an unanswered question awaiting future research.

In any case, however, the role of chronological age as a key search and organizing variable in the study of development is further challenged. Much of observed developmental change is not likely to be related to variables generally associated with age; therefore, age is not necessarily the most important initial search variable for explanatory analysis. Many of the findings on cohort effects in adolescence, adulthood, and aging indicate that systematic change is evident but that it is either specific to or related to cohort (and other events) rather than to age membership.

Cohort effects suggest, from a theory-construction point of view, that simple personological, intraorganismic models of development are insufficient.

The theoretical orientation deducible from cohort effects implies concerns for ecological relativity and correlated plasticity of behavioral development (see also Baltes & Baltes, 1977). Simple personological models are insufficient because large variability between cohorts and multidirectionality cannot be easily accounted for by a set of principles for development that assigns the major locus of developmental action to intraorganismic, genetically preprogrammed determinants.

Cohort effects suggest the need for explanatory models of development that are interactive, contextual, and ecological. The emerging formulation of a dialectical orientation to the study of behavioral development (Baltes & Cornelius, 1977; Huston-Stein & Baltes, 1976; Riegel, 1973, 1976a, 1976b) is an expression of the search for interactive and contextual models of development. The same is true for the parallel emergence of an ecological orientation as evidenced in the work of researchers such as Bronfenbrenner (1974, 1977).

As a corollary, research on cohort effects suggests the need for multi-

disciplinary approaches in order to capture the joint import of ontogenetic and historical-evolutionary components of change.

The existence of cohort effects, contrary to simple personological-ontogenetic models, focuses on both individual and biocultural change systems. In the past, the study of biocultural change has not been of great concern to psychologists. Traditionally, anthropologists and sociologists were more typical of the social scientists interested in the study of social change and evolutionary principles. Research on cohort effects suggests a rapprochement between disciplines of social and biological science in order to arrive at a comprehensive view of individual development in a changing biocultural context.

The suggestion is not that developmental psychologists expand their field to include biocultural change as a dependent variable. Rather, the suggestion is that biocultural change codetermines and interacts with individual development and that the joint consideration, on both the descriptive and explanatory level, of individual and biocultural change components is desirable (see also Baltes, 1979; Baltes & Willis, 1977; Elder, 1975; Keniston, 1971; Riegel, 1976a,1976b; Riley, 1976). A comprehensive understanding of behavioral development in a rapidly changing world cannot be accomplished if the forces and forms of individual development and biocultural change are treated as conceptually separate and without concern for their interactive relationships. On the contrary, the pervasiveness of cohort effects suggests the need for multidisciplinary collaboration and eventually "marriage," because, as Willems (1973) suggested in another context, "Courtship is not enough."

Chapter 4

Mathematical Description and Representation of Developmental Change Functions on the Intra- and Interindividual Levels

KENNETH E. GUIRE

CHARLES J. KOWALSKI

ABSTRACT

Methods of the analysis of longitudinal data are discussed. For the intraindividual case that deals with a single longitudinal series, a variety of curve fitting approaches are considered. For the interindividual case that deals with one or more samples of longitudinal observations, several methods, including univariate analysis of variance, multivariate analysis of variance, and polynomial growth curve models are considered. An attempt is made to relate these methods, which are widely used in biological applications, to the broader context of developmental research.

I. Introduction

In an earlier paper (Kowalski & Guire, 1974), we surveyed the then-available data-analytic strategies for several types of longitudinal data sets. In particular, we identified six distinct types of longitudinal data sets, namely, (1) univariate time series; (2) univariate one-sample data matrices; (3) univariate k-sample data matrices; (4) multivariate time series; (5) multivariate one-sample data matrices; and (6) multivariate k-sample data matrices, and the methodologies appropriate for each of these types were treated separately. The present chapter builds on this background, paying special attention to the mathematical description and representation of developmental-change functions on the intra- and interindividual levels. An overview of the available models and statistical procedures for the analysis of such data is presented. The aim of this presentation is to identify certain procedures that have proved to be useful in the biological, growth-oriented

89

LONGITUDINAL RESEARCH IN THE
STUDY OF BEHAVIOR AND DEVELOPMENT

sciences for possible application in behavioral developmental research. In so doing, we must carefully consider potential differences in the structure of the measurements to be analyzed, and, whenever possible, models that do not require monotonicity and nonparametric analogs for the statistical procedures discussed will be cited. On the other hand, more research—from the standpoint of both theory and practice—needs to be done before we can confidently analyze multivariate data sets in any field of application (cf. Kowalski, 1972); thus, any words of caution in this context should be tempered by the need for the entire developmental research community to gain some experience in the use of these techniques (Prahl-Andersen & Kowalski, 1973). It is in this spirit that this chapter is written. Behavioral scientists should be aware of the possibilities and limitations of statistical treatment of developmental data; the models presented were chosen to illustrate both ends of this spectrum, as well as many of the shady areas in between.

We begin with a general discussion of longitudinal data sets in the context of the design of developmental studies. The purpose of this section is to place the longitudinal approach into some perspective vis-à-vis the oft-heard dictum that "the design of a study is a function of the purposes of the investigation," and an attempt at delineating the class of studies for which longitudinal designs may be appropriate is made. It is recognized that development will often depend on factors other than simple chronological age, but it is argued that this does not imply that the class referred to above is empty. Since questions of this type are considered in great detail in the first part of this book, our discussion is brief and somewhat cursory. It is included only in an attempt to counteract some of the impact of much of the recent developmental literature that seems bent on condemning the longitudinal method. We then consider questions associated with the descriptive and explanatory study of intraindividual change. We focus on the implications of choosing one or another of the models that can be used for these purposes and thereby confront important philosophical problems ranging from the making of reasonable a priori assumptions to the validation of a model by the expedient of subjecting it to a goodness-of-fit test. Finally, we discuss techniques for the investigation of interindividual differences in development. We consider not only formal hypothesis-testing techniques but also less formal, descriptive, data-analytic procedures that may prove useful in unraveling some of the complex problems associated with the measurement of change (Harris, 1963b).

II. Designs for the Study of Development

Much of the current thinking in behavioral research concerning the study of development was generated by a series of papers by Schaie (1965, 1970,

1972). In 1965, Schaie introduced a trifactorial developmental model which views development, D, as a function of A = chronological age, C = cohort, and T = time-of-measurement. Perhaps the greatest contribution of this model was to focus attention on the implications it had for the choice of the design of developmental studies. In particular, Schaie (1970) pointed out that (1) cross-sectional designs confound the age and cohort effects; (2) longitudinal designs confound the age and time-of-measurement effects; and (3) time-lag designs confound the age and time-of-measurement effects. Though these facts were apparent long before Schaie introduced his model, the model provided a convenient conceptual framework that clearly illustrated the source of these problems. In an attempt to rectify the situation, the general notion of a mixed-longitudinal design was developed (Prahl-Andersen & Kowalski, 1973), and several special cases, namely, the cohort-sequential, time-sequential, and cross-sequential designs, were identified and proposed for use in certain well-defined types of developmental investigations (Wohlwill, 1970b). It was clear that Schaie viewed these mixed-longitudinal strategies as completely replacing the more traditional designs. Schaie (1972) was especially vociferous in condemning longitudinal designs, concluding that "the single cohort longitudinal study be used for no other purpose than that of the historian, the case history reporter, or to gather anecdotal material for the purpose of generating hypotheses." However, none of the Schaie designs completely solves the problem of confounding alluded to earlier, and a number of questions have arisen regarding both the analysis (van't Hof, Prahl-Andersen, & Kowalski, 1976) and the interpretation (Baltes, 1968b) of data collected using the mixed-longitudinal approach. Thus Hindley (1972) responded to Schaie by noting, "At the same time that he belabors the longitudinal method for resting on dubious assumptions, he seems prepared to make other assumptions which some might consider equally open to question. One example is his use of projected longitudinal gradients which, as he admits, depend on the assumption that environmental input will be approximately equal over past and future time intervals [p. 40]." It would appear, then, that there may be a bit of life left in longitudinal research despite the well-known and documented problems it presents in the data-collection (Jones, 1958), data-analytic (Kowalski & Guire, 1974), and interpretive (Cronbach & Furby, 1970) spheres.

We approach this question by summarizing the case against the longitudinal method in the context of Schaie's trifactorial developmental model. If we write $D = f(A, C, T)$ to represent Schaie's model, we see that there are two distinct problems to be faced. The first is that since longitudinal studies are indexed by but two of the three factors comprising Schaie's model, $D = f(A, T)$, we cannot generalize the results of any longitudinal investigation beyond the cohort selected for study. Otherwise stated, if we are to attempt to generalize the results of a longitudinal study, we must assume that the cohort effect is zero. The second problem, already mentioned, is that even if the cohort effect can reasonably be neglected, age differences will still be confounded with time-of-measurement effects, these being viewed as temporary variations or aberrations superimposed on the developmental function. What Schaie's argument comes down to, then, is that longitudinal studies are appropriate only in those cases when $C = T = 0$. But must every study answer all questions? It is our opinion that to adopt this attitude would stifle a good deal of potentially valuable research. There are situations in which the longitudinal approach must be employed since a number of questions cannot be answered in any other way. To cite but one example, if our concern is with intraindividual patterning of relationships among variables over time, there simply is no substitute for the longitudinal method (Wohlwill, 1970b). Whenever we wish to study the relationships between the amount or direction of change for two or more variables, or between such change and any other information about the individual, the only alternative to the longitudinal approach is the abandonment of the project. This does not mean that every project is worth doing, that one should flatly ignore potential time-of-measurement disturbances, and that cohort effects are mere figments of the imagination. It means simply that we should take care with the procedural conduct of the study and prudently limit our inferences to the population from which our sample was selected. We need not overreact to the point of jettisoning the longitudinal approach. As stated by Jones (1958), "If we wish . . . to achieve a body of developmental theory, we cannot eliminate developmental observation [p. 98]."

Though we certainly do not advocate the use of the longitudinal approach in every developmental investigation, it is our contention that there are situations in which time-of-measurement effects may be safely neglected—for example, in most studies of physical growth—and that when these effects are unimportant, most of the objections to the longitudinal approach disappear. This is primarily due to the fact that the remaining technical difficulties associated with the longitudinal method are counterbalanced by its great efficiency in estimating change scores. Wallis and Roberts (1956) for example, estimated that in analyzing the weights of men before and after a lapse of time, each of two independent samples would have to contain 2222 individuals (a total of 4444 observations) to provide the same sampling reliability as a single paired sample of 25 men measured before and after the lapse of time. Though the data they used to obtain these estimates were artificially generated, they do provide some idea of the increase in precision of the paired-sample approach that may be expected in practice (see also Rao & Rao, 1966).

We turn now to questions dealing with the study of intraindividual change. Some mathematical models that can be used to mirror these changes are presented and discussed in the context of their potential usefulness in developmental research.

III. Models for Intraindividual Change

We begin, following Kessen (1960), by agreeing that "a characteristic is said to be developmental if it can be related to age in an orderly or lawful way." Thus, given a series of measurements $x_1, x_2, \ldots, x_T$ on a given individual, we suppose that the tth such measurement ($t = 1, 2, \ldots, T$) can be expressed in the form

$$x_t = f(t) + \epsilon_t \tag{1}$$

in which the observations x_t are viewed as being composed of a systematic part, $f(t)$, and a random or stochastic part, ϵ_t, which obeys some probability law. The basic problem is then to fit a function, $f(t)$ to the observations in such a way that the function (1) provides a close fit to the data; (2) has a reasonably simple mathematical structure; and (3) has relatively few parameters, whose meanings are clear with a definite developmental significance (Israelsohn, 1960). A number of such functions have been proposed for use in a variety of developmental circumstances. Perhaps the simplest of these is the first-order autoregressive scheme, or Markov Process, in which

$$f(t) = \beta x_{t-1}$$

so that the value of the observation at time t is a simple linear function of the measurement made at the preceding time point. The next most complex form of linear autoregressive series is the Yule series, where

$$f(t) = \beta_1 x_{t-1} + \beta_2 x_{t-2}$$

and x_t is determined by the values of the observations made at the preceding two time points. This formulation can be extended in obvious ways, and a good account of autoregressive models is provided by Kendall and Stuart (1968). These and a number of other forms for $f(t)$ may be generated by characterizing the developmental process in terms of a differential equation. Here we sketch some examples of simple differential equations that have been used to this end. Letting t denote time and x denote magnitude of the measurement being taken, the differential coefficient dx/dt then denotes the rate of growth; that is, the increase in x per unit time. It is generally assumed that the growth process may be characterized by a differential equation

$$dx/dt = g(x, t)$$

which says that the growth rate depends on both time and current size. In the examples to follow, we consider only special cases of the type

$$dx/dt = g(x)h(t) \tag{2}$$

which may be written as

$$dx/g(x) = h(t)\, dt$$

or, solving,

$$\int [dx/g(x)] = H(t) \tag{3}$$

which determines x as a function of t. Turning to some specific examples, if we let $g(x) = 1$, x, $\lambda - x$ and $x(\lambda - x)$ for $0 < x < \lambda$ in Eq. (2), we obtain the differential equations

$$dx/dt = \begin{cases} h(t) \\ xh(t) \\ (\lambda - x)h(t) \\ x(\lambda - x)h(t) \end{cases} \tag{4}$$

where, in the last two equations, λ is interpreted as the maximum value of x. The four equations relate to quite different and varied types of growth processes. Specifically, the respective equations indicate that at a given time the growth rate (1) depends on time, but not on size; (2) is proportional to size and a function of time; (3) is proportional to the "growth potential"— that is, the maximum size minus current size—and a function of time; and (4) is proportional to both the current size and the growth potential, as well as a function of time.

If we now consider the "logarithmic differential coefficient" $d \log x/dt = dx/xdt$, which denotes the relative growth rate (i.e., the proportional increase per unit of time), the last three equations in (4) may be written

$$\frac{d \log x}{dt} = h(t)$$

$$\frac{-d \log(\lambda - x)}{dt} = h(t)$$

$$\frac{d \log x}{dt} - \frac{d \log(\lambda - x)}{dt} = h(t)$$

Solving these as in Eq. (3), the equations (4) yield

$$x = H(t)$$

$$\log x = H(t)$$

$$\log(\lambda - x) = \log \lambda - H(t)$$

$$\log(\lambda - x) - \log \lambda = -\lambda H(t)$$

or, if solved for x,

$$x = \begin{cases} H(t) \\ \exp[H(t)] \\ \lambda\{1 - \exp[-H(t)]\} \\ \lambda\{1 + \exp[-\lambda H(t)]\}^{-1} \end{cases} \tag{5}$$

Here $\exp[H(t)] = e^{H(t)}$ where e is the base of the natural logarithms. The equations include a constant of integration that may be determined from a given value of (x,t). By looking at particular values of $h(t)$ we can now generate a number of examples of growth curves satisfying the conditions set out following equation Eq. (4). If we take $h(t) = \beta$, for example, we obtain

$$x = \begin{cases} \alpha + \beta t \\ \exp(\alpha + \beta t) \\ \lambda[1 - \exp(-\alpha - \beta t)] \\ \lambda\{1 + \exp[-\lambda(\alpha + \beta t)]\}^{-1} \end{cases}$$

For $\beta > 0$ these are increasing functions of t, the last two having asymptote λ. The last of these expressions defines what is generally called the logistic growth curve. By retracing the steps that led to its derivation, we may be able to gain some appreciation for the sorts of growth processes it might reasonably be expected to characterize. The equation for growth rate is

$$dx/dt = \beta x(\lambda - x)$$

and for relative growth rate,

$$\frac{d \log x}{dt} - \frac{d \log(\lambda - x)}{dt} = \lambda\beta$$

or, since

$$\frac{d \log(\lambda - x)}{dt} = \frac{1}{\lambda - x}\frac{dx}{dt} = -\frac{1}{\lambda - x}\beta x(\lambda - x) = -\beta x$$

we can write

$$\frac{d \log x}{dt} = \beta(\lambda - x)$$

(i.e., the relative growth rate is a linear function of x). Thus, before fitting a logistic function to developmental data, we should be sure that the conditions implied by these equations do not violate our a priori knowledge of the process under consideration. Looked at the other way around, after fitting a logistic function to developmental data, a reasonable test of goodness of fit would be to plot the values of x on the abscissa and the values of $\Delta \log x/\Delta t$ on the ordinate to see whether or not a linear relationship obtains. But it should be noted that though goodness of fit is perhaps a necessary condition for the employment of a particular function to mirror a growth process, it is by no means sufficient to ensure transcending mere description to the real desiderata of explanation. This is due not only to technical, statistical difficulties (Kowalski, 1970, 1972), but also to the very philosophy underlying the use of goodness-of-fit tests in this context. As stated by Feller (1966), "The logistic distribution function . . . may serve as a warning. An unbelievably huge literature tried to establish a transcendental "law of logistic growth": measured in appropriate units, practically all growth processes were supposed to be represented by a function of this form. . . . [p. 52]." The problem is that a number of other distributions can be fit to the same data with as good or better goodness of fit.

Thus the proper emphasis in fitting a curve to longitudinal data is not on selecting a function on the basis of goodness of fit, but rather on selecting a function that accurately mirrors the biological structure of the process under consideration. There are certainly enough functions to choose from, each with its own set of assumptions that must be met if we are to go beyond a mere description of our developmental data. In addition to those already discussed, we should mention several others that have been proposed for use in relatively well-defined sets of circumstances. In the realm of physical growth, because of the adolescent growth spurt typical of the higher primates (which may or may not obtain in psychosocial investigations), a parameterization consisting of distinct components for prepubertal and adolescent growth is often recommended. Thus Deming (1957) suggested the use of

$$f(t) = \alpha + \beta t + \gamma \log(t)$$

for the period up to 9 years in girls and 10 in boys, and from that point to maturity, the Gompertz (1825) curve, namely,

$$f(t) = \alpha \exp[-\exp \beta - \gamma t)]$$

Similarly, Jenss and Bayley (1937) fit

$$f(t) = \alpha + \beta t - \exp(\gamma + \delta t)$$

over the prepubertal period and then used the Gompertz function. An analogous strategy was suggested by Count (1943). Examples were provided by Israelsohn (1960). But, as pointed out by Bock, Wainer, Petersen, Murray, & Rocher, (1973), the problem as to where one curve should end and the other begin is still an open question. They suggested instead the use of a mixture of logistic growth curves. In their notation,

$$f(t) = \frac{a_1}{1 + \exp[-b_1(t - c_1)]} + \frac{f - a_1}{1 + \exp[-b_2(t - c_2)]}$$

where a_1 is the upper limit of the prepubertal component; b_1 determines the initial slope of the prepubertal component, implicitly given by $v_1 = a_1 b_1/4$, the maximum velocity of growth in the prepubertal component; c_1 determines the location in time of the prepubertal component; f is mature size; $a_2 = f - a_1$ is the contribution of the adolescent component to mature size; b_2 determines the slope of the adolescent component, implicitly given by $v_2 = a_2 b_2/4$, the maximum velocity of growth of the adolescent component; c_2 is the age at maximum velocity of the adolescent component.

In fitting this model to data on stature, Bock *et al.* (1973) were given t, observed y, and assumed f known, and the remaining five parameters (a_1, b_1, c_1, b_2, c_2) were fit by nonlinear least-squares. Another parameterization that permits straightforward interpretation of the parameters comprising the model was suggested by Weinbach (1941). Here

$$f(t) = b_1 \exp(c_1 t) - b_2 \exp(-c_2 t)$$

where c_1 is the multiplicative rate of growth per unit time; b_1 is the size of the individual when he enters the time span of constant multiplicative growth in early or middle childhood; b_2 is birth weight and c_2 represents how rapidly the child decelerates from birth into the phase of constant multiplicative growth.

The rationale behind the use of this model is that since the growth of most physical measurements is decelerative in infancy and more nearly constant for some years thereafter, a convenient mathematical representation of the growth of an individual is one that estimates both this deceleration and the more constant phase of middle childhood. Presumably the use of another function would be required if the age range were extended to include the pubertal spurt.

We might also mention at this stage another model that can actually be used to test the hypothesis of a significant change in the pattern of growth due to some event E (e.g., puberty) occurring within the interval of observation. This is due to Box (1967), who considered the general problem of testing for a change in the level of a nonstationary time series. Potential applications in the context of the present discussion include checking on whether or not behavioral measurements exhibit a growth spurt and facilitating the choice of where different growth curves may be needed to mirror accurately changes in the processes governing development. Suppose we have a total of $T = n + m$ measurements, the first n of these being taken before E, the next m after. If then δ measures the shift in level of the series associated with the event E, Box's model is of the form

$$x_t = \begin{cases} L + \gamma_0 \sum_{j=1}^{t-1} \alpha_{t-j} + \alpha_t & \text{for} \quad t \leq n \\ \\ L + \delta + \gamma_0 \sum_{j=1}^{t-1} \alpha_{t-j} + \alpha_t & \text{for} \quad t > n \end{cases}$$

where L denotes the initial location of the series, γ_0 is a constant, $0 \leq \gamma_0 < 2$, presumed known, and the α's are independent normal deviates having variance σ^2. It may aid in the interpretation of this model to write

$$\gamma_0 \sum_{j=1}^{t-1} \alpha_{t-j} + \alpha_t = \gamma_0 \sum_{j=1}^{t-2} (1 - \gamma_0)^j x_{t-1-j} + (1 - \gamma_0)^{t-1} L + \alpha_t$$

which emphasizes its autoregressive structure. Box then shows how to estimate σ^2, L, and δ (say by s^2, $\hat{L}$, and $\hat{\delta}$) from the data, and the required test follows from the fact that

$$(\delta - \hat{\delta})\left\{\frac{[1 - (1 - \gamma_0)^{2n}][1 - (1 - \gamma_0)^{2m}]}{[1 - (1 - \gamma_0)^{2t}]\gamma_0(2 - \gamma_0)s^2}\right\}^{1/2} \tag{6}$$

has Student's t-distribution with $n + m - 2\ df$. Box approached this problem from the Bayesian point of view, in which certain (noninformative) prior distributions for the parameters in the model were assumed, Eq. (6) then representing the posterior distribution of δ. The test can, however, be directly applied in the more usual Neyman–Pearson framework, where no a priori information concerning these parameters is invoked. In either case, γ_0 is taken as known, but Box has shown that Eq. (6) is relatively insensitive to changes in the value of γ_0.

The point of the above examples is to acquaint the reader with a number of models that have been proposed for representing intraindividual physical growth. As already noted, it is important to realize that in the competition between these models, goodness of fit plays a relatively minor role. Though a poor fit of the model to the data should reasonably cause one to question the applicability of the model under consideration in the context of the current problem, a good fit to the data is not sufficient to ensure this applicability. A more prudent course is perhaps via the derivation of a model that satisfies certain definite a priori requirements imposed by the structure of the developmental process under consideration. This may be approached by the use of differential equations as sketched above (see also Shock, 1951). Alternatively, the properties of available models can be checked to see whether or not they conform to these a priori criteria. Thus, for example, if we wish to use a model that is consistent with allometric growth, the use of the Gompertz curve may be appropriate (Deakin, 1970).

On the other hand, if only a simple descriptive function is required and/ or little is known about the mechanisms governing the growth process, the class of polynomial functions

$$f(t) = a_0 + a_1 t + a_2 t^2 + \cdots + a_p t^p$$

is apt to be satisfactory and have the convenient property that the *mean curve* (that fitted to the observed growth patterns of a number of individuals) is equivalent to the *mean constant curve* (that obtained by fitting the individual records to a set of such polynomials and then averaging the coefficients a_i). This is not true for growth curves in general (e.g., Gompertz, logistic), and thus the character of the individual curves is subject to distortion through group averaging. This may be a critical point in practice, since indiscriminate averaging tends to oversmooth the growth curves, masking the inherent interindividual variability, which is often of prime importance in the study of growth. Thus, although polynomial growth curves may not lend themselves to easily interpretable explanatory models for growth processes, they may still be useful for the description of development and in the effective reduction of the observations to a small number of parameters characterizing the observed course of growth. This method was introduced by Wishart (1938, 1939), who suggested that the growth curve for each subject be broken down into its mean and linear, quadratic, etc. components, each of these being subjected to separate analysis. The effects of treatments on the average growth rate could then be seen from the analysis of the linear components, and analysis of the higher-order components would show to what extent the treatments were affecting the shapes of the growth curves. The method was valuable in that it succeeded in replacing the successive observations on growth by a few summary figures, which led to efficient comparisons between the groups being studied (Rao, 1958).

In an attempt to extend this approach, Rao (1958) considered the problem of transforming time by a function $\tau = G(t)$ in such a way that the growth rate is uniform with respect to this new time metameter, so that an adequate representation of growth would be available in terms of the initial value of the measurement and the redefined uniform rate. This method produces the required transformation from the data in hand and provides a valid test of the hypothesis that the average growth curve is the same under all treatment conditions irrespective of any assumptions on the nature of the growth curve; it is not even necessary to know the exact values of the time points at which the observations were made. Rao (1958) also considered the model

$$y_{t\alpha} = \lambda_\alpha g(t) + \epsilon_t \tag{7}$$

where $y_{t\alpha}$ is the increase in the tth interval, λ_a is a parameter specific to individual α, $g(t)$ is an unknown function of time only, and ϵ_t is a random error. Whereas the first method did not depend on any assumptions about the individual growth curves, Eq. (7) implies that, apart from a deterministic linear trend for growth with respect to some time metameter, there are independent disturbances taking place in small intervals of time. By a common transformation $\tau = g(t)$, all the individual growth curves can be made linear apart from random fluctuations.

Finally, Rao also considered extending Eq. (7) to its factor-analytic analog

$$y_{t\alpha} = \lambda_\alpha^{(1)} g_1(t) + \lambda_\alpha^{(2)} g_2(t) + \cdots + \epsilon_t \tag{8}$$

where $\lambda^{(1)}, \lambda^{(2)}, \ldots$, corresponds to the factors and $g_1, g_2 \ldots$ to the regression coefficients. If Eq. (8) holds, we should be able to replace the growth curve by its estimated factor values $\lambda^{(1)}, \lambda^{(2)}, \ldots$ and to single out the dominant ones for further analysis. Though this approach has obvious merit as a potentially valuable data-reduction technique, Eq. (8) differs enough from the standard factor-analysis model to require an entirely new set of associated significance tests, and these have not as yet been worked out. In case ϵ_t can be assumed independent of t, Hotelling's principal component analysis may be used to obtain the requisite factors, and standard tests can be applied (Rao, 1958).

In the following sections we consider how some of these models for intraindividual development are used in the study of interindividual differences in developmental patterns and in providing tests of hypothesis concerning the mean patterns of growth in several groups of individuals.

IV. Models for Interindividual Change

When an investigator is concerned with a single attribute measured longitudinally on one or more groups of individuals, there are a variety of analytical models that can be employed. These techniques, which are quite different from those described above for intraindividual analysis, fall into three main categories: (1) univariate analysis of variance; (2) multivariate analysis of variance; and (3) polynomial growth-curve (PGC) models. For any particular analysis problem, the choice of one of these three approaches should be made as a function of the extent to which the structure of the model is appropriate and the extent to which the statistical assumptions are met. In describing these three approaches, careful attention will be paid to these points. However, most attention will be given to the PGC models, which are least widely considered in applications.

The univariate analysis of variance is probably the most widely used, most widely documented (namely, Gaito & Wiley, 1963; Winer, 1962), and most problematic approach to the analysis of longitudinal data. In the case of a single sample of individuals, the approach is often referred to as trend analysis (Kowalski & Guire, 1974; Winer, 1962). In this model the total sum of squares is partitioned into components attributable to individual differences, time, and error under the assumption of no interaction between the time and individual factors. This model allows the investigator to test the overall hypothesis of no differences attributable to the time factor. It is also possible to subdivide the sum of squares for time into orthogonal polynomial components allowing hypotheses concerning the shape of the time response to be tested.

In the case of two or more samples of individuals measured longitudinally, a repeated-measures analysis of variance (Winer, 1962) can be employed. In this model, individuals are treated as a random factor nested within groups with repeated measurements over time. In the context of this model the main null hypotheses of interest are (1) no time effect; (2) no group effect; and (3) no time by group interaction. The last of these hypotheses is often of greatest interest since it can be thought of as a test that the time-response functions of the k groups are parallel. As in the simpler case described above, it is possible to partition the time effect into orthogonal polynomial components to gain greater insight into the shape of the time response. This k-sample repeated-measure design can be thought of as a prototype for a great variety of more complex models in which the k-groups are structured as the levels of a factorial or other design. It is also possible to structure the repeated measure as levels of a more complex experiment.

These analysis-of-variance models seem at first glance to be ideal for the analysis of longitudinal data, since they are relatively simple and the questions of interest correspond to hypotheses that can be tested in the context of these models. The problem, of course, has to do with the validity of the underlying statistical assumptions of the models. It is an unfortunate fact that the ratios of mean squares will have an exact F-distribution only under the rather restrictive assumptions described by Huynh and Feldt (1970). A sufficient condition for the result requires that the repeated measures be normally distributed, have equal variances, and either be mutually independent or have equal correlations (Greenhouse & Geisser, 1959). The assumption of mutual independence is virtually never tenable, and the assumption of equal correlations is seldom tenable when the repeated measures are indexed by time, since adjacent pairs of measures will almost always be more correlated than pairs separated by a greater time interval. If the investigator does not wish to prejudge the validity of the equal-correlation assumption, a test of equal correlation is available (Box, 1950). Box suggested that when the assumption of equal correlations clearly does not hold, it might hold if the analysis were performed on differences between adjacent measurements rather than on the original data. The only other approach to salvaging the univariate-analysis-of-variance models for the analysis of longitudinal data when the equal-correlation hypothesis is not tenable is an approximate procedure proposed by Greenhouse and Geisser (1959). They have shown that the ratios of mean squares have approximate F-distributions with modified degrees of freedom that are a function of the unknown population variance–covariance matrix. They further show that there is a lower bound on the degrees of freedom that is independent of the unknown parameters. Unfortunately, the use of this lower bound gives a test that is conservative in the sense that the null hypothesis will too often be accepted when it is not true. This loss of power may well be unacceptable.

Because of the restrictive assumptions of equal variances and covariances, it is clear that univariate-analysis-of-variance approaches are not applicable in most situations and that other models that are not dependent on this assumption are needed. Multivariate-analysis-of-variance techniques provide such a class of models. In the case of a single sample of individuals measured longitudinally, the multivariate analog of trend analysis can be thought of as a multivariate generalization of a paired t-test. In this situation, the data consist of the vectors $\mathbf{x}'_i = (x_{i1}, x_{i2},...,x_{ip})$ for $i = 1,...,N$ and the hypothesis of interest is that of no time effect; that is,

$$H_0: \quad \boldsymbol{\mu} = \mu \mathbf{j}$$

where $\boldsymbol{\mu}$ is the mean vector, μ is a scalar, and $\mathbf{j}' = (1, 1,...,1)$. Morrison (1972) has shown that under the assumption that the observations are an independent sample from a multivariate normal distribution, the maximum likelihood test of this hypothesis is equal to a test of the hypothesis

$$H_0: \quad \mathbf{C}\boldsymbol{\mu} = \mathbf{0}$$

where $\mathbf{C}$ is any $(p - 1)$ by p matrix with the property $\mathbf{Cj} = 0$. In practice, $\mathbf{C}$ is chosen so that the transformed observations are the successive differences of the original data.

This model also allows the investigator to obtain simultaneous confidence intervals for all contrasts $\mathbf{a}'\boldsymbol{\mu}$ of the repeated treatment means using Scheffé's method of multiple comparisons. When the null hypothesis is rejected, this capability allows more precise statements to be made about the nature of the time response. In particular, the contrasts $\mathbf{a}$ could be chosen to be orthogonal polynomial contrasts. In addition to this basic result, Morrison (1972) derives analogous test statistics and confidence intervals under the more restrictive assumptions of (1) equal variances and covariances; and (2) reducible form for the variance–covariance matrix. He then compares the lengths of the confidence intervals with those derived with no structural assumptions. It seems clear that these methods provide a reasonable alternative to trend analysis under a variety of conditions that an investigator might be willing to assume.

The multivariate-analysis-of-variance approach to the k-sample problem of repeated measures is known in the literature as profile analysis (Greenhouse & Geisser, 1959; Morrison, 1967). The basic model is that of a k-sample multivariate analysis of variance in which the observation on the jth individual in the ith group is denoted $\mathbf{y}'_{ij} = (y_{ij1}, y_{ij2},..., y_{ijp})$ and is assumed to have a multivariate normal distribution with mean $\boldsymbol{\mu}_i$ and variance–covariance matrix $\boldsymbol{\Sigma}$. The linear model for these N observations is

$$E(\mathbf{Y}) = \quad \mathbf{X} \quad \mathbf{B}$$
$$\begin{smallmatrix} (n \times p) & (n \times k)(k \times p) \end{smallmatrix}$$

where $\mathbf{X}$ is the k-sample design matrix and $\mathbf{B}$ is the matrix of group means. In the context of this model, it is possible to test hypotheses of the form $\mathbf{C} \mathbf{B} \mathbf{A} = \boldsymbol{\Gamma}$ for arbitrary $\mathbf{C}$, $\mathbf{A}$, and $\boldsymbol{\Gamma}$, satisfying the requirements of the general Gauss–Markoff theorem. In particular there exist choices of $\mathbf{C}$, $\mathbf{A}$, and $\boldsymbol{\Gamma}$ to test the three basic null hypotheses of interest.

The first of these null hypotheses, H_{01}, is that the k profiles are parallel, which is analogous to the test of no group-by-time interaction in the univariate-analysis-of-variance approach. For appropriate choice of $\mathbf{C}$, $\mathbf{A}$, and

Γ, this hypothesis has the form

$$H_{01}: \begin{bmatrix} \mu_{11} - \mu_{12} \\ \mu_{12} - \mu_{23} \\ \vdots \\ \mu_{1(p-1)} - \mu_{p} \end{bmatrix} = \cdots = \begin{bmatrix} \mu_{k1} - \mu_{k2} \\ \mu_{k2} - \mu_{k3} \\ \vdots \\ \mu_{k(p-1)} - \mu_{kp} \end{bmatrix}$$

which is equivalent to a one-way multivariate analysis of variance on the differences between measures made at adjacent times.

The second null hypothesis, H_{02}, is that there is no change through time; that is,

$$H_{02}: \begin{bmatrix} \mu_{11} \\ \vdots \\ \mu_{k1} \end{bmatrix} = \begin{bmatrix} \mu_{12} \\ \vdots \\ \mu_{k2} \end{bmatrix} = \cdots = \begin{bmatrix} \mu_{1p} \\ \vdots \\ \mu_{kp} \end{bmatrix}$$

Matrices C, A, and Γ can be found to test the hypothesis in this form, which assumes nothing about the parallelism of the profiles. However, Morrison (1967) proposes an alternative choice of the test matrix that causes the hypothesis tested to be based on equality of sums over groups for each variable. The test in this form is

$$H'_{02}: \sum_{j=1}^{k} \mu_{j1} = \sum_{j=1}^{k} \mu_{j2} = \cdots = \sum_{j=1}^{k} \mu_{jp}$$

which is interpretable only under the assumption of parallel profiles.

The third hypothesis, H_{03}, is that there are no group differences. Without the assumption of parallel profiles, this hypothesis has the form:

$$H_{03}: \begin{bmatrix} \mu_{11} \\ \vdots \\ \mu_{1p} \end{bmatrix} = \begin{bmatrix} \mu_{21} \\ \vdots \\ \mu_{2p} \end{bmatrix} = \cdots = \begin{bmatrix} \mu_{k1} \\ \vdots \\ \mu_{kp} \end{bmatrix}$$

As above under the assumption of parallel profiles, Morrison (1967) suggests an alternative hypothesis based on the sums over measurements, which has the form

$$H'_{03}: \sum_{j=1}^{p} \mu_{1j} = \sum_{j=1}^{p} \mu_{2j} = \cdots = \sum_{j=1}^{p} \mu_{kj}$$

As in the case of univariate analysis of variance, the basic k-sample MANOVA model can be generalized to more complex designs by considering the k-samples as levels of a factorial or other experiment or by assuming some structure for the repeated measures. McCall and Appelbaum (1973) present such a generalization with six repeated measures structured as a two by three factorial design. They then compare the univariate and multivariate results for this case and conclude that the multivariate approach is superior.

In the profile-analysis model, it is important to point out that the only assumptions made are that the longitudinal series for each individual has a multivariate normal distribution with the same variance–covariance matrix in each of the k groups. The assumption of parallel time-response functions in the k groups is not necessary. It should additionally be pointed out that the model does not assume anything about the structure of repeated measures. It is in fact not necessary that they be indexed by time of measurement, be equally spaced, or even be ordered. Because of this lack of structure, the model simply tests whether the time-response functions have the same shape without providing a model that describes the shape of the function.

The final major class of models we will consider is that of the polynomial growth-curve (PGC) models. This class of procedures differs from those already considered because the models are formulated as a function of the structure of the repeated measures. In the previous cases, this structure could be incorporated by considering appropriate contrasts but was not included in the overall tests of hypotheses.

The development of the PGC approaches goes back to the pioneering work of Wishart (1938), which was alluded to earlier as a way of summarizing an individual's time response with a few lower-order orthogonal polynomial regression coefficients. Rao (1958) improved on this basic idea by suggesting that the time scale be transformed so that more complex time-response functions could be adequately summarized by the linear coefficient computed with respect to the modified time axis. More recent developments in the area of estimating and testing hypotheses about the average PGC of one or more groups have been provided by Rao (1959, 1965, 1966), Potthoff and Roy (1964), Khatri (1966), and Grizzle and Allen (1969). These investigators have provided a variety of procedures that are equivalent under certain but not all conditions. Because of the extent of overlap between approaches, we will concentrate primarily on the Potthoff and Roy approach, since their basic model seems most appealing. However, we will point out relationships between their results and the work of Khatri and Rao.

As presented above, the usual MANOVA model can be written as

$$E(\mathbf{Y}) = \underset{(n\times m)}{\mathbf{X}} \quad \underset{(m\times p)}{\mathbf{B}}$$
$$\underset{(n\times p)}{}$$

where the rows of $\mathbf{Y}$ are assumed to be independent and follow a multivariate normal distribution with variance–covariance matrix $\boldsymbol{\Sigma}$, $\mathbf{X}$ is a design matrix of known constants, and $\mathbf{B}$ is a matrix of unknown parameters. In the context of this model, it is possible to test hypotheses of the form

$$H_0: \quad \underset{(q\times m)}{\mathbf{C}} \quad \underset{(m\times p)}{\mathbf{B}} \quad \underset{(p\times u)}{\mathbf{A}} = \underset{(q\times u)}{\boldsymbol{\Gamma}}$$

for appropriate choices of $\mathbf{C}$, $\mathbf{A}$, and $\boldsymbol{\Gamma}$, satisfying the generalized Gauss–Markoff theorem (Timm, 1975). It is also possible to provide simultaneous confidence intervals for functions of the form

$$\underset{(1\times q)}{\mathbf{b}'} \quad \underset{(q\times m)}{\mathbf{C}} \quad \underset{(m\times p)}{\mathbf{B}} \quad \underset{(p\times u)}{\mathbf{A}} \quad \underset{(u\times 1)}{\mathbf{f}} \qquad \text{for all } \mathbf{b} \text{ and } \mathbf{f}.$$

Potthoff and Roy (1964) propose a more general model of the form

$$E(\mathbf{Y}_0) = \underset{(n\times m)}{\mathbf{X}} \quad \underset{(m\times p)}{\mathbf{B}} \quad \underset{(p\times q)}{\mathbf{Q}}$$
$$\underset{(n\times q)}{}$$

where $\mathbf{Y}_0$ has rows that are independent and follow a multivariate normal distribution with variance–covariance matrix $\boldsymbol{\Sigma}_0$, $\mathbf{X}$ is the between-individual design matrix of known constants, $\mathbf{B}$ is a matrix of unknown parameters, and $\mathbf{Q}$ is the within-individual design matrix. Potthoff and Roy show that this model can be reduced to the previous MANOVA model with the same parameter matrix $\mathbf{B}$ by considering the transformed variable

$$\mathbf{Y} = \mathbf{Y}_0 \mathbf{G}^{-1} \mathbf{Q}' (\mathbf{Q}\mathbf{G}\mathbf{Q}')^{-1}$$

where $\mathbf{G}$ is an arbitrary q-by-q symmetric positive definite matrix. In their original discussion, Potthoff and Roy suggested that the choice $\mathbf{G} = \boldsymbol{\Sigma}_0$ would be optimum but that since $\boldsymbol{\Sigma}_0$ was unknown and the distribution theory of using a data-derived estimate of $\boldsymbol{\Sigma}_0$ was unknown, another choice that approximated $\boldsymbol{\Sigma}_0$ but that was not data-based would be appropriate. The choice of taking $\mathbf{G} = \mathbf{I}_q$ was also discussed. Subsequent results by Khatri (1966), Rao (1965), and Lee (1974) established the usefulness of choosing $\mathbf{G} = \hat{\boldsymbol{\Sigma}}_0$ where $\hat{\boldsymbol{\Sigma}}_0$ is the data-based estimate of $\boldsymbol{\Sigma}_0$.

Given this basic model, the one sample problem considered previously can be parameterized by choosing

$$\underset{(n\times 1)}{\mathbf{X}} = \begin{bmatrix} 1 \\ 1 \\ \vdots \\ 1 \end{bmatrix} \quad \text{and} \quad \mathbf{Q} = \begin{bmatrix} 1 & 1 & \cdots & 1 \\ t_1 & t_2 & \cdots & t_q \\ \vdots & & & \\ t_1^{p-1} & t_2^{p-1} & \cdots & t_q^{p-1} \end{bmatrix}$$

so that the expected value of the jth observation on the ith subject has the form

$$E(y_{ij}) = \beta_1 + \beta_2 t_j + \beta_3 t_j^2 + \cdots + \beta_p t_j^{p-1} \qquad \text{for all } i \text{ and } j.$$

It is important to point out that the form of the time response is assumed to be the same for each subject (i.e., have the same degree). For appropriate choices of matrices $\mathbf{C}$ and $\mathbf{A}$, this model allows an investigator to test hypotheses about the regression coefficients. In particular, one could test the adequacy of a model of a certain degree; or using the result for simultaneous confidence intervals, confidence bounds for the mean growth curve could be derived.

The generalization of this model to the case of k groups of individuals with N_i individuals in the ith group is straightforward. The matrix $\mathbf{X}(N,k)$

is constructed to contain N_1 rows of $(1,0,\ldots,0)$, N_2 rows of $(0,1,0,\ldots,0)$,…, and N_k rows of $(0,0,\ldots,1)$. The matrix $\mathbf{Q}$ is chosen as above. With this specification, the expected value of the jth observation on the ith subject in the kth group has the form

$$E(y_{kij}) = \beta_{k1} + \beta_{k2}t_j + \beta_{k3}t_j^2 + \cdots + \beta_{kp}t_j^{p-1}$$

With this model, matrices $\mathbf{C}$ and $\mathbf{A}$ could be chosen to test the complete equality of the k regressions, the parallelism of the regressions, or the adequacy of a model of some lower degree. As in the case of the other methodologies discussed, generalizations of the k-sample model to more complex situations are possible. Timm (1975) presents an example in which the k groups correspond to levels of a two-factor factorial experiment.

Alternatives to the use of the Potthoff–Roy model include the one sample PGC model proposed by Rao (1959) and the independent but essentially complementary developments by Khatri (1966) and Rao (1965, 1966, 1967), which are argued to be superior since they eliminate the arbitrary choice of the matrix $\mathbf{G}$. These models have the form

$$E(\mathbf{Y}) = \mathbf{XB} + \mathbf{Z\Gamma}$$

where $\mathbf{Y}$, $\mathbf{X}$, and $\mathbf{B}$ are as before, $\mathbf{Z}(N, p\text{-}q)$ is a matrix of covariates chosen from the higher-order orthogonal polynomial coefficients, and $\mathbf{\Gamma}$ is a matrix of unknown covariate coefficients. If the covariates are not included, the results are identical to the choice $G = I$ in the Potthoff–Roy formulation. If all of the q-p covariates are used, the Rao model is equivalent to the model proposed in Rao (1959) and to the choice $G = S$ in the Potthoff–Roy model where S is the data estimate of Σ_0. Rao (1966) and Grizzle and Allen (1969) recommend the use of some but not all of the p-q possible covariates with the decision of which covariates to include determined by the data. The important point of this rather technical discussion is that the various choices are more similar than different and that each formulation has its problems; that is, the choice of G for Potthoff and Roy and the choice of which covariates for Rao. In any case the class of models is rich and seems to answer most questions of interest.

The preceding sections discussed a variety of methods for interindividual analysis that (1) were derived under an assumption that the data were sampled from a univariate or multivariate normal distribution; (2) made inferences in classical statistical fashion on the basis of the sampling distribution of statistics; (3) made a tacit assumption that all data were present in all of the longitudinal series studied; and (4) considered only a single attribute measured longitudinally. It is the purpose of this section to discuss briefly approaches in the literature for which not all of these four conditions obtain.

The assumption of univariate normality usually does not present a problem in most data analyses, since the validity of assuming normality or the extent of deviation from normality can be assessed easily either by using a testing procedure or by inspecting histograms or probability plots. In contrast, the assumption of multivariate normality raises more serious problems, since testing and graphic procedures are not nearly as available and results concerning the robustness of procedures in the absence of normality are largely unknown (Kowalski, 1972). In order to avoid the assumption of normality, nonparametric approaches have been developed for many data contexts, but these approaches have been conspicuously absent from the longitudinal data-analysis literature. One exception is the paper by Ghosh, Grizzle, and Sen (1973). In this paper, two examples are considered in which the longitudinal series for each individual are replaced by a vector of regression coefficients that summarize the individual's time-response function. Under the assumption that these coefficients have a continuous but not necessarily multivariate normal distribution, statistics based on ranks of the coefficients are proposed, and inferences are based on the permutation distributions of these statistics that are asymptotically χ^2. The main hypothesis tested is equality of treatment groups in a design that includes a block factor. Though the precise results on the asymptotic relative efficiency of these procedures are not known, the authors assert that these approaches have high asymptotic relative efficiencies for distributions with heavy tails and that the procedures are robust in the presence of gross errors or outliers.

The second common attribute of the interindividual procedures discussed in the previous sections is the fact that they are all based on sampling distributions of statistics. This fact is not in any sense an assumption of the models analogous to the assumption of normality but rather a constraint on the type of inferential statements that can be made. The major alternative inferential context is the Bayesian approach, which, among other differences, allows prior information about parameters to be formally incorporated in the analysis. Unfortunately, there are few examples of the application of Bayesian inferential methods to longitudinal data-analysis problems. One such application is the work of Geisser (1965) and Geisser and Kappenman (1971). In these papers, the profile-analysis model is considered from a Bayesian point of view for, respectively, the two and k-group cases. Under the assumption of parallel profiles, a posterior region is derived for the difference between profiles in the case of two groups and for the vector of differences between the k-1 pairs of adjacent profiles in the case of k-groups. This derivation is considered for both "non-informative" and "natural conjugate" priors.

The third point concerns the presumption of complete longitudinal series. This requirement is, in practice, quite severe, since it is often the case in protracted studies that only a small percentage of the series are complete for all ages. The loss of data imposed by this constraint is even more serious inferentially if there is any reason to believe that the occurrence of missing data is in any way related to the value of the attribute being measured. This problem can be dealt with in at least a couple of ways. One method would be to take the approach used by Wishart (1938) to replace the longitudinal series by summary parameters that can be estimated even in the presence of a moderate amount of missing data. Such derived data, though not precisely identically distributed, should allow at least an approximate analysis using a larger sample size.

A more formal approach to this problem was suggested in a paper by Kleinbaum (1973), who generalized the polynomial growth-curve formulation of Potthoff and Roy (1964) to consider the presence of missing data. In the presence of complete data the model has the form

$$E(\mathbf{Y}) = \underset{(N \times q)}{\mathbf{}} \quad \underset{(N \times m)}{\mathbf{X}} \quad \underset{(m \times p)}{\mathbf{B}} \quad \underset{(p \times q)}{\mathbf{Q}}$$

If the structure of the data is such that there are l blocks of cases with N_l cases in block l and that within block l all cases are complete for some number q_l of the q observations, Kleinbaum proposes a modified model

$$E(\mathbf{Y}_l) = \underset{(N_l \times q_l)}{\mathbf{}} \quad \underset{(N_l \times m)}{\mathbf{X}_l} \quad \underset{(m \times p)}{\mathbf{B}} \quad \underset{(p \times q)}{\mathbf{Q}} \quad \underset{(q \times q_l)}{\mathbf{H}_l}$$

where $\mathbf{H}$ is an incidence matrix of zeros and ones. With this model it is possible to obtain best asymptotically normal estimates for linear functions of the parameters and to test hypotheses about such linear functions.

Whereas this approach may be useful in correcting for data missing by chance, it is also applicable to situations in which data are missing by design, as in the case of mixed longitudinal cross-sectional designs (Prahl-Andersen & Kowalski, 1973).

The fourth point concerns the fact that all of the preceding discussion at both the intra- and interindividual levels has been restricted to situations that are univariate in the sense that the data have consisted of a series of measurements of a single attribute indexed by time. The extension of these approaches to the case of a three-dimensional data matrix in which two or more variables are measured longitudinally introduces a new level of complexity. Several approaches to this problem have been suggested in the literature for both intra- and interindividual analyses (Kowalski & Guire, 1974). Of these, the approach most widely used in biological applications is bivariate allometry, which relates the growth of exactly two dimensions in a single sample of cases. Attempts to extend this approach to more than two dimensions have been made but not without introducing additional problems of interpretation. Another avenue of approach to this problem has been in the area of factor analysis generalized to the case of a three-dimensional data matrix. Such approaches, which go beyond the scope of this presentation, seem also to introduce difficult problems of interpretation.

Of the topics discussed in this chapter for the univariate case, two areas seem to offer a way of approaching the problem of a three-dimensional data matrix. The first approach is simply to reduce the problem to a two-dimensional one by summarizing the longitudinal series for each variable with one or more derived variables. The methods of Section III for intraindividual analysis provide a variety of possible ways in which this could be done. Possible candidates for such summary variables include orthogonal polynomial coefficients (Rao, 1958; Wishart, 1938), the parameters of an appropriate Gompertz or logistic model (Bock *et al.*, 1973), or the scores derived from a principal-components analysis of the longitudinal series as suggested by Rao (1958). Such summary parameters could then be used in a variety of multivariate analyses that either analyze the structure of a single sample or compare two or more samples. The utility of this approach obviously depends on the choice of summary variables, which introduces a certain degree of subjectivity into the analysis. However, it would seem that this approach makes considerable data-analytic sense.

The second approach is provided by the Potthoff and Roy polynomial growth-curve models, which can be applied directly to the case of two or more variables measured concurrently. This can be done simply by appropriate choice of the pre- and post-design matrices. One could, for example, specify a model in which a polynomial was fit separately for two or more variables, taking into account not only the correlations within a series but the correlations between series as well. Having fit such a model, one could test whether the several time-response functions were equal or parallel. More complex models involving more than a single sample could also be considered.

V. Summary

We have attempted to survey a variety of methods appropriate for the analysis of a single longitudinal series and for the analysis of one or more samples of longitudinal observations. We also attempted to place in perspective the role of such methodologies in the broader context of developmental research. Having done this, it seems appropriate to comment on the current state of the art from the point of view of both theory and practice.

In 1963 Bereiter observed that deficiencies of statistical methodology seriously impaired scientists' investigation of questions dealing with change. Since that observation was made, a great deal of theoretical work has been carried out. At the intraindividual level, new models have been proposed by Bock *et al.* (1973) that are parameterized in ways that facilitate biological interpretation of the fitted curve. At the interindividual level, the development of polynomial growth-curve models, which began with the work of Rao (1959) and Potthoff and Roy (1964), is certainly the most notable advance of the last few years. Because of these achievements and others, one would have to conclude that the state of the art has indeed improved.

One would also have to conclude that there are many interesting and challenging problems remaining. At the theoretical level, the problems of growth prediction for individual series, of multivariate data observed longitudinally, and of nonparametric alternatives to normal theory procedures stand out as areas of ongoing interest. At the applied level, the challenge of testing new methodologies in a variety of contexts always exists as statistical practice lags frustratingly far behind statistical theory.

Chapter 5

Time-Series Models and the
Study of Longitudinal Change

CARL H. FREDERIKSEN
JOHN A. ROTONDO

ABSTRACT

Statistical time-series models have been developed to represent a great variety of change patterns. Central problems in studying change include first determining whether or not growth or development is occurring and, if so, specifying the growth characteristics of the system being studied. In the present chapter time-series models are defined and a five-dimensional scheme for classification of models is introduced. Subsequently, a brief survey of time-series models is presented with special attention given to Markov models and linear stochastic process models.

The design of research, both for descriptive purposes and for the assessment of treatment effects, is discussed with particular emphasis placed on the nature of the entities being studied, the measurement scheme, and the interventions employed. Characteristics of the research purpose, the investigator's theoretical orientation, and existing empirical knowledge are all critical aspects to consider in designing a time-series study. Finally, approaches to the estimation of parameters and testing of hypothesis are discussed and sequential hypothesis testing procedures illustrated.

I. Introduction

The study of change in phenomena over time is an all-pervasive problem in the biological, behavioral, and social sciences in which no system is completely static or unchanging. The possible kinds of change can range from cyclical or periodic change in which systems return to prior states to

111

LONGITUDINAL RESEARCH IN THE
STUDY OF BEHAVIOR AND DEVELOPMENT

systems that learn, develop, mature, grow, decline, or in other ways exhibit changes that permanently alter the characteristics of the system. An important problem in the study of change is to determine whether a system is static, exhibits a periodic pattern of change, or exhibits growth or development. Once a system has been shown to exhibit growth or development, the central problem is to analyze the pattern of growth and to detect changes or discontinuities in the growth characteristics of the system that are associated with environmental changes or are the result of experimental intervention.

The purpose of this chapter is to review a variety of approaches that may be taken to the study of change in human characteristics, emphasizing psychological changes associated with learning, maturation, development, or effects of education. We begin with a definition and classification of statistical time-series models that have been developed to represent different kinds and patterns of change. We then present a brief survey of time-series models, many of which will be described in greater detail in subsequent chapters of this book. Finally, we present a brief survey of time-series research designs and discuss uses of time-series models in different longitudinal research situations.

There are two problems that we feel are of central importance in longitudinal research in psychology and education. The first is how to determine whether a system is exhibiting growth or change in its growth characteristics. This problem involves investigating the *stationarity* of a time series. The second problem involves the analysis of *correlated growth*—investigating how growth in one human characteristic is related to changes in other characteristics. Approaches to these two problems are discussed in the section on time-series research designs. The chapter also includes a brief discussion of approaches to estimation and hypothesis testing in time-series research.

II. The Definition and Classification of Time Series

Time series is a generic term denoting any of a wide variety of probability models that have been developed for analyzing the behavior of systems that vary in time. When a time-series model is employed together with an appropriate experimental design and suitable techniques for parameter estimation and hypothesis testing, the result is a powerful methodology for the conduct of longitudinal research. In psychology and education, many longitudinal studies focus on intraindividual change and individual and group differences in intraindividual change. Time-series models are intrinsically appropriate for the study of such changes.

Despite the wide variety of time-series models, there is a small core of unifying concepts common to all such models and the analytic procedures based on them. These concepts correspond to certain aspects of all time series having to do with the nature of the entity studied and the manner in which it is changing in time. Briefly, a time series is conceived of as consisting of an entity or system that can be in one of several states at any given time. When the system is monitored at a sequence of points in time, it is observed to pass through a sequence of states that define its path or trajectory.

Consider first the entity or system whose behavior through time is to be studied. A *system* may be defined roughly as any entity whose behavior at any point in time is governed by possibly nondeterministic (i.e., probabilistic) rules. Examples of systems that can be studied in longitudinal research are individuals, families and other social groups, school classes, schools, school systems, communities, and other social or political institutions. Thus, systems may be defined and studied at different levels of inclusiveness or complexity. At each moment in time, a system is assumed to be in one of a set of mutually exclusive and exhaustive states. The states in the above set can be uniquely numbered, and the resulting set of numbers is called the *state space*. We will denote the state space of a system by S. As a simple example, consider a set of five letter grades, (A, B, C, D, F), as indices of the "state" of an individual with respect to mastery of certain skills or concepts. These states may be numbered as follows: A-4, B-3, C-2, D-1, F-0. Hence $S = (0, 1, 2, 3, 4)$ is a state space. In this case the numbers assigned to the states are meant only to represent an ordinal level of measurement of mastery. Thus, any order-preserving transformation of these numbers would serve equally well as elements of the state space S. In other cases, the numbers in S might reflect nominal, interval, or ratio levels of measurement of the state of a system.

With the passage of time, a system moves through a sequence of states. Suppose x_t is a number representing the state of a system at time t. Plotting x_t against each value of t at which the system is measured yields a graphical representation of the sequence of states assumed by the system as it "moves through time." The time-ordered sequence $(x_0, x_1, \ldots)$ describes the *path* of a system through the state space. To continue the above example, let us assume that four "parallel" forms of a test are administered at four different times during a course of instruction. On each testing occasion an individual is assigned a letter grade. The paths of two hypothetical individuals through the state space may be represented graphically by plotting numerical values of states against time (Figure 5.1).

A mathematical model of a system whose paths are not purely deterministic is called a *stochastic process*. A stochastic process can be defined quite generally as any collection of random variables $X(t)$ defined on a common probability space where t is thought of as a set of points in time at which the system is measured, or, more accurately, t is a member of the

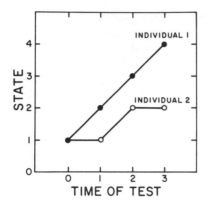

FIGURE 5.1. **Paths of two individuals through a state space.**

time parameter set T, which is a subset of $(-\infty, +\infty)$ (Hoel, Port, & Stone, 1972). Usually $X(t)$ represents the state of a system at time t, and hence $X(t)$ may assume the values contained in the state space in accordance with some probability law. The function $X(t)$ is called a *time series, stochastic process,* or *random function.*

Five dimensions may be used to classify stochastic processes: (1) the type of state space (e.g., finite, continuous); (2) the manner in which time is measured or represented (discrete, continuous); (3) the stationarity or nonstationarity of the probability structure of the time series; (4) the number of stochastic variables in the series; and (5) the presence or absence of error of measurement (Table 5.1). Each of these dimensions reflects an important theoretical or practical decision that must be made by a researcher in designing longitudinal research or selecting an appropriate statistical model to represent longitudinal data.

The first dimension of classification involves the state space of the system being studied. In the example of the previous section, the state space S was a finite set of numbers that represented five ordered levels of mastery of a concept. Any time series defined on a finite space will be classified as

TABLE 5.1
Classification of Time-Series Models

Dimension	Values
1. State space	(a) Finite; (b) countably infinite; (c) continuous
2. Time-parameter set	(a) Discrete; (b) continuous
3. Probability structure	(a) Stationary; (b) nonstationary
4. Number of variables	(a) Univariate; (b) multivariate
5. Presence–absence of measurement error	(a) Weak measurement (error); (b) strong measurement (no error)

a *finite state model*. Certain finite state models are among the most highly developed time-series models and among the least used for longitudinal research. Later we will give examples of several situations in which the use of such models seems appropriate.

A time series may also be defined on an infinite state space. We will be concerned particularly with two major types of infinite state spaces. The first type often arises when *counts* of events are used as indicators of the state of a system. For example, the state of an individual at time t might be indexed by the cumulative number of times that an individual exhibited a particular category of behavior in a time interval (e.g., raising a question of a certain type in a classroom). The counting numbers 0, 1, 2,..., serve as natural labels for these states. If an individual could be observed for an infinite period of time there would be no theoretical limit to how large such counts could become. Although observations are always made over a finite amount of time, it is often useful to define a state space so that the system can be adequately represented over arbitrarily long periods of time. Any time-series model defined on an infinite state space that can be put into one-to-one correspondence with the counting numbers will be classified as a *countably infinite state model*. A second type of infinite state space occurs when a system is conceived of as able to assume states corresponding to points on a continuum. A set of numbers capable of representing a continuum of states must be an infinite set that cannot be put into one-to-one correspondence with the counting numbers (positive integers); that is, an uncountably infinite set. In addition there may be no "gaps" in this set of numbers. Any time-series model defined on a state space satisfying the above requirements will be classified as a *continuous state model*. The assumption of a continuum of states is explicit in most theories of mental testing and is usually described in terms of a continuum of *true scores*. Hence, the use of mental tests based on this type of theory to assess the state of an individual over multiple occasions usually leads to the adoption of some continuous-state model.

The second dimension of classification concerns the time-parameter set on which a time series is defined. A time series $X(t)$ defined for all t belonging to a time-parameter set T is called a *discrete parameter process* if the set T is finite or countably infinite. Biological or social systems studied in longitudinal research are usually measured at discrete time intervals, unlike physical systems, which often permit continuous measurement. For this reason we shall devote most of our attention to discrete parameter processes in which t, the time at which the system is measured, takes on the values 0, ± 1, ± 2,.... Thus, we will usually assume that measurements of the system are taken at equally spaced intervals extending, if necessary, infinitely far into the past and future. A time series defined on a time-parameter set T in which T represents a continuum of time and thus consists of an uncountably infinite set in which there are no "gaps" will be classified as a *continuous-parameter process*. In a continuous-parameter process the system is being monitored continuously and there are no breaks or only negligible breaks in the measurement process. Although continuous measurement is unusual in longitudinal research, there are measurement situations that clearly call for continuous measurement, for example, when counts of events that may occur at any time are the basic index of the state of a system.

The *probability structure* of a time series is the concern cf our third dimension of classification. Let us denote the joint probability or density of a sequence of $(k + 1)$ observations taken at equally spaced intervals as follows:

$$P[X(t) = x_t, X(t + 1) = x_{t+1}, \ldots, X(t + k) = X_{t+k}].$$

We will now consider possible behaviors of this probability structure as t is increased or decreased. A time series is said to be *strictly stationary* if shifting the entire series forward or backward in time does not change the joint density of the observations; that is

$$P[X(t) = x_t, X(t + 1)$$

$$= x_{t+1}, \ldots, X(t + k) = x_{t+k}]$$

$$= P[X(t \pm u) = x_t, X(t + 1 \pm u)$$

$$= x_{t+1}, \ldots, X(t + k \pm u) = x_{t+k}]$$

for all possible t, k, and u. Strict stationary is one sort of "time invariance" property a time series can exhibit.

Another sort of time invariance is called *second-order* or *wide-sense stationarity*. A time series is second-order stationary if (1) $E[X(t)] = \mu$ for all t; (2) $\text{var}[X(t)] = \sigma^2$ for all t; and (3) the autocovariance $\text{cov}[X(t), X(t \pm u)] = \sigma^2$ if $u = 0$ (for all t) and $= \sigma(u)$ otherwise, for all t and u. The first condition states that the expected value of the series is the same for all t. Similarly, the second condition requires that the variance of the series be the same for all t. The third condition states that the covariance between any two observations separated by u units of time depends on u, the amount of separation, but not on t. A time series that is either strictly or second-order stationary will be classified as a stationary time series. All other series will be classified as nonstationary time series. Thus, there are a variety of ways in which a series may be nonstationary. These different possible sources of nonstationary are of great theoretical significance to the longitudinal researcher, especially in studies of learning or cognitive growth where means, variances, and covariances are not likely to exhibit any time-invariant properties. We will discuss this important topic in greater detail later.

The basis for our fourth dimension of classification is the natural division that can be made between *univariate* and *multivariate* time series. An observation at time t in a multivariate series consists of measurements on k random variables ($k \geq 2$), each of which is a univariate time series. The state space of a multivariate time series is therefore multidimensional. If the state spaces of k univariate series are denoted by $S_1, S_2, \ldots, S_k$, then the state space of the corresponding k-variate time series can be constructed by taking the Cartesian products of these sets; that is, $S_1 \otimes S_2 \otimes \cdots \otimes S_k$, where $\otimes$ stands for the Cartesian product operation. For example suppose $S_1 = (0, 1, 2)$ represents ordered levels of mastery of one skill and $S_2 = (0, 1, 2)$ represents mastery of another. Then the state space for a two-variate time-series model based on both S_1 and S_2 is given by

$$S_1 \otimes S_2 = \begin{Bmatrix} (0,0) & (0,1) & (0,2) \\ (1,0) & (1,1) & (1,2) \\ (2,0) & (2,1) & (2,2) \end{Bmatrix}.$$

A graphical representation of $S_1 \otimes S_2$ is shown in Figure 5.2. Each point in the graph represents an ordered pair in $S_1 \otimes S_2$. These ordered pairs are joint states that a two-variate time series defined on $S_1 \otimes S_2$ may assume. An important index of relationship between pairs of variables in a multivariate time series is the *cross-covariance* function. This function is simply the covariance between one univariate time series and another. The form of the cross-covariance functions and their behavior as t varies are theoretically important aspects of multivariate time series. The relationships among variables in a multivariate time series can provide valuable information for purposes of theory building, confirmation, or prediction. We will explore this subject more fully in a later section on the analysis of correlated growth.

The fifth and final order of classification concerns the possible presence of error, unreliability, or noise in measurements of the state of a system. When measurement error is present it is necessary to distinguish between the *observed* state of the system and the *true* state. The observed state may

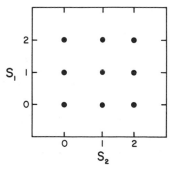

FIGURE 5.2. **Graphical representation of the multivariate state space defined by $S_1 \otimes S_2$ [S_1 = (0,1,2), S_2 = (0,1,2)].**

or may not correspond to the true state on any given measurement occasion. Time-series models that incorporate measurement error will be classified as *weak measurement models*. All other time-series models will be designated as *strong measurement models*. A summary of the classification system is presented in Table 5.1.

Any time series can be classified according to all five of these dimensions. For example, we may have a finite state process with a discrete parameter set, nonstationary probability structure, univariate state space, and no measurement error. An example of such a process is a set of mastery levels observed at discrete points in time in which the joint probability of the observations depends on time. Furthermore, the states are assumed to be observed without error. As a second example, we may have a continuous univariate state space with a discrete time-parameter set and weak measurement that is nonstationary. A possible example of such a process is a time series consisting of longitudinal measurements of cognitive ability in which the ability exhibits growth over the period at which the test is administered and the test score contains measurement error.

III. A Brief Survey of Time-Series Models

A. Markov Models

A large and extremely useful class of time-series models is the class of Markov models, which have representatives in many cells of the classification scheme of Table 5.1. The term *Markov* refers to an interesting property of the probability structures of these models that results in "memoryless" behavior of the system as it moves through time. A model has the Markov property if, given the *present* state of the system, *past* states have no influence on the probability of any future states of the system. Thus, Markov models have no "memory" of the states the system has already passed through; that is, of the past history of the system. Only the present state of the system has any effect on the probability of future states. The Markov property may be formally represented as follows:

$$P[X(t + 1) = x_{t+1} \mid X(0) = x_0, X(1) = x_1, \ldots, X(t) = x_t]$$

$$= P[X(t + 1) = x_{t+1} \mid X(t) = x_t'] \qquad \text{for all } t.$$

That is, the conditional probability of the system's being in state x_{t+1} at time $t + 1$ depends only on the state of the system at the immediately preceding time t and not on states prior to time t. The conditional probabilities, $P[X(t +1) = x_{t+1} \mid X(t) = x_t]$, are called *one-step transition probabilities*. They denote the probability of the system's moving to state x_{t+1} given that the system is currently in state x_t. Much of our discussion of Markov models will concern the form and behavior of these transition probabilities.

1. Markov Chains

A Markov model that has a finite or countably infinite state space and is defined on a discrete time parameter set $t = 0, 1, 2, \ldots$ is called a *Markov chain*. Recall the previous example in which the elements of state space $S = 0,1,2,3,4$ represented ordered levels of concept mastery. A finite-state Markov chain can be constructed for the above S. The transition probabilities we will use in this example are shown in Table 5.2. The number in the ith row and the jth column of the matrix in Table 5.2 is the probability of moving from state i to state j in the interval t to $t + 1$, for $t = 0, 1, 2, \ldots$. Here we have chosen one set of transition probabilities that serve for all t. Markov chains, such as this one, whose transition probabilities are constant from interval to interval are called *stationary* chains. However, the term *stationary* is misleading here, since the time series represented by a "stationary" chain is not necessarily a stationary process. More general Markov chains in which the transition probabilities may change with t have also been developed. The starting point of a Markov chain is a set of probabilities. For each state there is a probability that the system will be in that state at $t = 0$. Because the states are mutually exclusive and exhaustive, these probabilities must sum to 1. The set of "starting" probabilities is called the *initial distribution* of the chain. In the concept-mastery example, the initial distribution of the Markov chain would reflect the probability of a student's being at any given level of mastery at the beginning of instruction $(t = 0)$.

The pattern of transition probabilities determines the characteristic ways in which a system may move from state to state. Because of this pattern there may be states, for example, that once entered can never be left. Such states are called *absorbing* states. A state is absorbing if the transition

TABLE 5.2
Hypothetical Transition Probabilities in a Five-State Markov Chain

	State at time $t + 1$				
State at time t	0	1	2	3	4
4	0	0	0	0	1
3	.01	.02	.02	.40	.55
2	.02	.05	.13	.60	.20
1	.05	.20	.50	.20	.05
0	.10	.60	.25	.04	.01

probability from that state to itself is 1 and the transition probabilities to all other states are 0. A look at Table 5.2 shows that State 4 in our Markov-chain example is an absorbing state. Furthermore, depending upon the transition probabilities there may be states that will be revisited an infinite number of times if the process is allowed to continue indefinitely. A state that has this property is called a *recurrent* state. A state that is not recurrent is called a *transient* state. If a state is transient there is some positive probability that, once visited, the state will never be visited again. *Transient* also implies that the expected number of visits to the state must be finite. Note in Table 5.2 that State 4 is the only absorbing state (absorbing states are recurrent). If the process is allowed to continue indefinitely a system will always end up in State 4 and remain there with probability 1. The remaining states are all transient. They will be visited only a finite number of times before the system is finally absorbed into State 4. This is an example of a chain that eventually achieves a steady state.

For Markov chains that achieve some sort of steady state, we may speak of a *steady state* or *stationary distribution*. The stationary distribution of a Markov chain (if it exists) gives the limiting probability of the system's being in any given state as t approaches infinity. In our Markov-chain example, the probability of being in State 4 as t approaches infinity is 1. The probability of being in any other state is 0. In the general case, stationary probabilities other than 0 and 1 are also possible.

In addition to transition probabilities and initial and stationary distributions, a number of other descriptive measures can be calculated for a Markov chain. For example, it is possible to calculate the expected number of time intervals before a system enters some state y given that the system is starting from some other state x. This quantity is called the *mean first passage time* from x to y. One may also calculate the expected number of visits to a transient state, the expected number of intervals before a recurrent state is revisited, and a host of other measures that together capture practically every aspect of a Markov chain's behavior.

Markov-chain methodology has a natural application to the problem of comparing several treatment or subject populations longitudinally. Populations may differ in their transition probabilities, initial or stationary distributions, mean first passage times, etc. Within each population, intervention effects may appear in the form of abrupt or gradual changes in the transition probabilities. For additional information on Markov chains the reader is referred to Cox and Miller (1965), Feller (1957), Karlin (1966) and Parzen (1962).

2. Markov Pure Jump Processes

Like Markov chains, pure jump processes have finite or countably infinite state spaces. However, whereas chains are discrete time processes (for $t = 0, 1, 2, \ldots$), pure jump processes are defined in continuous time, for all

$t \geq 0$. In a pure jump process a system starting out from some state x_0 at $t = 0$ may jump at any time to a new state x_1. The system continues in state x_1 until it jumps at some later time to a new state x_2, etc. A pure jump process is *Markovian* if and only if the probability of remaining in any nonabsorbing state between time t and $t + u$ depends only on u, the length of the time interval. An interesting consequence of the Markov property for pure jump processes is that given the current state of the system, the remaining amount of time the system will spend in that state before jumping to a new one must have an exponential distribution. Markov pure jump processes are useful in situations in which a researcher is using counts of events that may occur at any time to index the state of a system. For example, the state of a child might be indexed by cumulative number of times a certain behavior was exhibited during a continuously monitored social activity. The state of an examinee might be indexed by a running count of the items passed or failed during the course of an examination.

Two general types of Markov pure jump processes that may be appropriate in situations such as these are *birth* and *death* processes. The state space of a birth or death process can be either $S = (0,1,...,N)$ or $S = (0,1,2,...)$. In a pure birth process, a system starting at some state x_0 at $t = 0$ may jump only to state $x_0 + 1$, the next higher state. From state $x_0 + 1$ the system may jump only to state $x_0 + 2$, etc. The familiar Poisson process is an example of a pure birth process. Meredith (1971) has used the Poisson process to model an examinee's behavior on speeded tests in which running counts are kept of the number of items failed. A sample path from a pure birth process is shown in Figure 5.3. In a pure death process, a system starting in some state x_0 at $t = 0$ may jump only to state $x_0 - 1$, the next lower state. From state $x_0 - 1$, the system may jump only to state $x_0 - 2$, etc. Similarly, one may define a combined birth and death process in which a system starting from state x_0 at $t = 0$ may jump only to state x_0

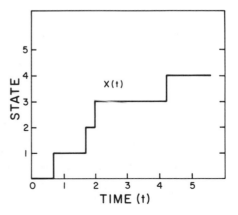

FIGURE 5.3. **A sample path from a pure birth process.**

+ 1 or to state $x_0 - 1$. From this new state the system may then jump to the next higher state or the next lower state, etc. For Markov pure jump processes, the quantities of primary interest to the researcher are the transition probabilities and the initial and stationary distributions. As with Markov chains, the states of a jump process may be classified as absorbing or nonabsorbing, recurrent or transient. The application of Markov jump processes to the problem of comparing several treatment or subject populations longitudinally and characterizing intervention effects is similar to the approach taken with Markov chains. For more information about jump processes, see references given for Markov chains.

3. First-Order Autoregressive Processes

The Markov models we have discussed so far have been defined on finite or countably infinite state spaces. We turn now to a class of Markov models that is defined on a *continuous* state space and for which measurements are taken at discrete intervals, $t = 0, \pm 1, \pm 2, \ldots$. To simplify the presentation, we will start with first-order autoregressive processes that are wide-sense stationary, that is,

$$E[X(t)] = \mu$$

$$\text{var}[X(t)] = \sigma^2$$

$$\text{cov}[X(t), X(t + u)] = \sigma(u) \qquad \text{for all } t.$$

A model equation for the first-order autoregressive process is

$$X(t) - \mu = \alpha[X(t - 1) - \mu] + Y(t) \tag{1}$$

where

$$|\alpha| < 1, \qquad E[Y(t)] = 0, \qquad \text{and} \qquad \text{Var}[Y(t)] = \sigma_y^2 \qquad \text{for all } t.$$

The random variables $Y(0)$, $Y(\pm 1)$, $Y(\pm 2), \ldots$ are assumed to be mutually independent. The stationary time series $Y(t)$, a series of independent random shocks, is sometimes called a *white-noise process*. White-noise processes are important components in many linear stochastic models.

The model equation states that the deviation score at time t consists of a regression on the deviation score at $t - 1$ plus an independent random shock specific to t. The model is autoregressive in the sense that $X(t)$ is regressed on its own history. It is *first-order* autoregressive because the only part of $X(t)$'s history that it depends on is $X(t - 1)$, the state of the system one interval earlier (this is also why it is Markovian). The above series oscillates about a fixed mean, μ, and the oscillations have fixed variance. The autocovariance of $X(t)$ and $X(t + u)$ may be shown to depend on u, the amount of separation, but not on t. The condition $|\alpha| < 1$ is necessary to ensure the stationarity of the process. The *lag u autocor-*

relation between $X(t)$ and $X(t + u)$ is defined as

$$\rho_u = \frac{\text{cov}[X(t), X(t + u)]}{\text{var}[X(t)]} .$$

The lag u autocorrelation of a first-order autoregressive process is

$$\rho_u = \alpha^{|u|} \qquad u = 0, \pm 1, \pm 2, \ldots$$

As u, the amount of separation, increases, the lag autocorrelation decays exponentially (for positive α). Table 5.3 displays a pattern of autorcorrelations from a hypothetical first-order autoregressive process in which $\alpha = .9$. Note that as one moves away from the main diagonal the correlations are exponentially decreasing. Observations immediately adjacent in time are most highly correlated. As the amount of time between observations increases, the correlations gradually decrease.

In many situations the assumption of a fixed mean and constant autoregression weight (α) will not be tenable. A more general first-order autoregressive model with nonstationary means and changing autoregression weights (α_t) is

$$X(t) - \mu_t = \alpha_t[X(t - 1) - \mu_{t-1}] + Y(t)$$

where $E[X(t)] = \mu_t$ is the arbitrary mean of the process at time t, α_t is a time-dependent regression weight, and $Y(t)$ is a white-noise process. A trend in the mean of the series may easily be incorporated in the model by letting μ_t be a function of t. For example, a quadratic trend in μ_t may be represented as

$$\mu_t = a + bt + ct^2.$$

In addition to changes in the mean of the series, the model also allows for changes in autoregression. For example, the dependency of $X(t)$ on $X(t$

TABLE 5.3
Autocorrelations of a First-Order Autoregressive Process with $\alpha = .90$ across Eight Time Intervals

Time interval	1	2	3	4	5	6	7
1	1.–						
2	.90	1.–					
3	.81	.90	1.–				
4	.73	.81	.90	1.–			
5	.66	.73	.81	.90	1.–		
6	.59	.66	.73	.81	.90	1.–	
7	.53	.59	.66	.73	.81	.90	1.–
8	.48	.53	.59	.66	.73	.81	.90

$-$ 1) may change with t. Thus the regression weight α_t may assume different values for different values of t. Since the means, variances, and covariances all depend on t, the process is not wide-sense stationary.

Markov Simplexes. An alternative representation of a first-order autoregressive process is the Markov simplex. A stationary Markov simplex is defined by

$$E[X(t)] = 0, \tag{2}$$

$$\text{var}[X(t)] = 1, \tag{3}$$

$$\text{cov}[X(t), X(t + u)] = \alpha^{|u|}(0 < \alpha < 1). \tag{4}$$

From Eqs. (2), (3), and (4) it is apparent that the process $X(t)$ is wide-sense stationary. The covariance function is exponentially decaying as u increases in absolute value and is identical in form to the autocorrelation function of the first-order autoregression process in Eq. (1).

Jöreskog (1970a) has observed that for most applications in the behavioral sciences the assumption of a common zero mean and unit variances is too restrictive. He considers the following nonstationary Markov simplex with arbitrary means and variances:

$$Z(t) = \mu_t + \beta_t X(t)$$

where $E[Z(t)] = \mu_t$, $\text{Var}[Z(t)] = \beta_t^2$ and $X(t)$ is defined by Eqs. (2)–(4). Jöreskog shows that this model is equivalent to a nonstationary first-order autoregressive process.

Markov simplexes may also accommodate measurement error. A model in which the "true variates" have a Markov simplex structure but are measured with imperfect reliability is called a *quasi-Markov simplex*. Because imperfectly reliable measurement is the rule rather than the exception in behavioral science research, weak measurement models such as the quasi-Markov simplex may prove to be highly useful. Table 5.4 contains a

TABLE 5.4
Intercorrelations of Semester Grades in Electrical Engineering[a]

Semester	1	2	3	4	5	6	7	8
1	1.–							
2	.69	1.–						
3	.55	.65	1.–					
4	.46	.58	.65	1.–				
5	.45	.50	.59	.67	1.–			
6	.41	.60	.60	.63	.61	1.–		
7	.34	.41	.56	.66	.64	.68	1.–	
8	.33	.44	.52	.53	.68	.69	.72	1.–

[a] After Humphreys (1960).

pattern of correlations that approximate the pattern typical of a Markov simplex. Notice that as the amount of time between observations increases, the correlations gradually decrease (although the pattern is not perfect). Jöreskog found that a quasi-Markov simplex fits this data reasonably well. Additional information about simplex models may be found in Jöreskog (1970a), Humphreys (1960), and Guttman (1954).

4. First-order Moving-Average Processes

Another simple Markov process, which is fundamentally different from the autoregressive and simplex processes, is the *moving-average process*. The model equation for the process is

$$X(t) - \mu = Y(t) + \gamma Y(t - 1) \tag{5}$$

where $E[X(t)] = \mu$ for all t, γ is a regression weight, and $Y(t)$ is a white-noise process. The model states that the deviation score at time t consists of an independent random shock at t plus a weighting of the independent random shock at $t - 1$, the immediately preceding interval. Thus, the effect of an independent shock in one interval is "carried over" to the next interval with the size of the effect increased or diminished by a weight. If we denote the common variance of the white-noise process by σ_y^2, then

$$\text{var}[X(t)] = (1 + \gamma^2)\sigma_y^2 \qquad \text{for all } t$$

and the covariance function is

$$\text{cov}[X(t), X(t + u)] = \begin{cases} \gamma\sigma_y^2 & \text{for } |u| = 1 \\ 0 & \text{for } |u| > 1. \end{cases}$$

Hence the lag u autocorrelation is

$$\rho_u = \begin{cases} \dfrac{\gamma}{1 + \gamma^2} & \text{for } u = \pm 1 \\ 0 & \text{for } |u| > 1 \end{cases}$$

From inspection of ρ_u it is apparent that an observation is correlated only with its immediately adjacent neighbors. Any two observations separated by more than one interval are uncorrelated. This pattern of correlation distinguishes the moving-average process from the autoregressive process. A pattern of autocorrelations for a hypothetical moving-average process with $\gamma = .90$ is shown in Table 5.5.

B. Linear Stochastic Processes

A time-series model that is expressed as a weighted sum of random variables is called a *linear stochastic process*. The first-order autoregressive and first-order moving-average processes are simple examples of linear

TABLE 5.5
Autocorrelations of a Moving Average Process with =.90 across Eight Occasions

Occasions	2	3	4	5	6	7	8
1	.497						
2	0	.497					
3	0	0	.497				
4	0	0	0	.497			
5	0	0	0	0	.497		
6	0	0	0	0	0	.497	
7	0	0	0	0	0	0	.497

stochastic processes. In this section we focus on some useful generalizations of these two important processes. The models presented here are discrete parameter processes (i.e., $t = 0, \pm 1, \pm 2, \ldots$) and are defined on continuous state spaces. An assumption commonly made about a linear stochastic process $X(t)$ is that $X(t)$ has a normal distribution for all t. If normality is assumed, then the series is said to be a *Gaussian,* or *normal,* process. The models we will be discussing are usually treated as Gaussian processes.

1. Autoregressive Processes of Order p

The following model is a straightforward generalization of the first-order autoregressive process defined in Eq. (1). A model equation for the process is

$$X(t) - \mu = \alpha_1[X(t-1) - \mu] + \alpha_2[X(t-2) - \mu] + \cdots$$
$$+ \alpha_p[X(t-p) - \mu] + Y(t) \tag{6}$$

where $E[X(t)] = \mu$ for all t, $\alpha_1, \alpha_2, \ldots, \alpha_p$ are regression weights, and $Y(t)$ is a white-noise process. The model states that the deviation score at time t consists of a part that is predictable from a weighting of the deviation scores over the p previous intervals plus an independent unpredictable part. If $p \geq 2$, the process is not Markovian.

To obtain another useful representation of a pth-order autoregressive process we define the backward shift operator, B, as follows:

$$BX(t) = X(t-1)$$
$$B^2X(t) = X(t-2)'$$
$$\vdots$$
$$B^pX(t) = X(t-p)$$

Using the B operator an equivalent expression for the model in Eq. (6) is

$$F_p(B)[X(t) - \mu] = Y(t) \tag{7}$$

where

$$F_p(B) = (1 - \alpha_1 B - \alpha_2 B^2 - \cdots - \alpha_p B^p).$$

Autoregressive processes that do not oscillate about a fixed mean and that have time-dependent regression weights are also possible. Such models are necessarily nonstationary.

2. Moving-Average Processes of Order q

A generalization of the first-order moving-average process shown in Eq. (5) is given by

$$X(t) - \mu = Y(t) + \gamma_1 Y(t-1) + \gamma_2 Y(t-2) + \cdots + \gamma_q Y(t-q) \quad (8)$$

where $\gamma_1, \gamma_2, \ldots, \gamma_q$ are regression weights and $Y(t)$ is a white-noise process. The deviation score at time t is expressed as a weighted sum of white-noise processes over the q previous intervals. The white-noise processes are usually assumed to have independent and identical normal distributions. In this model an independent random shock at time t—that is, $Y(t)$—continues to exert an influence on future states of the system for the next q intervals. The effect of the shock is increased or diminished by a weight in each of the succeeding q intervals. The effect of a new independent random shock is added to the process before the effect of the previous shocks dies out.

Using the backward shift operator, B, an equivalent expression for the model in Eq. (8) can be written as

$$X(t) - \mu = G_q(B) Y(t) \quad (9)$$

where

$$G_q(B) = (1 + \gamma_1 B + \gamma_2 B^2 + \cdots + \gamma_q B^q).$$

The moving-average model may be further extended to the case where the series oscillates around a changing mean. Models with time-dependent regression weights have also been considered.

3. Autoregressive Moving-Average Processes

A combination of the autoregressive and moving-average models can be obtained by equating the left side of Eq. (7) with the right side of Eq. (9):

$$F_p(B)[X(t) - \mu] = G_q(B) Y(t). \quad (10)$$

The process represented by Eq. (10) is an autoregressive moving-average process of order (p,q). A more interpretable equation for the same process is

$$X(t) - \mu = \alpha_1[X(t-1) - \mu] + \cdots + \alpha_p[X(t-p) - \mu] + Z(t) \quad (11)$$

where

$$Z(t) = Y(t) + \gamma_1 Y(t-1) + \cdots + \gamma_q Y(t-q)$$

The first p terms on the right side of Eq. (11) represent the autoregressive part of the process. The residual $Z(t)$ is a moving-average process. The form of the model in Eq. (11) is called an *autoregressive process with moving-average residuals*. Note that if $q = 0$, then $G_q(B) = 1$ and Eq. (10) simplifies to a pth-order autoregressive process. Similarly, if $p = 0$, the $F_p(B) = 1$ and Eq. (10) simplifies to a qth-order moving-average process. If either $p \geq 2$ or $q \geq 2$, the process is not Markovian. Autoregressive moving-average processes that do not oscillate about a fixed mean or that have time-dependent regression weights have also been considered.

4. Autoregressive Integrated Moving-Average Processes

In many longitudinal studies it is reasonable to expect some degree of growth or trend in the mean of the series. It is often the case that this trend may be what is most significant to the researcher. For other applications all or part of the trend in the mean is not of major interest and only serves to complicate model building, estimation, and testing. If there is polynomial trend in the mean of the series it may be eliminated by applying a simple differencing operation to the sequence of observations in the series. The differencing operation Δ is defined as follows:

$$\Delta X(t) = X(t) - X(t - 1).$$

Applying the difference operator to the series of observations 5, 7, 9, 11,... results in a flat series 2, 2, 2,.... Differencing the observations once will eliminate linear trend; differencing the observations twice—that is, taking differences between differences—will eliminate quadratic trend, etc. In general, by applying the difference operator d times, $\Delta^d X(t)$, a polynomial trend of degree d or less will be eliminated. Once a trend of some degree is eliminated there may still be variability in the series. To characterize this remaining variability, a model can be imposed on the differenced series rather than on the original series. When an autoregressive moving-average process of order (p,q) is imposed on a series differenced d times, the resulting model is called an *autoregressive integrated moving-average process of order* (p, d, q). A model equation for the process is

$$F_p(B)\Delta^d X(t) = G_q(B) Y(t) \tag{12}$$

where $Y(t)$ is a white-noise process.

Although the variate-difference method is useful for eliminating deterministic trend in the mean function, it is often the case that the trend itself may be what is most significant to the researcher. An alternative to variate differencing is to incorporate the deterministic trend in the mean function directly into the model. Suppose that the mean function can be represented as a polynomial in time; that is,

$$\mu_t = E[X(t)] = \lambda_0 + \lambda_1 t + \lambda_2 t^2 + \cdots + \lambda_d t^d.$$

The deviation score $X(t) - \mu_t$ may be substituted for $X(t) - \mu$ in Eq. (10), the autoregressive moving-average model. The resulting process oscillates around a mean that has a deterministic polynomial trend of degree d.

Trend in the mean of a series also can be viewed as resulting from trend in the mean of the white-noise component of the series. Consider, for example, the first-order autoregressive process in Eq. (1). The white-noise process, $Y(t)$, on the right side of Eq. (1) may be slightly altered so that it has a nonzero expected value. Let us define a new process $Z(t)$ such that

$$E[Z(t)] = \mu$$

$$\text{var}[Z(t)] = \sigma^2 \qquad \text{for all } t$$

and $Z(0)$, $Z(\pm 1)$, $Z(\pm 2),\ldots$, are mutually independent random variables. If $Z(t)$ is substituted for $Y(t)$ in Eq. (1) the resulting autoregressive process, $X(t)$, has a constant drift; that is, the expected value of the new autoregressive process is

$$E[X(t)] = t\mu.$$

Thus the process can be expected to drift upward t units (for μ positive) by time t.

The uses of linear stochastic models for assessing the effects of interventions in longitudinal studies are discussed in detail by Glass, Willson, and Gottman (1972). More about the mathematical and statistical foundations of the models can be found in Anderson (1971), Box and Jenkins (1970), and Kendall and Stuart (1968).

To appreciate better the significance and meaning of different linear time-series models, it may be useful to consider some hypothetical situations in which different models would be expected to account for longitudinal changes in behavior, learning, or development. To facilitate comparisons among different time-series models, our examples will all involve classroom learning situations. Consider a classroom situation involving one or more lessons consisting of ordered sequences of learning tasks or exercises. Children's responses during each exercise are observed and scored in terms of number of correct responses. The temporal sequence of scores constitutes a time series. By making different assumptions about sequences of learning tasks and the situational context in which learning takes place, we can define situations in which different stochastic processes would be expected to account for the data. These different assumptions are summarized in Table 5.6. Note that no examples of stationary processes are given, since plausible conditions leading to stationary processes would not be expected to occur in the classroom learning situation being considered.

In Example 1, the exercises are assumed to form a cumulative sequence in which performance at step t in the sequence depends on learning on the immediately prior step $t - 1$. However, earlier learning affects current learning (at step t) only through the cumulative stepwise dependence of

TABLE 5.6
Hypothetical Situations Illustrating Different Linear Stochastic Processes

Linear stochastic process[a]	Classroom example
Autoregressive processes	
First-order (nonstationary)	Cumulative learning occurs in which performance at time t depends on that at time $t - 1$, but not on learning prior to trial $t - 1$.
p^{th} order (nonstationary)	Learning does not consist of a simple cumulative sequence of dependent states. Rather, learning on trial t depends on prior learning on trial $t - 1$ and on earlier trials.
Moving-average processes	
First-order (nonstationary)	Children perform on a sequence of independent classroom exercises in an environment in which feedback ("shock") occurs during each exercise. Performance on the tth exercise is affected by the shock at time t and that at time $t - 1$ (but no earlier shocks).
q^{th} order (nonstationary)	Shocks have a cumulative effect over time on children's performance on the exercises; that is, performance at time t is affected by shocks at time t, $t - 1$, and earlier shocks.
Autoregressive moving-average processes	
Simple (order 1,1)	Cumulative learning occurs in which learning on the exercise at time t depends on that at time $t - 1$, but **not** on prior exercises, and learning at time t is affected by shocks at time t and at time $t - 1$.
Simple (order p,q)	Learning occurs on the exercise at time t that depends on the prior learning history and the cumulative effects of prior shocks.

[a] Deterministic trend in the mean can be incorporated directly or by differencing (integrated model), or the model can incorporate nondeterministic drift.

learning tasks. This "Markovian" assumption would appear to be plausible for many task sequences or subsequences. In Example 2, the relationship among learning tasks is more complex: Learning on a current task (t) depends on learning that occurred not only on the immediately prior task ($t - 1$) but also on earlier tasks. This situation would be plausible for task sequences in which prior tasks involve different knowledge and skills that are required to perform successfully on subsequent tasks.

In contrast, Examples (3) and (4) do not assume that learning involves a cumulative dependency of a sequence of tasks. Rather, they are concerned with cumulative effects (positive or negative) of "shocks," or influences (e.g., rewards, information, feedback, disruptions) that occur at each stage of the lesson sequence. In Example 3, such shocks are assumed to affect current performance (at time $t - 1$) and performance during the next exercise (at time t). In Example 4, the shocks are assumed to have cumulative effects on learning.

Examples 5 and 6 combine the effects of shocks with situations involving cumulative learning on related tasks. In Example 5, the cumulative effects of learning and shocks are *local;* that is, learning at time t depends only on learning at time $t - 1$ and shocks at time $t - 1$. For example, the cumulative learning might represent effects of positive or negative feedback. In Example 6 these effects are more complex—current learning is affected by a more extended prior history of learning and, for example, feedback. Any of these models can incorporate deterministic or nondeterministic change in the mean function. The characterization of a time series in terms of a linear stochastic process enables one to make important inferences and descriptive statements about the nature of the time series being investigated.

IV. Time-Series Research Design

Now that we have reviewed the types of time-series models that have been developed to represent properties of systems that are changing over time, we can examine how time-series models may be employed in the conduct of longitudinal research. Our objective in this section will be to sketch the logic of time-series research design and to convey an appreciation of some of the available strategies that can enable a longitudinal researcher to make interesting observations and conclusions concerning the behavior of a time series. First we will consider important *design features* in time-series research: (1) the nature of the groups studied; (2) the nature and type of time-series measurements; and (3) the nature of any interventions that are made in the series. Then we will identify important *classes of time-series designs* and examine *properties of time series* that may be studied in descriptive and experimental time-series research.

Designing a longitudinal study involves decisions that reflect several important kinds and levels of design features. These decisions usually begin with the general and specific objectives of the research and proceed to involve (1) *choices of populations and selection of samples* for study; (2) adoption of a *measurement strategy* involving decisions concerning the nature and number of measurements, measurement procedures and properties, and the distribution of observations over a selected time interval; and (3) selection of an *intervention plan* involving decisions concerning the nature and distribution of any interventions in the time series. These decisions will determine what time-series model and methodology are appropriate.

Time-series research is often recommended in discussions of experimental and quasi-experimental research design as desirable principally because it allows one to eliminate various sources of invalidity associated with single observation or pretest–posttest designs that are intended to evaluate the effects of an experimental intervention (e.g., see Campbell & Stanley, 1963; Cook & Campbell, 1975; Glass, Willson & Gottman, 1972). The advantages of time-series designs in which observations are made repeatedly prior to an intervention and repeatedly after are that they enable a researcher to make conclusions concerning extended or delayed effects of an intervention and to examine effects in the context of how individuals were changing prior to an intervention. Furthermore, interventions can be studied that are protracted in time or repeatedly administered. In these discussions, the use of time-series designs and models to evaluate the effects of an intervention and to isolate the causes of time-series effects is emphasized. Time-series studies designed to evaluate intervention effects may be *true experiments,* in which there is random assignment of individuals (or other sampling units) to treatment conditions, or they may be *quasi-experiments,* in which groups are not equivalent; that is, are not randomly constituted.

Whereas time-series research designed to evaluate the effects of interventions constitutes one important class of objectives of longitudinal research, time-series observations often may be made on one or more nonequivalent groups solely for the purpose of providing descriptive information concerning the processes of growth or change that occur in these groups. Such *descriptive* longitudinal research has traditionally held an important place in developmental psychology and should receive as much attention in a discussion of time-series research design as research designed to evaluate intervention effects. In descriptive longitudinal research, interest centers on describing the properties of a time series and group differences in these properties, whereas intervention research (experimental or quasi-experimental) is typically less concerned with the properties of the series and more with detecting effects or changes resulting from an intervention. Descriptive longitudinal research is often multivariate, whereas intervention studies are usually univariate. The discussion that follows will concentrate on descriptive and experimental time-series research. Quasi-experiments (and their problems) have been discussed thoroughly elsewhere (Campbell & Stanley, 1963; Cook & Campbell, 1975). From a design standpoint, it seems reasonable to focus on the logic and possibilities of descriptive and experimental studies of change. The reader is referred to these other sources for discussion of time-series designs as means of gaining greater validity in intervention studies that are not true experiments.

A. Design Features of Time-Series Research

Descriptive research and experimental time-series research both involve design decisions concerning the nature and type of time series measurements and the nature of populations and samples selected for study. Experimental time-series research involves in addition design decisions that reflect the nature and distribution of interventions that are made during the series. We will discuss first design features and decisions that are common to both descriptive and experimental time series research and then discuss design decisions concerned with interventions in time-series experiments.

1. Time-Series Measurements

The starting point for longitudinal research in psychology and education is a conception of what developmental trait or class of behaviors one wants to characterize as a time series. In some educational situations, the behaviors of interest may consist of directly observable classes of responses such as may be exhibited in classrooms, and the research focuses on the changes that take place in these observed classes of behavior over time. In a time-series experiment the focus would be on the effects of an intervention on these behaviors. The behaviors selected for study might consist of a single-response class (univariate measure) or multiple-response classes (multivariate measures). In either case, the variables of interest are considered to be directly observable without error (strong measurement).

In other longitudinal research situations, interest may center on changes in traits, abilities, knowledge states, skills, or other cognitive or personality characteristics that underlie observable behavior. Such *latent traits* are not directly observable but must be inferred from overt behavior. In the simplest case, a latent trait may be indexed by a single observable response class, leading to a conception of weak measurement in which an observed response is considered to represent both an underlying trait and a specific (nontrait) and error component. In more complex cases, a single trait may be indexed by multiple observed variables, each of which reflects the common trait together with other specific and error factors. In the most complex cases of multivariate time series with structural relationships among variables, changes in multiple traits are studied, each of which may be indexed by more than one variable (multivariate series with weak measurement and structural relationships among variables). As we shall see, in some cases these structural relationships among variables may be incorporated directly into time-series models (Frederiksen, 1974; Jöreskog & Sörbom, 1976a). Though latent traits are usually conceived of as varying continuously, situations are also possible in which finite (discrete) states or countably infinite states occur.

As an examination of Table 5.1 reveals, these decisions concerning the nature of time-series measurements are closely associated with the particular class of time-series models that will be appropriate to represent and analyze the data. Thus, measurement decisions determine the nature of the state space (finite, countably infinite, continuous), the number of variables (univariate, multivariate), and the presence or absence of measurement error (weak or strong measurement). One other attribute of time-series models is also associated with a measurement decision—the nature of the time-parameter set. However, most longitudinal research conducted in psychology or education will involve *discrete* time sampling. Decisions concerning the frequency of observations in time and the extent of the series may be extremely important in determining the characteristics (probability structure) of the series. Infrequent time sampling will tend to pick up long-term changes while obscuring more local changes in a behavior or trait. Too frequent time sampling may lead one to overlook longer-term developmental changes.

Measurement decisions in longitudinal research should reflect a mix of theory, empirical observation, and knowledge of the time-series models that are appropriate to different situations. In cases in which more than one approach to measurement is possible, an awareness of what stochastic models are appropriate under different approaches can help ensure that data are gathered that are adequate or appropriate to the requirements of the model and that the model will enable one to derive descriptions and make inferences from a time series that are appropriate to the substantive issues being investigated in the research.

2. Groups Studied

From the standpoint of time-series models and analysis, the two most important design decisions concerning the nature of the groups studied are the number of groups and their identity; that is, whether they are equivalent or stratified. Descriptive time-series research can involve a single group— a random sample from a single population, or multiple stratified groups— random samples from different populations, or, alternatively, stratified samples from a single population. In *single-group* descriptive research the primary interest is in the characteristics of the growth process in a single group. Examples of single-group descriptive studies are studies of physical growth that are concerned with characteristic growth patterns and "spurts" and studies of cognitive development that are designed to examine growth patterns and discontinuities in development such as shifts from one developmental stage to another. Single-group studies can also be multivariate, investigating the relationship of growth in one trait to growth in other traits.

In *multiple-group* studies, interest centers on differences between natural *stratified groups* in their developmental characteristics. Natural groups may be based on cultural, linguistic, or socioeconomic variables; on situational differences—that is, differences in the geographic, social, or demographic features of the environment in which the groups develop—or on their previous history of development or exposure to different situations. Groups may also be stratified on the basis of test scores, school performance, or other ability or performance measurements. In such instances, it may be wise to consider obtaining repeated measurements of the stratifying variables; that is, adopting a single-group multivariate time-series design rather than a stratified group design. The multivariate design would permit one to examine the nature of the dependency of development of the trait or behavior of interest on the "stratifying" variable over time, permitting stronger inferences concerning the nature of the dependency.

Equivalent groups are groups that are constructed by random sampling from a single population with random assignment to groups. Equivalent groups might be studied in a descriptive study if the principal interest were in the generalizability of the characteristics of a time series. However, most research employing equivalent groups is experimental, involving the introduction of an intervention to one or more of the groups. Research designs that combine descriptive and experimental objectives are also possible and involve both equivalent and stratified groups. Interest in such studies would focus both on differences in the developmental characteristics of different stratified groups and on how these groups differ in their reactions to an intervention in the time series, as, for example, to a new method of instruction.

3. Interventions in Time-Series Experiments

In a single observation or pretest–posttest experiment, specifying an intervention involves only specifying the number and types of interventions. However, in time-series experiments in which an intervention can be applied at different times in a series, the design of an intervention plan involves decisions concerning the time, duration, and pattern of interventions as well as their number and type. In general five design dimensions may be used to specify an intervention plan in time-series experiments: (1) the *number and types of interventions;* (2) the *time* at which an intervention occurs in a series; (3) the *duration* of an intervention; (4) the number of *repetitions* of an intervention; and (5) the *sequence* of different types of interventions in designs involving the application of more than one type of intervention to a group. The intervention plan in any time-series experiment can be characterized in terms of these five dimensions.

Figure 5.4 introduces a simple notation (adapted from Glass, Willson, & Gottman, 1972) that may be used to illustrate these different aspects of an intervention plan. We assume first that measurement decisions have been made resulting in a time-parameter set consisting of T equally spaced times, and that T independent observations of a stochastic variable $X(t)$ have been made, one at each point in the time-parameter set. We will let I_r denote an intervention of type r and an O denote the absence of an intervention on a measurement occasion. A sequence $O\ O\ I_r\ O\ O$ denotes a sequence of observations and interventions at points in the series (see Figure 5.4). In a time-series experiment consisting of equivalent groups, each of which has associated with it an intervention sequence, a separate line will be used to denote the sequence for each group. Groups will be

Time _____

Time-parameter Set	$t :$	I	2	3	...	t	... T
Measurements	$X(t)$:	$X(I)$	$X(2)$	$X(3)$	... $X(t)$	... $X(T)$	
Intervention of Type r in a Sequence of Observations		O	O	I_r	... O	... O	
Equivalent Groups	$R_1 :$ $R_2 :$	O O	O O	O I	... O ... O	... O ... O	
Stratified Groups	$S_1 :$ $S_2 :$	O O	O O	I I	... O ... O	... O ... O	

FIGURE 5.4. **Basic notation for time-series designs.**

numbered R_i (for the ith random group) and separated by a line. Stratified groups are represented in the same manner and are numbered S_i (for the ith stratified group).

The five design dimensions together with certain other intervention sequences that are of interest are illustrated in Figure 5.5. The simplest design

BASIC DESIGNS

Single Group – Single I

    O O O I O O O

Multiple Group – Multiple I

R_1: O O O I_1 O O O

R_2: O O O I_2 O O O

Intervention Time Designs

R_1: O O I O O O O

R_2:   O O I O O O O

Intervention Duration Designs

R_1: O O I O O O O O

R_2: O O / I / O O O O

R_3: O O / I / O O O

R_4: O O / I   / O O

Repetition Effect Designs

R_1: O O I O O O O O O

R_2: O O I O I O O O O

R_3: O O I O I O I O O

Sequential Designs

R_1: O O I_1 O O I_2 O O

R_2: O O I_2 O O I_1 O O

SPECIAL PURPOSE DESIGNS

Interaction Designs

   O O I_1 O O I_2 O O (I_1, I_2) O O

R_1: O O O   O O

R_2: O O I_1 O O

R_3: O O I_2 O O

R_4: O O (I_1, I_2) O O

Multiple Group – Single I
(Generalizability Design)

R_1: O O O I O O O

R_2: O O O I O O O

R_3: O O O I O O O

Stratified Multiple Group Designs

S_1: O O O I O O O

S_2: O O O I O O O

"Operant" Design

   O O I O I O O O I O O I O

Single Group – Multiple I

   O O O I_1 O O O I_2 O O O

FIGURE 5.5. **Examples of types of time-series designs.**

involving an intervention is the basic design consisting of a single group and single intervention administered once during a time series. An experiment having more than one type of intervention is illustrated by the Multiple Group–Multiple *I* design. Here interventions of different types are administered to equivalent groups at the same time. If one of the "interventions" is *the absence* of an intervention, we have a no-treatment control group. Multiple interventions can, of course, be designed that control for different aspects of the intervention treatment according to the usual logic of experimental design.

The other four dimensions involve the temporal and sequential aspects of an intervention. Design types are illustrated in Figure 5.5 that represent experiments investigating each of these design dimensions. Thus, in the Intervention Time Design, a single intervention type is administered at different *times* while occupying the same place in the sequence of observations for a group. The only difference between groups in this design is the time at which the series begins. Such a design would be important in situations in which the real time at which the series is observed might be expected to influence the nature of an intervention's effects; for example, the time during a school year might be expected to influence the "potency" of an instructional treatment. The Intervention Duration Design provides a means for investigating the effects of the *duration* of an intervention in situations in which an intervention can be applied for varying lengths of time. In this design, equivalent groups differ only in the duration of an intervention measured in terms of the number of time intervals in the time-parameter set it spans. The *repetition* dimension is illustrated by the Repetition Effects Design in which equivalent groups differ only in the number of times a treatment is applied (the pattern of observations and interventions is kept fixed). Finally, the intervention *sequence* dimension is illustrated by the Sequential Design in Figure 5.5. Here, equivalent groups are given different sequences of two intervention types, every other dimension being held constant. Of course, designs that combine these features may be constructed by constituting equivalent groups that contrast the dimensions of intervention sequence that are of interest.

Several other types of designs have been presented in the literature (cf. Glass, Willson, & Gottman, 1972) and merit discussion. The first of these recognizes still another important kind of intervention in a time series. In many situations it may be possible to apply two types of intervention simultaneously to examine possible interactions between intervention types. Thus two interventions applied together may be additive, their effects consisting of a sum of their individual effects, or they may interact, having greater or less effect than would be expected under the assumption of independent additive effects. The Interaction Design in Figure 5.5 illustrates this possibility.

The remaining designs illustrated in Figure 5.5 represent various special designs that are of interest in particular situations or for special purposes. For example, the Multiple Group–Single I Design is a special case of the Multiple Group–Multiple I Design in which a single intervention type is applied at the same time to two or more equivalent groups. Such a design enables one to explore the generalizability of the conclusions one would draw across equivalent groups. In many natural research situations having equivalent groups (random assignment), though the groups may be given the same intervention, that intervention is applied against a background of uncontrolled, possibly random variation in the situation in which observations are made; for example, in situations in which treatments are applied in interactive social group settings such as classrooms. This design would permit one to assess the importance of these "background" factors to conclusions concerning the effects of an intervention and hence the generalizability of the intervention effects. Related to this Generalizability Design is the case in which the groups are stratified rather than randomly constituted. This Stratified Multiple-Group Design would be appropriate when sufficient knowledge about "background" factors exists that groups can be stratified according to these factors. Together, these two designs are very important in research conducted in natural settings.

Also important in situations in which observations are made in natural settings are designs involving a single group. Though these designs are not experiments, situations frequently exist in which an investigator is content to confine his or her interest to the characteristics of a single group. This might occur, for example, in an exploratory study of a single group prior to systematic experimental evaluation of intervention effects or studies of the generalizability of effects. Three examples of single-group designs are given in Figure 5.5. In the so-called Operant Design (Glass, Willson, & Gottman, 1972), a single intervention is applied repeatedly and the effect of each intervention is studied. Often (as in operant experiments in which a pigeon is reinforced for pressing a bar) an intervention is made contingent on a person's response, so that controlled studies of repetition effects are not possible. In Single Group–Multiple I designs, an existing group such as a classroom is the setting studied, and different types of interventions may be introduced at different times. Usually, sufficient time between interventions will be allowed to elapse that sequential effects are thought to be unlikely. This design, of course, confounds intervention type with time of intervention as well as sequence. Untangling these factors would require follow-up experiments employing sequential and intervention-time design features. Nevertheless, as a preliminary to other more controlled studies, Single Group–Multiple I Designs may be useful. Single-group Interaction Designs have a similar role in situations in which interactions among interventions are of interest. The reader is referred to Glass et al. (1972) for examples and more extended discussion of various time-series designs.

B. Properties of Time Series

Combinations of the design features that we have summarized describe a vast array of possible time-series studies involving varied longitudinal measurements, groups, and intervention sequences. Time-series models may be employed in conjunction with a time-series design to enable the longitudinal researcher to investigate the stochastic properties of a time series and to contrast groups and investigate effects of an intervention on the properties of a time series. Our approach to this topic will be first to review the properties of time series that can be studied and then to explore the descriptive properties, group contrasts, and intervention effects that are of potential interest in time-series research. Table 5.7 lists properties of time series separately for *univariate* time series, in which there is one measurement at each occasion of observation, and *multivariate* time series, in which multiple measurements are made on each occasion. We will consider the properties of univariate and multivariate time series separately.

1. Univariate Time Series

The first property of a univariate time series, the *type of stochastic process,* is determined largely by the nature of the time-series measurements. For example, is the level of measurement discrete? a frequency count? a continuous variable? Is there a presence or absence of measurement error; that is, is there weak or strong measurement? Often there may be alternative answers to questions such as these. For example, frequency data may often be treated as continuous, and measurements may often be regarded as either weak or strong. In such situations alternative models may be fit to the data and compared with respect to their ability to account for the data (see the next section, on approaches to estimation).

TABLE 5.7
Properties of Time Series

Univariate series	Multivariate series
Type of stochastic process	Types of stochastic processes[a]
Stationarity properties of process	Stationarity properties of processes[a]
Strict stationarity	Strict stationarity
Wide-sense stationarity	Wide-sense stationarity
Mean	Mean
Covariance	Covariance
Parameter values of process	Parameter values of processes[a]
	Cross-covariance functions
	Structural relationships among stochastic variables

[a] One or more stochastic processes depending on the structural relationships among stochastic variables (see text).

Once a particular time-series model has been selected to represent the data, two kinds of model properties are of interest in describing a time series. The first is the *stationarity properties* of the process. In most instances, interest will center on wide-sense stationarity; that is, stationarity in the means, variances and covariances of the series. The question being asked when the *mean* stationarity of a time series is investigated is, Is there evidence that the series is changing in level? When stationarity of *variance* is investigated, the question concerns whether or not the system exhibits change in its variability. A system may also exhibit a pattern of *autocorrelation* that is stationary or nonstationary; that is, the autocorrelations of a series may or may not depend on the times at which the system is observed. If a series is wide-sense stationary—that is, is stationary with respect to means, variances, and autocovariances—the series oscillates about a fixed mean showing cyclical or periodic change, but fails to exhibit growth or developmental change. A series that is mean nonstationary but stationary in its variance and covariance is one that exhibits growth or developmental change in level. Stationarity of autocovariance might be expected to occur for relatively simple cumulative learning tasks. However, in most situations of learning or development, nonstationarity of covariances would be expected to occur.

Once a system has been found to be *nonstationary,* the properties of the time series of primary interest are the values of the parameters of the stochastic model that describes the series. For example, if the process is a nonstationary first-order autoregressive process, the parameters of the process are μ_t, σ_t^2, and α_t, all time-dependent parameters. Changes in the mean μ_t as a function of time reflect trends in the level and direction of the process. Changes in the variance σ_t^2 as a function of time may reveal unsystematic fluctuations in the variability of the process or systematic damping, for example, reductions or increases in the variability of the process. Changes in the autoregression weights α_t as a function of time reflect changes in the extent to which a response reflects the effects of random shocks on a specific occasion or reflects the prior state of the system. Thus, an increase in regression weights would indicate a system whose current state is increasingly dependent on preceding states of the system.

In *stratified multiple-group* studies, the interest is in comparing two or more groups with respect to properties of the time series occurring for each group. Group differences can occur with respect to both the stationarity and the parameter values of the process. For example, one group of children might be found to show nonstationary means and covariances, the parameter values indicating an increasing trend in the mean of the process and positive increasing autoregression weights. Another group might be found to exhibit a less pronounced upward trend in the means and a stationary small positive autoregression weight. Such an outcome in a learning study would be consistent with the interpretation that the first group shows improvement attributable to an increasing cumulative learning process, whereas the second group shows a slower rate of improvement attributable to a less pronounced and stable cumulative learning process.

Experimental *interventions* may also affect both the stationarity and the parameter values of a process. The introduction of an intervention may affect the stationarity of a time series by transforming a stationary process into one that is nonstationary. Such would be the case if systematic instruction were introduced in a learning domain in which no instruction was previously occurring. Performance on assessment tasks sampled from the domain before the introduction of instruction would be expected to exhibit stationarity, whereas departures from stationarity in the means and covariances would be expected to occur after the onset of instruction. There are, of course, many kinds of possible effects of an intervention on the parameter values of a process. Glass *et al.* (1972) discuss a variety of possible intervention effects on the *mean* of a process including changes in *level* that are abrupt, delayed, temporary, or decaying in their effects, and changes in *direction* that are abrupt, delayed, temporary, accelerated, or "evolutionary" in their effects (see Glass *et al.,* 1972 for a full discussion of these different possibilities). An intervention may also affect the variability of a process, and interventions may influence the fundamental stochastic nature of a series as reflected in the regression weights of the process. For example, an intervention might reduce (or increase) the regression weights of the process. Finally, an intervention might alter the stochastic nature of the process in such a way that the process changes in type. For example, a first-order autoregressive model might, as a result of an intervention, fail to account for the stochastic nature of a time series, the series becoming a more complex linear stochastic process; that is, an autoregressive moving-average process of order greater than (1,0).

2. Multivariate Time Series

In a multivariate time series, instead of a single stochastic variable $X(t)$ measured on each occasion t, a set of p stochastic variables $X_1(t)$, $X_2(t), \ldots, X_p(t)$ are observed on each measurement occasion t in the time-parameter set. A multivariate time series may be thought of as a collection of p univariate time series. If the p univariate series were mutually independent, then each series could be treated as a separate univariate series. The complexity of multivariate time series comes from the fact that the p stochastic variables may in general be correlated.

There are two approaches that may be taken to multivariate time series. In one approach, univariate linear stochastic process models are generalized to the multivariate case. In this approach the problem is to estimate simultaneously the parameters of p-dependent time series; that is, the parameters of a p-variate time series. For example, in a p-variate first-order autoregressive series, the problem is to estimate the *matrix* of autoregression weights of the series consisting of a vector of T weights for each of the p variates. The properties that were discussed in conjunction with univariate series have their counterparts for multivariate time series. In general, interest has centered on the stationarity of a multivariate series of a given type, for example, first-order autoregressive or moving-average processes. Group differences in the stationarity or parameters of a multivariate series can be considered, as can intervention effects. For example, Jones, Crowell and Kupuniai (1970) describe a model for detecting change from stationarity in multivariate stationary linear stochastic processes. For further discussion of multivariate generalizations of linear stochastic processes, see Kendall and Stuart (1968).

In most research on longitudinal change in psychology and education that involves change in multiple traits or behaviors, the most important problem is not to detect nonstationarity but to explore the relationships that hold among correlated traits or behaviors and changes in these relationships over time. For example, in a learning study, simultaneous observations on two or more measures of learning may be obtained on successive trials in a learning task, or assessments of two or more cognitive traits may be made on repeated occasions in a longitudinal study of cognitive growth. In such situations it is likely that the stochastic variables will be correlated; that is, there will be some interval of time in which the variables are not statistically independent. In such situations the question arises as to whether the change or growth that is observed in one variable may be attributed to growth in the stochastic variable with which it is correlated. In a learning study the change that is taking place in one measure of learning may result from changes in other measured aspects of learning, and in a longitudinal study of development, one may want to investigate the extent to which changes in one developmental trait are attributable to contemporaneous changes in a second trait. The problem in such studies is to analyze *correlated growth* in concomitantly observed stochastic variables and changes that take place in the statistical dependencies of stochastic variables. This problem may be explored descriptively in one or more groups. It may also be investigated in conjunction with evaluating the effects of natural or experimental interventions. Here the problem is that of *detecting change* in the statistical dependencies of correlated stochastic variables.

The second approach to multivariate time series explores the *linear structural relationships* that occur among multiple stochastic variables. The general method used to investigate structural relationships among variables is to employ a general linear model that can be used to fit systems of linear structural equations to multivariate data (Jöreskog, 1970c, 1973a; Jöreskog & Sörbom, 1976a). This model allows one to fit structural equations to multivariate time series in which the stochastic variables are first-order autoregressive. The approach involves expressing alternative hypothesis concerning the relationships among different stochastic variables in the form of linear equations and then fitting these equations to the covariance matrix of the stochastic variables consisting of the autocovariances and cross-covariances of the p stochastic variables. Alternative models are compared with respect to their goodness of fit, and parameter estimates are obtained for models that adequately account for the data. Though this approach is presently limited to the number of variables and types of time-series models that can be considered, the model does enable one to fit nonstationary first-order autoregressive models. In our experience, first-order autoregressive models are likely to be applicable to most learning or developmental data in psychology and education if the models are allowed to be nonstationary. The application of linear structural models to longitudinal data is thoroughly discussed and illustrated by Jöreskog in Chapter 11 (also see Frederiksen, 1974; Jöreskog & Sörbom, 1976a).

The properties of multivariate time series described in terms of linear structural equation systems that are of potential interest to the longitudinal investigator are summarized in Table 6.7. Suppose that a structural model has been fit to a time series that attributes change in p observed variables to two underlying stochastic variables. For example, suppose scores on p different measures of learning reflect two underlying types of learning, each score being a weighted linear combination of the two types of learning. Each underlying stochastic variable is first-order autoregressive. Let us first consider for this example the properties of the model that would be of interest in a descriptive study. First, the type of stochastic process is given (both are first-order autoregressive). Interest in this example would center on the stationarity properties of the two autoregressive processes, the parameter values of the processes, their cross-covariances and the structural relationships of the p observed variables.

With respect to mean stationarity, the observed variables may exhibit different upward trends in their means that are a result of their dependence on the two underlying stochastic variables. Covariance stationarity can be investigated for each underlying process by comparing the fit of the model that constrains the autoregression weights for a process to be equal to a single fixed value to the model that estimates a different autoregression weight for each occasion. The parameter values of each process, particularly the autoregression weights, may be estimated for each process and compared across the two processes. The cross-covariances of the two processes reflect the extent to which the two learning processes are independent. One hypothesis of interest is that of independence of the two processes. If the two processes are not found to be independent aspects of learning, changes in their cross-covariances over time are descriptive parameters that would be of great interest. Finally, particular structural relationships among the p observed variables are of interest because they reflect changes in the extent to which an observed indicator of learning reflects the two kinds of learning.

Thus, a particular observed learning measure may show change in its dependence on an underlying stochastic variable and different observed variables may be compared with respect to the extent of their linear dependence on an underlying variable.

An experimental intervention may affect any of these properties of a multivariate time series. The general approach taken to detecting change produced by an intervention would be to fit a structural model to a multivariate time-series prior to an intervention and then determine whether a significant shift has occurred in the properties of the model by attempting to fit it to the time series obtained after the intervention. Shifts in stationarity properties, parameter values of a process, cross-covariances, and structural relations among the observed variables are all possible and are of great interest. In the next section, we will consider a framework for testing hypotheses concerning the properties of time series.

V. Approaches to Estimation and Hypothesis Testing

A. Testing in the Absence of a Stochastic Process Model

A longitudinal researcher's initial questions about a time series often may be simple enough to answer without employing an elaborate stochastic model. One basic question is whether or not there is anything systematic (i.e., nonrandom) in the series. When systematization is not obvious from examining the data, it may be advantageous to test the series first for *randomness*. A number of tests for randomness are available that are distribution-free and relatively easy to compute. One simple test involves counting the number of peaks or troughs in the series. A peak is defined as a value that is greater than the values of its two adjacent neighbors. Both peaks and troughs are called "turning points" of the series. The observed number of turning points may be compared with the expected number under the hypothesis that the distribution of peaks and troughs is random. The turning-points test performs poorly when there is random oscillation around a line of gentle trend. A second test of randomness involves the interval between two turning points, called a *phase*. The length of this interval is the *phase length*. In this test of randomness, the observed numbers of phases of each possible length are compared with the expected numbers under the hypothesis that the distribution of phase lengths is random.

Tests of randomness differ with respect to the characteristic of the series that is presumed to be random and the nature of the nonrandomness specified by the alternative hypothesis. Certain tests, for example, specify *monotonic trend* as the alternative. The difference-sign test, for example, involves counting the number of points where the series increases and has been advocated primarily as a test of randomness against an alternative hypothesis of monotonic trend. The test performs poorly when there is monotonic trend but the number of upward and downward movements in the series is about the same. In this case the turning-points test is preferable. Still better tests of randomness against an alternative of monotonic trend are the rank-correlation tests. Given the series of observations x_1, x_2, . . . , x_p, a rank-order correlation coefficient such as Kendall's τ or Spearman's ρ may be computed on the pairs $(x_1, 1)$, $(x_2, 2)$,...,(x_p, p). For a random series the expected value of τ and ρ is zero. Tests of the hypothesis $\tau = 0$ or $\rho = 0$ are particularly powerful against an alternative of linear trend. These and other *nonparametric tests of randomness* are described in Kendall and Stuart (1968).

When trend is present, the researcher may seek a simple parametric description of the series as a polynomial function of time, or in the case of cyclical trend, as a periodic function of time. A regression model frequently used for fitting curves to trends is

$$X(t) = f(t) + U(t)$$

where $f(t)$ is a polynomial or periodic function of time and $U(t)$ is a random component with zero expectation. In many cases it is possible to obtain least squares, maximum likelihood, or other types of parameter estimates along with goodness-of-fit tests. A classic application of these *curve-fitting* procedures concerns the problem of finding the best-fitting polynomial or periodic function for a series. The use of regression analyses for investigating polynomial and cyclical trends is given detailed mathematical treatment in Anderson (1971).

Within the framework of multivariate analysis of variance (MANOVA) it is possible to compare time series across independent samples from different experimental or natural populations. Three important null hypotheses are *parallelism, coincidence,* and *flatness.* Parallelism holds when the upward and downward *changes* in the mean function in each series are identical across the populations sampled. Shown in Figure 5.6 are series for two groups that exhibit parallelism. If series are parallel, further testing is done to determine whether they are at the same level; that is, are coincident. Figure 5.7 illustrates two coincident series. If coincident, the series are then tested for flatness; that is, the absence of change across occasions. These procedures, usually discussed under the rubrics of *repeated measures* and *profile analysis,* are detailed in Bock (1975), Morrison (1967) and Winer (1971).

There are several weaknesses in the nonparametric, curve-fitting, and MANOVA approaches to the analysis of time series. The results of testing, particularly nonparametric testing, are often ambiguous. If randomness, monotonicity, or linearity can be rejected, for example, the experimenter

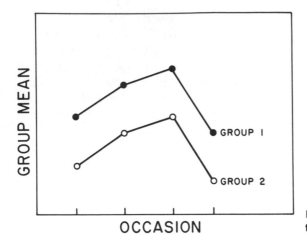

FIGURE 5.6. **Parallel series for two groups.**

is still left with the question of which alternative to the null hypothesis is responsible for the rejection. Similarly, if parallelism is rejected, there remains the problem of interpreting the differing shapes or profiles of the series in each group. Consequently, these procedures usually afford only a weak test of theory. The rejection of randomness or the finding of an adequately descriptive polynomial or periodic function will rarely provide more than marginal support for a theory of longitudinal change. Furthermore, these procedures do not lend themselves well to the examination of some important kinds of structural relationships between multiple time series arising from multimeasure, multioccasion research designs. The use of stochastic process models in the analysis of time series makes possible more precise investigation of the characteristics of time series and of structural relations in multivariate time series.

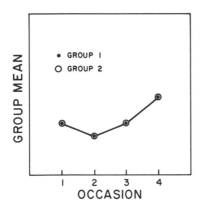

FIGURE 5.7. **Coincident series for two groups.**

B. Testing Sequences of Stochastic Models

Statistical inference with time-series models can be usefully viewed as a process of comparative model fitting. The researcher's inferential problem is basically one of comparing n classes of models on m samples from natural or experimental populations. Let us suppose that because of theoretical and practical constraints, attention can be restricted to model classes C_1, $C_2, \ldots, C_n$. For example an investigator may initially assume that the series in a single population study can be adequately described by either a Gaussian second-order autoregressive process (C_1) or a Gaussian second-order moving-average process (C_2). The union of C_1 and C_2 is the class of models whose members are either members of C_1 or members of C_2 or both. This union defines the *class of admissible hypotheses* for the above study. In general the union $A = C_1 \cup C_2 \cup \cdots \cup C_n$ describes the class of admissible hypotheses. Sometimes it is advantageous to consider a sequence of *nested classes of models* in which each model class is completely contained within the class that procedes it in the sequence. A model class C_i is said to be *properly nested* in model class C_j if every member of C_i is also a member of C_j but some members of C_j are not members of C_i. If C_i is properly nested in C_j, we may write $C_j \subset C_i$; that is, class j properly includes class i. Suppose, for example, that C_1 is the class of Gaussian, stationary autoregressive processes of Order 3 (GSAR3). If C_2 is the class of GSAR2, then $C_1 \subset C_2$. Similarly, if C_3 is the class of GSAR1, then $C_2 \subset C_3$. Hence, the sequence of model classes C_1, C_2, C_3 is ordered from most to least inclusive; that is, $C_1 \subset C_2 \subset C_3$.

Testing a sequence of nested models corresponds to a "top down" approach to comparative model fitting. As one proceeds through the sequence $C_1, C_2, C_3, \ldots$, progressively more restricted models are tested until a model that fits poorly is encountered. At this point the investigator concludes in favor of the model that immediately preceded the rejected model in the sequence. The first model class, C_1, in a nested sequence is never tested. Since C_1 properly includes all subsequent model classes it is equivalent to the class of admissible hypotheses $A = C_1 = C_1 \cup C_2 \cup \cdots \cup C_n$. By assumption the correct model is a member of A, and hence only model classes properly included in A need to be tested. The inability to test the fit of C_1 is not really a problem since one can usually let C_2 be the most general model for which a test of fit is desired and choose C_1 to be some model sufficiently general to include C_2 properly. As will be seen, there is sometimes a "natural" choice for C_1.

As in all hypothesis testing, the statistical power of any test of a model's goodness of fit will depend upon sample size and the alternative against which the model is tested. Here we will focus on the problem of choosing "good" alternative hypotheses. Let $H: C$ denote the hypothesis that some member of model class C is the correct model; for example, $C = $ GSAR1.

The most general alternative hypothesis is that the correct model is a member of admissible class A and not a member of C. We denote the alternative hypothesis by $K : A \cap \bar{C}$. For instance, if A is the class of Gaussian processes and H:GSARl, then the most general alternative hypothesis is that the correct model is a Gaussian process but not a Gaussian, stationary, autoregressive process of Order 1. However, the most general alternative to a model is not always the most appropriate choice for a test of the model.

Consider a sequence of properly nested models, $C_1, C_2, \ldots, C_n$, in which each succeeding model, starting with C_2, is tested against the most general alternative to that model; that is,

$$H: C_2 \quad \text{versus} \quad K: C_1 \cap \bar{C}_2$$

$$H: C_3 \quad \text{versus} \quad K: C_1 \cap \bar{C}_3$$

$$\vdots$$

$$H: C_n \quad \text{versus} \quad K: C_1 \cap \bar{C}_n$$

Testing terminates when the first rejectable hypothesis is encounted. In testing each model against its most general alternative, no advantage is taken of the fact that the models are nested and that the results of tests earlier in the sequence can be used to choose more restricted alternatives for models tested later in the sequence. A better sequence of alternatives is

$$H: C_2 \quad \text{versus} \quad K: C_1 \cap \bar{C}_2$$

$$H: C_3 \quad \text{versus} \quad K: C_2 \cap \bar{C}_3$$

$$\vdots$$

$$H: C_n \quad \text{versus} \quad K: C_{n-1} \cap \bar{C}_n$$

Testing begins, as before, with a test of C_2 against $C_1 \cap \bar{C}_2$. If C_2 cannot be rejected, then C_3 can be tested against $C_2 \cap \bar{C}_3$, the model class whose members are members of C_2 and not members of C_3. This alternative is the most general one for C_3 when the class of admissible hypotheses is restricted to C_2. If C_3 cannot be rejected, then C_4 is tested against $C_3 \cap \bar{C}_4$, etc. Testing terminates when the first rejectable model is encountered. The advantage of sequentially restricting the alternative hypothesis based on the results of earlier testing is that the "restricted" tests against these properly nested alternatives are usually more powerful than unrestricted tests against general alternatives in C_1. When restricted tests are used, testing will usually terminate earlier in a sequence.

To illustrate many of the principles described thus far, we consider a simple time-series experiment in which an experimental group is subjected to a single intervention between measurement occasions I and $I + 1$. The control group is not subjected to the intervention and engages in "normal activity" during the intervention interval. The object of the study is to assess the effect of the intervention through a comparison of the experimental and control series. The sequence of nested hypotheses to be tested is shown in Table 5.8. The class of admissible hypotheses, C_1, restricts attention to Gaussian processes; that is, it is assumed that the series in each group has a multivariate normal distribution. Gaussian processes are a natural choice for C_1 in many instances. Multivariate normality is assumed in many statistical models but is rarely tested in practice. It is a reasonable simplifying assumption even when only approximately true.

The first hypothesis tested, C_2, is that the process in each group is some Gaussian (nonstationary autoregressive moving-average) model of Order (1,1); that is, GNS–ARMA (1,1), in which the means, variances, and covariances in each series may be time-dependent. The hypothesis also allows that parameter values of GNS–ARMA (1,1) process in the experimental series may differ from those in the control series. Model class C_2 is tested against the alternative that the process in each group is Gaussian but not GNS–ARMA (1,1). Given that C_2 cannot be rejected, the next hypothesis tested, C_3, is that the series in each group is some Gaussian nonstationary autoregressive process of Order 1; that is, GNS–ARI. As before, the parameters of the processes are allowed to differ between groups. Hypothesis C_3 is tested against the restricted alternative that the process in each group is GNS–ARMA (1,1) but not GNS–ARI. Failure to reject C_3 indicates that responses at time t in both series depend on earlier responses only through the response at time $t - 1$ and that a moving-average residual component is unnecessary.

Given that C_3 cannot be rejected, one may proceed to test hypothesis C_4, that the value of the autoregression weight in each series prior to the intervention—that is, for $t = 0,1,2,\ldots,I$—is constant but possibly a different

TABLE 5.8

A Sequence of Nested Hypotheses for Comparing on Experimental and Control Series

H	Experimental series	Control series	K
C_1	A Gaussian process	A Gaussian process	
C_2	GNS-ARMA(1,1)	GNS-ARMA(1,1)	$C_1 \cap \bar{C}_2$
C_3	GNS-ARI	GNS-ARI	$C_2 \cap \bar{C}_3$
C_4	GNS-ARI: α_E	GNS-ARI: α_C	$C_3 \cap \bar{C}_4$
C_5	GNS-ARI: α	GNS-ARI: α	$C_4 \cap \bar{C}_5$
C_6	GNS-ARI: $\alpha,\ \mu_E,\ \mu_E + \delta_E$	GNS-ARI: $\alpha,\ \mu_C,\ \mu_C + \delta_C$	$C_5 \cap \bar{C}_6$
C_7	GNS-ARI: $\alpha,\ \mu,\ \mu + \delta_E$	GNS-ARI: $\alpha,\ \mu,\ \mu + \delta_C$	$C_6 \cap \bar{C}_7$
C_8	GNS-ARI: $\alpha,\ \mu,\ \mu + \delta$	GNS-ARI: $\alpha,\ \mu,\ \mu + \delta$	$C_7 \cap \bar{C}_8$
C_9	GNS-ARI: $\alpha,\ \mu,\ \mu + \delta,\ \beta_E$	GNS-ARI: $\alpha,\ \mu,\ \mu + \delta,\ \beta_C$	$C_8 \cap \bar{C}_9$
C_{10}	GNS-ARI: $\alpha,\ \mu,\ \mu + \delta,\ \beta$	GNS-ARI: $\alpha,\ \mu,\ \mu + \delta,\ \beta$	$C_9 \cap \bar{C}_{10}$

constant in each series. Let α_E and α_C denote the constant preintervention autoregression weights in the experimental and control series, respectively. Hypothesis C_4 is tested against the restricted alternative that the process in each group is GNS–AR1 but that the preintervention autoregression weight in one or both groups is not constant; that is, the weight is time-dependent. Failure to reject C_4 indicates that, in both series, the response at time t has a constant amount of dependency upon the response at time $t - 1$ for all t prior to the intervention.

If C_4 cannot be rejected, then test C_5, the hypothesis that the preintervention autoregression weight is not only constant in both groups but the same constant; that is, $\alpha_E = \alpha_C$. Let α denote the common value of the preintervention weight. Hypothesis C_5 is tested against the restricted alternative that the preintervention weights are constant but not the same constant in both groups. Failure to reject C_5 indicates that prior to the intervention, the responses at time t have exactly the same amount of dependency on the responses at $t - 1$ in both series. If C_4 were rejectable, then preintervention differences between groups in autoregression would be indicated and further comparisons to isolate the intervention effect would be invalid.

Provided that C_5 cannot be rejected, hypothesis C_6, which concerns the mean functions of the two series, may be tested. This hypothesis holds that the preintervention mean functions are constant in both series but not necessarily the same constant. In addition, C_6 requires that the postintervention mean functions be constant but not necessarily the same constant for both series. The hypothesis allows that the constant preintervention mean may differ from the constant post-intervention mean in either group. Let μ_E and μ_C denote the constant preintervention means of the experimental and control series, respectively. In addition, let $\mu_E + \delta_E$ and $\mu_C + \delta_C$ denote the constant postintervention means of the experimental and control series, respectively. Failure to reject C_6 indicates that the series in both groups prior to the intervention oscillates around a fixed level where the fixed level in one group may differ from the fixed level in the other, and that after the intervention the series may shift to a new fixed level where, again, the new level in one group may differ from the new level in the other.

Given that C_6 cannot be rejected, one goes on to test C_7, the hypothesis that the constant preintervention means are exactly the same in both groups; that is, $\mu_E = \mu_C$. Let μ denote the common preintervention mean. Failure to reject C_7 indicates that both series oscillate around the same fixed level prior to the intervention. If C_7 were rejectable, a preintervention difference in mean functions between the experimental and control series would be indicated, and further comparisons to isolate an intervention effect would be invalid.

If C_7 is accepted, then one proceeds to test C_8, the hypothesis that the shift from the common preintervention mean is the same in both series; that is, $\delta_E = \delta_C$. Let δ denote the common value of the shift after the intervention. Failure to reject C_7 indicates that there is no differential effect, because of the intervention, in the postintervention means of the two series. For example, both the experimental and control series may shift from a constant mean of 10 before the intervention interval to a constant mean of 20 after. Since the intervention in the experimental group produces no *differential* change in the mean of the series relative to the control, one concludes that there is no intervention effect on mean functions. If C_7 can be rejected, then the change in mean level of the series following the intervention is not the same for both series and hence there is a true intervention effect upon the mean function of the experimental series.

Provided C_8 is not rejectable, the next hypothesis tested, C_9, is that the postintervention autoregression weights are constant. Let β_E and β_C denote the constant postintervention regression weights in the experimental and control series, respectively. Failure to reject C_9 indicates that following the intervention—that is, for $t = I + 1, I + 2, \ldots$—a response at time t has a fixed amount of dependence upon the response at $t - 1$, although the fixed amount in the experimental series may differ from the fixed amount in the control series. If C_9 can be accepted, then C_{10}, the hypothesis that the constant postintervention autoregression weights in both series are the same—that is, $\beta_E = \beta_C$—is tested. We let β denote this common postintervention weight.

Suppose that C_{10} is the first rejectable hypothesis encountered in the sequence. Then the overall conclusion is that the shift (if any) in the mean function of the experimental series is not attributable to the intervention but the intervention does produce a differential change in autoregression relative to the control series. Hence the sole effect of the experimental intervention is to produce a different degree of dependency among postintervention responses than is found in the control series. Should C_{10} be accepted, one might go on to test flatness in both series—that is, $\delta = 0$—or equality of the pre- and postintervention autoregression in both series; that is, $\alpha = \beta$.

The sequence of hypotheses in our example is obviously not the only sequence that might be considered. The particular sequence chosen by an investigator will depend upon what hypotheses seem plausible for the data and what kinds of potential intervention effects are most important to detect and isolate. It should also be noted that when a rejectable hypothesis is encountered, the testing sequence may be restarted from the last acceptable hypothesis provided that no models in a new nested sequence have any members in common with the first rejectable model in the original sequence.

C. A Note on Estimation

Because there are so many different methods for parameter estimation, each yielding estimates having somewhat different properties, we will not attempt to enumerate them and provide technical discussions of each procedure. Instead we will restrict attention to just two methods that are among the most generally applicable and efficient methods available, with the intention of conveying a nontechnical appreciation of approaches to estimation.

One important method, yielding estimates having several "desirable" properties, is the method of *maximum likelihood*. To use this method one must be able to specify the joint density or probability of all the observations in the sample. Since joint-density functions of time-series models are often complex, the computation of a density function can be quite difficult. The numerical value of the density depends upon the numerical values of all the model parameters, for example, the variance of the white-noise process. When the density is regarded as a function of the model parameters, it is called a *likelihood function*. Those values of the model parameters that make the likelihood as large as possible are called the *maximum likelihood estimates* (MLEs) of the parameters. Finding the parameter values that maximize the likelihood is a calculus problem that, for some models, has a simple, closed-form algebraic solution. In other cases trial values for the parameters must be used and then successively improved until the maximum is found. Procedures for successively improving trial estimates are called *iterative procedures*. In most cases the use of a computer program is the only practical means for obtaining maximum likelihood estimates, even when closed-form solutions exist. Some generally desirable properties of MLEs are that they are consistent, asymptotically unbiased, and efficient. In addition, when sample size is "large," each estimate will have approximately a normal distribution, and appropriate standard errors of estimate may be computed. If MLEs can be obtained, they may be used in conjunction with likelihood ratio testing procedures that generally permit the testing of time-series models against both restricted and unrestricted alternative hypotheses.

Another important method of estimation is *generalized least squares*. A special case of this method is the ordinary-least-squares procedure familiar from the topic of linear regression analysis. In the generalized-least-squares (GLS) approach each observation is regarded as being composed of two parts: a part that can be represented as a nonrandom function of the model parameters and another part representing a random disturbance or error. The GLS method allows that the random disturbances in the observations may be correlated with each other as would generally be the case for time-series models. The ordinary-least-squares procedure, by contrast, is most appropriate when the random disturbances are uncorrelated. The GLS criterion is a measure of the sum of squared deviations from expected values under the model that take the correlated disturbances into account. This criterion is a function of the model parameters as well as the observations. Those values of the model parameters that make the GLS criterion as small as possible are called the *GLS estimates*. Finding the parameter values that minimize the GLS criterion is a calculus problem that is handled in much the same way as the maximization problem for MLEs. The GLS estimates also have many of the same desirable properties as MLEs. However, the model-testing procedures based on the GLS criterion usually do not permit tests against restricted alternatives. These and other estimation methods are discussed in many of the references mentioned earlier in this chapter and in other chapters in this volume.

Chapter 6

Mathematical Representations of Development Theories[1]

BURTON SINGER
SEYMOUR SPILERMAN

ABSTRACT

In this chapter we explore the consequences of particular stage linkage structures for the evolution of a population. We first argue the importance of constructing "dynamic" models of developmental theories and show through a series of examples the implications of various stage connections for population movements. In discussing dynamic models, one thrust of our comments is to identify the sorts of process features about which assumptions must be made in order to convert a static theory about stage connections (the sort of specification commonly presented in life-span psychology) into a dynamic model. A second focus of our discussion concerns inverse problems: How to utilize a model formulation so that the stage linkage structure may be recovered from survey data of the kind collected by developmental psychologists.

I. Introduction

Although time, usually in the guise of age, is a crucial variable in developmental psychology, formal models of developmental phenomena rarely have the character of dynamic representations, in the sense of mimicking the evolution of an empirical process through time. The analytic procedures employed most extensively by life-span psychologists are factor analysis, regression, analysis of variance, scaling, clustering, and variants of these methods (see, for instance, Nesselroade & Reese, 1973). These are powerful

[1] The work reported here was supported by National Science Foundation Grants SOC76-17706 at Columbia University and SOC76-07698 at University of Wisconsin (Madison). Assistance was also provided by the Institute for Research on Poverty at the University of Wisconsin.

155

LONGITUDINAL RESEARCH IN THE
STUDY OF BEHAVIOR AND DEVELOPMENT

techniques for identifying variables that are central to the course of development in a particular substantive area (e.g., intellectual maturation, acquisition of moral values). Also, when applied to panel data, the procedures can yield insights into how the salience of key variables shifts over the life cycle, or over a portion thereof (e.g., stages in infancy, youth, adulthood).

These analytic methods do not, however, lead to *dynamic* formulations of developmental theories, which can be useful in testing predictions from a theory about the evolution of an empirical process, or in comparing the implications of competing explanations. By a dynamic formulation we mean a representation that incorporates into the mathematics the main assumptions about a developmental phenomenon and is specified in such a way that the relevant variables, and their postulated interrelations, are functions of time or subjects's age. In this sense, like the empirical process, it too constitutes an evolving system. As a simple illustration of such a model, consider the following statements of alternative evolutionary mechanisms:

1. *The growth of a process at each instant is proportional to its potential for future growth.*
2. *The growth of a process at each instant is proportional to the product of its current size and its potential for further growth.*

These statements might be proposed as competing explanations of the manner by which information is diffused in a population of size N. In Formulation (1), it does not matter how many persons $y(t)$ know the information of concern at instant t; only those yet to hear, numbering $N - y(t)$, are salient to the diffusion rate. If the information were propagated by a mass-media source, such as radio or television, rather than by interpersonal communication, this model might apply. Formulation (2), in comparison, is consistent with a process in which those already aware of the information "infect" the uninitiated through contact and conversation. Assuming that the informed and the uninformed mix randomly, the variable governing the

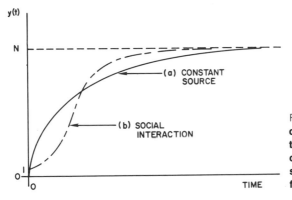

FIGURE 6.1. **Illustrative growth curves for diffusion via social interaction and diffusion from a constant source. N = population size; $y(t)$ = number aware of information at time t.**

evolution of the process would be $y(t)[N - y(t)]$, which measures the rate at which individuals from the two groups come into contact.

The evolutionary mechanisms, (1) and (2), can be represented by the differential Eq. (1) and (2), respectively,

$$dy(t)/d(t) = k_1[N - y(t)], \qquad y(0) = 0 \qquad (1)$$

$$dy(t)/d(t) = k_2 y(t)[N - y(t)], \qquad y(0) = 1 \qquad (2)$$

where k_1 and k_2 are constants that adjust for the time unit (e.g., day, year) used in the measurements.[2] Equations (1) and (2) have for solutions Eq. (3) and Eq. (4),

$$y(t) = N[1 - \exp(-k_1 t)] \qquad (3)$$

$$y(t) = [N \exp(Nk_2 t)]/[N - 1 + \exp(Nk_2 t)] \qquad (4)$$

which predict the different evolutionary paths displayed in Figure 6.1.

These formulations are *dynamic* in that time appears explicitly as a variable; they are *process models* in that the predicted value of $y(t)$ evolves according to the assumptions of a particular theory. If a researcher has data on the time course of an empirical process, he can test whether Eq. (3), Eq. (4), or a specification of an equivalent sort best approximates his observations. By this exercise it is often possible to select among competing explanations of the mechanism underlying a developmental process. Indeed, these very models have been applied by Coleman, Katz, and Menzel (1957) to data on drug adoptions by physicians (also see Coleman, 1964, pp. 43–45). They concluded that the drug acquisition pattern by socially integrated M.D.'s is best represented by a logistic curve (implying Mechanism 2), whereas isolated M.D.'s adopt according to the constant source model (Mechanism 1), as they are influenced principally by drug advertisements in trade journals. To our knowledge, although developmental psychologists emphasize ontogenetic processes and employ the imagery of an evolutionary system, few attempts have been made to translate their theories into formal models such as the preceding.

In this chapter, we describe the formulation of dynamic models where the objective is to test developmental theories against data or ascertain the consequences of particular assumptions about the structure of a process. To delimit our task, we focus on the sort of mathematics that is appropriate for studying qualitative change. As a result, the tools we introduce are pertinent to theories that postulate stage sequences, a variety of explanation with considerable precedent in developmental psychology (Ausubel & Sullivan, 1970; Kohlberg, 1968; Piaget, 1960). To the degree possible we have written this chapter with a view toward substantive issues and have con-

---

[2] The initial condition, $y(0) = 1$, in Eq. (2) is necessary because diffusion through communication cannot begin until at least one person is knowledgeable.

centrated on the translation of theoretical specifications into mathematical formalism; the reader is usually referred elsewhere for mathematical details and estimation procedures. The organization of the chapter is as follows: In the next section we introduce a class of models that is suitable for studying evolutionary processes that incorporate the notion of stage. In section III we describe how particular stage theories can be cast in the framework of the general model. In the fourth section we relax several requirements of the basic model so that it can more realistically represent developmental phenomena.

II. The Concept of Development Stages and a Mathematical Formulation of Stage Progressions

Stage sequences have been postulated for a variety of developmental processes—the evolution of moral behavior (Kohlberg, 1973), cognition (Piaget, 1954), personality (Loevinger, 1966a), and motor skills (Shirley, 1933), to cite but a few topics. There also exist diverse formulations of stage models in the literature of life-span psychology. These differ with respect to the presumed sources of the stages and with regard to the rules governing movement between them. In regard to stage origins, some authors have emphasized maturational considerations, in which individuals are viewed as programmed genetically for particular behaviors or abilities to emerge (Gesell, 1954). The specification of psychosexual stages, keyed to biological activation of the sex glands, provides an illustration (Kohlberg, 1973, p. 181). Others view stages as arising from interactions with the social environment. Kohlberg (1968, pp. 1016–1024), for example, contends that experience with the cultural and physical world is necessary for cognitive stages to take the shapes they do. Still other researchers have adopted the position that stages are a useful research construct around which to discuss development, without insisting that they have an empirical existence (Kaplan, 1966; Reese, 1970).

We shall not discuss further the very important issues concerning the etiology of stages, but will focus instead on the mathematical representation of theories about stage connections and on the consequences of various linkage structures for the evolution of individuals among the stages. Formulations of stage connections in a developmental process differ according to whether the progression is viewed as unilineal or multilineal, whether stages in the sequence can be skipped, and whether regression to an earlier level is possible. A second set of considerations pertinent to the structure of developmental theories concerns the age specificity of a stage and the related matter of the variability of duration in a stage. For discussions of these topics in the context of particular substantive processes, the reader is referred to Emmerich (1968) and Kessen (1962).

To develop the mathematical apparatus for ascertaining the implications of particular stage connections, we discuss both the simplest prototype of a stage theory (for concreteness) and the general mathematical formulation.[3] Consider, then, a developmental progression consisting of n stages, in which the linkage is unilineal and there is no possibility of stage skipping or regression. An example of such a structure, with $n = 5$, is presented in panel A of Figure 6.2; henceforth this model is referred to as Example 1. It will be convenient to have available also a matrix representation of the stage linkages. For an arbitrary n-stage structure, we define a matrix $\mathbf{M}$,

$$\mathbf{M} = \begin{bmatrix} m_{11} & m_{12} & \cdots & m_{1n} \\ m_{21} & m_{22} & \cdots & m_{2n} \\ \vdots & & & \vdots \\ m_{n1} & m_{n2} & \cdots & m_{nn} \end{bmatrix} \tag{5}$$

whose elements are $m_{ij} = \{$probability of transferring from stage i to stage j when a transition occurs$\}$, where $0 \le m_{ij} \le 1$, and $\sum_{j=1}^{n} m_{ij} = 1$. These restrictions on the elements of $\mathbf{M}$ ensure that each row of the matrix constitutes a probability distribution. We require, in addition, that $m_{ii} = 0$ for each stage i that is not an absorbing state of the process; that is, from which individuals can exit. This means we exclude the possibility of within-stage transitions, a type of move that is undefined in most developmental theories. Also, we set $m_{ii} = 1$ for each stage that is an absorbing state of the process.

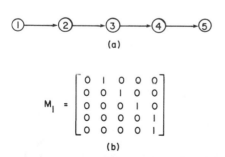

(a)

$$M_1 = \begin{bmatrix} 0 & 1 & 0 & 0 & 0 \\ 0 & 0 & 1 & 0 & 0 \\ 0 & 0 & 0 & 1 & 0 \\ 0 & 0 & 0 & 0 & 1 \\ 0 & 0 & 0 & 0 & 1 \end{bmatrix}$$

(b)

FIGURE 6.2. **(a) Representation of a simple unilineal stage structure. (b) Each row of M_1 is a vector of destination probabilities. Thus, if an individual were in Stage 1 before a transition, the Row 1 entries would pertain, and they indicate movement to Stage 2 with probability equal to 1. The main diagonal entries are set equal to 0 (with the exception of Row 5) to indicate that a "move" is not defined apart from a stage transition; that is, there is no notion of movement within a stage. The main diagonal entry of Row 5 is set equal to 1 because this stage is an absorbing state ($m_{5j} = 0$ for $j \ne 5$), and the definition of M_1 (see text) requires $\Sigma_j m_{5j} = 1$.**

[3] For a more technical presentation of continuous-time Markov processes see Feller (1968, chapter 17) and Singer and Spilerman (1974). For discussions on the superimposition of theoretical structures on stochastic models see Coleman (1964, chapters 5, 6).

This is done for mathematical convenience and, as we shall see, carries no substantive implications. In the particular case of the unilineal progression (Figure 6.2a), we have the further requirements on $\mathbf{M}$: $m_{i,i+1} = 1$, and $m_{ij} = 0$ otherwise (except that $m_{55} = 1$). This matrix, $\mathbf{M}_1$, is reported in Figure 6.2b.

To this point, though matrix $\mathbf{M}$ conveys important structural information about the process, the description of the stage progression is a static representation. To elaborate the model we must indicate how stage-transition events occur. At a general level of description we assume that the time τ_k spent by an individual in stage i follows some probability distribution,

$$\mathrm{Prob}_i(\tau_k < t \,|\, \tau_1, \ldots , \tau_{k-1}) \tag{6}$$

where $\tau_1, \ldots , \tau_{k-1}$ report the sojourn times in earlier stages. Our imagery, therefore, is the following. An individual originates in stage i at the beginning of the process, $t_0 = 0$. He remains there for an interval τ_1, specified by a distribution function $\mathrm{Prob}_i(\tau_1 < t)$, and then transfers to stage j with probability m_{ij}. He remains in this stage for a period τ_2, specified by a conditional probability distribution $\mathrm{Prob}_j(\tau_2 < t \,|\, \tau_1)$, then transfers to stage k with probability m_{jk}; and so forth.[4] The process continues until some absorbing state is reached, at which point the evolution is terminated. The time path for the unilineal progression associated with the stage linkages of matrix $\mathbf{M}_1$ is presented in Figure 6.3.

Several further assumptions are necessary to complete the specification of the model. One matter concerns the relevance of an individual's past

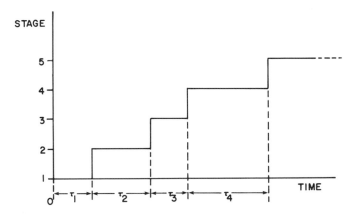

FIGURE 6.3. **A sample path description corresponding to the unilineal stage structure of Figure 6.2. It is assumed that there are five stages, which must be traversed sequentially.** τ_i **is the value of a random variable and denotes the sojourn time for an individual in stage** i**. Stage 5 is an absorbing state of the process.**

[4] In the present example i, j, k = 1, 2, 3, respectively.

movement history to the course of his subsequent evolution among the stages. We assume

1. *Knowlege of current stage conveys all information that is relevant to forecasting future movements.*

Stated technically, if $m_{ij,ab\cdots f}$ = {probability of moving from stage i to stage j at the occurrence of a transition, given prior sojourns in stages $a,b, \ldots ,f$}, then

$$m_{ij,ab\cdots f} = m_{ij}.$$

(This assumption is superfluous in the current example of a unilineal progression since there is only one possible path, but it is relevant to the evolution of a population in less restrictive models.) We indicate in the next section that this specification has been employed in descriptions of stage linkages in developmental psychology.

For an initial baseline class of models, we further assume

2. *The sojourn time in stage i is exponentially distributed; that is,*

$$\text{Prob}_i(\tau_k < t \mid \tau_1, \ldots , \tau_{k-1}) = \text{Prob}_i(\tau_k < t)$$

$$= F_i(t) = 1 - e^{-\lambda_i t}. \tag{7}$$

Use of the exponential distribution amounts to specifying that the probability of departing from stage i during the infinitesimal interval $(t, t + dt)$, conditional on being in stage i at time t, equals

$$\frac{f_i(t)\, dt}{1 - F_i(t)} = \frac{\lambda_i \exp(-\lambda_i t)\, dt}{1 - [1 - \exp(-\lambda_i t)]} = \lambda_i\, dt$$

where $f_i(t)$ is the density function corresponding to $F_i(t)$. This result, in turn, indicates that the probability of leaving stage i is independent of duration in the stage, and is tantamount to specifying an absence of aging. So new entrants have the same likelihood of departing as individuals who have been in the stage for some period of time. The parameter λ_i, incidentally, has an interpretation as the rate of movement out of stage i; consequently, $1/\lambda_i$ equals the expected duration in stage i.

3. *Finally, we require that if the data pertain to the movements of a population, rather than to the transitions of a single individual, the population is homogeneous with respect to the structure of the evolutionary process.*

This does not mean that all persons have the same duration τ_i in stage i, but that τ_{ic}, the time spent in stage i by individual c, follows the single exponential distribution $F_i(t) = 1 - \exp(-\lambda_i t)$. Stated less formally, duration in a stage is a random variable with the underlying distribution of holding times the same for all individuals. Similarly, where alternative destinations are available to persons in stage i, homogeneity means that all have the same list of probabilities for making the various transitions, not that they move identically.

It is worth dwelling on the conceptual status of the preceding assumptions. The question of the structure of **M** is a familiar topic to developmental psychologists, since stage theories are commonly specified at this level. Assumptions (1)-(3) can be viewed as "side conditions," aspects of the process to which researchers have generally not been sensitive, though see Kessen (1960) and Emmerich (1968) for provocative comments on precisely these matters. What is made evident by formulating a dynamic model is that development theorists must address these auxiliary questions if complete models are to be specified. The particular assumptions we have made constitute a gross simplification of reality; this is especially true of Specification (2), which postulates an absence of duration effects, and Specification (3), which postulates population homogeneity. These assumptions do, however, provide a convenient starting point from which to consider more realistic formulations, which are developed in the next sections.

We now wish to convey the implications of Assumptions (1)-(3) for the movements of individuals among the stages. We denote by $p_{ij}(t)$ the probability that an individual in stage i at time 0 moves to stage j by time t. (This probability differs from m_{ij} in that the latter refers to movement proclivities at the occurrence of a transition, not over widely spaced time intervals.) With this specification in hand, the evolution of a population among the stages is described by the system of integral equations,

$$p_{ij}(t) = \delta_{ij} \exp(-\lambda_i t) + \sum_k \int_0^t \lambda_i \exp(-\lambda_i u) m_{ik} p_{kj}(t - u) \, du \qquad (8)$$

$$0 \le i, \quad j \le n$$

where $\delta_{ij} = 1$ if $i = j$, and 0 otherwise. This expression, known as the backward equations for a continuous-time Markov process (Feller, 1971, p. 484), is amenable to the following interpretation:

1. When $i \ne j$, $p_{ij}(t)$ consists of the sum of products of three factors: the probability of a first departure from stage i at time u, the probability of a stage i to stage k transition at that instant, and the probability of transferring to stage j by some combination of moves in the interval $t - u$. The summation is over all intermediate stages k and over all time divisions u in the interval $(0, t)$.
2. When $i = j$, in addition to the above term, there is the possibility of not transferring out of stage i during $(0, t)$. This probability is given by the first term.

If we represent by $\mathbf{P}(t)$ the matrix of elements $p_{ij}(t)$.

$$\mathbf{P}(t) = \begin{bmatrix} p_{11}(t) & \cdots & p_{1n}(t) \\ \vdots & & \vdots \\ p_{n1}(t) & \cdots & p_{nn}(t) \end{bmatrix}$$

$0 \le p_{ij}(t) \le 1$, $\Sigma_j\, p_{ij}(t) = 1$, then the integral equations (Eq. 8) have the convenient solution,

$$\mathbf{P}(t) = e^{\,\mathbf{\Lambda}[\mathbf{M}-\mathbf{I}]t}, \qquad \mathbf{P}(0) = \mathbf{I}. \tag{9}$$

In this representation $\mathbf{\Lambda}$ is a diagonal matrix,

$$\mathbf{\Lambda} = \begin{bmatrix} \lambda_1 & & & 0 \\ & \lambda_2 & & \\ & & \ddots & \\ 0 & & & \lambda_n \end{bmatrix}$$

whose entries are the reciprocals of the expected duration times in each stage, $\mathbf{I}$ is the identity matrix, and $\mathbf{M}$ is the array specified in Eq. (5), which describes the pattern of movement between the stages. Furthermore, by the expression $e^{\mathbf{A}}$, $\mathbf{A}$ an arbitrary square matrix, we mean the power series in $\mathbf{A}$,

$$e^{\mathbf{A}} = \sum_{n=0}^{\infty} \frac{\mathbf{A}^n}{n!} \tag{10}$$

which can be evaluated by standard numerical methods (see, e.g., Gantmacher, 1960).

It is useful to recapitulate what is accomplished by this mathematical formulation. The matrix $\mathbf{P}(t)$ relates the distribution of a population among stages at time t to its distribution at time 0, in the sense that a typical entry, $p_{ij}(t)$, conveys the probability of moving from stage i to stage j during the interval $(0,t)$. The model is dynamic in that $\mathbf{P}(t)$ is a function of time; with the passage of time, $\mathbf{P}(t)$ describes the evolution of the population among the stages. Equation (9) shows how the matrix $\mathbf{P}(t)$ is built up from the arrays $\mathbf{M}$ and $\mathbf{\Lambda}$. However, while this equation is useful as a calculating formula, the logic of the process is conveyed more adequately by the integral equation (8).

To illustrate this model in the setting of a simple unilineal progression (matrix $\mathbf{M}_1$ of Figure 6.2), we must specify average waiting times in Stages 1, 2, 3, and 4. We assume these to be .5, 1, 2, and 5 years, respectively.

Consequently, we have for matrix Λ,

$$\Lambda = \begin{bmatrix} 2 & 0 & 0 & 0 & 0 \\ 0 & 1 & 0 & 0 & 0 \\ 0 & 0 & .5 & 0 & 0 \\ 0 & 0 & 0 & .2 & 0 \\ 0 & 0 & 0 & 0 & \lambda_5 \end{bmatrix} \tag{11}$$

where the choice of λ_5 is arbitrary. Since Stage 5 is an absorbing state, the notion of waiting time to a departure has no meaning. (Mathematically, $[\mathbf{M} - \mathbf{I}]_{55} = [m_{55} - 1] = [1 - 1] = 0$, so λ_5 bears no influence on the calculations.) Now, from $\mathbf{M}_1$, Λ, and $\mathbf{I}$, we have

$$\Lambda(\mathbf{M}_1 - \mathbf{I}) = \begin{bmatrix} -2 & 2 & 0 & 0 & 0 \\ 0 & -1 & 1 & 0 & 0 \\ 0 & 0 & -.5 & .5 & 0 \\ 0 & 0 & 0 & -.2 & .2 \\ 0 & 0 & 0 & 0 & 0 \end{bmatrix}. \tag{12}$$

For the illustrative times $t = 1$, 2, and 4 years, we obtain, from Eq. (9) for $\mathbf{P}(t)$,

$$\mathbf{P}(1) = \begin{bmatrix} .1353 & .4651 & .3263 & .0691 & .0041 \\ .0000 & .3679 & .4773 & .1438 & .0110 \\ .0000 & .0000 & .6065 & .3537 & .0398 \\ .0000 & .0000 & .0000 & .8187 & .1813 \\ .0000 & .0000 & .0000 & .0000 & 1.0000 \end{bmatrix}, \tag{13}$$

$$\mathbf{P}(2) = \begin{bmatrix} .0183 & .2340 & .4641 & .2482 & .0354 \\ .0000 & .1353 & .4651 & .3394 & .0602 \\ .0000 & .0000 & .3679 & .5041 & .1281 \\ .0000 & .0000 & .0000 & .6703 & .3297 \\ .0000 & .0000 & .0000 & .0000 & 1.0000 \end{bmatrix}, \tag{14}$$

and

$$\mathbf{P}(4) = \begin{bmatrix} .0003 & .0360 & .2881 & .4843 & .1913 \\ .0000 & .0183 & .2340 & .5079 & .2398 \\ .0000 & .0000 & .1353 & .5233 & .3413 \\ .0000 & .0000 & .0000 & .4493 & .5507 \\ .0000 & .0000 & .0000 & .0000 & 1.0000 \end{bmatrix}. \tag{15}$$

These values of $\mathbf{P}(t)$ describe the evolution of individuals among the stages, subject to the assumptions about the process structure detailed above. The entries $p_{ij}(t)$ refer to proportions[5] of the population who have

---

[5] If the observations are on a single individual the interpretation of $p_{ij}(t)$ is in terms of the *probability* of a stage i to stage j move between times 0 and t.

moved between particular stages in the relevant time interval. For example, according to the entries in the top row of $\mathbf{P}(1)$, if observations are taken 1 year apart, we would expect 13% of the population in Stage 1 at time 0 to still be there, 46% to have moved to Stage 2, and 33% to have reached Stage 3. By comparison, over a 4-year interval, less than 1% would remain in Stage 1, 48% would have reached Stage 4, and 19% would be in the terminal stage of the process.

The results from the three calculations reveal that, even though the progression is unilineal with all individuals characterized by the same parameters, if observations were taken on the population at two time points, $t = 0$ and $t = t_1$, the array[6] $\hat{\mathbf{P}}(t_1)$ might be interpreted as evidence for a more complex theory, such as one permitting stage skipping or population heterogeneity in the rate or pattern of movement. Furthermore, the correspondence between the matrix constructed from the population locations at two time points, $\hat{\mathbf{P}}(t_1)$, and the rule governing stage transitions, $\mathbf{M}_1$, decreases with time. Thus, different researchers observing the same population at two time points but with different spacing intervals might draw contrary conclusions about the stage-linkage structure even though the single mechanism, $\mathbf{M}_1$ of Figure 6.2 governs its evolution. Only with a formal model of the process could one hope to uncover its underlying structure.

III. Models of More Elaborate Stage Theories

The matrix $\mathbf{M}$ contains structural information about stage linkages. Since theories of development are commonly posed at the level of specifying this array, flexibility in incorporating a variety of particular formulations would appear to be an important feature of a general framework for describing evolutionary behavior. In this section we focus on the issue of translating stage theories into $\mathbf{M}$-matrices, and illustrate the evolution of $\mathbf{P}(t)$, the transition matrix for a population based on its locations at times 0 and t, under alternative specifications of $\mathbf{M}$. As we have noted, auxiliary information about the process, concerning the distribution of waiting-time intervals and the form of population heterogeneity, is required for a full description of a dynamic model. In the next section we therefore elaborate upon these "side conditions" and outline ways in which our initial assumptions can be relaxed.

No technical difficulties arise in reformulating the continuous-time Markov model to accommodate more elaborate theories of stage linkages than

---

[6] A caret over a matrix or over an element in a matrix will mean that it should be viewed as estimated directly from data rather than calculated from a mathematical model.

the structure in Figure 6.2. We illustrate the procedure with a few examples.[7]

A. Unilineal Progressions

1. A Unilineal Progression that Permits Stage Skipping

The formulation of such a structure is diagrammed in Figure 6.4a its translation into an **M**-matrix is reported in Figure 6.4b. The principal new feature is that, supplementing the deterministic sequence of Figure 6.2, it is now possible to move directly from Stage 2 to Stage 4 and from Stage 3 to Stage 5, when transition out of the relevant origin location takes place. We must also specify the probabilities of following the alternate paths. In the present example, lacking information as to the relative magnitudes of the various probabilities, we assume all destinations to be equally likely; that is, we prescribe $m_{23} = m_{24} = .5$, and $m_{34} = m_{35} = .5$. In practice, estimates of the transition probabilities would be assigned on the basis of theory or from observation on the empirical process.

Using matrix $\mathbf{M}_2$, together with the Λ array of Eq. (11), whose entries describe the rate of movement by individuals out of each stage, we obtain for $\mathbf{P}(1)$ and $\mathbf{P}(4)$, from Eq. (9):

$$\mathbf{P}(1) = \begin{bmatrix} .1353 & .4651 & .1632 & .2012 & .0352 \\ .0000 & .3679 & .2387 & .3177 & .0757 \\ .0000 & .0000 & .6065 & .1768 & .2166 \\ .0000 & .0000 & .0000 & .8187 & .1813 \\ .0000 & .0000 & .0000 & .0000 & 1.0000 \end{bmatrix}, \tag{16}$$

$$\mathbf{P}(4) = \begin{bmatrix} .0003 & .0360 & .1440 & .4104 & .4093 \\ .0000 & .0183 & .1170 & .3964 & .4683 \\ .0000 & .0000 & .1353 & .2617 & .6030 \\ .0000 & .0000 & .0000 & .4493 & .5507 \\ .0000 & .0000 & .0000 & .0000 & 1.0000 \end{bmatrix}. \tag{17}$$

These $\mathbf{P}(t)$ arrays are the transition matrices a researcher should expect to observe if the stage locations of individuals are surveyed 1 year or 4 years apart, assuming that the population evolves according to the linkage specification $\mathbf{M}_2$ together with the auxiliary conditions outlined in the preceding section. The entries are different from those obtained with the simple unilineal progression [Eq. (13) and (15)], yet the same pattern of zeros and nonzeros is present. Without a formal model of the evolution of the process, a researcher would be unable to predict the different implications of these structures.

---

[7] We begin here with Example 2; Example 1 refers to the structure in Figure 6.2.

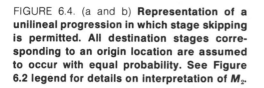

(a)

FIGURE 6.4. (a and b) **Representation of a unilineal progression in which stage skipping is permitted. All destination stages corresponding to an origin location are assumed to occur with equal probability. See Figure 6.2 legend for details on interpretation of M_2.**

$$M_2 = \begin{bmatrix} 0 & 1 & 0 & 0 & 0 \\ 0 & 0 & .5 & .5 & 0 \\ 0 & 0 & 0 & .5 & .5 \\ 0 & 0 & 0 & 0 & 1 \\ 0 & 0 & 0 & 0 & 1 \end{bmatrix}$$

(b)

2. A Unilineal Progression with Stage Skipping and the Possibility of Regression

We now superimpose on the linkage structure the possibility of reverting to an earlier stage. This arrangement is diagrammed in Figure 6.5a, in which we have provided for the possibility of backward flows from Stage 2 to Stage 1, from Stage 3 to Stage 2, and from Stage 5 to Stage 4. The M-matrix corresponding to this model is reported in Figure 6.5b. Again, where multiple destinations correspond to an origin stage, we have arbitrarily assigned equal values to the m_{ij}'s. There is one additional alteration in M_3, in comparison with the M-matrices of earlier examples. Because there now exists a possibility of regressing from the terminal stage to an earlier level, $m_{55} \neq 1$. To maintain our conceptual imagery, in which within-stage transitions are undefined, we set $m_{54} = 1$ and $m_{55} = 0$. Note that the former value does not imply a high rate of departure from Stage 5, since the rate of movement is controlled by λ_5. It only means that all transitions from Stage 5 are directed to Stage 4.

To obtain $P(t)$ we use M_3 and Λ in conjunction with Eq. (9). Here the element λ_5 in Eq. (11) is no longer arbitrary, as movement out of Stage 5 is a possibility. We shall assume that such reversions are rare, and hence

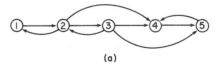

(a)

FIGURE 6.5. (a and b) **Representation of a unilineal progression in which stage skipping and regression to an earlier level are permitted. All destination stages corresponding to an origin location are assumed to occur with equal probability. See Figure 6.2 legend for additional details on interpretation.**

$$M_3 = \begin{bmatrix} 0 & 1 & 0 & 0 & 0 \\ .33 & 0 & .34 & .33 & 0 \\ 0 & .33 & 0 & .34 & .33 \\ 0 & 0 & 0 & 0 & 1 \\ 0 & 0 & 0 & 1 & 0 \end{bmatrix}$$

(b)

specify the average waiting time to a transition from Stage 5 to be 8 years; that is, $\lambda_5 = .125$. With these assumptions, we obtain for our illustrative calculations at $t = 1, 4$:

$$\mathbf{P}(1) = \begin{bmatrix} .2043 & .5240 & .1153 & .1374 & .0190 \\ .0871 & .4758 & .1742 & .2217 & .0411 \\ .0094 & .0858 & .6215 & .1461 & .1371 \\ .0000 & .0000 & .0000 & .8292 & .1708 \\ .0000 & .0000 & .0000 & .1067 & .8933 \end{bmatrix}, \quad (18)$$

$$\mathbf{P}(4) = \begin{bmatrix} .0330 & .1560 & .1652 & .4025 & .2433 \\ .0259 & .1246 & .1500 & .4174 & .2820 \\ .0135 & .0739 & .1846 & .3542 & .3738 \\ .0000 & .0000 & .0000 & .5523 & .4477 \\ .0000 & .0000 & .0000 & .2798 & .7202 \end{bmatrix}. \quad (19)$$

If we compare the $\mathbf{P}(1)$ matrices and the $\mathbf{P}(4)$ matrices from the three examples [i.e., Eqs. (13), (16), (18), and (15), (17), (19)], we can acquire a fair idea of the implications of different stage interconnections for the evolution of a population among the statuses. We also emphasize the fact that if a population is surveyed at two time points, especially widely spaced time points, the structure of the stage linkages (matrix $\mathbf{M}$) that generated the observations may not be obvious from inspecting the empirically determined transition array, $\hat{\mathbf{P}}(t_1)$. We will return to the issue of identifying the correct structure and recovering matrix $\mathbf{M}$ when the observations on a process are widely spaced; we conclude this discussion on translating theoretical specifications of stage linkages into $\mathbf{M}$-matrices with two examples of multilineal sequences that have been described in the developmental psychology literature.

3. A Divergent Multiple Progression

This stage linkage structure (see Van den Daele, 1969, Figures 2, 4) has the diagrammatic representation of Figure 6.6a; its corresponding $\mathbf{M}$-matrix is presented in Figure 6.6b. Because Stages 4–7 are specified to be terminal states of the process, the corresponding rows of $\mathbf{M}_4$ have 1's in the main diagonal. Van den Daele provides no discussion of waiting time distributions to departure from the various stages; hence the model remains incomplete as an evolutionary process.

4. A Convergent Multiple Progression

This stage sequence (see Van den Daele, 1969, Figure 2) is depicted in Figure 6.7a, and its associated $\mathbf{M}$–matrix is reported in Figure 6.7b. In this instance, the structure consists of a collection of deterministic unilineal progressions, the specific sequence for an individual being contingent upon his entry stage. Note also that the assumption of irrelevance of past history,

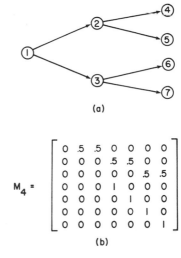

$$
M_4 = \begin{bmatrix}
0 & .5 & .5 & 0 & 0 & 0 & 0 \\
0 & 0 & 0 & .5 & .5 & 0 & 0 \\
0 & 0 & 0 & 0 & 0 & .5 & .5 \\
0 & 0 & 0 & 1 & 0 & 0 & 0 \\
0 & 0 & 0 & 0 & 1 & 0 & 0 \\
0 & 0 & 0 & 0 & 0 & 1 & 0 \\
0 & 0 & 0 & 0 & 0 & 0 & 1
\end{bmatrix}
$$

FIGURE 6.6. (a and b) **Representation of a divergent multiple progression. [Source: Van den Daele (1969, Figures 2,3).]**

(b)

which is posited in this formulation, is one of the side conditions we have required (Assumption 1 in the preceding section). In particular, this specification appears in the fact that knowledge of the path by which one has reached Stage 5 (or Stage 6) is of no value in forecasting, or understanding, an individual's subsequent movements. Van den Daele (1969) discusses several additional models of stage linkages, such as "partially convergent, divergent progression," and "partially divergent, convergent progression." Since the procedure used in converting flow structures into M-matrices should be evident at this point, discussions of these specifications are not presented.

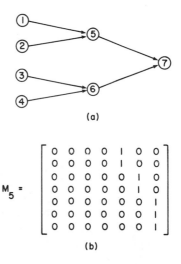

$$
M_5 = \begin{bmatrix}
0 & 0 & 0 & 0 & 1 & 0 & 0 \\
0 & 0 & 0 & 0 & 1 & 0 & 0 \\
0 & 0 & 0 & 0 & 0 & 1 & 0 \\
0 & 0 & 0 & 0 & 0 & 1 & 0 \\
0 & 0 & 0 & 0 & 0 & 0 & 1 \\
0 & 0 & 0 & 0 & 0 & 0 & 1 \\
0 & 0 & 0 & 0 & 0 & 0 & 1
\end{bmatrix}
$$

FIGURE 6.7. (a and b) **Representation of a convergent multiple progression. [Source: Van den Daele (1969, Figure 2).]**

(b)

To recapitulate, we have shown that, subject to several side conditions, it is possible to construct formulations of a range of developmental phenomena that mimic the evolutionary character of the observed process. With such a model one can forecast the movements of a population among the stages. By carrying out the requisite calculations for different specifications of the stage linkages and comparing the predictions, it is possible to ascertain the ways in which rather complex theories produce divergent implications and to design testing schemes that maximize the possibility of rejecting one or another formulation as a description of the empirical process. Of equal importance, it is often possible to work backward, starting with observations on the stage locations of a population at a few widely spaced time points, and derive the structure of the stage linkages compatible with the data.

B. An Inverse Problem

Until this point we have assumed that observations have been made on an empirical process in a way such that M and Λ can be estimated directly from the data, or that theories are available that specify the values of their entries. We then sought to derive the evolution of the process subject to the presumed structure. In developmental psychology, it is not uncommon for a researcher to have many observations on a few individuals (e.g., Piaget, 1954). Such a data-collection scheme approximates *sample path information*, a complete history of movements and waiting times of the sort illustrated in Figure 6.3. Detailed observation of a few subjects is a research strategy not without its costs, however. One learns little about the frequency of rare events (e.g., regression to an earlier stage, stage skipping, rare development paths) and acquires only the most rudimentary knowledge about the variation of duration times in a stage. It is therefore not surprising that investigators who rely on this approach tend to be oriented to uncovering universal rules (e.g., Piaget, 1960) rather than to elucidating individual differences and ascertaining the variety of developmental patterns.

Partly because of the limitations of small data sets, it is becoming increasingly common to employ survey methods in which a large population, sometimes thousands of individuals, is observed (or interrogated) at a very few time points (e.g., Baltes & Nesselroade, 1972). The spacing intervals in such panel studies are usually wide—often 1 or more years elapse between interviews—so it is not unusual for some subjects to have made multiple moves while others have made one or zero shifts between stages. The transition matrices that can be constructed directly from such observations are $P(t)$ arrays, rather than M arrays, and the stage linkages may not be readily discernible. Indeed, determination of the movement structure that underlies the evolution of the population can be a difficult task.

One approach to ascertaining the stage linkages from survey data involves consideration of the *inverse problem* to the mathematical formulation of the evolutionary model [Eq. (9)]. Stated formally, we have available the matrix $\hat{P}(t_1)$, constructed from observations on the stage locations of individuals at time 0 and t_1. The typical entry in this matrix is $\hat{p}_{ij}(t_1) = n_{ij}(t_1)/n_i$, where n_i = {number of individuals in stage i at time 0} and $n_{ij}(t_1)$ = {number of persons who started in stage i at time 0 and are in stage j at time t_1}. We wish to inquire whether it is possible to recover a unique M-matrix for the process and, where the answer is affirmative, we wish to estimate this matrix.

The first step in solving the inverse problem is to take the logarithm of both sides of Eq. (9).

$$\mathbf{Q} = \Lambda[\mathbf{M} - \mathbf{I}] = t_1^{-1} \ln \hat{\mathbf{P}}(t_1). \tag{20}$$

Just what we mean by the logarithm of matrix $\hat{P}(t_1)$, the conditions under which a solution to Eq. (20) will exist, and the circumstances under which the solution will be unique are complex issues that are discussed at length in Singer and Spilerman (1976). Assuming we can obtain a valid and unique Q-matrix from these calculations, a second task, separating M from Λ, still remains. In many instances, though, this matter is of little concern, since the pattern of zeros and nonzeros in Q and M − I will be identical, and development theories are often posed at the level of identifying permissible transitions. Moreover, because zeros are typically present in many main diagonal cells of M in models of developmental structures, a complete or near complete separation between M and Λ can frequently be effected.

We conclude this section with an example of the calculations associated with the inverse problem. Suppose observations taken on a population at times 0 and t_1 have produced the transition matrix.

$$\hat{\mathbf{P}}(t_1) = \begin{bmatrix} .0224 & .2633 & .2402 & .1262 & .3479 \\ .0064 & .1758 & .2460 & .1735 & .3983 \\ .0216 & .0288 & .3758 & .5060 & .0678 \\ .0365 & .0744 & .0288 & .6794 & .1809 \\ .0005 & .0960 & .0460 & .0178 & .8397 \end{bmatrix} \tag{21}$$

Such data would appear to be consistent with a variety of evolutionary mechanisms. From inspection of $\hat{P}(t_1)$ we **do** know that regression to some earlier stage must be possible; otherwise all entries below the main diagonal would be zero. Little else about the structure of M, however, can be inferred from inspection of $\hat{P}(t_1)$. Indeed, because of the sizable nonzero elements in most cells of the matrix, a researcher might conclude that direct transitions are possible between most pairs of stages.

If we are willing to assume that matrix $\hat{P}(t_1)$ was generated by a continuous-time Markov process—that is, via the evolution of the structure $P(t) = e^{\Lambda(M-I)t}$, for some matrices Λ and M, that satisfy the definitional restrictions enumerated in connection with Eqs. (5) and (9)—we can solve for $\Lambda(M - I)t_1$ using Eq. (20). This yields the array,

$$\Lambda(M - I)t_1 = \begin{bmatrix} -4 & 4 & 0 & 0 & 0 \\ 0 & -2 & 1 & 0 & 1 \\ 0 & 0 & -1 & 1 & 0 \\ .20 & 0 & 0 & -.40 & .20 \\ 0 & .25 & 0 & 0 & -.25 \end{bmatrix}. \tag{22}$$

In this instance Λt_1 and M can be separated by employing the following argument. From our earlier examples we know that a main diagonal element m_{ii} of M will equal zero if any off-diagonal entry in the same row, m_{ij}, is different from zero. According to Eq. (22), each row of matrix M must have at least one nonzero off-diagonal element; therefore, $m_{ij} = 0$ for all values of i. With this information we can obtain Λt_1 uniquely,

$$\Lambda t_1 = \begin{bmatrix} 4 & 0 & 0 & 0 & 0 \\ 0 & 2 & 0 & 0 & 0 \\ 0 & 0 & 1 & 0 & 0 \\ 0 & 0 & 0 & .4 & 0 \\ 0 & 0 & 0 & 0 & .25 \end{bmatrix} \tag{23}$$

and solving for M provides the structure M_4 reported in Figure 6.8a. The schematic representation of the stage linkages implied by M_4 is shown in Figure 6.8b, in which probabilities of the various moves have been appended to the paths.

The point to be emphasized is that it is not apparent from inspecting matrix $\hat{P}(t_1)$ in Eq. (21) that the underlying stage linkages are those reported in Figure 6.8, nor would any static analytic procedure be likely to lead a researcher to the correct conclusion. What is necessary is to construct a model of the evolution of the process and solve the implied inverse problem for the parameters that correspond to the particular data set. (In the present example, we have assumed that the underlying model is a continuous-time

$$M_4 = \begin{bmatrix} 0 & 1 & 0 & 0 & 0 \\ 0 & 0 & .5 & 0 & .5 \\ 0 & 0 & 0 & 1 & 0 \\ .5 & 0 & 0 & 0 & .5 \\ 0 & 1 & 0 & 0 & 0 \end{bmatrix}$$

(a)

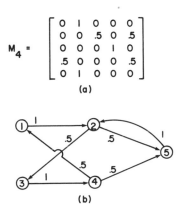

(b)

FIGURE 6.8. (a and b) **Stage sequence structure implied by $\hat{P}(t_1)$ in Eq.(21). The process is assumed to evolve according to a continuous-time Markov formulation. Entries indicate the probability of a stage i to stage j move when transition takes place. Probabilities of the various transitions are attached to the appropriate paths.**

Markov process (i.e., Specifications 1–3 of the preceding section) and have solved for the matrices Λt_1 and $\mathbf{M}$ that are compatible with the observed array $\hat{\mathbf{P}}(t_1)$, in that they would have given rise to this array if the postulated evolutionary process were approximately correct.

IV. Alternative Specifications of the Side Conditions

In this section we discuss relaxing two of the more burdensome specifications of the model, in the sense that they are likely to be inappropriate as characterizations of developmental processes. We first consider the requirement that the duration intervals in a stage must follow an exponential distribution (Assumption 2 of the second section). Following these comments we turn to the requirement that the population be homogeneous with respect to the process parameters Λ and $\mathbf{M}$ (Assumption 3).

A. More General Waiting Times than Exponential

The exponential distribution is frequently employed in the literature of reliability theory to describe duration intervals in a system state (stage in the current application). It has the advantages of being mathematically tractable and approximating reality in situations where the probability of a state change is uninfluenced by aging or time in the state. For example, if the process states are "alive" and "not alive," then over the middle age ranges of many animal species, the age-specific mortality rate is relatively constant and the duration intervals (in the "alive" state) are reasonably well captured by the exponential distribution. Similarly, when mortality results from exogenous events—accidents—the distribution of ages at failure can often be approximated by the exponential.

In a great many situations in social research, however, we know that proneness to changing state is a function of duration. In particular, this has been suggested with respect to residence location (McGinnis, 1968) and employment affiliation (Ginsberg, 1971). In these applications it has been argued that the duration-specific departure rate decreases with time, giving rise to the phenomenon of *cumulative inertia*—the longer an individual remains in a state the less likely he is to leave in the immediate future. The substantive explanations for a declining departure rate involve the growing investment an individual has made, with duration, in friendships (in the first instance) and in seniority in his place of work (in the second). There is no mathematical reason, however, to assume a declining departure rate in choosing $F_i(t)$; and in other substantive contexts a different specification may be more appropriate. For a superb review of stochastic models incorporating the notion of duration dependence, see Hoem (1972).

A convenient way to generalize the Markov model to accommodate a variety of duration–time distributions is to begin with the integral equation representation for transition probabilities. Equation (8) is a special case of the formulation,

$$p_{ij}(t) = \delta_{ij}[1 - F_i(t)] + \sum_k \int_0^t f_i(u) m_{ik} p_{kj}(t - u) \, du \qquad 0 \le i, j \le n \qquad (24)$$

in which the terms are identical with those of the earlier equation except that $f_i(u)$ replaces the exponential density $\lambda_i \exp(-\lambda_i u)$, and $F_i(t)$ [the distribution function corresponding to $f_i(t)$], replaces $[1 - \exp(-\lambda_i t)]$. A theoretically appropriate choice may now be made for $F_i(t)$.

As an illustration, one candidate for $F_i(t)$, in the case of a declining departure rate, is the two-parameter family of functions

$$F_i(t) = 1 - \exp(-\lambda_i t^{\gamma_i}) \qquad \lambda_i > 0, \quad 0 < \gamma_i < 1. \qquad (25)$$

Here the probability of departing from state i during the infinitesimal interval $(t, t + dt)$, conditional on the process being in state i at time t, equals

$$\frac{f_i(t) \, dt}{1 - F_i(t)} = \frac{(\lambda_i \gamma_i t^{\gamma_i - 1}) \exp(-\lambda_i t^{\gamma_i})}{\exp(-\lambda_i t^{\gamma_i})} \, dt = \lambda_i \gamma_i t^{\gamma_i - 1} \, dt.$$

Because of the restriction on γ_i in Eq. (25), $t^{\gamma_i - 1}$ is a decreasing function of time, and the declining failure-rate aspect of the distribution is evident.

The general formulation in Eq. (24), built up from duration–time distributions and transition probabilities between states, generates a class of models known as semi-Markov processes. These generally do not have simple representations for the matrices $P(t)$, analogous to Eq. (9), and the solution of the system of Eq. (24) requires numerical integration methods.

B. Population Heterogeneity

To this point we have assumed that the matrices Λ and M of Eq. (9) are identical for all individuals. This does not mean that all persons move identically since the process is probabilistic; it does imply, though, that individual-level characteristics are unrelated to the structural parameters of the process. In other words, homogeneity means that considerations of genetic makeup, intelligence, sensory stimulation, and other factors by which individuals differ from one another do not portend distinct evolutionary paths in the developmental process under consideration.

There is reason to believe, however, that individual differences are present in the course of development in many processes (Kohlberg, 1968, p. 1024; Werner, 1957). We therefore desire a formulation in which the movement pattern is paramerized in terms of variables that differentiate among persons. To construct a general specification of heterogeneity within the conceptual framework of a Markov process, we assume that, corresponding to Eq. (9), the stage transitions by individual c have the structure

$$\mathbf{P}_c(t) = \exp[\Lambda_c(\mathbf{M}_c - \mathbf{I})t].\tag{26}$$

This formula indicates that each person is characterized by a pair of matrices, Λ_c and $\mathbf{M}_c$, and his evolution, in turn, is described by $\mathbf{P}_c(t)$. Thus, our formulation begins with a separate Markov process for each individual.

This approach directs a researcher to identify the variables that describe heterogeneity; that is, to ascertain which factors account for individual differences in the matrices $\mathbf{M}$ and Λ. Thus, not only does a heterogeneity formulation lead to more realistic models of evolutionary processes, in that allowance is made for individual differences, but it stresses the analytic tasks of specifying the variety of developmental patterns in a population and ascertaining which attributes make an individual more prone to following one set of paths rather than another.

One form of heterogeneity involves the distribution of $\mathbf{M}$-matrices in a population. Focusing on these arrays serves to emphasize individual differences in proneness to making particular moves when a transition takes place. We shall not discuss this form of heterogeneity in the present chapter and direct the interested reader instead to McFarland (1970), Spilerman (1972a), and Singer and Spilerman (1974). A second form of heterogeneity stresses individual differences in the Λ-matrix; that is, in the rates at which departures occur for persons in the various states. We conclude this section with a simple formulation of population heterogeneity in which it is assumed that the individual differences can be expressed in the latter way.

To simplify the discussion, we further require the nonzero entries in the diagonal matrix Λ to be equal for an individual; that is, $\lambda_i = \lambda$ for all i. This means we are specifying identical departure rates from all states. As a result, Eq. (9) reduces to

$$\mathbf{P}(t|\lambda) = e^{\lambda t(\mathbf{M}-\mathbf{I})}\tag{27}$$

where $\mathbf{P}(t|\lambda)$ denotes the transition matrix for an *individual* having a rate of movement value equal to λ. We shall assume that Eq. (27) describes the evolution of an individual drawn at random from the population.

Heterogeneity is incorporated into the formulation by specifying a density function $g(\lambda)$ that describes the distribution of λ-values in the population. We now define the *population-level* transition matrix corresponding to times 0 and t to be

$$\mathbf{P}(t) = \int_0^\infty \mathbf{P}(t|\lambda)g(\lambda)\,d\lambda = \int_0^\infty e^{t\lambda(\mathbf{M}-\mathbf{I})}g(\lambda)\,d\lambda.\tag{28}$$

This formula expresses the population-level matrix as a weighted average of the individual-level arrays, $P(t|\lambda)$, the weights reflecting the population proportions associated with particular λ-values.

To complete this specification of heterogeneity it is necessary to select a density function $g(\lambda)$ to describe the distribution of λ-values. One useful choice is the gamma family of functions

$$g(\lambda) = \frac{\beta^\alpha \lambda^{\alpha-1} e^{-\beta\lambda}}{\Gamma(\alpha)} \qquad \lambda > 0, \quad \alpha > 0, \quad \beta > 0 \qquad (29)$$

which is flexible enough to describe a variety of unimodal curves. With this selection of $g(\lambda)$, a convenient representation of the population-level matrix $P(t)$ is obtained (Spilerman, 1972b, p. 608):

$$\mathbf{P}(t) = \left(\frac{\beta}{\beta + t}\right)^\alpha \left[\mathbf{I} - \frac{t}{\beta + t}\mathbf{M}\right]^{-\alpha}. \qquad (30)$$

The transition probabilities [Eq. (30)] do not describe the evolution of a Markov process; however, they do describe the movement of a population *in which each individual follows a Markov process*, with individual differences being specified by $g(\lambda)$ in Eq. (29).

In analogy with our earlier discussion of the inverse problem for Markov chains, the present formulation can be used with observations taken at widely spaced time points, 0 and t_1, together with estimates of α and β to yield an estimate of the underlying transition mechanism $\mathbf{M}$, according to the matrix equation

$$\mathbf{M} = \left(\frac{\beta + t_1}{t_1}\right)\left(\mathbf{I} - \frac{\beta}{\beta + t_1}[\hat{\mathbf{P}}(t_1)]^{-1/\alpha}\right). \qquad (31)$$

Thus, from observations of the sort collected in many surveys, even under an assumption of population heterogeneity in the rate of movement, it may be possible to recover the matrix of stage linkages that governs the evolution of the process.

V. Conclusions

In this chapter we have explored the consequences of particular stage-linkage structures for the evolution of a population. One thrust of our comments has been to identify the sorts of process features concerning which assumptions must be made in order to convert a static theory about stage connections into a dynamic model. A second focus in our discussion has been on inverse problems; how to utilize a model formulation so that the stage-linkage structure (matrix $\mathbf{M}$) may be recovered from survey data of the kind usually collected by developmental psychologists.

We have presented only the most rudimentary sorts of stage structures.

Indeed, even within the Markov framework we have limited our consideration to a subset of these models; namely, those that are time-stationary (i.e., Λ and M are not functions of time). By this specification we have excluded the possibility of accommodating age-dependent transition laws, a consideration of substantial importance in developmental psychology. (An extension of the models discussed here to incorporate both age dependence and cohort effects is, however, a feasible undertaking but one with an increase in mathematical complexity.) Furthermore, all the models we have discussed entail a low dependence of future movements on the transition history of an individual, given his current stage.[8] Restrictions of these sorts are likely to be reasonable for some processes, unreasonable for others. Appropriate models of developmental phenomena must, therefore, be constructed from a list of known characteristics about an empirical process.

We also point out that the concept of stage merges with the notion of state as the number and sorts of permissible transitions increase. "Stage" seems conceptually rooted to the idea of progress (i.e., development) and would be an appropriate component of a theory that sees the system's statuses as genetically determined or as facilitating the conditions for succeeding statuses to come into play.[9] The mathematical framework we have introduced is also compatible with a notion of state, in which there is extensive opportunity to cycle among the statuses. State formulations have been suggested in the psychology literature in relation to anxiety, moods, etc. (e.g., Kessen, 1962, pp. 72–73).

As a final set of considerations in relation to the structure of stage models, we note that all the formulations we have addressed are models of solitary processes. We have proceeded as if intelligence, cognition, motor skills, and personality development unfolded autonomously. In reality there no doubt exist extensive dependencies among some of these processes. Mathematical models of interacting developmental phenomena could be formulated, but clear empirically based specifications of such dependencies are still lacking.

---

[8] The time-stationary Markov formulations postulate irrelevance of prior stage affiliations, durations in those stages, and duration in current stage. The last two of these restrictions can be eliminated by introducing nonstationary semi-Markov models as delineated, for example, in Hoem (1972).

[9] Stages in childhood such as "walking" or "reading" expose an individual to entirely new sets of experiences that may be prerequisites for the onset of more advanced behaviors.

Chapter 7

Assessment and Statistical Control of Subject Variables in Longitudinal Designs

PAUL A. GAMES

ABSTRACT

An experimental design notational system is described. A "minimal power" check is recommended for use with complex analyses of covariance structures. Longitudinal models always include repeated measures. Conventional ANOVA longitudinal analyses are contrasted with covariance type linear models. The covariance models have the virtue of permitting the use of P different organismic (X) variables, while conventional ANOVA usually is limited to one. Tests of homogeneity of regression slopes are illustrated for covariance type models with a repeated measure factor and: (1) X's available on subjects but not each separate occasion; or (2) X's available for each occasion.

I. Introduction

Longitudinal studies automatically imply that there will be one or more repeated-measure factors (Kirk, 1968; Winer, 1971). For convenience we shall label one repeated-measure factor T, the time factor. The simplest possible design is to obtain several subjects drawn at random from some meaningful population and record the dependent variable Y upon those subjects over the T factor. This permits the plotting of individual "growth," or T curves, on Y. Unfortunately, when we note that the curves for John Smith and for Tom Johnson are different, we have gained little useful knowledge. Since these individuals differ in many ways, we have no basis for distinguishing future individuals who are likely to show the "Smith curve" instead of the "Johnson curve." To obtain useful information it is necessary to have available data on other trait or organismic variables that may be used to classify or group the individual subjects. We shall label

179

LONGITUDINAL RESEARCH IN THE
STUDY OF BEHAVIOR AND DEVELOPMENT

these variables X. What we designate as X may be something as easily observed as sex, or something that must be measured by instrumentation or psychological tests. Thus we may have a study in which children are grouped into those with internal locus of control versus those with external locus of control. If these groups now show divergent T curves on Y, we have obtained useful information such that other children may be assessed on this X and predictions made about the type of T curve expected. Thus the minimum useful design is one where there is at least one X in addition to the dependent variable Y.

II. Representation of Experimental Designs

It is helpful to have a concise notation to express the information available in a given design. We need two basic terms. Two factors are *crossed* if each level of each factor appears with each level of the other factor. Since each subject S appears with each level of T, we say S and T are crossed, and represent this as $S \times T$. We may use subscripts on the factors to represent the number of levels. Thus $S_n \times T_5$ indicates that n subjects are crossed with five levels of time.

If a level of factor A occurs within only one level of factor B, then we say A is nested in B. This is represented as A in (B). In a completely randomized one-factor design where 50 subjects are randomly divided into 10 subjects under each of five levels of factor A, we would write S_{10} in (A_5). A completely randomized factoral design with two levels of A, and three of B may be represented as S_n in $(A_2 \times B_3)$. Since subjects are nested in the AB crossing, this shows that any one subject appears in only one of the six cells formed by the AB crossing. Lee (1975) has written an ANOVA text using crossing and nesting notations throughout that should be consulted if an expansion of this brief explanation is desired.

We must also add a notation to express the role of X. We shall use X to stand for any continuous variable available other than the dependent variable, Y. We shall arrange the terms so that when X is present, it implies an X in every unit prior to the appearance of X. Thus S_n w $X \times T_4$ implies that there is an X available with every subject, or here, a total of n values of X. However, if there is an X available on each observation, this would be represented by placing the "w X" last. Thus, $S_6 \times T_4$ w X implies that there are 24 values of X available, or an X associated with each of the 24 observations of Y. The "w" is for mnemonic value since the S w $X \times T$ would be read as: Subjects, with an X value on each, crossed with Time.

These symbols may be combined to represent more complex designs. As an example with one repeated measure B and one between-subjects measure A Winer has an $[S_3$ in $(A_2)] \times B_4$ design (1971, p. 525). The square brackets indicate that B is crossed with both A and with subjects. We must distinguish whether there is only one X for each subject, or one X for each observation. An example of the former is an $[S_4 \text{ w } X \text{ in } (A_2)] \times B_2$ in Winer (1971, p. 803), whereas an example of the latter is an $[S_3 \text{ in } (A_3)] \times B_2 \text{ w } X$ (Winer, 1971, p. 806).

Naturally it is possible to have more than one organismic variable in a study. To indicate more than one, we will add extra values of X. We shall designate the number of X variables as P, and may represent a more general case of Winer's covariance example (1971, p. 803) as $[S \text{ w } X_1 \cdots X_p \text{ in } (A_2)] \times B_2$.

III. Possible Roles of Organismic Variables

A. Reduction of Error Term

There are several possible roles of organismic variables in longitudinal designs. In some designs they may be included primarily as a device to reduce the error term and increase the power and precision of the comparisons made. If we have variable X, we may divide it into four adjacent intervals, and treat these four levels as a factor with subjects nested in the four levels. If the initial design involves a manipulative factor A, the design may be expanded by adding the additional O factor with four levels. Thus an initial $[S_{40} \text{ in } (A_3)] \times T_2$ design may be expanded to an $[S_{10} \text{ in } (A_3 \times O_4)] \times T_2$ design. In the latter design the addition of the O factor should reduce the error term for the A effect, $\text{MS}_{S(AO)}$, just as in a treatment by levels design. The statistical considerations of such usage are well covered in Lindquist (1953, chapter 5) and Myers (1972, chapter 6).

An alternative way of using an organismic variable to reduce mean-square error (MS_E) is to use X as a covariate in a legitimate experimental design. With an $[S \text{ w } X \text{ in } (A)] \times T$ design where subjects were randomly assigned to the A conditions so the $\bar{X}$ values vary only by chance, the major role of a covariate would be in reducing $\text{MS}_{S(A)}$ term, the error term for the A main effect. A test for heterogeneous slopes in such a design is illustrated later in the present chapter.

B. Identifying Variable by Time Interactions

A second role of organismic variables is in a search for organismic variable by time interactions, or a search for organismic variable by treatment interactions that occur over time. In an $[S \text{ in } (A \times O)] \times T$ design, the AO interaction would be an example of an "aptitude by treatment" interaction. The presence of an OT interaction would indicate different growth curves for the several O levels. A significant AOT interaction would indicate that the aptitude by treatment interaction changed over time.

Similar searches for O interactions are possible without subdividing X into levels and using it as an additional factor in an analysis of variance. In an $[S \text{ w } X \text{ in } (A)] \times T$ design the check of homogeneous regression slopes is equivalent to a test for a linear AO interaction. Thus the finding of heterogeneous slopes in a covariance model is another way of discovering an "aptitude by treatment" interaction.

Similarly, if there is interest in a possible X by T interaction, it is possible to build vectors consisting of the X vector multiplied by contrasts of the T factor to determine whether there is an XT interaction. Unfortunately, this involves methodology that is less likely to be used. Similarly, the search for a triple interaction by use of AXT vectors is even less common. The beginning student is probably well advised to use the blocking method of forming an O variable, and AOV when he has only a single X variable. The complexity of the other methods is mainly needed when there are several X variables.

C. Clarifying the Nature of Relationships

The third role of organismic variables is in an attempt to "eliminate" the effect of other "extraneous" organismic variables to provide "clear" interpretations. This is the role of partial correlations, part correlations, and sometimes of analysis of covariance when the $\bar{X}$'s differ systematically because of the fact that a legitimate randomization of experimental subjects has not been carried out. Unfortunately, such usage is easy to misinterpret. Campbell and Erlebacher (1970) give a long, detailed presentation of such problems.

Some such studies take a multiple regression form. We may ask, for example, how much effect education has on income at age 40 after IQ, SES, and parental income have been "partialed out." Such a study computes the residual increment in $R^2_{Y \cdot 1234} - R^2_{Y \cdot 123}$ where education is the fourth variable of the four highly intercorrelated variables. The problem is, each of the four variables may have a very low "additional contribution" so that no matter which of the variables is placed last, it will contribute very little once the other variables have entered. Thus $R^2_{Y \cdot 1234} - R^2_{Y \cdot 124}$ may be equally low, suggesting that parental income is a very minor contribution once education, SES, and IQ have been partialed out. Unfortunately, some authors (e.g., Bowles & Gintis, 1972) report only the one type of partialing that fits the investigators' intellectual framework. The statistically naive reader is left with the impression that this has been a dramatic demonstration that education has no effect on future income. Such a study merely reveals high intercorrelations between the predictors, so that no one predictor makes a unique contribution once the others have been used.

Unfortunately, there is no solution to obtaining clear causative conclusions in the absence of manipulative studies. Studies in which subjects cannot be assigned at random can yield tentative guesses of causative chains, but no more. Sometimes, these tentative guesses can be strengthened by attempts that show the same trends exist even after a possible extraneous uncontrolled factor has been partialed out. Thus, if an $[RS$ in $(O)] \times T$ experiment shows that low-anxiety subjects have a more rapidly rising learning curve than high-anxiety groups, the interpretative or theoretical value of this result may be questioned when it turns out that the low-anxiety group had a mean IQ of 110 and the high anxiety group had a mean IQ of 100. Partialing out the IQ variable may restore part of the credibility of the finding, if the same results are obtained. However, such results never have the interpretative clarity that can be obtained when "anxiety" is determined from a manipulated condition rather than a biographical inventory. If several manipulative conditions all supposed to produce anxiety yield consistent results, clear causative conclusions are possible. Unfortunately, longitudinal studies must often use organismic variables to designate their groups. From such studies many alternative explanations are always possible.

D. Use of Organismic Variables in Complex Structures

A fourth use of organismic variables here must be a catchall category. We shall call it use of organismic variables in complex structures. This is meant to include factor analysis, analysis of covariance structures, and the models Jöreskog identifies as LISREL models (Jöreskog & Sörbom, 1976a; see also Chapter 12, this volume). The latter refers to a very general model that Jöreskog has incorporated into a computer program that permits specification and testing of a measurement model of latent variables in the X's, a measurement model of latent variables in the Y's, and a structural analysis relating the X latent variables and the Y latent variables. This general structure includes many multivariate analyses as special cases. It permits specification of simplex models on the Y's with X's as additional predictors.

The numerous possibilities are too many and too complicated to comment on here, except for a brief philosophical note. We will be seeing many complex models formulated on behavioral data sets. In many cases, the authors report a given model, say it is compatible with the data, and let it go at that. Jöreskog's programs permit maximum likelihood tests of specified models. It is hoped that readers will learn to take such tests in a sensible fashion, without some of the habits that seem to exist in the interpretation of simpler hypotheses tests. One of the most superficial review practices is to take a given area of content, or a given experimental question, and then to obtain all references on that topic and tabulate the number of significant differences. In asking whether A is greater than B, some review articles say 15 were significant with $A > B$, 25 were nonsignificant, so $A = B$ was retained, and 2 were significant with $B > A$. Therefore the $A = B$'s have it, and further research is needed. Such reviews often ignore the fact that many of the studies may have had such small N's that for any reasonable $A-B$ effect, the power was minimal, and retention of the null is quite likely. Until reviewers consider power problems and the adequacy of the experimental design, such compilations are of little value. A modicum of statistical sophistication is needed to yield worthwhile reviews that separate the wheat from the chaff, the signal from the noise.

As we go to more complex models, for more complex questions, still more sophistication will be needed. It is clear that for most sets of data, many different models could be built. If N is small enough, the power will be small, so that almost any model will "fit" in that the null will be retained. On the other hand, if N is large enough, almost any model will not fit, in that the chi square on the model fit will be significant because some specified parameter in the model will be a little bit different in reality than it is in the model. Readers who use the "significant versus nonsignificant" gauge as their sole evaluation tool for published research are going to be hopelessly lost when it comes to the use of complex models. It is difficult to provide guidance rules that will always apply, but the author would like to add one suggestion.

It is often very difficult to express the adequacy of fit of these complex models. The more interesting publications are often those that at least explore alternative models. Madaus, Woods, and Nuttall (1973) present an interesting study based on a very large N, on the hierarchical model of Bloom's taxonomy of cognitive objectives. They construct a model that knowledge items must be mastered before one can master comprehension items, and that comprehensive items must be mastered before one can master application items on that topic, etc. They compare a model without a general intelligence factor, and a model with a general IQ factor, and conclude that the latter is needed to fit the data. Basically, their final model supports the notion of a hierarchical structure from knowledge to comprehension to application. However, no hierarchy is indicated for analysis, synthesis, or evaluation. Their study is especially interesting because it compares several feasible models with one another. (Further statistics and further models to be included may be desired by the reader; this is a very tough problem for the editors and reviewers of studies testing complex structures. We can only ask that authors make copies of their data available to those who request it.)

To provide at least a minimum basis for publication of such studies, it would be desirable to know that the experiment at least had enough power so that it could reject some "outrageous models." In the Madaus *et al.* (1973) study, it would be possible to reverse the hierarchy and test a model in which evaluation, synthesis, and analysis are taken as prerequisites to successful mastery of knowledge and comprehension items. That is, an outrageous model might be one in which the direction of the hierarchy is reversed. If the study has so little power it is unable to reject this outrageous alternative, there certainly is little basis for taking the model that is retained very seriously. As we get complex models, we must recognize that many, many different models may adequately fit the same data. We can only hope to improve our models, much as the physical sciences have done. We must not consider that every model that is not rejected is true, or that every model that is rejected is useless.

Rather than continue in this general vein, let us turn to the class of models probably used most often in longitudinal studies, covariance-type models. The author is somewhat skeptical about interpretations of such models when the $\bar{X}$'s differ considerably (Campbell & Erlebacher, 1973; Games, 1976), but feels that a major problem with covariance usage is that many, or even most, users readily adopt a covariance model without first looking at the more general models that permit heterogeneous slopes. Even modern computer programs (e.g., BMDP2V) do not provide a test for the homogeneous-slopes assumption in covariance. The following two sections illustrate such tests in repeated-measure-type designs.

IV. Covariance-type Models with a Nested Factor and a Repeated Measure, but with X Values Available Only on Subjects, Not on Each Separate Observation

In this design, we have only one set of X's per subject. It is possible to have several variables in X, as in $[RS_n \text{ w } X_1 \cdots X_p \text{ in } (A_a)] \times B_b$, and such designs would be carried out using the steps we will illustrate below, only with several vectors of X. For convenience, we shall use data with a single X vector. Winer (1971, p. 803) has such a set of data analyzed by covariance. One of the assumptions of covariance is that the regression coefficient within groups is the same. Winer does not illustrate how to test this assumption on any designs with repeated measures, nor does any other source I know of. To illustrate the procedures needed in a more general context, we shall add a third (A_3) group of independent subjects to Winer's data, thus resulting in an $[RS_4 \text{ w } X \text{ in } (A_3)] \times B_2$ design. Here, B is used instead of T to match Winer's notation.

A. Linear Models for a Test of Heterogeneous Regression Slopes

The data are given in Table 7.1, with various vectors needed for a linear-models solution with homogeneous- or heterogeneous-slope solutions. The first three columns are the usual subscripts for the design factors. Column

TABLE 7.1
Data and Vectors Characteristic of an $[RS_4 \text{ w } X \text{ in } (A_3)] \times B_2$ Design[a]

1	2	3	4	5	6	7	8	9	10	11	12	13
						COLUMN NUMBER						
						VECTOR						
A	S	B	Y	U	X	ψ_{A1}	ψ_{A2}	ψ_B	$\dot{\psi}_{A1B}$	ψ_{A2B}	$X\psi_{A1}$	$X\psi_{A2}$
1	1	1	10.0	1	3.0	−2	0	+1	−2	0	−6.0	0
1	1	2	8.0	1	3.0	−2	0	−1	+2	0	−6.0	0
1	2	1	15.0	1	5.0	−2	0	+1	−2	0	−10.0	0
1	2	2	12.0	1	5.0	−2	0	−1	+2	0	−10.0	0
1	3	1	20.0	1	8.0	−2	0	+1	−2	0	−16.0	0
1	3	2	14.0	1	8.0	−2	0	−1	+2	0	−16.0	0
1	4	1	12.0	1	2.0	−2	0	+1	−2	0	−4.0	0
1	4	2	6.0	1	2.0	−2	0	−1	+2	0	−4.0	0
2	1	1	15.0	1	1.0	1	−1	+1	+1	−1	1.0	−1.0
2	1	2	10.0	1	1.0	1	−1	−1	−1	+1	1.0	−1.0
2	2	1	25.0	1	8.0	1	−1	+1	+1	−1	8.0	−8.0
2	2	2	20.0	1	8.0	1	−1	−1	−1	+1	8.0	−8.0
2	3	1	20.0	1	10.0	1	−1	+1	+1	−1	10.0	−10.0
2	3	2	15.0	1	10.0	1	−1	−1	−1	+1	10.0	−10.0
2	4	1	15.0	1	2.0	1	−1	+1	+1	−1	2.0	−2.0
2	4	2	10.0	1	2.0	1	−1	−1	−1	+1	2.0	−2.0
3	1	1	11.0	1	2.0	1	+1	+1	+1	+1	2.0	2.0
3	1	2	8.0	1	2.0	1	+1	−1	−1	−1	2.0	2.0
3	2	1	15.0	1	6.0	1	+1	+1	+1	+1	6.0	6.0
3	2	2	13.0	1	6.0	1	+1	−1	−1	−1	6.0	6.0
3	3	1	19.0	1	9.0	1	+1	+1	+1	+1	9.0	9.0
3	3	2	15.0	1	9.0	1	+1	−1	−1	−1	9.0	9.0
3	4	1	12.0	1	3.0	1	+1	+1	+1	+1	3.0	3.0
3	4	2	7.0	1	3.0	1	+1	−1	−1	−1	3.0	3.0
Σ			327.0		118.0	0	0	0	0	0		
Means			13.625	7.4167	4.917	.45833	−2.125	−2.125			.375	
Cov B's					1.250					0.0		

[a] After Winer (1971, p. 802).

4 is the dependent variable, Y. There are two Y's for each subject (because of the repeated-measure factor B with two levels); here each observation is found in a different row, with the corresponding B level indicated in the third column. The unity vector of all 1's (for estimation of μ_y) is Column 5. The control variable X is given in Column 6. Since there is only one X per subject, we repeat the X value for each of the two rows of that subject. Thus Subject 1 has a 3 punched in both of the first two rows ($X_{11} = 3$). The X value is given twice for all subjects. Since X varies only over the different subjects, it can influence only the results on the between-subject factors, A and $S(A)$. Columns 7 and 8 are vectors expressing the three levels of A in two orthogonal contrasts: $-2, +1, +1$, and $0, -1, +1$.

Similarly, Column 9 expresses the $B +1, -1$ contrast as a vector. If there were more than two levels of b, we would need $(b - 1)$ such vectors, each an orthogonal contrast. In addition, we need vectors for the subjects, but since these are both numerous and constant for any of the analyses we shall consider, we shall not clutter up the table with them; they are implied (see Cohen & Cohen, 1975, chapter 10). The final vectors needed are for the interaction. When we multiply a main-effect contrast vector for A by a main-effect contrast vector for B in a balanced design, we obtain an orthogonal interaction vector, as in Columns 10 or 11. Thus we have a set of five mutually orthogonal experimental design vectors.

If we use Columns 5, 7–11, and the subject vectors as predictors in the X matrix of a multiple regression on Y, we may obtain the usual ANOVA as given in Table 7.2.

TABLE 7.2
AOV of Data of $[RS_4 \, w \, X \, in \, (A_3)] \times B_2$ Example Analysis of Variance Table

Source	Degrees of freedom	Sum of squares	Mean square	F	P
Between subjects					
A	2	83.250	41.6250	1.213	>.25
$S(A) = E$	9	308.880	34.3190		
Within subjects					
B	1	108.370	108.3700	109.896	<.01
AB	2	2.250	1.1250	1.141	>.25
$SB(A) = EW$	9	8.875	0.9861		
Total (adj.)	23	511.625			

Y means, $\bar{Y}_{.jk}$	B_1	B_2	$\bar{Y}_{.j.}$	$\Delta_j = \bar{Y}_{.j1} - \bar{Y}_{.j2}$
A_1	14.25	10.00	12.125	4.25
A_2	18.75	13.75	16.250	5.00
A_3	14.25	10.75	12.500	3.50
$\bar{Y}_{..k}$	15.75	11.50	13.625	

Since the five experimental vectors are mutually orthogonal, we could obtain an SS with 1 df for each vector and these would sum to SS_{cells}. However, it is conventional to sum the single degrees of freedom into the usual omnibus SS for a factor or interaction, as given in Table 7.2. (When apriori reasons specify a particular interaction or main-effect vector as of prime interest, it is advisable to test that one vector alone.) The summary table of the ANOVA has ignored the presence of the X vector as a predictor.

To obtain an analysis of covariance, we merely include the X vector (Column 6) in the predictor variable matrix of multiple regression. However, if we insert this *one* X vector alone, we are assuming that X acts the same way in all three of the independent groups of the A factor. We are assuming that the subject means (summed over the B factor) have the same regression from X in all three groups. Before making such an assumption, it is wise to test it.

To test for homogeneity of regression, we add not only Column 6, but also Columns 12 and 13 to the predictor matrix. Given that Vector 6 is already in the analysis, Column 12 is testing H_0: $\beta_1 = (\beta_2 + \beta_3)/2$ where the β's are the raw-score regression coefficients in the population for the three respective A populations, A_1, A_2, and A_3. Similarly, Column 13 is testing H_0: $\beta_2 = \beta_3$. If both of these are true, then $\beta_1 = \beta_2 = \beta_3$; that is, we have homogeneity of all three regression slopes. The common procedure is to combine these into a single familywise test. This may be carried out several ways, depending upon the computer programs available. If only general multiple regression programs are available, it may be necessary to punch the data as in Table 7.1, and obtain two different SS (regression) values.

We can simplify the analysis by ignoring the within-subject variables. These are orthogonal to all of the between-subject variables; and only the latter are influenced by the between-subject covariate vectors in the present design. If we use Columns 5, 6, 7, 8, 12, and 13 as predictors for the heterogeneous A-slopes model, we obtain SS (regression) = 339.16 with df = 5. Then dropping to the homogeneous A-slopes model, we would use Columns 5, 6, 7, and 8 only and obtain SS (regression) = 328.46 with df = 3. Taking the difference between these two SS's we obtain the SS associated with heterogeneous slopes = 339.16 − 328.46 = 10.70. The df = 5 − 3 = 2, so MS (heterogeneous slopes) = 5.35. This should be tested using the adjusted $MS_{S(A)}$ of the heterogeneous slopes model of 8.8269 as MS_E, yielding an F of .606. With $F < 1$, we would retain the hypothesis of homogeneous slopes, thus justifying adoption of the covariance model.

If the regression slopes were heterogeneous, it would be necessary to proceed using different regression slopes for each of the three levels of A. Probably the simplest way would be to obtain the subject means of $\bar{Y}_{ij}$. (averaged over B) and solve for a separate regression equation for each of the three groups. The procedures are illustrated in Cohen and Cohen (1975, pp. 314–319). If you use the simple $\hat{Y} = b_0 + b_1 X$ for each group separately, you may insert the value of the grand mean of the X's, $\bar{X}$ . . . , to obtain a predicted value of Y for each of the three groups when X is at its mean value. This plus graphs of the three regression equations will provide useful information. The statistically sophisticated may wish to use the Johnson–Neyman technique as illustrated in Walker and Lev (1953, pp. 398–404), or the extensions discussed by Cahen and Linn (1971).

B. A Linear Model for Covariance

With the above results, it is possible to proceed by covariance, using Vectors 5–11. In this case, we obtain the analysis given in Table 7.3. Note that only the between-subjects factors SS's have changed. Any time we have only one set of X's per subject, only the between-subjects factors may change. In this case, the covariate is successful in reducing the error term, $MS_{S(A)}$, from 34.319 in the AOV to 7.958 in the COV. Thus there will be more power in the COV than in the AOV. This is the major virtue of COV in a legitimate experimental design. When S's are assigned randomly and X is obtained prior to the treatments, the $\bar{X}_{.j}$'s will differ only by random fluctuation. Hence the adjusted $\bar{Y}_{.j}$'s for the A groups will not differ from the original $\bar{Y}_{.j}$'s by very much. When the groups are not assigned at random, and the $\bar{X}_{.j}$'s are substantially different, then we get into complex-

TABLE 7.3

COV of Data of $[RS_4 \text{ w } X \text{ in } (A_3)] \times B_2$ Example Analysis of Variance Table

Source	Degrees of freedom	Sum of squares	Mean square	F	P
Between subjects					
Reg. X_1	1	266.730			
A	2	61.728	30.864	3.879	<.05
$S(A)$	8	63.663	7.958		
Within subjects					
B	1	108.380	108.370	109.896	<.01
AB	2	2.250	1.125	1.141	>.25
$SB(A)$	9	8.875	0.986		
Total (adj.)	23	511.625			

Adj. means, $\bar{Y}_{.jk}$	B_1	B_2	$\bar{Y}_{.j.}$	Δ_j
A_1	14.771	10.521	12.646	4.25
A_2	18.333	13.333	15.833	5.00
A_3	14.146	10.646	12.396	3.50
$\bar{Y}_{..k}$	15.750	11.500	13.625	

ities of interpretation. We are then working on estimates of the effects of A when substantial differences in X have been partialed out. Interpretations are now similar to those of partial correlations.

Note that the adjusted means of the covariance have changed just slightly from the original $\bar{Y}$ means of Table 7.3. The B means and SS have not changed at all, since the covariance here may change only the between-subjects effects. The AB interaction SS also is exactly the same, and correspondingly the difference between the two cell means for a given row of A is exactly the same in Table 7.4 as in Table 7.3. Only the A main effects have been changed by the covariance (the cell means reflect this effect also). The A main means have changed only a little, because the $\bar{X}._{.j}$ differ only by small amounts, as would be expected if only random sampling produced the differences. The covariance has now increased the precision so the main A effect is significant, whereas it was not in Table 7.2. The

TABLE 7.4
Additional Vectors Needed with a Second Covariate, X_2

COLUMN NUMBER		
14	15	16
	VECTOR	
X_2	$\psi_{A_1X_2}$	$\psi_{A_2X_2}$
2.0	-4.0	0
2.0	-4.0	0
7.0	-14.0	0
7.0	-14.0	0
9.0	-18.0	0
9.0	-18.0	0
4.0	-8.0	0
4.0	-8.0	0
7.0	7.0	-7.0
7.0	7.0	-7.0
9.0	9.0	-9.0
9.0	9.0	-9.0
8.0	8.0	-8.0
8.0	8.0	-8.0
5.0	5.0	-5.0
5.0	5.0	-5.0
3.0	3.0	3.0
3.0	3.0	3.0
6.0	6.0	6.0
6.0	6.0	6.0
8.0	8.0	8.0
8.0	8.0	8.0
4.0	4.0	4.0
4.0	4.0	4.0

Tukey WSD value for the A means is 1.9697 so the A_2 mean is found to be significantly larger than either the A_1 or A_3 means, the latter two not being significantly different.

There are two different procedures that may be used to solve for the "adjusted A means." Some programs and texts solve for the "adjusted mean" as the predicted Y value using the observed $\bar{X}._{.j.}$ of that particular group. The present solution uses the grand mean of the X's (4.9167) for all three A groups, so the "adjusted means" are the predicted values of Y for that common point.

C. Linear Models Using More Than One X Vector

One of the virtues of the general linear-model approach is that it readily facilitates the use of as many covariates as available, whereas the conventional procedures covered in Winer (1971), Kirk (1968), Dayton (1970), or Myers (1972) become very awkward with more than one covariant. We shall illustrate the expanded case by adding a second covariate, X_2, to the data of Table 7.1. The new vector, and the vectors generated from it are found in Table 7.4. These should be considered a continuation of Table 7.1.

The heterogeneous-slopes model would now use all vectors from 5 to 16 as predictors. The homogeneous slopes model includes Vectors 5–11, plus the new vector 14 (X_2). There are now four vectors included in the heterogeneous-slopes model that are not in the homogeneous-slopes model. Thus, subtracting the SS regression from the two models yields the SS (heterogeneous slopes) = 8.4974 with $df = 4$. This value converts to MS of 2.1244. The new value of the adjusted $MS_{S(A)}$ error terms (8.9137) when divided into the above MS yields an F less than 1, so we retain the hypothesis of homogeneous slopes, and would proceed with the usual covariance.

The covariance table and adjusted means are contained in Table 7.5. We see that the second covariate has further reduced the MS error term, since it accounts for much of the subject variance (within A). The error term has been reduced from 7.96 in the COV with X_1 alone, to 5.03 in the analysis with both X_1 and X_2 as covariates. However, whereas the A effect was significant in Table 7.4, it no longer is significant in Table 7.5. Partialing out X_2 removes more variance from SS_A than it does from $SS_{S(A)}$, so the test of the A effect is no longer significant. Those who believe that covariance will always decrease p values are in for disappointments.

The observant reader will have noted that the within-subjects effects SS_B and SS_{AB} have been completely unaffected by all of the above. This is because the A, X_1, and X_2 vectors are all orthogonal to the within-subject effects. Thus, analysis of covariance, when there is just a single X set of values for each subject, will only influence the between-subjects effects. The within-subjects effects are here reflected by the B main means (here always 15.75 and 11.5) and the differences between the cell means for each

TABLE 7.5
COV with X_1 and X_2 as Covariates

Source	Degrees of freedom	Sum of squares	Mean square	F
Between subjects				
Reg. X_1 and X_2	2	339.373		
A	2	17.509	8.755	1.739
$S(A)$	7	35.238	5.034	
Within subjects				
B	1	108.380	108.370	96.229
AB	2	2.250	1.125	
$SB(A)$	9	8.875	0.986	
Total (adj.)	23	511.625		

Adj. means, $\bar{Y}'_{.jk}$	B_1	B_2	$\bar{Y}'_{.j.}$	Δ_j
A_1	13.938	9.688	11.813	4.25
A_2	22.187	17.187	19.687	5.00
A_3	11.125	7.625	9.375	3.50
$\bar{Y}'_{..k}$	15.75	11.5	13.625	

A row (here always 4.25, 5.00, and 3.50). These terms stay the same regardless of any between-subject covariate effect. This same difference in between-subject and within-subject effects would hold on more complex repeated-measure designs exactly as it holds here.

It would be possible to add a third covariate vector to the present set. However, to test for homogeneity of regression would require a total of three additional vectors, as in Table 7.5, and this would leave 0 *df* for the adjusted error term, $MS_{S(A)}$. In reality, we should have many more subjects to achieve stability when using many covariates.

V. Covariance-type Models with One Covariate Value per Observation (Several per Subject)

In this situation, we have the entire design available in both the X and the Y values. There is one X paired with each Y. This may be represented in our notational form by placing the w X term after the last term in the design. This is in contrast to the previous case where w X was placed after the subject term to indicate X's are available only for each subject. Winer (1971, p. 806) has an example design that is an $[S_3$ in $(A_3)] \times B_2$ w X. We shall use these data to illustrate the linear-model analyses needed to test for homogeneity of slopes, and the covariance analysis.

Winer's data are given in Table 7.6. The first three columns contain the

TABLE 7.6
Linear Model Vectors of Winer's $[RS_3$ in $(A_3)] \times B_2$ w X Data

1	2	3	4	5	6	7	8	9	10	11	12	13	14	15	16	17
								COLUMN NUMBER								
								VECTOR								
A	S	B	X	Y	SX	WX	ψ_B	$X\psi_B$	ψ_{A_1}	$SX\psi_{A_1}$	ψ_{A_2}	$SX\psi_{A_2}$	ψ_{AB_1}	$X\psi_{AB_1}$	ψ_{AB_2}	$X\psi_{AB_2}$
1	1	1	3.0	8.0	3.5	-.5	-1	-3.0	-2	-7.0	0	0	+2	6.0	0	0
1	1	2	4.0	14.0	3.5	+.5	+1	4.0	-2	-7.0	0	0	-2	-8.0	0	0
1	2	1	5.0	11.0	7.0	-2.0	-1	-5.0	-2	-14.0	0	0	+2	10.0	0	0
1	2	2	9.0	18.0	7.0	+2.0	+1	9.0	-2	-14.0	0	0	-2	-18.0	0	0
1	3	1	11.0	16.0	12.5	-1.5	-1	-11.0	-2	-25.0	0	0	+2	22.0	0	0
1	3	2	14.0	22.0	12.5	+1.5	+1	14.0	-2	-25.0	0	0	-2	-28.0	0	0
2	1	1	2.0	6.0	1.5	+.5	-1	-2.0	1	1.5	-1	-1.5	-1	-2.0	+1	2.0
2	1	2	1.0	8.0	1.5	-.5	+1	1.0	1	1.5	-1	-1.5	+1	1.0	-1	-1.0
2	2	1	8.0	12.0	8.5	-.5	-1	-8.0	1	8.5	-1	-8.5	-1	-8.0	+1	8.0
2	2	2	9.0	14.0	8.5	+.5	+1	9.0	1	8.5	-1	-8.5	+1	9.0	-1	-9.0
2	3	1	10.0	9.0	9.5	+.5	-1	-10.0	1	9.5	-1	-9.5	-1	-10.0	+1	10.0
2	3	2	9.0	10.0	9.5	-.5	+1	9.0	1	9.5	-1	-9.5	+1	9.0	-1	-9.0
3	1	1	7.0	10.0	5.5	+1.5	-1	-7.0	1	5.5	+1	5.5	-1	-7.0	-1	-7.0
3	1	2	4.0	10.0	5.5	-1.5	+1	4.0	1	5.5	+1	5.5	+1	4.0	+1	4.0
3	2	1	8.0	14.0	9.0	-1.0	-1	-8.0	1	9.0	+1	9.0	-1	-8.0	-1	-8.0
3	2	2	10.0	18.0	9.0	+1.0	+1	10.0	1	9.0	+1	9.0	+1	10.0	+1	10.0
3	3	1	9.0	15.0	10.5	-1.5	-1	-9.0	1	10.5	+1	10.5	-1	-9.0	-1	-9.0
3	3	2	12.0	22.0	10.5	+1.5	+1	12.0	1	10.5	+1	10.5	+1	12.0	+1	12.0

subscripts for the A, S, and B factors, respectively. Column 4 contains the X values and Column 5 has the Y's. Unlike the prior example, note that X varies from row to row of the same subject. In this design, it is necessary to obtain a covariate for the between-subjects terms (here A and $S(A)$ and a different covariate for the within-subjects effects (here B, AB, and $SB(A)$). Column 6 has been created by averaging the two X values for a given subject. Column 6 will then be used in exactly the same manner the X vector was used in the previous example; that is, as the between-subjects predictor variable. We shall label it here as SX to indicate it has just one value per subject.

Column 7 is created by subtracting Column 6 from Column 4. It is labeled as the WX vector to indicate it is the regression vector to be used on within-subjects effects. (The same results may be obtained by using Column 4 as long as all models include Column 6 prior to Column 4 or other columns derived from Column 4. The use of Column 7 is desired only to improve the clarity of the example).

Vectors 8, 10, 12, 14, and 16 are created to reflect the orthogonal contrasts in the design. The B factor is in Column 8, the A effects are in Columns 10 and 12, and the AB interaction in Columns 14 and 16. Use of a unity vector and these vectors (plus subject vectors) in a multiple regression will yield the AOV summary table reported as Table 10.6.7 (ii) in Winer (1971, p. 807).

A. Tests for Heterogeneous Slopes

Vectors 6 and 7 would be added as predictors to yield a COV summary table. However, prior to doing this, it is desirable to test for homogeneity of slopes. There are two types of regression slopes present in such a design, and they must be tested separately since they will have different error terms. Heterogeneity of between-subjects regressions (in the three A groups) is tested using the adjusted $MS_{S(A)}$. Heterogeneity of slopes on the within-subjects factors is tested using adjusted $MS_{SB(A)}$. To provide a test of heterogeneous slopes on the A groups, multiply the SX vector by the A contrasts, yielding Columns 11 and 13. To provide for a test of heterogeneous slopes on the within-subject factors, we multiply Column 7 by the B contrast and the AB contrast vectors. This yields Columns 9, 15, and 17. Using a unity vector and Vectors 6–17 of Table 7.6 in one or more computer runs (depending on the programs available) in a process similar to that illustrated in the prior example yields the summary table of Table 7.7.

The SS in the SX and WX rows are the sum of squares of regression associated with Columns 6 and 7, respectively. (These would not be included in some program outputs.) They clearly indicate the effectiveness of both covariants. The main interest in this model is whether we may assume

TABLE 7.7
Summary Table of the Completely Heterogeneous-slopes Model Using Vectors 6–17 of Table 7.6

Source	Degrees of freedom	Sum of squares	Mean square	F	P
Between subjects					
SX reg.	1	178.370			
A	2	54.259	27.129	4.926	>.10
Het A	2	27.849	13.924	2.528	>.20
(Cols. 11 and 13)					
$S(A)$	3	16.522	5.507		
Within subjects					
WX reg.	1	62.745			
B	1	29.418	29.418	126.551	<.01
Het B	1	1.118	1.118	4.804	>.10
(Col. 9)					
AB	2	1.923	0.961	4.136	>.10
Het AB	2	1.832	0.916	3.940	>.10
Cols. 16 and 17)					
Pooled 9, 16, and 17	3	2.950	0.983	4.230	>.10
$SB(A)$	2	0.465	0.232		
Total (adj.)	17	374.500			

homogeneity of slopes of the Column 7 vector over the several within-subjects effects.

The between-subjects homogeneity is tested by $MS_{\text{Het }A}/MS_{S(A)} = 2.528$. This value has a probability greater than .20, which leads to a retention of homogeneous slopes of the SX vector on the three A groups.

There are two different possible heterogeneous-slopes tests for the within-subjects vector WX. Using Column 9 we may test for heterogeneous slopes over the B main effect, whereas using Columns 16 and 17 we may test for heterogeneous slopes over the AB interaction contrasts. Unless there is an a priori reason for believing that these would differ, these would be combined into a single test of heterogeneous slopes for the WX vector over all within-subjects effects. This is shown in Table 7.7 in the row with the pooled SS from Vectors 9, 16, and 17. Since this test has a probability greater than .10 (as do the individual tests), the null hypothesis of homogeneity of slopes is again retained. If the pooled test leads to the conclusion of heterogenity, it would be appropriate to test for homogeneity on B and on AB separately.

B. Covariance Models

In the absence of heterogeneity, the covariance (homogeneous slopes) model is appropriate. This is given in Table 7.8. The table differs slightly

TABLE 7.8
Summary Table of the Covariance Model Using Vectors 6–8, 10, 12, and 14 of Table 7.6 and the Adjusted Means

Source	Degrees of freedom	Sum of squares	Mean square	F	P
Between subjects					
SX reg.	1	178.370			
A	2	54.259	27.129	3.057	$>.10$
$S(A)$	5	44.370	8.874		
Within subjects					
WX reg.	1	62.745			
B	1	29.418	29.418	49.063	$<.001$
AB	2	2.339	1.170	1.951	$>.20$
$SB(A)$	5	2.998	0.600		
Total (adj.)	17	374.50			

Adj. means, $\bar{Y}'_{jk}$	B_1	B_2	$\bar{Y}'_{.j.}$
A_1	12.516	16.595	14.556
A_2	10.526	12.474	11.500
A_3	11.893	14.996	13.444
$\bar{Y}'_{..k}$	11.645	14.688	13.166

from Winer's (1971, p. 807, iii) because Winer chose to use the regression coefficient for the WX vector also as the regression coefficient for the SX vector (they were quite close). The present solution uses the two vectors separately. Again the grand mean of the X's (7.5) is used to find the "adjusted means" as the predicted values of Y. In this case, the A main means, the B main means, and the cell means all will have changed somewhat because of the "adjustment" by covariance, since this included regression by both a between-subjects vector and a within-subjects vector.

It is possible in some examples that only one of these two covariate vectors (Column 6 and Column 7) would have a significant regression, so you may wish to go to a simpler model with only one of the two. Since the previous section illustrated the use of only the between-subjects vector, we shall illustrate an example where only the WX vector is retained and the SX vector is dropped. Table 7.9 contains this summary table, and the adjusted means corresponding to it. The between-subjects SS's are changed by dropping the SX vector, but we see that this has no effect on the within-subjects SS's since the SX vector is orthogonal to all within-subjects contrasts. For the same reason, the between-subjects SS's are the same as in the AOV table, and the main A means (a between-subjects effect) are the same as in the ANOVA analysis ignoring Column 7. With the WX vector as a lone covariate, the SS's within subjects and the B main means are

TABLE 7.9
Analysis of Covariance with Only the *WX* Vector as a Covariate

Source	Degrees of freedom	Sum of squares	Mean square	F	P
Between subjects					
A	2	100.000	50.000	1.695	>.20
S(A)	6	177.000	29.500		
Within subjects					
WX reg.	1	62.745			
B	1	29.418	29.418	49.063	<.001
AB	2	2.339	1.170	1.951	>.20
SB(A)	5	2.998	0.600		
Total (adj.)	17	374.500			

Adj. means, $\bar{Y}'_{\cdot jk}$	B_1	B_2	$\bar{Y}'_{\cdot j \cdot}$
	12.794	16.873	14.833
	8.859	10.808	9.833
	13.282	16.385	14.833
$\bar{Y}'_{\cdot \cdot k}$	11.645	14.688	13.166

identical to what they were in the complete covariance analysis of Table 7.8. The cell means have been "adjusted" with respect to the *WX* covariate also. The general point is that in such an analysis of covariance you are always working with two orthogonal sets of effects. The between-subjects effects require one covariate, Column 6, and will be changed by it, but the between-subjects effects are orthogonal to the within-subjects effects and the within-subjects covariate, Column 7. Correspondingly, the within-subject effects are orthogonal to the between-subjects effects and Column 6, the between-subjects covariate. Neither set is influenced by the decisions made on the other set.

This kind of covariance can be conceptualized as doing two different covariate analyses, one for the between-subjects effects and one for the within-subjects effects. In each case, we should start by testing for heterogeneity of slopes, and proceed with the covariance only if the condition of homogeneous slopes is feasible. It is perfectly possible to have heterogeneous slopes on the between-subjects portion, and homogeneous slopes on the within-subjects effects, or vice versa.

VI. Conclusions and Summary

When working with organismic variables, one must face the fact that clear interpretative conclusions are not as easy to come by as when working with manipulative variables. The investigator must recognize that the organismic variables he has used are correlated with many other organismic variables, and it is impossible to be 100% confident that it is "rigidity" rather than some other variable correlated with rigidity that has produced the observed differences. The limitations of cross-sectional studies can be viewed as the problem that the observed organismic variable, age, is confounded with other variables of educational differences, historical differences, environmental differences, etc., of cohorts. This same problem is present, in a different and lesser extent, when an organismic variable, X, is used in a longitudinal study.

Although covariance can be used as one method to try to eliminate some of the possible alternative interpretations, it is often used incautiously without testing even the basic assumption of homogeneous regression slopes. Least-squares analyses are possible for either heterogeneous- or homogeneous-slopes models, with or without repeated measures. Since longitudinal studies require at least one repeated measure, such analyses have been illustrated in the present article. Unfortunately, even if all statistical assumptions have been met, it is still a matter of considerable controversy whether clear interpretations after a covariance analysis are justified if the $\bar{X}$'s are considerably different. Evans and Anastasio (1968), Ferguson (1966), and McNemar (1969) say yes, but Cronbach and Furby (1970), Campbell and Erlebacher (1970), and Games (1976) say no. The author thus recommends caution in such interpretations, and a willingness to look at the data from alternative interpretations.

Most longitudinal studies are investigations, as distinguished from experiments (Games & Klare, 1967). We must recognize we are mere observers in situations in which nature pulls a thousand strings. The strings we are watching may not be the crucial ones. Only by careful observation over many studies and many situations are the crucial strings likely to be identified, and only after they are identified are we likely to learn the crucial cues that indicate a desired response will shortly follow. The longitudinal investigator needs considerable patience, not only for the collection of his data, but also for the processes to yield clear interpretations.

Chapter 8

Univariate and Multivariate Analysis of Variance of Time-Structured Data[1]

R. DARRELL BOCK

ABSTRACT

Analysis of variance and its multivariate extensions are among the most dependable and effective methods available for detecting and describing trends in cross-sectional and longitudinal time-structured data. Although adaptable to many types of data, these methods are best suited to the analysis of trends in group (population) means when the times of observation are fixed in advance in equal intervals and the trends or differences in trend between groups is sufficiently regular to be described by simple polynomial models. Cross-sectional data are especially easy to analyze, because, if subjects are sampled randomly, the residuals are independent from one time point to another. Longitudinal data present a more difficult problem for analysis because the residuals are in general correlated between time points and the pattern of correlation can rarely be specified in advance. Provided the number of time points is not too large, multivariate repeated measures analysis effectively deals with this problem by using the within-group variation to estimate the covariance structure of the residuals. This estimate can be incorporated into the analysis to obtain exact unweighted tests of trend assuming that the distribution of residuals is multivariate normal. Or, the estimate can be used in large-sample tests based on efficient, weighted estimates of trend coefficients. Either type of analysis is conveniently carried out by computer methods of multivariate analysis of variance specialized for repeated measures analysis.

Data are time-structured when the observations can be identified with a number of preassigned points on the time continuum. In behavioral studies, we have the option of introducing time structure on more than one level: To study secular change in populations, we locate the observations in historical time (years, decades, centuries); to describe the growth and development of individual subjects within populations, we typically observe

[1] Preparation of this chapter was supported in part by NSF Grant BNS76-02849.

199

the subject at fixed intervals (days, months, years) on a time scale originating at his conception or birth; to characterize time-dependent response processes within subjects, we can record the subject's responses during intervals beginning at various elapsed times (seconds, minutes, hours) after the onset of an experimentally imposed condition or stimulus.

As a general technique for the statistical treatment of time-structured data, analysis of variance is virtually unique in its capacity to detect and summarize systematic time-dependent variation and covariation in observations from all of these levels, separately or jointly. In one unified analysis, it can encompass the possibly multiple outcomes of an experiment represented at several points in historical time, based on responses from subjects at different stages of development, and repeated within each subject on a number of occasions or trials. Given this structure, we can with the aid of analysis of variance and its multivariate extensions, extract the shape of the average response curve as a function of trial times, test for differences in shape due to the conditions imposed by the experimenter or to existing characteristics of natural populations, and investigate all possible interactions of these factors.

Even in these complex applications the analysis-of-variance approach is surprisingly modest in its demands on mental effort to formulate the problem and on computing resources to perform the calculations. It should be borne in mind, however, that this conceptual and computational economy is not purchased without a certain price. Because analysis of variance is part of linear least-squares (Gauss–Markov) estimation, it requires simplifying assumptions if we are to benefit from its advantages, and we have to be cognizant of these limitations. We must not attempt to extend this general-purpose technique into realms where more specialized methods (often involving nonlinear estimation) are required. Obviously, we must begin our investigation with a complete plan of the data analysis and with its assumptions and limitations clearly in view. Some of the points to be considered at the planning stage are discussed in the next section.

I. Assumptions and Limitations

For time-structured data to be accessible to analysis of variance, not only must each observation carry a time identification, but the method of measuring response, the sampling plan, the arrangement of the time points, the assumed form of time dependency, and the nature of the error distribution must be restricted in certain ways.

A. Interval Measurement

If the object of the analysis is to describe systematic trend over time, it is mandatory that the response variables be measured on a scale whose units are commensurate throughout the relevant range of variation; that is, the measurement must be on a so-called *interval scale* with units everywhere of constant size in some well-defined sense. Otherwise, the shape of the trend line is arbitrary, straight lines cannot be distinguished from curves, and parallel lines at different elevations may appear nonparallel. Even when the measures are known to be equal on one scale (e.g., physical units such as gram, centimeter, seconds), it may be desirable to transform them to equality on another scale in order to see clearly the essential form of the trend line. For example, variables measuring exponential growth may be better analyzed in log units rather than the original units.

The problem of commensurate units can be especially severe when the measures arise from behavioral responses. Bock and Jones (1968, Chapter 1) discuss the issue of defining measurement scales for behavioral data that have some of the properties of, for example, the c.g.s. system in physical measurement. They point out that physical units are intrinsically defined not by the method by which the measurements are taken, but by their role in the mathematical models that connect one observable phenomenon with another. Thus, the units of length take on meaning when the formula for computing area can be used at every point on the scale of measurement, and that area can be used to translate pressure into force in terms of units of mass, and so on. Specifically, it is the invariance of a great variety of mathematical models with respect to location on the measurement scale that gives meaning, utility, and generality to systems such as c.g.s.

With admittedly weak theoretical underpinning, we can perhaps accept as having commensurate units any behavioral-measurement scale that has a validated linear relationship with another variable of interest. By this criterion we might be willing to accept the Binet Mental Age scale as interval measurement on the grounds that in the interval from 5 to 15 years it exhibits a linear relationship with many other physiological and psychological indices of maturation. To the extent that Binet Mental Age differences translate proportionately into increases in these measures, the assumption that the Mental Age scale has well-defined units is not entirely gratuitous.

But stronger definitions of behavioral scales are possible. Bock and Jones (1968) consider Thurstone's psychological scaling to be interval measurement defined by a system of linearly related response models. They present a number of models for judgment and choice that are connected by a common scale making possible mutual prediction of one form of choice behavior from another. Using units on this scale, they exploit analyses of variance to study factorial models for experimental effects on sensation and preference.

In much the same sense, modern psychometric methods of latent-trait measurement produce scales with commensurate units by defining a model relating differences on the scale to item–response probabilities (Bock, 1972; Lord, 1974a; Rasch, 1960; Samejima, 1969). These scales appear also to yield linear relationships with other variables (Andersen & Madsen, 1976;

Bock, 1976; Bock & Thrash, 1977). Because much of research on human behavior at the individual level depends on objective test instruments, it is of considerable interest that latent-trait theory can open this domain to statistical methods, such as curve fitting and complex analysis of variance, that assume interval measurement.

B. Group Comparisons

The analysis of variance is most straightforward when its purpose is estimation or comparison of group means. In this case, the questions the investigator can ask of the data are limited to those concerning the shape of the curve of population means as a function of time, or the shape of differences between the means of two or more populations as a function of time. Whether or not these are interesting questions depends critically upon the practical meaningfulness of group averages. It has long been recognized that such averages are not completely informative about individual development. A well-known example is the unsatisfactory characterization of the adolescent growth spurt in plots of mean stature versus age. The spurt is apparent in such data, but few if any subjects follow the mean curve in their own growth. The group mean curve tends to show a more gentle spurt because of the averaging of individual growth spurts occurring at different times. But even this generalization is not entirely true because there are usually some subjects, especially among the boys, who show a more gentle and protracted slope than is seen in the average data.

The positive thing that can be said of average data is that, if there is some weak but consistent trend in the population, the average growth curve may detect it, whereas the examination of individual growth curves separately may not. An example of this phenomenon is presented in Bock (1976). In early stages of research or when the quantity or quality of longitudinal data required for fitting nonlinear individual growth models is not available, useful information about growth trends may still be accessible through the analysis of group means discussed here.

C. Fixed Time Points

Analysis of variance can be applied conveniently to time-dependent data only when the time points are fixed in advance and are moderate in number. In studies where chronological age is the time variable, this requirement can be met by measuring a subject at preselected ages. In growth studies such as the Fels or Berkeley studies, for example, the children were measured on or near their birthdays and in certain age ranges at their half-year anniversaries. If this degree of planning is not possible, the subjects will have a more or less random distribution of age at the time of measurement, and for purposes of the analysis of variance, the data must then be grouped into age ranges and the mean or median age used to represent the group. In educational work, similar use of grade in school as a time point may be defended on grounds that the relevant dimension for growth of achievement is years of schooling rather than chronological age. Although not a mandatory requirement, it is also convenient for the time points to be evenly spaced. As we shall see, the analysis-of-variance of trend is then more easily carried out.

D. Short-Term Moderate Change

For a number of reasons, analysis-of-variance techniques may become difficult to apply when there are many time points encompassing substantial change in the variables of interest. This is not simply a matter of the computational labor in analyzing designs with many time points, but one of increasing difficulty in justifying the assumptions of conventional trend analysis. As discussed in the next section, we typically use a low-degree polynomial to represent group mean curves and differences in mean curves. This is quite satisfactory for short-run change, but may not be suitable over a wider range. The curve for average growth in stature, for example, has no very satisfactory polynomial representation over the entire growth cycle. Only nonlinear models such as the three-component logistic model (Bock & Thissen, 1979), or the two-component model of Preece and Bains (1978) seem capable of describing growth in stature from near birth to maturity. Fitting and testing of these models requires nonlinear estimation and cannot be approached by the elementary methods of univariate or multivariate analysis of variance discussed here. However, growth over a more limited range can be so described, as will be apparent in the examples in Sections III and IV.

E. Freedom from Outliers

Like all least-squares techniques, analysis of variance is adversely affected by a few aberrant observations far removed from the main body of the data. In behavioral and biological measurement, such aberrant values are almost always due to clerical or technical errors, or to subjects in the sample who do not belong to the target population. Fortunately, outliers are easy to detect when prescreening the data and can be removed from the sample before the analysis begins.

To justify linear least-square estimation in terms of unbiasedness and minimum variance, it is only necessary to assume that the error distribution has finite mean and finite constant variance throughout the range of measurement. (The presence of outliers indicates that the assumption of homogeneous variance has been violated.) To justify the nominal error rates of the significance tests associated with analysis of variance, it is necessary to add the assumption of normally distributed error or large-sample assumptions. Because many of the measures used in behavioral studies are essentially additive combinations of many more or less independent sources of environmental, biological, and physiological variation, the assumption of a normal error distribution, after systematic effects have been absorbed into the model, is broadly justified. The only notable exceptions are response-time measures, which tend to have a log-normal rather than a normal distribution. In many applications, the logarithms of response times are satisfactory quantities for analysis of variance (see Thissen, 1976).

II. Types of Time-Structured Data

Insofar as it affects the method of analysis, the main distinction to be made is between cross-sectional and longitudinal data.

A. Cross-Sectional Data

In cross-sectional data, different subjects are sampled at each time point and all measures in the sample are assumed to be statistically independent. As a result, in the crossed design of (experimental or sampling) groups × time points, the observations are independent both within and between cells. They may therefore be analyzed in a conventional two-way or multiway analysis of variance with but one feature particularly related to time dependence—that in the partition of the sum of squares for the time way of classification and its interactions, single-degree-of-freedom terms are isolated for each component of trend.

If proportionate numbers of subjects in each group appear in each time-point class, a straightforward orthogonal analysis of variance applies. If the numbers are disproportionate, *a nonorthogonal* analysis will be necessary and will require the investigator to fix the order of the partition of sum of squares by choosing an order of priority among hypotheses about various effects in the model. This issue will be clarified in the discussion of analysis of variance of cross-sectional data illustrated by an example from anthropology, presented in the third section.

B. Longitudinal Data

Time-structured data are longitudinal when each subject is measured on a scale commensurate at each time point. Note that, though a longitudinal study resulting in this type of data is *prospective,* not all prospective studies are longitudinal or even time-structured. A study that obtains one set of measures at an earlier time and a second qualitatively distinct set at some later time is prospective and may enable prediction of later characteristics from earlier. But it is not longitudinal or time-structured, does not describe change or growth over some period of time, and cannot be subjected to analysis of variance. Longitudinal studies are both prospective and time-structured, enable both prediction and description of growth and change, and are amenable to analysis of variance.

The analysis of variance of longitudinal data is more complex and interesting than that of cross-sectional data. In the psychological and behavioral literature, the statistical treatment of longitudinal data is often called *repeated-measures analysis* (Bock, 1975, Chapter 7; Winer, 1971). In the biometric and statistical literature, this topic is usually referred to as *analysis of growth* or of *growth curves* (Khatri, 1966; Lee, 1974; Pottoff & Roy, 1964). Basically, three forms of repeated measures analysis have been proposed:

1. Mixed-model univariate analysis of variance (Lindquist, 1953; Winer, 1971)
2. Unweighted (exact) multivariate analysis of variance (Bock, 1963)
3. Weighted (large-sample) multivariate analysis of variance (Khatri, 1966; Pottoff & Roy, 1964)

The choice among these methods depends upon the nature of the time dependency and on the structure of the variance–covariance matrix of the residuals from the fitted trend line. In most cases, this choice can be made only after some preliminary inspection of the data. How this inspection is carried out and the subsequent analysis performed is discussed and illustrated in Section IV.

C. Other Characteristics of Longitudinal Data

A sometimes troublesome limitation on the multivariate analysis of longitudinal data is that the data for each subject must be complete. Although recent work on the problem of incomplete data appears promising (Kleinbaum, 1973; Rubin, 1974; Trawinski & Bargmann, 1964), the practical implementation of these developments is still several years off.

In the meantime, the investigator faced with missing data has the option of (1) omitting subjects with incomplete data records (if this makes the experimental or sampling design unbalanced, a nonorthogonal multivariate analysis of variance will be required); (2) proceeding under mixed-model assumptions with a nonorthogonal univariate analysis of variance (because subjects must be included as a way of classification in this analysis, the computations will be extremely heavy if the number of subjects is large); (3) using some method of interpolating data points if relatively few records are incomplete (the so-called EM algorithm [Dempster, Laird, & Rubin, 1977] is the method of choice). Considering the problems that may attend any of these options, it is more advisable for the investigator to expend energy on collecting complete data initially than to attempt a patch-up later.

As a preface to the discussion of statistical methods, it should perhaps be mentioned that, except in the simplest cases, the computations will require the use of a fairly large-scale computer program. Of the several multivariate analysis-of-variance programs available, the MULTIVARIANCE program of Jeremy Finn (1974) is the most convenient for repeated-measures analysis, and Version VI greatly extends this facility (Finn, 1976). (The examples in the present chapter were prepared with Version V.) A discussion of the use of the MULTIVARIANCE program in the analysis of time-structured data appears in Finn and Mattsson (1977).

III. Analysis of Cross-Sectional Data[2]

In studies of human growth and development, limited time and resources may leave the investigator no option except to collect cross-sectional data. A good example is the measures of height and weight, collected by Haller, Scott, and Hammes (1967) and more recently by Jamison (1977), among children indigenous to the Alaskan North Slope. Although purely cross-sectional, these data are quite adequate to check on anecdotal reports that these children grow more slowly than children living in the south 48 states. An analysis of some of Jamison's results in comparison with a control group of children the same age is presented in the computing example at the end of this section.

A. Form of Cross-Sectional Data

Cross-sectional data may be represented in the form of a so-called *crossed analysis* of variance design (groups × occasions) shown in Table 8.1. Note that the necessary limitation to time points identical for all groups is represented in Table 8.1 by the recurring value of x_k. Note also that the numbers N_{jk} of independently sampled subjects in the Group × Occasion subclasses are not necessarily assumed equal—indeed, a nonorthogonal analysis of these data is still possible even when some of the N_{jk} are zero.

The sample statistics required for least-squares analysis of this form of data are the subclass means $y_{\cdot jk} = \sum y_{ijk}/N_{jk}$, the subclass numbers N_{jk}, and the pooled within-subclass variance estimate,

$$\hat{\sigma}_N^2 = \left[\sum_{j=1}^{n} \sum_{k=1}^{m} \left(\sum_{i=1}^{N_{jk}} y_{ijk}^2 - N_{jk} y_{\cdot jk}^2 \right) \right] \bigg/ (N - mn),$$

---

[2] This section is based on Section 5.2.5 of Bock, R. D. *Multivariate statistical methods in behavioral research.* McGraw-Hill, 1975 (hereafter referred to as MSMBR).

TABLE 8.1
Form of Time-Structured Cross-Sectional Data

Groups j	Time points x_k	Observations y_{ijk} $(i = 1, 2, \ldots, N_{jk})$
1	x_1	y_{i11}
	x_2	y_{i12}
	$\vdots$	$\vdots$
	x_m	y_{i1m}
2	x_1	y_{i21}
	x_2	y_{i22}
	$\vdots$	$\vdots$
	x_m	y_{i2m}
$\vdots$	$\vdots$	$\vdots$
n	x_1	y_{in1}
	x_2	y_{in2}
	$\vdots$	$\vdots$
	x_m	y_{inm}

where

$$N = \sum_{j=1}^{n} \sum_{k=1}^{m} N_{jk}.$$

The first objective of the data analysis is selection of the linear model that describes systematic effects in the observations. The criterion for this choice is one of plausibility and parsimony—namely, that the model should comprise the least number of effects consistent with theory concerning the phenomenon in question and with acceptable fit of the model as judged by a formal test statistic.

The second objective is, given the model, to estimate the effects and their standard errors, to compute from the estimated effects the expected trend lines for the groups, and to show the expected dispersion of observations about the trend line, possibly in the form of a tolerance interval for a new observation at given time points. Methods for choosing the model and estimating effects in cross-sectional data are discussed in the remainder of this section.

B. Polynomial Models for Time Trend

If an interval-measured time-dependent variable y has been observed on N_k, different subjects at successive distinct fixed time points x_k, $k = 1$,

2,...,m, and m is not too large nor the change in y discontinuous in this interval, a suitable statistical model for time trend may be $q < m$ degree polynomial with additive error,

$$y = \beta_0 + \beta_1 x + \beta_2 x^2 + \cdots + \beta_q x^q + \epsilon. \tag{1}$$

The random error ϵ is assumed to be independently distributed with mean 0 and unknown variance σ^2. The β's are in general unknown, but may be estimated from the means of the observations at each time point

$$y_{\cdot k} = \frac{1}{N_k} \sum_{i=1}^{N_k} y_{ik},$$

by the so-called Gauss–Markov (least-squares) estimator,

$$\hat{\beta} = (\mathbf{X}'\mathbf{D}\mathbf{X})^{-1}\mathbf{X}'\mathbf{D}_{y\cdot}, \qquad \text{for} \qquad |\mathbf{X}'\mathbf{D}\mathbf{X}| \neq 0, \tag{2}$$

where

$$\hat{\beta}' = [\beta_0, \beta_1, \beta_2, \ldots, \beta_q]$$

$$\hat{y}\cdot' = [y_{\cdot 1}, y_{\cdot 2}, \ldots, y_{\cdot m}],$$

$$\mathbf{D} = \text{diag}[N_1, N_2, \ldots, N_m],$$

and

$$\begin{bmatrix} 1 & x_1 & x_1^2 & \cdots & x_1^q \\ 1 & x_2 & x_2^2 & \cdots & x_2^q \\ \vdots & \vdots & \vdots & \vdots & \vdots \\ 1 & x_m & x_m^2 & \cdots & x_m^q \end{bmatrix} \tag{3}$$

The $m \times (q + 1)$ matrix $\mathbf{X}$ contains the leading $q + 1$ rows of the Vandermonde matrix of order m. Since $\mathbf{X}$ is of rank $q + 1$, $m > q$ when all x are distinct (Browne, 1958), $|\mathbf{X}'\mathbf{D}\mathbf{X}| \neq 0$, in general. The expected value of this (unbiased, minimum-variance linear) estimator is β and its sampling variance–covariance matrix is $\sigma^2(\mathbf{X}'\mathbf{D}\mathbf{X})^{-1}$ (see MSMBR, Sec. 4.1).

Although satisfactory in most other respects, this method of fitting the polynomial model by estimating the β's has the disadvantage of requiring the degree q to be specified in advance. In general, all elements of $(\mathbf{X}'\mathbf{D}\mathbf{X})^{-1}$ and of $\hat{\beta}$ change when columns are added to or deleted from $\mathbf{X}$. Yet in many cases the investigator is uncertain about the least degree that will give a good account of the data and will wish to inspect the goodness of fit of several successively lower-degree models before deciding.

To facilitate this form of stepwise testing of polynomial models and to make the calculations easier, Fisher (1921) introduced a method of reparameterizing (Eq. [1]) as a so-called *orthogonal polynomial* model. The reparameterization is equivalent to applying to $\mathbf{X}$ the Gram–Schmidt orthogonalization with respect to the metric matrix $\mathbf{D}$, beginning in the leftmost column of $\mathbf{X}$ and working to the right (see MSMBR, Sec. 2.2.4). The result is to decompose X into an $m \times (q + 1)$ orthogonal matrix P and an upper triangular matrix S'. This is,

$$X = PS', \tag{4}$$

where $P'DP = I$ and $X'DX = SS'$.

Then Eq. (1) may be expressed in terms of the orthogonal coefficients $\gamma = S'\beta$, which are estimated from the group means by

$$\hat{\gamma} = P'Dy. = u = \begin{bmatrix} u_0 \\ u_1 \\ \vdots \\ u_q \end{bmatrix} \tag{5}$$

The elements of the $(q + 1) \times 1$ vector u have expected value $S'\beta$; their variance–covariance matrix is the $(q + 1) \times (q + 1)$ identity matrix; that is, they have unit variance and are uncorrelated. The convenience of this parameterization is due to the implied statistical independence of the orthogonal estimates when the observations are normally distributed and to the fact that S' is upper triangular with strictly positive diagonal elements. The former property implies that, on the hypothesis that the corresponding orthogonal coefficient is null, the square of each element in u is distributed independently as a central chi-square on one degree of freedom. The latter implies that accepting the null hypothesis for the last q_2 orthogonal coefficients is equivalent to accepting $q_1 = q - q_2$ for the degree of the polynomial model for trend. Together, they justify the averaging of squares of the last q_2 elements of u for use as the numerator mean square of an F statistic testing goodness of fit of the degree q_1 polynomial versus the degree q polynomial. The denominator is either the within-group mean square or the residual mean square for the degree q model obtained by pooling the residual between-groups sum of squares and the within-group sum of squares. The calculations involved in this test are summarized in Table 8.2. If on the basis of this test, the degree q_1 model is adopted, the $q_1 + 1$ estimated coefficients of the polynomial are given by

$$\hat{\beta}_1 = (S'_{11})^{-1}u_1, \tag{6}$$

where S_{11} is the leading $(q_1 + 1) \times (q_1 + 1)$ submatrix of S', and u_1 contains the leading $q + 1$ elements of u. The variance–covariance matrix of this estimator is $\sigma^2(S'_{11})^{-1}S_{11}^{-1}$. The error variance, σ^2, is estimated by the denominator mean square in the goodness-of-fit statistic.

But it is not always necessary to compute the estimated β-coefficients. In most cases the trend line can be plotted from the fitted values at the assigned time points, and these may be computed from the orthogonal estimates by

$$\hat{y} = P_1u_1. \tag{7}$$

TABLE 8.2
Cross-Sectional Data: Analysis of Variance for Testing the Fit of a q_1 Degree Polynomial, Given that the q Degree Model Has Been Found to Fit[a]

Source of variation	Degrees of freedom	Sums of squares	F-statistic[b]
Constant	1	$ssm = u_0^2$	
Linear	1	u_1^2	
Quadratic	1		
$\vdots$	$\vdots$	$\vdots$	
$q_1 - ic$	1	$u_{q_1}^2$	
q_1 degree model	q_1	$ssr_1 = \sum_{l=1}^{q_1} u_l^2$	
q degree model, given q_1 degree	$q_2 = q - q_1$	$ssr_2 = \sum_{l=q_1+1}^{q} u_l^2$	$F = \dfrac{ssr_2/q_2}{(sse + ssw)/(N - q - 1)}$
Between-groups residual	$m - q$	$sse = ssg - ssr_1 - ssr_2 - ssm$	
Group means	m	$ssg = \sum_{k=1}^{m} N_k y_{.k}^2$	
Within groups	$N - m$	$ssw = sst - ssg$	
Total	$N = \sum_{k=1}^{m} N_k$	$sst = \sum_{k=1}^{m} \sum_{i=1}^{N_k} y_{ik}^2$	

[a] The regression sums of squares are computed from the orthogonal estimates $u = P'Dy$.
[b] Or $(ssr_2/q_2)/[ssw/(N - m)]$.

where P_1 contains the leading $q_1 + 1$ columns of P. Similarly, the 2σ tolerance interval for a new observation at the point x_j is

$$\hat{y}_{.j} \pm 2\sigma(1 + [P_1]_j'[P_1]_j)^{1/2}, \tag{8}$$

where $[P_1]_j$ is the jth row of P_1 written as a column. (See MSMBR, Sec. 4.1.13.)

B. The Fisher–Tchebycheff Orthogonal Polynomials

The true merit of Fisher's method of fitting the polynomial model for trend is most evident when the time points are spaced equally (i.e., when $x_{j+1} - x_j$ is constant for $j = 1, 2, \ldots, m - 1$). For then, P is invariant with respect to the origin and units of the time measure and is, in fact, precisely the tabled Fisher–Tchebycheff orthogonal polynomial. Provided the values of x belong to the rational numbers, the elements of **P** are rational and may be given in integer form with respect to a largest common denominator, as may the square of the normalizing constants for the columns of **P**. As a result, the orthogonal estimates can, for given data, be computed up to the limit of the tables without any rounding error whatsoever. Similarly, the matrix **S** may be tabled in integers and inverted in integer operations to obtain estimates of β without error. Thus, the problem of round-off error, which plagues least-squares fitting of high-order polynomials (Wampler, 1970) is completely solved if the orthogonal polynomials are used. The tables given in MSMBR, Appendix B, for polynomials up to $q = 9$ include the integer forms of the **P** matrix, the normalizing constants, and the **S** matrix. They are convenient for orthogonal polynomial trend analysis when the number of time points does not exceed 10. For greater numbers of points, the DeLury (1950) and Fisher–Yates (1963) tables are available.

C. Orthogonal Polynomial Trend Analysis in Cross-Sectional Data

For cross-sectional designs in which, say, m time points are equally spaced, the orthogonal polynomial matrix of order m may be incorporated into the analysis of variance to provide up to $m - 1$ single-degree-of-freedom components of the sum of squares for the time dimension and for its interaction with the other ways of classification in the design. Except for the additional ways of classification of the groups, this analysis is similar to that shown in Table 8.2 for the time classification only. In the numerical illustration to follow, the subjects are classified by the location of the communities from which the subjects were sampled (which in this case reflects differences in the ethnic origin of the samples) and further classified by sex and by years of age. Thus, the design may be described as a Location × Sex × Age cross-classification. Using the conventional model for crossed designs (see MSMBR, Sec. 5.3), the parameter space of the model, and corresponding sums of squares in the analysis of variance, is partitioned into the following subspaces: General mean, Location, Sex, Age, Location × Sex, Location × Age, Sex × Age, and Location × Sex × Age.

The purpose of the analysis of variance for this type of design is to aid in the choice of the least complex model for effects of the sample classes (in this case the Location and Sex groups) and the lowest degree model for polynomial trend in any of these effects. If there is a significant way of classification in the analysis, the corresponding parameter space is retained in the model. If there is a significant two-factor interaction involving a given way of classification, then the two-factor space and the main-class space of that way of classification are retained. Similarly, if there is a significant three-factor interaction involving a given way of classification, the spaces corresponding to that interaction, to the two-factor interactions involving that classification and the main-class space are retained. And so on, to the highest order of interaction.

In any of these spaces, if a q_1 degree polynomial is required for a given way of classification in any main class or interaction space, then the q_1 degree polynomial is used in all spaces involving that way of classification when fitting the final model. Trend in the data is depicted by computing, from the fitted degree q_1 polynomial, the marginal or group means required for plotting interaction or main-class effects as appropriate. A plot of trend lines is included in the computing example (Figure 8.1 on p. 215).

If the design is nonorthogonal (i.e., the subclass numbers are disproportionate), the order in which the subspaces enter the model must be specified by the investigator. In general, the strategy is to enter effects with more prior certainty of existence before those with less prior certainty. This provides a critical test of the more dubious effects, unconfounded by effects that are presumed to exist and are necessary in the model.

In the case of the Location × Sex × Age design, age effects are a foregone conclusion, sex effects are always possible, but there is little prior knowledge about location effects. If interactions are considered less certain than main effects, a reasonable ordering of spaces for the analysis of variance might be Mean, Age, Sex, Location, Age × Sex, Age × Location, Location × Sex, Age × Location × Sex.

When there is ambiguity as to the ordering, the analysis may be carried in more than one order. But such analyses are in general not independent and should be held to a minimum to avoid incurring Type I errors considerably more frequently than their nominal rates.

D. Example 1: Cross-Sectional Comparison of Growth in Stature of Children Aged 6–14 Years from Two Populations

To illustrate the analysis of variance of trend in cross-sectional data, we compare some data reported by Jamison (1977) giving the stature of boys and girls aged 6–14 years from the villages of Barrow and Wainwright, Alaska, with data of Tuddenham and Snyder (1954, p. 199) for boys and girls in the Berkeley Guidance Study. Strictly speaking, this is not a rigorous analysis because the Berkeley data are actually longitudinal (and will be analyzed longitudinally in Example 2). But it clarifies the calculations and gives some indication of the results that might be expected from actual cross-sectional data.

Sample statistics required in the calculations are shown in Table 8.3. The within-age-group standard deviation estimate is reconstructed from the age-group sample standard deviations reported in the original sources by converting standard deviations to sums of squares, summing and dividing by the pooled degrees of freedom.

TABLE 8.3
Mean Stature of Boys and Girls Aged 6–14: North Slope and Berkeley Samples[a]

Age (years)	North Slope[b]				Berkeley[c]			
	Boys mean (cm)	N	Girls mean (cm)	N	Boys mean (cm)	N	Girls mean (cm)	N
6	113.0	22	113.4	11	117.5	66	117.2	70
7	117.8	15	118.2	22	124.0	66	123.4	70
8	122.4	15	122.5	19	130.1	66	129.2	70
9	129.9	20	129.2	22	135.9	66	135.2	70
10	132.2	23	130.1	16	141.3	66	141.0	70
11	137.9	14	137.6	18	146.5	66	147.6	70
12	144.1	26	147.2	19	152.2	66	154.5	70
13	145.1	14	148.1	16	158.8	66	159.8	70
14	154.0	13	155.1	12	165.8	66	163.1	70

[a] Common within-group standard deviation = 6.23.
[b] Jamison (1977).
[c] Tuddenham and Snyder (1954, p. 199).

The calculations outlined in Section III were carried out on these data by means of the MULTIVARIANCE program (Finn, 1974). This program provides both the nonorthogonal analysis of variance and the orthogonal polynomial trend analysis required in this problem. After the terms to be retained in the model are chosen, the program computes the estimated orthogonal polynomial coefficients and the predicted values for the mean-trend lines for the groups.

In this application, the groups are cross-classified by location (North Slope, Berkeley) and by sex (male, female), and the between-group and group × occasion interaction degrees of freedom are partitioned accordingly in the analysis of variance shown in Table 8.4. Note also that degrees of freedom for polynomial trend of higher degree than quartic are pooled in this table.

The results of the analysis of variance in Table 8.4 are clear enough, with one minor exception. There is some evidence of Location × Occasion trend effects of degree 5 through 8 ($p = .046$). Significant high-degree orthogonal polynomial components almost always indicate the presence of one or two irregular points in the data, often because of procedural or clerical errors. From the plot of the group means in Figure 8.1, it appears that Age Groups 10 and 13 are out of line for both boys and girls in Jamison's data. This is undoubtedly due to nonrandom sampling aggravated by the pooling of samples from several sites and by elevated coefficients of consanguinity in the North Slope villages.

If the significant higher-degree Age × Location interaction is discounted, the only significant effect greater than linear is the cubic Age × Sex interaction ($p = .004$). Because girls reach mature stature before boys, this type

TABLE 8.4
Cross-Sectional Trend Analysis of Average Stature of Children Aged 6–14 from Berkeley, California, and the Alaskan North Slope (Age × Sex × Location)

Source of variation	Degrees of freedom	Sum of squares	F	p
General mean	1	—	—	—
Linear Age	1	336,242	8666	<.0001
Quadratic Age	1	11.96	.30	.58
Cubic Age	1	4.48	.11	.74
Higher Age	5	98.91	.51	.77
Sex	1	6.11	.16	.69
Location	1	15,766	406	<.0001
Linear Age × Sex	1	36.75	.95	.33
Quadratic Age × Sex	1	73.55	1.90	.17
Cubic Age × Sex	1	319.40	8.23	.004
Higher Age × Sex	5	190.36	.98	.43
Linear Age × Location	1	1004.6	25.89	<.0001
Quadratic Age × Location	1	18.75	.48	.49
Cubic Age × Location	1	.002	.000	.99.
Higher Age × Location	5	437.35	2.25	.046
Location × Sex	1	21.25	.55	.46
Age × Location × Sex	5	140.97	.45	.89
Within groups	1505	58,394		

of interaction is to be expected as the children enter adolescence. It is clearly seen in the group means in Table 8.3 as an inversion in the order of the means for the two sexes in the Berkeley data. That there is no similar inversion in the North Slope data might suggest an Age × Sex × Location interaction, but the analysis does not confirm its presence.

If the Cubic Age × Sex term is included in the model, the Sex main effect and Age main effects up to Degree 3 must also be retained along with the highly significant Location effect and the Linear Age × Location interaction. The latter confirms the reality of a difference in growth rate between the Berkeley and North Slope populations during the long period of essentially linear-in-age preadolescent growth in stature. From the fact that the Location contrast is North Slope minus Berkeley $(A - B)$, and the Linear Age × Location contrast is negative, we deduce that the Berkeley population is growing faster. This is confirmed by the plot, in Figure 8.1, of the fitted group means calculated from the orthogonal estimates in Table 8.5. Between 8 and 14 years of age, the rate of growth of the Berkeley children

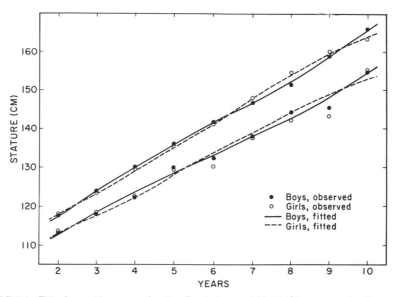

FIGURE 8.1. **Fitted growth curves for the Berkeley and North Slope samples (upper two curves, Berkeley; lower two curves, North Slope).**

is about .8 cm/year greater than that of the North Slope children. This figure is obtained by dividing the orthogonal estimate by the normalizing coefficient for the linear orthogonal polynomial of Order 9:

$$-6.3038/\sqrt{60} = -0.8138$$

(See MSMBR, Appendix B.)

TABLE 8.5
Orthogonal Estimates: Rank 10 Polynomial Model

Effect	Estimate	Standard error
Constant	137.3027	.1968
Linear Age	42.5591	.6143
Quadratic Age	−0.2143	.4805
Cubic Age	−0.0620	.4782
Sex (boys–girls)	0.0096	.3176
Location (NS–B)	−7.9580	.3937
Linear Age × Sex	−0.6483	.9625
Quadratic Age × Sex	1.1824	.9603
Cubic Age × Sex	2.9167	.9567
Linear Age × Location	−6.3038	1.2294

IV. Analysis of Longitudinal Data

In a fully longitudinal study, each subject is measured at the same or equivalent, preassigned time points.[3] The formal layout of data from such a study is shown in Table 8.6. Note that the measure repeated on each subject is indexed by the superscript $k = 1, 2, \ldots, p$ (in parentheses to distinguish it from an exponent). The subscript is reserved for the identification of experimental or sampling group j and for subject i within group j. The (arbitrary) number of subjects in each group is N_j. If the groups are further classified according to experimental factors and/or sampling attributes, j may be replaced by a multiple subscript indicating the treatment or attribute combination.

A. Sample Statistics

All computations of a linear least-squares analysis of longitudinal data may be performed starting from the following summary information:

1. The group vector means

$$\mathbf{y}'_{\cdot j} = [y^{(1)}_{\cdot j} y^{(2)}_{\cdot j} \cdots y^{(p)}_{\cdot j}], \tag{9}$$

where

$$y^{(k)}_{\cdot j} = \frac{1}{N_j} \sum_{i=1}^{N_j} y^{(k)}_{ij}.$$

2. The subclass numbers N_j, $j = 1, 2, \ldots, n$.

3. The pooled within-group variance–covariance matrix $\hat{\mathbf{\Sigma}}$ in which the

TABLE 8.6
Form of Longitudinal Time-Structured Data

Groups j	$x_1 x_2 \cdots x_p$	
1	$y^{(1)}_{i1} y^{(2)}_{i1} \cdots y^{(p)}_{i1}$;	$i = 1, 2, \ldots, N_1$
2	$y^{(1)}_{i2} y^{(2)}_{i2} \cdots y^{(p)}_{i2}$;	$i = 1, 2, \ldots, N_2$
$\vdots$		
n	$y^{(1)}_{in} y^{(2)}_{in} \cdots y^{(p)}_{in}$;	$i = 1, 2, \ldots, N_n$

[3] Various designs for semilongitudinal studies have been proposed (Schaie, 1965). Their analysis is beyond the scope of this chapter.

diagonal elements are the unbiased variance estimates,

$$\hat{\sigma}_k^2 = \frac{1}{N-n}\left\{ \sum_{j=1}^{n} \sum_{i=1}^{N_j} [y_{ij}^{(k)}]^2 - \sum_{j=1}^{n} N_j [y_{\cdot j}^{(k)}]^2 \right\}, \tag{10}$$

and the off-diagonal elements are the unbiased covariance estimates

$$\hat{\sigma}_{kl} = \frac{1}{N-n}\left\{ \sum_{j=1}^{n} \sum_{i=1}^{N_j} y_{ij}^{(k)} y_{ij}^{(l)} - \sum_{j=1}^{n} N_j y_{\cdot j}^{(k)} y_{\cdot j}^{(l)} \right\},$$

$$l \neq k \tag{11}$$

where

$$N = \sum_{j=1}^{n} N_j.$$

A typical example of longitudinal data summarized in this form is shown in Table 8.7. The upper section of Table 8.7 contains the mean yearly measures of stature (cm) for boys and girls ages 2–8 in the Berkeley study as published by Tuddenham and Snyder (1954). The lower section contains the unbiased estimate of the common within-sex-group variation and covariation. Note that to facilitate visual inspection, the latter is shown in the form of standard deviations and correlations rather than variances and covariances.

B. The Polynomial Model for Longitudinal Data

A general linear model suitable for repeated-measures data was first given by Roy (1957, p. 83) and applied to the analysis of change in Bock (1963) and to the analysis of growth curves by Khatri (1966), Pottoff and Roy (1964), and numerous subsequent workers (Kleinbaum, 1973; Lee, 1974; MSMBR, Sec. 7.2; Timm, 1975, Sec. 5.16; Tubbs, Lewis, & Duran, 1975). For present purposes, it is most convenient to express this model in terms of the $n \times p$ matrix $\mathbf{Y}.$ of vector means for the experimental or sampling groups:

$$\mathbf{Y}. = \mathbf{A}\boldsymbol{\beta}\mathbf{X}' + \boldsymbol{\xi}. \tag{12}$$

In Eq. (12), the $n \times m$ design matrix $\mathbf{A}$ contains 1 and 0 elements specifying how the trend effects enter additively into the expected values of the group means.

The columns of the $m \times s$ matrix $\boldsymbol{\beta}$ pertain to the unknown coefficients of the degree $s - 1$ polynomial model, and the rows pertain to main class and possible interactive effects of the experimental factors or sampling attributes.

The $p \times s$ matrix $\mathbf{X}$ contains the leading $s \leq p$ columns of the order-p Vandermonde matrix shown in Eq. (3).

TABLE 8.7
Sample Statistics for Stature of 129 Complete Cases Aged 2–8 from the Berkeley Guidance Study[a]

					Year means (cm)			
Age	1	2	3	4	5	6	7	8
Group	*N*							
Boys	65	88.174	96.579	104.118	110.962	117.335	123.852	129.932
Girls	64	87.123	95.489	103.072	110.430	117.541	123.639	129.367
Within-group S.D.		3.1875	3.4445	3.8021	4.1688	4.5479	4.8241	5.1267
Correlations								
2		1.0000						
3		.8706	1.0000					
4		.8243	.9352	1.0000				
5		.8050	.9214	.9603	1.0000			
6		.7821	.8904	.9187	.9701	1.0000		
7		.7755	.8941	.9107	.9621	.9856	1.0000	
8		.7583	.8790	.9047	.9474	.9723	.9889	1.0000

[a] These are the same cases studied by Thissen, Bock, Wainer, and Roche (1976).

Row j of the $n \times p$ matrix $\boldsymbol{\xi}$. contains the means of errors due to random sampling of subjects within group j. The expected value of $\boldsymbol{\xi}$. is the $n \times p$ null matrix. Different rows of $\boldsymbol{\xi}$. are statistically independent, but elements within rows are in general correlated and their covariance matrix is $\dfrac{1}{N_j} \boldsymbol{\Sigma}$, where $\boldsymbol{\Sigma}$ is the covariance matrix of the p-variate vector observations.

Although $\mathbf{X}$ is of full column rank when the x_k are distinct, $\mathbf{A}$ is in general **not** of full column rank. When $\mathbf{A}$ is of deficient column rank $r < m$, $|\mathbf{A}'\mathbf{DA}| = 0$ and, in consequence, the elements of $\boldsymbol{\beta}$ are not all estimable. Nevertheless, the normal equations arising from routine application of least-squares to Eq. (12) are consistent, and the various mathematical methods of expressing their solution (such as placing independent restrictions on the rows of $\boldsymbol{\beta}$) can be shown to be equivalent to decomposing the model matrix into

$$\mathbf{A} = \mathbf{KL}, \tag{13}$$

where the $n \times r$ matrix $\mathbf{K}$ is a rank r column basis for A, and the $r \times m$ matrix $\mathbf{L}$, also of rank r, contains the coefficients of certain selected linear parametric functions of the rows of $\boldsymbol{\beta}$. (Bock, 1963; MSMBR, Sec. 5.1.) When $\mathbf{L}$ is specified, $\mathbf{K}$ is obtained by $\mathbf{K} = \mathbf{AL}'(\mathbf{LL}')^{-1}$.

Substituting Eq. (13) in Eq. (12), and at the same time introducing the orthogonal reparameterization of the polynomials as in Section II, we may write Eq. (12) as

$$\mathbf{Y}. = \mathbf{K}(\mathbf{L}\boldsymbol{\beta}\mathbf{S})\mathbf{P}' + \boldsymbol{\xi}.$$
$$= \underset{n\times r \;\; r\times s \;\; s\times p}{\mathbf{K} \quad \boldsymbol{\Gamma} \quad \mathbf{P}'} + \boldsymbol{\xi}. \tag{14}$$

Then the weighted least-squares (Gauss–Markov) estimator of $\boldsymbol{\Gamma}$ is (Lee, 1974)

$$\hat{\boldsymbol{\Gamma}} = (\mathbf{K}'\mathbf{DK})^{-1}\mathbf{K}'\mathbf{DY}.\boldsymbol{\Sigma}^{-1}\mathbf{P}(\mathbf{P}'\boldsymbol{\Sigma}^{-1}\mathbf{P})^{-1}. \tag{15}$$

The expected value of this estimator is $\boldsymbol{\Gamma}$ and its sampling variance–covariance matrix is given by the Kronecker product (see MSMBR, p. 212),

$$(\mathbf{K}'\mathbf{DK})^{-1} \otimes (\mathbf{P}'\boldsymbol{\Sigma}^{-1}\mathbf{P})^{-1}. \tag{16}$$

We notice, however, that Eq. (15) contains the error variance–covariance matrix $\boldsymbol{\Sigma}$ and cannot be applied in general unless $\boldsymbol{\Sigma}$ is known. Fortunately, there are a number of straightforward methods of dealing with this problem:

1. Timm (1975, Sec. 5.16) has pointed out that if the degree of the polynomial model is set equal to $p - 1$, then $\mathbf{P}$ is nonsingular, $\mathbf{P}^{-1} = \mathbf{P}'$, and the matrix $\boldsymbol{\Sigma}^{-1}$ cancels out of Eq. (15); that is,

$$\boldsymbol{\Sigma}^{-1}\mathbf{P}(\mathbf{P}'\boldsymbol{\Sigma}^{-1}\mathbf{P}) - 1 = \boldsymbol{\Sigma}^{-1}\mathbf{PP}'\boldsymbol{\Sigma}\mathbf{P} = \mathbf{P}.$$

Thus, if p is not large and there is no advantage in using a less than p

-1 degree trend polynomial, the Gauss–Markov estimator of the orthogonal coefficients is obtained in an unweighted analysis simply by transforming the vector observations by the $p \times p$ matrix of Fisher–Tshebycheff orthogonal polynomials $\mathbf{P}'$.

2. If the structure of Σ is such that

$$\underset{p \times p}{\Lambda} = \mathbf{P}'\Sigma\mathbf{P} \tag{17}$$

is a diagonal matrix, the weight matrix cancels out of Eq. (15) for all values of $s \leq p$. This is true because, if $\mathbf{P}$ is an orthogonal matrix and Eq. (17) is diagonal, the columns of $\mathbf{P}$ are the characteristic vectors of Σ and corresponding elements of Λ are the characteristic values associated with each. Thus $\Sigma\mathbf{P} = \mathbf{P}\Lambda$, $\Sigma = \mathbf{P}\Lambda\mathbf{P}'$ and $\Sigma^{-1} = \mathbf{P}'\Lambda^{-1}\mathbf{P}$. Then if the $n \times s$ matrix $\mathbf{P}_1$ contains the leading s columns of $\mathbf{P}$, and the $s \times s$ diagonal matrix Λ_s contains the corresponding characteristic values, we have

$$\Sigma^{-1}\mathbf{P}_1(\mathbf{P}'\Sigma^{-1}\mathbf{P}_1)^{-1} = \mathbf{P}_1\Lambda_1^{-1}(\Lambda_1^{-1})^{-1} = \mathbf{P}_1,$$

and the unweighted estimator is Gauss–Markov.

This result is of considerable practical interest because it can be shown under mixed-model assumptions (Bock, 1960, 1963; MSMBR, Sec. 7.1.2) that Σ belongs to a class of covariance structures diagonalized by a class of orthogonal transformations of which $\mathbf{P}$ is a member. The former is the class of so-called "reducible" covariance structures studied by Bargmann (1957; see also Huynh and Feldt, 1970).[4] Thus, unweighted multivariate analysis of repeated measures given in Bock (1963) and MSMBR (Chapter 7) is justified when applied under mixed-model assumptions, or more generally when $\mathbf{P}'\Sigma\mathbf{P}$ can be assumed diagonal, even when s is less than p.

This result also suggests that, in the presence of nonzero association in $\mathbf{P}'\hat{\Sigma}\mathbf{P}$, the transformed covariance matrix may be so greatly dominated by its diagonal elements that the unweighted estimates will differ but little from the weighted estimates.

The analysis in Example 2 is an instance in which this is the case.

3. Finally, if $\mathbf{P}'\Sigma\mathbf{P}$ is not diagonal, the most practical alternative would seem to be to forgo an exact analysis and proceed by maximum-likelihood estimation under large-sample assumptions. It can be shown (Khatri, 1966; Tubbs *et al.*, 1975) that, if a maximum-likelihood estimator of Σ is available independent of $\mathbf{Y}$ (e.g., the within-group covariance matrix $\hat{\Sigma}$), then, for $|\hat{\Sigma}| \neq 0$,

$$\hat{\hat{\Gamma}} = (\mathbf{K}'\mathbf{D}\mathbf{K})^{-1}\mathbf{K}'\mathbf{D}\mathbf{Y}.\hat{\Sigma}^{-1}\mathbf{P}(\mathbf{P}'\hat{\Sigma}^{-1}\mathbf{P})^{-1} \tag{18}$$

is a consistent estimator of Γ with large-sample variance–covariance ma-

---

[4] The hypothesis that the population transformed error matrix is diagonal may be tested by a likelihood ratio test of no-association in the transformed sample matrix $\mathbf{P}'\hat{\Sigma}\mathbf{P}$. (See Anderson, 1958, Chapter 9.)

trix given by the Kronecker product

$$(\mathbf{K'DK})^{-1} \otimes (\mathbf{P'\hat{\Sigma}^{-1}P})^{-1}. \tag{19}$$

Associated with Eq. (18) is a multivariate analysis of variance that plays the same role in longitudinal data as does the univariate analysis of variance of cross-sectional data discussed earlier. For purposes of the multivariate analysis of variance, the columns may be orthogonalized from left to right with respect to $\mathbf{D}$ to obtain, say, $\mathbf{K}^*$, where $\mathbf{K}^{*'}\mathbf{DK}^* = \mathbf{I}_r$. Similarly, the columns of $\mathbf{P}_1$ are orthogonalized from left to right with respect to $\mathbf{\Sigma}^{-1}$ to obtain, say $\mathbf{P}_1^*$, where $\mathbf{P}_1^{*'}\mathbf{\Sigma}^{-1}\mathbf{P}_1^* = \mathbf{I}_s$. Then, letting $\mathbf{M}^* = \mathbf{K}^{*'}\mathbf{D}$ and $\mathbf{Q}_1^* = \mathbf{\Sigma}^{-1}\mathbf{P}_1^*$,

$$\hat{\mathbf{\Gamma}}^*_{r \times s} = \mathbf{M}^*\mathbf{Y}.\mathbf{Q}_1^* = \mathbf{U} = \begin{bmatrix} \mathbf{u}_0' \\ \mathbf{u}_1' \\ \vdots \\ \mathbf{u}_{r-1}' \end{bmatrix} \tag{20}$$

is a maximum likelihood estimator of orthogonal parameters, $\mathbf{\Gamma}^*$, with large-sample covariance matrix $\mathbf{I}_r \otimes \mathbf{I}_s$. The partition of the $s \times s$ matrix of sum of squares and cross-products (briefly "sums of products") for the multivariate analysis of variance may therefore be computed as shown in Table 8.8.

TABLE 8.8
Longitudinal Data: Multivariate Analysis of Variance of an $s - 1$ Degree Polynomial Model for r Group Effects[a]

Source of dispersion	Degrees of freedom	Sums of squares and cross-products $(s \times s)$
General mean	1	$\mathbf{SSM} = \mathbf{u}_0\mathbf{u}_0'$
Between-groups effects (leading effects eliminated and following effects ignored)	1	$\mathbf{SSB}_1 = \mathbf{u}_1\mathbf{u}_1'$
	1	$\mathbf{SSB}_2 = \mathbf{u}_2\mathbf{u}_2'$
	$\vdots$	
	1	$\mathbf{SSB}_{r-1} = \mathbf{u}_{r-1}\mathbf{u}_{r-1}'$
Between-groups effects	$r - 1$	$\mathbf{SSB}$
Between-groups residual	$n - r$	$\mathbf{SSE} = \mathbf{SSG} - \mathbf{SSB} - \mathbf{SSM}$
Group means	n	$\mathbf{SSG} = \mathbf{Q}\left[\sum\limits_{j=1}^{n} N_j\mathbf{y}_{\cdot j}\mathbf{y}_{\cdot j}'\right]\mathbf{Q}'$
Within groups	$N - n$	$\mathbf{SSW} = \mathbf{SST} - \mathbf{SSG} = \mathbf{I}_s$
Total	$N = \sum\limits_{j=1}^{n} N_j$	$\mathbf{SST} = \mathbf{Q}\left[\sum\limits_{j=1}^{n}\sum\limits_{i=1}^{N_j} \mathbf{y}_{ij}\mathbf{y}_{ij}'\right]\mathbf{Q}'$

[a] The sums of squares and cross-products are computed from the orthogonal estimates $\mathbf{U} = \mathbf{MY}.\mathbf{Q}'$.

The sums of products matrices are employed in tests of multivariate hypotheses of trend as follows:

Suppose it is desired to test the hypothesis that orthogonal polynomial coefficients greater than degree $s_1 - 1$ are null for some between-groups effect represented by the sum of products

$$\mathbf{SSH} = \sum_{k=c+1}^{c+n_h} \mathbf{SSB}_k$$

on n_h degrees of freedom. For this test, an error sum of products independent of SSH is extracted from the table. For example,

$$\mathbf{SSE}^* = \mathbf{SSE} + \mathbf{SSW},$$

on $n_e = (N - r) \geq s - s_1$ degrees of freedom.

Then, for $s_2 = s - s_1$, the $s_2 \times s_2$ submatrices $\mathbf{SSH}_2$ and $\mathbf{SSE}_2^*$ are extracted from the lower right corners of $\mathbf{SSH}$ and $\mathbf{SSE}^*$, respectively, and the $\min(n_h, s_2)$ nonzero roots of the determinantal equation

$$|\mathbf{SSH}_2 - \lambda\mathbf{SSE}_2^*| = 0$$

are found and ordered from largest to smallest. From these roots, the following test statistics may be computed:

1. Roy's largest-root statistic, for example, in the form of the generalized F with arguments r and t and $s = \min(n_h, s_2)$ (MSMBR, Sec. 3.4.7):

$$F_0 = (t/r)\lambda_1, \tag{21}$$

where

$$\lambda_1 = \max \lambda_l, \, l = 1, 2, \ldots, \min(n_h, s_2)$$

$$r = |n_h - s_2| + 1$$

$$t = n_e - s_2 + 1$$

Critical points for F_0 may be read from the table for $\min(n_h, s_2)$ roots in Appendix A of MSMBR.

2. Hotelling trace statistic:

$$T_0^2 = n_e \sum_{l=1}^{\min(n_h, s_2)} \lambda_l \tag{22}$$

An F approximation for this statistic has been given by McKeon (1974):

$$F_M^{(K,D)} = \frac{mD}{s_2 n_h(D - 2)n_e} T_0^2$$

where

$$m = n_e - s_2 - 1$$

$$K = s_2 n_h$$

$$D = 4 + \frac{K + 2}{B - 1}$$

$$B = \frac{(m + s_2)(m + n_h)}{(m - 2)(m + 1)}$$

Exact .05 and .01 points for T_0^2 are available in Pillai (1960) and Pillai and Jayachandran (1970).

3. The likelihood ratio statistic:

$$\Lambda = \prod_{l=1}^{\min(n_h, s_2)} \frac{1}{1 + \lambda_l} \tag{23}$$

Rao's F approximation (see MSMBR, Sec. 3.4.9) may be used to compute probability levels for Λ.

Note that, since the weighted analysis is based on an estimated Σ and assumes large-sample statistics, critical points of the distribution of $\chi^2 / n_h s_2$ on $n_h s_2$ degrees of freedom (given, for example, by Hald, 1952) could be used in place of F_0, F_M, or F_R.

Both the weighted and the unweighted analyses include univariate F statistics for the separate terms of the polynomial. If the condition obtains that $P'\Sigma P$ is diagonal, these F statistics are statistically independent under multivariate normality. Thus, a union–intersection test—namely, that the hypothesis is rejected if the F_k is significant at the α_k level—is a quite satisfactory multivariate test with joint significance level

$$\alpha^* = 1 - \prod_{k=1}^{s_2} (1 - \alpha_k) \tag{24}$$

(cf. Roy and Bargmann, 1958; J. Roy, 1958).

In the weighted case, where the terms are orthogonalized in the sample, Eq. (24) applies in large samples. Because of the greater diagnostic and descriptive detail in the F's for the separate functions, the union–intersection test is in general more useful in repeated-measures analysis than are statistics 1, 2 and 3 above. This is the test used in Example 2 in this section.

When the rank r of the model for the sampling or experimental effects and the rank s of the polynomial trend model have been chosen, possibly with the aid of the foregoing tests, estimates of the parameters in Eq. (14)

are obtained from Eq. (20) as follows:

$$\Gamma = (S_r^{-1})' \Gamma^* T_s^{-1} \tag{25}$$

where S_r is the leading r rows and columns of the Cholesky factor of $K'DK$, and T_s is the s leading rows and columns of the Cholesky factor of $P'\hat{\Sigma}^{-1}P$ (see MSMBR, Sec. 2.7.2). These factors are given by the ORTHM subroutine of MATCAL (Bock and Repp, 1974) during the orthonormalization of K with respect to D and P with respect to $\hat{\Sigma}^{-1}$.

The fitted values of the group means may then be computed from

$$\hat{Y}. = \underset{r \times s}{K \hat{\Gamma} P'}. \tag{26}$$

The variance–covariance matrix of the elements of Eq. (26), rolled out across rows, is

$$(K \otimes P)[(K'DK)^{-1} \otimes (P'\hat{\Sigma}^{-1}P)^{-1}](K \otimes P)$$
$$= K(K'DK)^{-1}K' \otimes P(P'\hat{\Sigma}^{-1}P)^{-1}P' \tag{27}$$

The 2σ tolerance interval on a new observation in group j at time point k is, therefore,

$$\hat{Y}.j^{(k)} \pm 2\{1 + [K]_j'(K'DK)^{-1}[K]_j \cdot [P]_k(P'\hat{\Sigma}^{-1}P)^{-1}[P]_k'\}^{1/2}, \tag{28}$$

where $[K]_j$ is the jth row of K, written as a column, and $[P]_k$ is the kth row of P, similarly written.

C. Example 2: Longitudinal Comparison of Growth in Stature of Boys and Girls Aged 2–8

Although sex differences in preadolescent stature are only weakly detected by the cross-sectional analysis in Example 1, they are clearly revealed in the present example when the inherently more powerful repeated-measures analysis is brought to bear on longitudinal data. Table 8.7 summarizes measures of stature of boys and girls aged 2–8 from the Berkeley Guidance Study as reported by Tuddenham and Snyder (1954). Table 8.7, which includes standard deviations and product-moment correlations in addition to means and sample sizes, contains all of the information needed for a multivariate analysis of variance of mean trend in the two sex groups.

The first step in examining these data is to test their conformity to the assumptions of the mixed-model, unweighted, or weighted analysis. With the aid of the MULTIVARIANCE program, the common within-group covariance matrix is reconstructed from the standard deviations and correlations, and is transformed by the Order 8 matrix of orthogonal polynomials in normalized form. (The MULTIVARIANCE program gives the user the option of such a transformation and generates the required matrix.) The result of this transformation is shown in Table 8.9.

TABLE 8.9

Orthogonal Polynomial Transformation of Statistics in Table 8.7

		Term					
		Constant	Linear	Quadratic	Cubic	Quartic	Quintic	Sextic
Group	*N*							
Boys	65	291.392	36.481	-1.9287	.5175	-0.1188	-0.1366	-0.0626
Girls	64	289.771	37.324	-2.3025	-.1531	-0.0995	-0.2169	.0762
Within-group	S.D.	10.5552	2.9507	1.2480	1.0299	.7507	.6770	.5814
	Constant	1.0000						
	Linear	.6737	1.0000					
	Quadratic	-.1934	-.2896	1.0000				
Correlations[a]	Cubic	-.0031	-.0714	-.3716	1.0000			
	Quartic	-.0169	.0732	-.1141	-.2413	1.0000		
	Quintic	.0658	.2170	.0790	-.3062	-.4563	1.0000	
	Sextic	-.0311	-.0090	.0208	-.0041	.1888	-.2531	1.0000

[a] Characteristic roots of the within-group correlation matrix:

$$[\lambda_\ell] = [1.8899, 1.6498, 1.3464, .8845, .6907, .2911, .2475].$$

225

Inspecting the transformed correlations in Table 8.9, we see that the values in the first subdiagonal are large enough to suggest that the population matrix is not diagonal. We confirm this impression by calculating, from the characteristic roots of the correlation matrix shown in the footnote of Table 8.9, the likelihood ratio χ^2 statistic for testing the hypothesis of no association in a $p \times p$ correlation matrix (Anderson, 1958, Chapter 9):

$$\chi^2_{p(p-1)/2} = -\{N - n[(2p + 5)/6]\} \sum_{l=1}^{p} \ln \lambda_l = 209.10 \qquad (29)$$

On the null hypothesis and multivariate normal distribution of the within-group residuals, this statistic is distributed in large samples as a central χ^2 variate on $p(p - 1)/2$ degrees of freedom. In this instance, the number of degrees of freedom is 21 and the value of the χ^2 clearly contradicts the hypothesis that the correlation matrix (and thus the covariance matrix) is diagonal. We therefore conclude that a weighted analysis is necessary.

Had we accepted the hypothesis that the population covariance matrix is diagonal, we would have tested the variances of the linear through sextic terms for homogeneity. (The Hartley variance–range test is suitable for this purpose [Pearson & Hartley, 1966, p. 202].) If these variances had appeared homogeneous, we could then have pooled them to obtain for the F ratios a denominator with $6 \times 127 = 762$ degrees of freedom. Because of the resulting increase in power of the F tests, this "mixed-model" form of analysis is obviously the preferred approach to repeated-measures data when it is justified (see Bock, 1963; Huynh & Feldt, 1970).

If the population covariance matrix is assumed diagonal but the variances in multiple-degree-of-freedom subspaces of the within-subject variation are not assumed homogeneous, the unweighted repeated-measures analysis is indicated. This type of analysis is simply a multivariate analysis of variance of the orthogonal polynomial transform of the original data. In the MUL-TIVARIANCE program, it is performed by transforming the summary statistics before entering the estimation of tests-of-hypothesis phases of the program. The estimation phase computes the basis matrix K in Eq. (14) and estimates effects associated with the experimental or sampling structure of the data. In the present study, the sampling structure consists simply of the classification of the subjects as male and female. Since there are only two sample groups, the K matrix generated by the program is

$$K_2 = \begin{bmatrix} 1 & \frac{1}{2} \\ 1 & -\frac{1}{2} \end{bmatrix}.$$

The first column of K_2 corresponds to the one degree of freedom for the general mean, ignoring the sex classification, and the second column corresponds to the one degree of freedom between groups. Associated with each of these degrees of freedom is an F statistic for each of the terms in

TABLE 8.10
Inverse of the Sample Within-Group Covariance Matrix

	1	2	3	4	5	6	7
1	.4154			(Symmetric)			
2	−.3141	1.0020					
3	−.0570	− .4520	1.2923				
4	.0564	− .0905	− .0244	2.1499			
5	−.0989	.2362	.0192	− .8347	2.2599		
6	.0127	− .4584	.6559	− .6421	− .6296	4.2315	
7	.0579	.1522	− .4108	.3753	.1045	−2.2124	1.8759

the polynomial; these statistics are independent if the transformed covariance matrix $\mathbf{P'\Sigma P}$ is diagonal.

When the transformed covariance matrix is not diagonal and the weighted analysis is required, an additional step must be interposed between the calculation of the summary statistics and the multivariate analysis of variance: The matrix of orthogonal polynomials must be orthogonalized again with respect to the inverse sample covariance matrix. The MATCAL subroutine ORTHM performs this operation (Bock & Repp, 1974). For the present data, this inverse is shown in Table 8.10. The polynomials orthogonalized with respect to this matrix are shown in Table 8.11. The (upper triangular) matrix of the transformation of the Order 7 orthogonal polynomials (i.e., the $\mathbf{T}_s^{-1}$ matrix of Eq. [25] is given in Table 8.12. Tables 8.10 and 8.11 contain the matrices required for the computation of the transformation matrix for the weighted analysis as given by $\mathbf{Q}^* = \hat{\mathbf{\Sigma}}^{-1}\mathbf{P}^*$. Since the MULTIVARIANCE program has a provision for any arbitrary linear transformation of the sample data, it is a simple matter to perform the weighted analysis with the transformation matrix $\mathbf{Q}^*$.

For purposes of comparison, the results of both the weighted and unweighted repeated-measures trend analysis are shown in Table 8.13. Despite

TABLE 8.11
Orthogonal Polynomials for Weighted Trend Analysis

Age	Terms						
	Constant	Linear	Quadratic	Cubic	Quartic	Quintic	Sextic
2	2.9204	1.0426	.3385	−.5765	.2984	−.0876	−.0211
3	2.9204	1.5517	− .4531	.4506	−.5169	.3225	−.3853
4	2.9204	2.0609	−1.0041	.6411	−.0364	−.4368	.2625
5	2.9204	2.5700	−1.3146	.3519	.4538	.0383	−.4495
6	2.9204	3.0791	− 1.3844	−.0601	.3468	.7924	.0688
7	2.9204	3.5883	−1.2137	−.2379	−.1057	.5130	−.2525
8	2.9204	4.0974	− .8024	.1754	.0268	.5308	−.0921

TABLE 8.12
Coefficient Transformation from Unweighted to Weighted Orthogonal Polynomials

	Unweighted						
Weighted	1	2	3	4	5	6	7
1	7.7266	6.7996	−2.2050	.2813	.1697	.6322	−.3285
2		2.6941	−1.0062	.0336	.0739	.6549	−.0267
3			1.1025	−.5626	−.1144	.1086	.0260
4				.8742	−.4352	−.3271	−.0042
5					.6656	−.3170	.1417
6						.6550	−.1714
7		(Triangular)					.5814

the apparent smooth progression of sample means shown in Table 8.7, the differences between the sex groups are not a simple function of age. Both the weighted and unweighted analyses show a significant Degree 5 trend component in the differences between the means of the sex groups. To represent completely systematic differences in average stature of boys and girls in this age range therefore requires a Rank 2 model for sample classes ($r = 2$) and a Rank 6 model for trend ($s = 6$).

If the subjects regarded as a sample from a single population and the sex groups are combined, the curve of mean growth is considerably simpler. Both analyses show at most a marginally significant cubic component.

TABLE 8.13
Test Statistic for Longitudinal Trend Analysis of Growth in Stature of Children Aged 2–8 in the Berkeley Guidance Study (within-groups $df = 127$)

Source of variation	Degrees of freedom	Weighted		Unweighted	
		F	p	F	p
General mean	1				
Constant		84,805	<.0001	97,770	<.0001
Linear		21,770	<.0001	20,172	<.0001
Quadratic		443.0	<.0001	370.2	<.0001
Cubic		3.577	.061	4.154	.043
Quartic		2.416	.122	2.729	.101
Quintic		0.4969	.482	.4223	.517
Sextic		.0150	.903	.0150	.903
Between sexes	1				
Constant		4.210	.042	.762	.385
Linear		.0867	.769	2.631	.107
Quadratic		11.040	.001	2.893	.091
Cubic		5.388	.022	13.672	.004
Quartic		2.264	.135	.0213	.884
Quintic		11.692	.001	8.792	.004
Sextic		1.836	.178	1.836	.178

TABLE 8.14
Longitudinal Trend Analysis: Estimated Orthogonal Polynomial Coefficients

	Weighted		
Effect	Degree 5	Degree 3	Unweighted
General mean			
Constant	290.5870	290.5694	290.5816
Linear	36.9030	36.8709	36.9026
Quadratic	−2.1160	−2.1386	−2.1156
Cubic	.1823	.1442	.1822
Quartic	.1109		−.1091
Quintic	.0422		.0401
Sex (B − G)	1.5436	1.9692	1,6220
Age × Sex			
Linear	−.8492	−.4353	−.8429
Quadratic	.3800	.4151	.3738
Cubic	.6696	.3573	.6706
Quartic	.0145		−.0193
Quintic	−.3944		−.3535

Ignoring the sex classification thus leads to a Rank 1 ($r = 1$) model for the sample and a rank 4 ($s = 4$) model for trend.

The weighted and unweighted estimates of the orthogonal polynomial coefficients for these models are shown in Table 8.14. Note that when the quintic polynomial is assumed, the weighted and unweighted solutions give essentially the same result. This is a consequence of the very small corre-

TABLE 8.15
Observed and Fitted Age-Group Means for the Berkeley Guidance Study Data

	Mean stature (cm)					
	Observed		Fitted[a]			
			Degree 5		Degree 3	
Age (yr)	Boys	Girls	Boys	Girls	Boys	Girls
2	88.17	87.12	88.17	87.13	88.23	87.16
3	96.58	95.49	96.54	95.54	96.48	95.42
4	104.12	103.07	104.15	103.04	104.03	103.20
5	110.96	110.43	110.91	110.49	111.04	110.48
6	117.34	117.54	117.34	117.53	117.62	117.24
7	123.85	123.64	123.83	123.67	123.92	123.48
8	129.93	129.37	129.92	129.38	130.06	129.18

[a] From the weighted estimates.

lations between the sixth-degree term and the remaining terms of the polynomial (Table 8.9). With respect to the last term, the transformed error covariance matrix is nearly diagonal, and the weighted and unweighted analyses become nearly identical at the fifth-degree term.

When the cubic polynomial is assumed, on the other hand, the effects of the weights are more evident, especially in the sex effect and sex × age interactions, which are sensitive to the greater weight assigned at younger ages where the within-sex variation is smaller. Despite the significant failure of fit of the Degree-3 model, the fitted means reproduce the observed means almost as well as the much less parsimonious Degree-5 model. This is apparent in Table 8.15, where the observed means in Table 8.7 are reproduced along with means computed by Eq. (26) from the weighted estimates in Table 8.14. The figures in Table 8.15 demonstrate the efficacy of low-degree polynomial models for growth when a limited age span is examined.

V. Summary

A methodological problem widely encountered in the study of secular trend, growth and development, or experimental manipulation of behavior is that of detecting and describing systematic change over time. With certain restrictions on the design of the study and the method of measurement, this problem has a ready solution in analysis of variance and its multivariate extensions. To be amenable to this technique, the observations should be time-structured (i.e., limited to a moderate number of preassigned time points, preferably equally spaced), and the measurement of the trait or response in question should be made on a scale with commensurate units throughout the relevant range. The analysis is further facilitated if, in cross-sectional data, the observations are replicated at each time point, or, in longitudinal data, all subjects are observed at precisely the same or comparable time points.

When the data are cross-sectional (i.e., independent samples of subjects are drawn contemporaneously at the several time points), the shape of the curve describing time dependency of the population mean, and differences in the shape between populations, can be investigated in a polynomial trend analysis. A single-degree-of-freedom univariate analysis of variance of successive orthogonal polynomial components of trend and trend differences provides a convenient, exact, unbiased minimum-variance method of performing this analysis. Although the calculations for this analysis are most straightforward when the time points are equally spaced and the equal numbers of subjects are sampled at each time point, the statistical theory and computer methods for unequal spacing and unbalanced sampling are fully worked out and available if needed.

When the data are longitudinal (i.e., each subject is measured at each time point), trend analysis of the population time-point means, or differences in trend between populations, can be carried out by multivariate repeated-measures analysis or, in favorable cases, by mixed-model univariate analysis of variance. If the variance–covariance structure of the sampling errors is transformed to no-association (i.e., uncorrelated) by a suitable orthogonal matrix independent of the data (e.g., a matrix of Fisher–Tchebycheff orthogonal polynomials), an exact analysis of trend is provided by a multivariate analysis of variance in which the orthogonal components of trend appears as variates but are tested in a manner analogous to, but in general more powerful than, the single-degree-of-freedom tests in the univariate analysis of variance of cross-sectional data. If the transformed errors are uncorrelated and the error-trend components exclusive of the constant component are homogeneous in variance, a pooled estimate of the error components may be used and the multivariate repeated-measures analysis specializes to a still more powerful single-degree-of-freedom mixed-model univariate analysis of variance.

If the error covariance structure cannot be reduced to no-association by a suitable orthogonal matrix independent of the data, a consistent, efficient, large-sample, weighted method of repeated-measures analysis based on the Pottoff–Roy formulation is available. It is shown here that this analysis is conveniently implemented by orthogonalizing the Fisher–Tshebycheff orthogonal polynomials with respect to the inverse of the sample within-group covariance matrix. The statistical tests of conventional multivariate analysis of variance of trend components computed with this reorthogonalized matrix weighted by the inverse sample covariance matrix may then be interpreted in a large-sample sense.

An example is presented showing in cross-sectional data that a polynomial trend analysis easily detects a difference in growth rate between the children represented in the Berkeley growth study and children indigenous to the Alaskan North Slope. A weighted analysis of longitudinal data from the Berkeley Growth Study shows that, in the years 2–8 when there is no difference in the size or average rate of growth of boys and girls, the analysis is able to detect subtle differences in curvilinear components of the average growth curves of the two sexes.

Chapter 9

The Analysis of Categorical Data in Longitudinal Studies of Behavioral Development

J. RICHARD LANDIS
GARY G. KOCH

ABSTRACT

This chapter is concerned with the analysis of multivariate categorical data which are obtained from longitudinal studies of human growth and development. An expository discussion of pertinent hypotheses for such situations is provided within the context of two methodologically illustrated examples, and appropriate test statistics are developed through the application of weighted least squares. These procedures are illustrated with extensive analyses of each of the data sets.

I. Introduction

Many longitudinal investigations dealing with behavioral and/or educational development are concerned with intraindividual change for variables that are measured in terms of discrete categories (based on nominal or ordinal as opposed to interval scales). Examples of such categorical (qualitative) variables include measures of

1. Child competencies in task performance
2. Verbalization patterns
3. Coping ability in stress situations
4. Self-concept
5. Parent–child interaction
6. Developmental stages

Thus, the basic research design for such studies involves the classification of each subject with respect to each categorical variable (which is called an

233

LONGITUDINAL RESEARCH IN THE
STUDY OF BEHAVIOR AND DEVELOPMENT

attribute) at each of several successive time points. Moreover, the subjects may also be classified into a set of subpopulations on the basis of other categorical variables such as

7. Demographic characteristics
8. Health status with respect to the presence or absence of certain traits (e.g., dyslexia)
9. Program status with respect to certain specialized types of training

Within the context of this framework, the data resulting from longitudinal studies can be conceptually arrayed in (potentially very large) multidimensional contingency tables for which the corresponding dimensions are the classifications according to each attribute like 1–6 at each time point, together with the respective subpopulation variables like 7–9. For this reason, the various questions of interest for data analysis may be regarded as equivalent to statistical models for the cell probabilities in such contingency tables. Thus, in principle, data analysis can be undertaken in terms of various computational algorithms for contingency table-model fitting. As will be demonstrated in a later section, the weighted least-squares methods discussed by Grizzle, Starmer, and Koch (1969), and Koch, Landis, Freeman, Freeman and Lehnen (1977), and Landis, Stanish, Freeman, and Koch (1976) can be used to deal with questions pertaining to

1. The nature and extent of intraindividual change for the respective attributes over time, both separately and simultaneously
2. The nature and extent of interindividual differences among two or more subpopulations with respect to intraindividual change over time for the respective attributes
3. The nature and extent of the variation over time of the relationship among two or more attributes as reflected by certain measures of association

In this regard, the basic approach is in the same spirit as multivariate analysis of variance (profile analysis and/or growth analysis) with respect to analogous intervally scaled quantitative data situations. For this reason, explaining its application to longitudinal data is the primary purpose of this chapter. The types of examples where weighted least-squares methods are potentially most useful are briefly described in the next section. Specific formulations of the various hypotheses of interest are then presented in Section III, and their evaluation is illustrated in Section IV with respect to the examples in Section II. The chapter concludes with a brief discussion of certain special computational considerations for dealing with very large contingency tables, together with other potential difficulties that may arise in the analysis of longitudinal data.

Alternatively, in many investigations, the questions of interest pertain to the identification of the underlying structure of a large number of attributes in terms of a small number of implicit dimensions, and hence are analogous to those for which factor analysis is used with quantitative data. This topic is outside the scope of the present chapter. However, it is discussed to some extent by Goodman (1974) in the context of latent structure analysis. Similarly, the analysis of transition patterns over time for one or more attributes in terms of stochastic process models is also outside the scope of this chapter. Further information with respect to this general subject area is given in Bishop, Fienberg, and Holland (1975, Chapter 7).

II. Longitudinal Data Examples

In this section, we present two examples that may be regarded as methodologically illustrative data sets from longitudinal studies in human growth and development. In particular, a simple one-population study involving two attributes measured at two time points is considered in Section II.A to indicate the full range of hypotheses that can be tested. In addition, in Section II.B a two-population study involving one attribute measured at three points in time is used to illustrate the types of hypotheses associated with comparing growth curves among several groups. Although these examples involve hypothetical data and are much smaller in scope than those usually encountered in research situations, the extension to more complex designs is straightforward as developed in the Section III.

A. A Single-Population Example

The following hypothetical example arose from a longitudinal study in which two developmental attributes labeled $A1$ and $A2$ were measured at two time points labeled $T1$ and $T2$ for an age cohort of 354 children. In this regard, each subject was classified as absent (1) or present (2) for each of the attributes at each of the specified time points. The frequency data corresponding to each of the 16 possible response profiles is shown in Table 9.1.

The statistical issues concerning intraindividual change can be summarized within the framework of the following basic questions.

1. Are there any differences between the occurrence rates of the two attributes at each of the time points?
2. Are there any differences between the two time points with respect to the set of individual occurrence rates of the two attributes?
3. Is there any Attribute × Time interaction in the occurrence rates of the two attributes?
4. Are there any differences between the two time points with respect to the overall joint distribution of the two attributes?

TABLE 9.1
Attribute Data for Longitudinal Study

		Response profile for $A1$ and $A2$ at $T1$ and $T2$														
$T1$	$A1$	1	1	1	1	1	1	1	1	2	2	2	2	2	2	2	2
	$A2$	1	1	1	1	2	2	2	2	1	1	1	1	2	2	2	2
$T2$	$A1$	1	1	2	2	1	1	2	2	1	1	2	2	1	1	2	2
	$A2$	1	2	1	2	1	2	1	2	1	2	1	2	1	2	1	2
Frequency		57	36	18	69	0	0	0	33	0	3	0	15	0	0	0	123
Total		354

5. Is there any difference between the two time points with respect to a selected measure of association or agreement between the two attributes?

The first three questions, which involve the occurrence rates of the two attributes, are essentially similar to the hypotheses of interest in repeated-measurement (or mixed-model) experiments as discussed in further detail in Koch and Reinfurt (1971), Koch *et al.* (1977), and Landis and Koch (1977a). More specifically, Question 1 addresses differences among attributes, Question 2 involves the issue of time-point differences, and Question 3 is concerned with the Attribute × Time interaction as measured by the individual occurrence rates of the attributes. Thus, the first-order (univariate) marginal distributions of response for each of the attributes within each time point contain the relevant information for dealing with these questions. In contrast to overall average differences among the occurrence rates, Questions 4 and 5 address the relationship between the attributes on specific subjects across the time periods. As a result, these questions involve measures of association or agreement between the attributes such as those discussed in Bishop, Fienberg, and Holland (1975) and Landis and Koch (1975a, 1975b). Hence, certain functions of the diagonal cells of various subtables are used to provide information for dealing with these questions.

B. A Two-Population Example

The following hypothetical example arose from a longitudinal study to compare boys and girls from a selected age cohort with respect to their ability to perform a particular behavioral task. In this regard, each subject was graded as success (S) or failure (F) at the end of 1 year, 2 years, and 4 years of follow-up. These resulting data are shown in Table 9.2.

Accordingly, the statistical issues concerning these differences in growth patterns can be summarized within the framework of the following basic questions:

1. Are there any differences between the boys and the girls with respect to the behavioral-task success rates at the three time points?

TABLE 9.2
Longitudinal Data for Behavioral Task

| | \multicolumn{9}{c}{Response Profile at Year 1 versus Year 2 versus Year 4} |
	SSS	SSF	SFS	SFF	FSS	FSF	FFS	FFF	Total
Boys	0	0	5	0	21	14	51	71	162
Girls	16	5	12	5	71	12	74	14	209

2. Are there any differences among the three time points with respect to the behavioral-task success rates across the two groups of children?
3. Is there any Sex Group × Time interaction with respect to the behavioral-task success rate?

These three questions involving the success rates are directly analogous to the hypotheses of "no whole-plot effects," "no split-plot effects," and no whole-plot × split-plot interaction in standard split-plot experiments as described in Anderson and Bancroft (1952), Federer (1955), or Steel and Torrie (1960). In particular, since time is the split-plot factor, these resulting success rates give rise to growth profiles for each sex group. In this context, Question 1 addresses group differences, Question 2 involves the issue of time differences, and Question 3 is concerned with the hypothesis of parallelism among corresponding segments of the growth profiles. Consequently, the joint set of first-order (univariate) marginal distributions for each of the time points within each sex group contains the relevant information for dealing with these questions.

III. Methodology

This section is concerned with a general methodology for answering the types of questions outlined in Section II in terms of specific hypotheses. Because the measurement scales of the response variables (hereafter referred to as attributes) are categorical, the conceptual formulation of such hypotheses must be undertaken in terms of an underlying $(s \times r)$ contingency table, where s is the number of subpopulations and r is the number of possible multivariate response profiles. Test statistics for such hypotheses and the estimators for parameters of underlying linear regression models are obtained through weighted least squares computations by methods originally described in Grizzle, Starmer, and Koch (1969) (hereafter referenced as GSK) as reviewed in the Appendix. Consequently, this methodology represents a categorical data analogue to more well-known counterparts for quantitative data like multivariate analysis of variance as described by Cole and Grizzle (1966) and Morrison (1967) in the parametric case and multivariate rank analysis as described by Koch (1969, 1970) in the nonparametric case.

For longitudinal studies, each subject is measured on the same set of d attributes at each of t time points. In accordance with the general framework in the Appendix, let $i = 1, 2, \ldots, s$ index a set of subpopulations from which random samples have been selected. Let $m = 1, 2, \ldots, d$ index a set of d characteristics or attributes corresponding to behavioral tasks which are measured at each time point using an L_m-point scale. Then let the $r = (L_1 L_2 \cdots L_d)^t$ response profiles be indexed by a vector subscript $\mathbf{j} = (\mathbf{j}_1, \mathbf{j}_2, \ldots, \mathbf{j}_t)$ with $\mathbf{j}_g = (j_{g1}, j_{g2}, \ldots, j_{gd})$, where $j_{gm} = 1, 2, \ldots, L_m$ for $m = 1, 2, \ldots, d$ and $g = 1, 2, \ldots, t$. Furthermore, let $\pi_{i\mathbf{j}} = \pi_{i j_1, j_2, \ldots, j_t}$ represent the joint probability of response profile $\mathbf{j}$ for randomly selected subjects from the ith subpopulation. Then the first-order marginal probability

$$\phi_{igmk} = \sum_{\mathbf{j} \text{ with } j_{gm} = k} \cdots \sum \pi_{i j_1, j_2, \ldots, j_t} \tag{1}$$

for

$$i = 1, 2, \ldots, s \qquad g = 1, 2, \ldots, t$$
$$m = 1, 2, \ldots, d \qquad k = 1, 2, \ldots, L_m$$

represents the probability of the kth response category of the mth attribute at the gth time point in the ith subpopulation.

In addition, it should be noted here that this formulation for longitudinal studies presumes the following conditions:

1. There is no assumed structure on the attributes, so that all possible attribute combinations or response profiles are observable; that is, $\pi_{i\mathbf{j}} > 0$ for all $\mathbf{j}$ and for $i = 1, 2, \ldots, s$.
2. Every subject entering the study is followed until completion of the study; that is, there are no lost-to-follow-up cases.
3. Every subject is measured on each attribute at each time point; that is, there is no incomplete data.

Further discussion of these potential difficulties is given in the concluding section of the chapter.

A. Hypotheses Involving Marginal Distributions

Hypotheses directed at questions pertaining to average differences among subpopulations, attributes, and time points involve the first-order marginal distributions of the response profiles and can be expressed in terms of constraints on the corresponding probabilities $\{\phi_{igmk}\}$. More specifically, the hypotheses associated with Questions 1–3 of each of the examples in Section II can be formulated within the scope of one of the following statements:

1. If there are no differences among the marginal distributions of the

respective attributes at each time point for the s subpopulations, then the $\{\phi_{igmk}\}$ satisfy the hypothesis

$$H_{\text{SM}}: \quad \phi_{1gmk} = \phi_{2gmk} = \cdots = \phi_{sgmk} \tag{2}$$

for

$$g = 1, 2, \ldots, t, \qquad m = 1, 2, \ldots, d, \qquad k = 1, 2, \ldots, L_m,$$

where SM denotes subpopulations means.

2. If there are no differences among the marginal distributions of the respective attributes over the t time points within each of the subpopulations, then the $\{\phi_{igmk}\}$ satisfy the hypothesis of composite first-order marginal homogeneity (symmetry)

$$H_{\text{TMH}}: \quad \phi_{i1mk} = \phi_{i2mk} = \cdots = \phi_{itmk} \tag{3}$$

for

$$i = 1, 2, \ldots, s, \qquad m = 1, 2, \ldots, d, \qquad k = 1, 2, \ldots, L_m,$$

where TMH denotes time marginal homogeneity.

3. If there is no Time $\times$ Subgroup interaction (with respect to the marginal distributions of the respective attributes at the t time points), then the $\{\phi_{igmk}\}$ can be written in terms of an additive model

$$H_{\text{ST}}: \quad \phi_{igmk} = \mu_{mk} + \xi_{i*mk} + \tau_{*gmk} \tag{4}$$

for

$$i = 1, 2, \ldots, s, \qquad g = 1, 2, \ldots, t,$$

$$m = 1, 2, \ldots, d, \qquad k = 1, 2, \ldots, L_m,$$

where ST denotes subgroup $\times$ time, and where for the mth attribute, μ_{mk} is an overall mean associated with the kth response category, ξ_{i*mk} is an effect due to the ith subpopulation, and τ_{*gmk} is an effect due to the gth time point, and where it is understood that the $\{\mu_{mk}\}$, $\{\xi_{i*mk}\}$, and $\{\tau_{*gmk}\}$ satisfy the usual analysis of variance constraints.

Moreover, if the d attributes are all measured on the same L-point scale, it follows that $L_m = L$ for $m = 1, 2, \ldots, d$. For example, each attribute may be classified as present or absent as proposed in the single-population example presented earlier, or each attribute may represent a different scheme of classifying development under the assumption that there exists an identical number of stages as discussed in Wohlwill (1973). In such situations, several additional hypotheses of this type may become of interest.

4. If there are no differences among the marginal distributions of the

attributes at each of the time points within each of the subpopulations, then the $\{\phi_{igmk}\}$ satisfy the hypothesis of marginal homogeneity (symmetry) among the attributes

$$H_{\text{AMH}}: \quad \phi_{ig1k} = \phi_{ig2k} = \cdots = \phi_{igmk} \tag{5}$$

for

$$i = 1, 2, \ldots, s, \quad g = 1, 2, \ldots, t, \quad k = 1, 2, \ldots, L,$$

where AMH denotes attribute marginal homogeneity.

5. If there is no interaction between the marginal distributions of the attributes and time within each subpopulation, then the $\{\phi_{igmk}\}$ may be written in terms of an additive model

$$H_{\text{AT}}: \quad \phi_{igmk} = \mu_{ik} + \xi_{ig*k} + \tau_{i*mk} \tag{6}$$

for

$$i = 1, 2, \ldots, s, \quad g = 1, 2, \ldots, t,$$

$$m = 1, 2, \ldots, d, \quad k = 1, 2, \ldots, L,$$

where AT denotes Attribute × Time, and where for the ith subpopulation, μ_{ik} is an overall mean associated with the kth response category, ξ_{ig*k} is an effect due to the gth time point, and τ_{i*mk} is an effect due to the mth attribute, and where it is understood that the $\{\mu_{ik}\}$, $\{\xi_{ig*k}\}$, and $\{\tau_{i*mk}\}$ satisfy the usual analysis-of-variance constraints.

All of these considerations can be extended somewhat further if the response categories $k = 1, 2, \ldots, L_m$ for $m = 1, 2, \ldots, d$ are ordinally scaled with progressively large intensities. In this situation, the effects of the respective subpopulations, attributes, and time points can be compared in terms of summary indexes

$$\eta_{igm} = \sum_{k=1}^{L_m} a_{mk}\phi_{igmk} \tag{7}$$

for

$$i = 1, 2, \ldots, s, \quad g = 1, 2, \ldots, t, \quad m = 1, 2, \ldots, d.$$

Here η_{igm} can be regarded as a mean score for the mth attribute at the gth time period in the ith subpopulation with respect to an underlying numerical scaling $a_{m1}, a_{m2}, \ldots, a_{mL_m}$ of the L_m categories. In this context, the $\{\eta_{igm}\}$ are equivalent to mean scores derived from strictly quantitatively scaled response categories as discussed in Bhapkar (1966). Thus, the hypotheses in Eqs. (2–6) can also be expressed in terms of constraints on the $\{\eta_{igm}\}$ in Eq. (7). Expressions of these hypotheses in terms of the $\{\eta_{igm}\}$ are discussed in more detail in Koch *et al.* (1977) and are illustrated in Landis (1975).

B. Hypotheses Involving Measures of Association

Whereas the hypotheses in Section IIIA were addressed to comparisons among subpopulations, time points, and attributes within the context of first-order marginal distributions, the hypotheses in this section are directed at relationships among the attributes at a given time point, and the extent to which those relationships change across time. These hypotheses can be formulated in terms of comparisons among full joint distributions or second and higher-order joint marginal distributions across time periods or in terms of measures of association such as the log cross-product ratio for nominal data as discussed in Bhapkar and Koch (1968a, 1968b) or the Goodman-Kruskal rank correlation coefficient for ordinal data as discussed in Forthofer and Koch (1973).

In general, these hypotheses can be expressed as a set of constraint equations on the joint probabilities of specified response profiles. For purposes of simplicity, we will focus on the joint distributions of two selected attributes (relabeled as 1 and 2) at each of the t time points for each of the s subpopulations. Consequently, the joint probability of the k_1th category on the m_1th attribute and the k_2th category on the m_2th attribute at the gth time point in the ith subpopulation can be written as

$$\Psi_{igk_1k_2} = \sum_{j \text{ with } j_{gm_1}=k_1 \text{ and } j_{gm_2}=} \cdots \sum_{k_2} \pi_{ij_1,j_2,\ldots,j_t}. \tag{8}$$

Using this notation, the log cross-product measures of association between the two attributes can then be expressed as

$$\Delta_{igk_1k_2} = \log_e \left\{ \frac{\Psi_{igk_1k_2} \Psi_{igL_1L_2}}{\Psi_{igL_1k_2} \Psi_{igk_1L_2}} \right\} \tag{9}$$

for

$$i = 1, 2, \ldots, s, \qquad g = 1, 2, \ldots, t,$$
$$k_1 = 1, 2, \ldots, L_1 - 1, \qquad k_2 = 1, 2, \ldots, L_2 - 1.$$

In particular, for two dichotomous attributes ($L_1 = L_2 = 2$), the measures of association $\{\Delta_{igk_1k_2}\}$ in Eq. (9) reduce to the familiar log cross-product ratio for a 2×2 table

$$\Delta_{ig} = \log_e \left\{ \frac{\Psi_{ig11} \Psi_{ig22}}{\Psi_{ig21} \Psi_{ig12}} \right\} \tag{10}$$

for

$$i = 1, 2, \ldots, s, \qquad g = 1, 2, \ldots, t.$$

Otherwise, an alternative measure of association for 2×2 tables due to Yule can be formulated as

$$Q_{ig} = \frac{\Psi_{ig11} \Psi_{ig22} - \Psi_{ig21} \Psi_{ig12}}{\Psi_{ig11} \Psi_{ig22} + \Psi_{ig21} \Psi_{ig12}} \tag{11}$$

for

$$i = 1, 2, \ldots, s, \qquad g = 1, 2, \ldots, t.$$

(For a more complete discussion of measures of association, see Bishop, Fienberg, and Holland, 1975, Chapter 11.)

Hypotheses concerning comparisons among full joint distributions of the attributes can now be expressed in terms of constraints on the joint probabilities $\{\Psi_{igk_1k_2}\}$. More specifically, hypotheses associated with questions such as 4 in Section IIA can be formulated within the scope of one of the following statements:

6. If there are no differences among the joint distributions of the two attributes among the subpopulations, then the $\{\Psi_{igk_1k_2}\}$ satisfy the hypothesis

$$H_{\mathrm{SJD}}: \quad \Psi_{1gk_1k_2} = \Psi_{2gk_1k_2} = \cdots = \Psi_{sgk_1k_2} \tag{12}$$

for

$$g = 1, 2, \ldots, t, \qquad k_1 = 1, 2, \ldots, L_1, \qquad k_2 = 1, 2, \ldots, L_2,$$

where SJD denotes subpopulation joint distributions.

7. If there are no differences among the joint distributions of the two attributes among the time points, then the $\{\Psi_{igk_1k_2}\}$ satisfy the hypothesis

$$H_{\mathrm{TJD}}: \quad \Psi_{i1k_1k_2} = \Psi_{i2k_1k_2} = \cdots = \Psi_{itk_1k_2} \tag{13}$$

for

$$i = 1, 2, \ldots, s, \qquad k_1 = 1, 2, \ldots, L_1, \qquad k_2 = 1, 2, \ldots, L_2,$$

where TJD denotes time joint distributions.

Additional hypotheses involving the joint-distribution probabilities in Eq. (8), such as an additive model implying no interaction between subpopulations and time periods directly analogous to Eq. (4), could also be considered here. Moreover, hypothesis of "no interaction" among higher-order joint distributions involving more than two attributes simultaneously can be developed as direct extensions of these results, although the notation for corresponding expressions becomes more cumbersome. Similar considerations also apply to hypotheses of "no interaction" for the joint distribution over time of each separate attribute and/or simultaneous sets of attributes. Finally, a log-linear model can be fitted to the joint distribution of the attributes at each time point under appropriate hypotheses of "no interaction" as discussed in Koch *et al.* (1977). This approach then permits hypothesis testing for relationship across the time points in terms of the resulting log-linear-model parameters.

Alternatively, several hypotheses associated with questions such as 5 in Section IIA involving the measures of association in Eq. (9) can be formulated as follows:

8. If the two selected attributes are independent of each other at each time point within each subpopulation, then the $\{\Delta_{igk_1k_2}\}$ satisfy the hypothesis

$$H_{\text{PI}}: \quad \Delta_{igk_1k_2} = 0 \tag{14}$$

for

$$i = 1, 2, \ldots, s, \qquad g = 1, 2, \ldots, t,$$
$$k_1 = 1, 2, \ldots, L_1 - 1, \qquad k_2 = 1, 2, \ldots, L_2 - 1,$$

where PI denotes pairwise independence.

9. If the relationship between the two attributes as measured by the log cross-product ratio is the same across the time points for each subpopulation, then the $\{\Delta_{igk_1k_2}\}$ satisfy the hypothesis.

$$H_{\text{TA}}: \quad \Delta_{i1k_1k_2} = \Delta_{i2k_1k_2} = \cdots = \Delta_{itk_1k_2} \tag{15}$$

for

$$i = 1, 2, \ldots, s, \quad k_1 = 1, 2, \ldots, L_1 - 1, \quad k_2 = 1, 2, \ldots, L_2 - 1,$$

where TA denotes time association.

10. If the relationship between the two attributes as measured by the log cross-product ratio is the same across subpopulations at each time point, then the $\{\Delta_{igk_1k_2}\}$ satisfy the hypothesis

$$H_{\text{SA}}: \quad \Delta_{1gk_1k_2} = \Delta_{2gk_1k_2} = \cdots = \Delta_{sgk_1k_2} \tag{16}$$

for

$$g = 1, 2, \ldots, t, \quad k_1 = 1, 2, \ldots, L_1 - 1, \quad k_2 = 1, 2, \ldots, L_2 - 1,$$

where SA denotes subpopulation association.

11. If there is no Subpopulation × Time interaction with respect to the log cross-product ratio measure of association, then the $\{\Delta_{igk_1k_2}\}$ can be written in terms of an additive model

$$H_{\text{STA}}: \quad \Delta_{igk_1k_2} = \mu_{k_1k_2} + \xi_{i*k_1k_2} + \tau_{*gk_1k_2} \tag{17}$$

for

$$i = 1, 2, \ldots, s, \qquad g = 1, 2, \ldots, t,$$

$$k_1 = 1, 2, \ldots, L_1 - 1, \qquad k_2 = 1, 2, \ldots, L_2 - 1,$$

where STA denotes Subpopulation $\times$ Time Association, and where $\mu_{k_1 k_2}$ is an overall mean effect, $\xi_{i*k_1 k_2}$ is a subpopulation effect, and $\tau_{*gk_1 k_2}$ is a time effect, and where it is understood that the $\{\mu_{k_1 k_2}\}$, $\{\xi_{i*k_1 k_2}\}$ and $\{\tau_{*gk_1 k_2}\}$ satisfy the usual analysis-of-variance constraints. For an application of this type of additive model to measures of association, see Grizzle and Williams (1972).

Moreover, if the d attributes are all measured on the same L-point scale, hypotheses directed at the extent to which individual subjects are classified into the same category for each attribute can be investigated. For example, agreement on the classification of developmental stages by several different criteria is of considerable importance in establishing certain theories of behavioral growth (see Wohlwill, 1973). These problems are similar to those raised in the general area concerned with the measurement of agreement, and as such have received attention in a wide range of research areas as reviewed recently in Landis and Koch (1975a, 1975b). In this regard, numerous measures of observer agreement have been proposed for categorical data—for example, Goodman and Kruskal (1954), Cohen (1960, 1968), Fleiss (1971), Light (1971), and Cicchetti (1972). Most of these quantities are of the form

$$\kappa = (\pi_0 - \pi_e)/(1 - \pi_e) \tag{18}$$

where π_0 is an observational probability of agreement and π_e is a hypothetical expected probability of agreement under an appropriate set of baseline constraints such as total independence of attribute classifications.

Furthermore, kappa-type measures of agreement directly analogous to Eq. (18) can be developed to investigate the joint agreement of several attributes, as well as the pairwise agreements of two selected attributes. In addition, sets of weights that reflect the role of each response profile in a given agreement index can be selected to investigate "path" models of development among several behavioral tasks as discussed in Wohlwill (1973). Applications of such generalized kappa-type measures of agreement to clinical diagnosis data involving several observers is discussed in Landis and Koch (1977a, 1977b). In particular, the choice of weights that are in a hierarchical relationship with each other can be used to investigate hypothesized patterns of development such as synchronous progression, convergent "decalage," divergent "decalage," and reciprocal interaction (see Wohlwill, 1973, p. 215).

C. Estimation and Hypothesis Testing

Test statistics for the hypotheses considered in the previous sections as well as estimators for corresponding model parameters can be obtained by using the general approach for the analysis of multivariate categorical data discussed by GSK (1969). This procedure can be implemented by constructing the appropriate functions of the observed proportions that are directed at the relationships under investigation by a sequence of matrix operations. Then a weighted least-squares computational algorithm is used to generate linearized minimum modified chi-square test statistics. The basic elements of the GSK procedure that pertain to this chapter are summarized in the Appendix.

All the hypotheses involving constraints on the first-order marginal probabilities, discussed earlier, can be tested by expressing the estimates of the $\{\phi_{igmk}\}$ or the $\{\eta_{igm}\}$ as linear functions of the type given in the Appendix, Eq. (A.14). Although these particular matrix expressions have already been discussed in considerable detail in Koch and Reinfurt (1971) and Koch *et al.* (1977) they will be presented within the context of the data analysis in the next section. Otherwise, their specific construction for hypotheses like Eq. (2)–Eq (6) is also documented in Landis (1975).

In contrast to the linear functions that pertain to the hypotheses involving marginal distributions, all the hypotheses involving measures of association and agreement require the expression of the corresponding ratio estimates as compounded logarithmic–exponential–linear functions of the observed proportions as formulated in the Appendix, Eqs. (A.20) and (A.21). As a result, the test statistics for these hypotheses can also be generated by the corresponding expression given in the Appendix, Eq. (A.11).

IV. Analysis of Longitudinal Data Examples

This section is concerned with the analysis of the longitudinal data from the examples presented in Tables 9.1 and 9.2 with primary emphasis given to illustrating the methodology in Section III. In this regard, tests of significance are used in a descriptive context to identify important sources of variation as opposed to a rigorous inferential context; thus, issues pertaining to multiple comparisons are ignored here. These, however, can be handled by the Scheffé-type procedures given in GSK (1969).

A. Analysis of One-Population Example

The comparisons required to answer the questions associated with this example can be described more clearly within the context of two subtables of Table 9.1 corresponding to the cross-classification of the two attributes at each time point as shown in Table 9.3.

This study involves $s = 1$ subpopulation, $t = 2$ time points ($T1$ and $T2$), $d = 2$ attributes ($A1$ and $A2$), $L_1 = 2$ response categories for A_1 and $L_2 = 2$ response categories for A_2. Thus, there are $r = (L_1 L_2)^t = 4^2 = 16$ possible multivariate response profiles.

The functions required to test the hypotheses involving the first-order marginal distributions can be generated in the formulation of Eq. (A.14) by using

$$\mathbf{A}_1 = \begin{bmatrix} 0000 & 0000 & 1111 & 1111 \\ 0000 & 1111 & 0000 & 1111 \\ 0011 & 0011 & 0011 & 0011 \\ 0101 & 0101 & 0101 & 0101 \end{bmatrix}. \tag{19}$$

This yields the function vector

$$\mathbf{F}' = (.398, .441, .729, .788), \tag{20}$$

which contains the occurrence rates of $A1$ and $A2$ at each of the time points as shown in Figure 9.1. Consequently, the hypotheses associated with Questions (1)–(3) can be tested in the linear-models phase of the analysis by setting $\mathbf{X} = \mathbf{I}_4$ and testing each of the following contrast matrices:

$$\mathbf{C}_1 = \begin{bmatrix} 1 & -1 & 0 & 0 \\ 0 & 0 & 1 & -1 \end{bmatrix}, \tag{21}$$

$$\mathbf{C}_2 = [1 \quad -1 \quad 0 \quad 0], \tag{22}$$

$$\mathbf{C}_3 = [0 \quad 0 \quad 1 \quad -1], \tag{23}$$

$$\mathbf{C}_4 = \begin{bmatrix} 1 & 0 & -1 & 0 \\ 0 & 1 & 0 & -1 \end{bmatrix}, \tag{24}$$

$$\mathbf{C}_5 = [1 \quad 0 \quad -1 \quad 0], \tag{25}$$

$$\mathbf{C}_6 = [0 \quad 1 \quad 0 \quad -1], \tag{26}$$

$$\mathbf{C}_7 = [1 \quad -1 \quad -1 \quad 1]. \tag{27}$$

TABLE 9.3
Cross-Classification of Attribute Data by Time Points

Time point × Attribute	$T1 \times A2$				$T2 \times A2$			
	Category	1	2	Total	Category	1	2	Total
$A1$	1	180	33	213	1	57	39	96
	2	18	123	141	2	18	240	258
	Total	198	156	354	Total	75	279	354

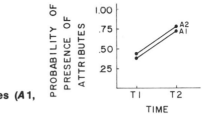

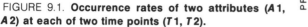

FIGURE 9.1. **Occurrence rates of two attributes (A 1, A 2) at each of two time points (T 1, T 2).**

The hypotheses from Section III that correspond to the **C** matrices and the resulting test statistics are given in Table 9.4. These results suggest that significant differences ($\alpha = .05$) exist between the occurrence rates of the attributes at each of the time points, and that the occurrence rates of each attribute are significantly different ($\alpha = .01$) between the time points. Otherwise, the attribute $\times$ time interaction is not significant ($\alpha = .25$), which indicates the similarity of the change over time in the occurrence rates of the two attributes.

The data from Table 9.1 can be displayed in terms of the joint distribution of the two attributes cross-classified by the time points as shown in Table 9.5. In this context, the bivariate distributions of the two attributes for $T1$ and $T2$ are summarized in the row and column margins respectively. This joint distribution can be generated for each time point in the formulation of Eq. (A.14) by using

$$\mathbf{A}_1 = \begin{bmatrix} 1111 & 0000 & 0000 & 0000 \\ 0000 & 1111 & 0000 & 0000 \\ 0000 & 0000 & 1111 & 0000 \\ 1000 & 1000 & 1000 & 1000 \\ 0100 & 0100 & 0100 & 0100 \\ 0010 & 0010 & 0010 & 0010 \end{bmatrix} . \tag{28}$$

Then by setting $\mathbf{X} = \mathbf{I}_6$, the hypothesis H_{TJD} in Eq. (13) associated with Question 4 concerning differences between the two time points can be tested by using

$$\mathbf{C} = \begin{bmatrix} 1 & 0 & 0 & -1 & 0 & 0 \\ 0 & 1 & 0 & 0 & -1 & 0 \\ 0 & 0 & 1 & 0 & 0 & -1 \end{bmatrix} . \tag{29}$$

For these data, the test statistic for H_{TJD} is $Q_C = 268.53$ with $df = 3$, which implies significant differences ($\alpha = .01$) between the joint distributions of $A1$ and $A2$ at the two time points. In particular, we observe in Table 9.5 that the major difference in the bivariate distributions is the shift from the large proportion (180/354) of the subjects who had neither attribute present at $T1$ to the large proportion (240/354) who had both attributes present at $T2$. However, we also note that this shift was not attributable

TABLE 9.4
Tests of Hypotheses Involving Marginal Distributions

Hypothesis	Degrees of freedom	Q_C
H_{AMH}: Attributes		
C_1 ($T1$ and $T2$)	2	13.32^a
C_2 ($T1$)	1	4.47^b
C_3 ($T2$)	1	7.91^a
H_{TMH}: Time		
C_4 ($A1$ and $A2$)	2	268.52^a
C_5 ($A1$)	1	162.33^a
C_6 ($A2$)	1	188.49^a
H_{AT}: Attribute × Time		
C_7	1	.32

[a] Significant at $\alpha = 0.01$
[b] Significant at $\alpha = 0.05$

only to individual subjects moving directly from (11) to (22). In fact, this distributional change is due to the high proportion (48/51) of subjects who had only one of the attributes present at $T1$ moving to the state of having both attributes present at $T2$, together with the tendency for those who had neither attribute present at $T1$ to progress to having either one or both of the attributes present at $T2$.

Although observed frequencies of zero as displayed in Table 9.5 can cause computational problems in certain applications, their presence is not troublesome here. In principle, this table has 15 df but in terms of the observed data there are effectively only 7 df that can be manipulated (without computational singularities as discussed in the Appendix), unless certain zero cells are replaced by 0.5. However, the six functions associated with the bivariate distributions specified in Eq. (28) do not require such artificial data adjustments; thus, they can be analyzed directly. For a more

TABLE 9.5
Joint Distribution of Attributes Cross-Classified by Time Points

	Attribute categories ($A1$, $A2$)	Time point ($T2$)				Total
		11	12	21	22	
Time point	11	57	36	18	69	180
($T1$)	12	0	0	0	33	33
	21	0	3	0	15	18
	22	0	0	0	123	123
	Total	57	39	18	240	354

detailed discussion concerning the treatment of observed zeros, see Koch *et al.* (1977).

Furthermore, the measures of association and agreement between $A1$ and $A2$ in the preceeding section can be generated as compounded functions of the underlying vector of proportions. In particular, for each of the two time points, the log cross-product ratio in Eq. (10) can be generated in the formulation of Eq. (A.20) by using

$$\mathbf{A}_1 = \begin{bmatrix} 1111 & 0000 & 0000 & 0000 \\ 0000 & 1111 & 0000 & 0000 \\ 0000 & 0000 & 1111 & 0000 \\ 0000 & 0000 & 0000 & 1111 \\ 1000 & 1000 & 1000 & 1000 \\ 0100 & 0100 & 0100 & 0100 \\ 0010 & 0010 & 0010 & 0010 \\ 0001 & 0001 & 0001 & 0001 \end{bmatrix}, \tag{30}$$

$$\mathbf{A}_2 = \begin{bmatrix} 1 & -1 & -1 & 1 & 0 & 0 & 0 & 0 \\ 0 & 0 & 0 & 0 & 1 & -1 & -1 & 1 \end{bmatrix}, \tag{31}$$

the measure of association Q in Eq. (11) can be estimated in the formulation of Eq. (A.21) by using $\mathbf{A}_1$ in Eq. (30);

$$\mathbf{A}_2 = \begin{bmatrix} 1001 & 0000 \\ 0110 & 0000 \\ 0000 & 1001 \\ 0000 & 0110 \end{bmatrix}, \tag{32}$$

$$\mathbf{A}_3 = \begin{bmatrix} 1 & -1 & 0 & 0 \\ 1 & 1 & 0 & 0 \\ 0 & 0 & 1 & -1 \\ 0 & 0 & 1 & 1 \end{bmatrix}, \tag{33}$$

$$\mathbf{A}_4 = \begin{bmatrix} 1 & -1 \end{bmatrix} \tag{34}$$

and finally, Cohen's kappa in Eq. (18) under the baseline constraints of independence can be computed in the formulation of Eq. (A.21) by letting

$$\mathbf{A}_1 = \begin{bmatrix} 1111 & 1111 & 0000 & 0000 \\ 0000 & 0000 & 1111 & 1111 \\ 1111 & 0000 & 1111 & 0000 \\ 0000 & 1111 & 0000 & 1111 \\ 1111 & 0000 & 0000 & 1111 \\ 1100 & 1100 & 1100 & 1100 \\ 0011 & 0011 & 0011 & 0011 \\ 1010 & 1010 & 1010 & 1010 \\ 0101 & 0101 & 0101 & 0101 \\ 1001 & 1001 & 1001 & 1001 \end{bmatrix}, \tag{35}$$

$$\mathbf{A}_2 = \begin{bmatrix} 10100 & 00000 \\ 10010 & 00000 \\ 01100 & 00000 \\ 01010 & 00000 \\ 00001 & 00000 \\ 00000 & 10100 \\ 00000 & 10010 \\ 00000 & 01100 \\ 00000 & 01010 \\ 00000 & 00001 \end{bmatrix}, \tag{36}$$

$$\mathbf{A}_3 = \begin{bmatrix} -1 & 0 & 0 & -1 & 1 & 0 & 0 & 0 & 0 & 0 \\ 0 & 1 & 1 & 0 & 0 & 0 & 0 & 0 & 0 & 0 \\ 0 & 0 & 0 & 0 & 0 & -1 & 0 & 0 & -1 & 1 \\ 0 & 0 & 0 & 0 & 0 & 0 & 1 & 1 & 0 & 0 \end{bmatrix}, \tag{37}$$

$$\mathbf{A}_4 = \begin{bmatrix} 1 & -1 & 0 & 0 \\ 0 & 0 & 1 & -1 \end{bmatrix}. \tag{38}$$

The estimates of these measures of association and agreement between $A1$ and $A2$ for the data in Table 9.1, together with their estimated standard errors are displayed in Table 9.6. Furthermore, the difference between the two time points with respect to each of these measures of association can be tested individually by setting $\mathbf{X} = \mathbf{I}_2$ and $\mathbf{C} = [1 - 1]$ for Δ, Q, and κ respectively. In this regard, the corresponding test statistics for this hypothesis in Eq. (15) associated with Question (5) are displayed in Table 9.7. Here we note that although the correlation structure between $A1$ and $A2$ (as measured either by Δ or Q) did not change between $T1$ and $T2$, the agreement between $A1$ and $A2$ is significantly different ($\alpha = .05$) between the two time points. This decrease in the agreement statistic from .70 to .56 is due largely to the increase in the expected value for the presence of both attributes (22), without a corresponding increase in the observed proportion of overall agreement.

TABLE 9.6
Measures of Association and Agreement between A1 and A2

	Time period ($T1$)		Time period ($T2$)	
	Estimate	Estimated standard error	Estimate	Estimated standard error
Δ	3.62	.316	2.97	.321
Q	.95	.016	.90	.030
κ	.70	.038	.56	.051

TABLE 9.7
Test Statistics for Time Differences in Measures of Association and Agreement between A1 and A2

Hypothesis	Degrees of freedom	Q_C
$\Delta_1 = \Delta_2$	1	2.02
$Q_1 = Q_2$	1	1.76
$\kappa_1 = \kappa_2$	1	5.03[a]

[a] Significant at $\alpha = 0.05$.

B. Analysis of Two-Population Example

The example in the second section involves $s = 2$ subpopulations (boys, girls), $t = 3$ time periods (Year 1, Year 2, Year 4), $d = 1$ behavioral task, and $L = 2$ response categories (success S and failure F). Thus, there are $r = L^t = 2^3 = 8$ possible multivariate response profiles. In this regard, differences in the growth profiles for the boys and girls can be investigated by using

$$\mathbf{A}_1 = \begin{bmatrix} 1 & 1 & 1 & 1 & 0 & 0 & 0 & 0 \\ 0 & 0 & 0 & 0 & 1 & 1 & 1 & 1 \\ 1 & 1 & 0 & 0 & 1 & 1 & 0 & 0 \\ 0 & 0 & 1 & 1 & 0 & 0 & 1 & 1 \\ 1 & 0 & 1 & 0 & 1 & 0 & 1 & 0 \\ 0 & 1 & 0 & 1 & 0 & 1 & 0 & 1 \end{bmatrix} \otimes \mathbf{I}_2 \qquad (39)$$

to generate estimates for the first-order marginal probabilities of success (S) shown in Figure 9.2 and failure (F) for each time × sex group combination in the formulation of Eq. (A.14), where $\otimes$ denotes Kronecker product of matrices and $\mathbf{I}_u$ is the $u \times u$ identity matrix. Although a straightforward profile analysis could be performed directly on these estimated marginal probabilities, we will illustrate an alternative approach involving an under-

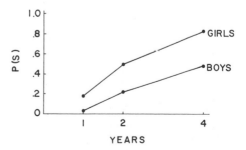

FIGURE 9.2. **Probability of success [P(S)] on a behavioral task for boys and girls at three different years of age.**

lying logistic model that is often of interest in growth studies (e.g., see Guire & Kowalski, Chapter 5, this volume, and Kowalski & Guire, 1974). These involve log ratios or logit functions that can be generated in the formulation of Eq. (A.20) by selecting $A_2 = [1 - 1] \otimes I_6$, together with A_1 in Eq. (39). These estimated probabilities of success and their corresponding logits, together with their respective estimated standard errors are shown in Table 9.8.

For this analysis, let λ_{ig} denote the asymptotic expected value of the logit corresponding to the ith sex and gth year. If time is assumed to represent a metric that is analogous to drug dosage in quantal bioassay research, then the linear logistic model with respect to log time represents a reasonable model by analogy to well-known results discussed by Berkson (1944, 1953, 1955) or Finney (1964). More specifically, we first consider the model

$$\lambda_{ig} = \mu_i + \gamma_i x_{ig} \qquad \text{for} \quad i = 1, 2; \quad g = 1, 2, 3; \tag{40}$$

where μ_i represents an intercept parameter in reference to Year 1 that is associated with the ith sex, γ_i represents a corresponding continuous slope effect over time, and x_{ig} is the log to the base 2 of year g for the ith sex. In matrix notation, this model can be fitted via the regression model

$$
E_A\{F\} = X_1\beta_1 =
\begin{bmatrix}
1 & 0 & 0 & 0 \\
1 & 1 & 0 & 0 \\
1 & 2 & 0 & 0 \\
0 & 0 & 1 & 0 \\
0 & 0 & 1 & 1 \\
0 & 0 & 1 & 2
\end{bmatrix}
\begin{bmatrix}
\mu_1 \\
\gamma_1 \\
\mu_2 \\
\gamma_2
\end{bmatrix},
\tag{41}
$$

for which the goodness-of-fit statistic is $Q = 2.29$ with $df = 2$. The hypotheses and test statistics in Table 9.9 suggest differences exist among the respective sex groups with respect to the intercept, but not the slope. On

TABLE 9.8

Observed and Predicted Estimates for First-Order Marginal Probabilities of Success and Corresponding Logits

Sex Group	Year	Observed est. prob. success	Est. s.e.	Observed est. logit	Est. s.e.	Predicted est. logit	Est. s.e.	Predicted est. prob. success	Est. s.e.
Boys	1	.03	.01	-3.45	.45	-2.99	.20	.05	.01
Boys	2	.22	.03	-1.29	.19	-1.50	.14	.18	.02
Boys	4	.48	.04	$-.10$	.16	.00	.14	.50	.03
Girls	1	.18	.03	-1.50	.18	-1.48	.14	.19	.02
Girls	2	.50	.03	$-.01$	.14	.01	.09	.50	.02
Girls	4	.83	.03	1.57	.18	1.51	.14	.82	.02

TABLE 9.9
Statistical Tests for X_1 Model

Hypothesis	Degrees of freedom	Q_C
$\mu_1 = \mu_2$	1	18.95[a]
$\gamma_1 = \gamma_2$	1	.22

[a] Significant at $\alpha = .01$

the basis of these results, the original model can be simplifed to

$$E_A\{F\} = X_2\beta_2 = \begin{bmatrix} 1 & 0 & 0 \\ 1 & 0 & 1 \\ 1 & 0 & 2 \\ 0 & 1 & 0 \\ 0 & 1 & 1 \\ 0 & 1 & 2 \end{bmatrix} \begin{bmatrix} \mu_1 \\ \mu_2 \\ \gamma \end{bmatrix} \tag{42}$$

where μ_i is the intercept parameter for the ith sex group and γ is an overall slope parameter. For this model, the goodness-of-fit statistic is $Q = 2.51$ with $df = 3$, which suggests that this reduced model provides a satisfactory characterization of the variation among the logits. The corresponding estimated parameter vector b_2 and its estimated covariance matrix V_{b_2} are given in Eq. (43).

$$b_2 = \begin{bmatrix} -2.99 \\ -1.48 \\ 1.50 \end{bmatrix} ; \quad V_{b_2} = \begin{bmatrix} 3.99 & & \\ 1.60 & 1.94 & \\ -1.60 & -1.07 & 1.07 \end{bmatrix} \times 10^{-2} \tag{43}$$

From these results, the predicted logits shown in Table 9.8 can be determined via Eq. (A.12). These can be used to obtain the predicted values for the first-order marginal probabilities of success (S) responses by reverse transformation, which are illustrated in considerably more detail in Koch *et al.* (1977) and Landis *et al.* (1976). These quantities are also shown in Table 9.8 and are plotted in Figure 9.3 within the context of fitted logistic curves. Estimated standard errors for these predicted values obtained through suitable manipulations of Eq. (A.13) are substantially smaller than those for the corresponding observed estimates, and thus reflect the extent to which the fitted model X_2 enhances statistical efficiency.

Finally, it can be shown that for this linear logistic model the parametric functions $(-\mu_i/\gamma)$ represent the median ages for successful performance of the behavioral task (the ED-50 analogue from bioassay studies) in the ith sex group. Estimates for these quantities are obtained as corresponding functions of b_2 and are shown in Table 9.10.

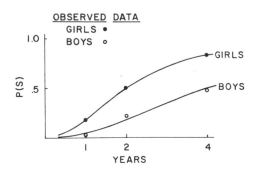

FIGURE 9.3. **Fitted logistic curves to probability of success [P(S)] on a behavioral task for boys and girls at three different years of age.**

V. Dicussion

Although the methodology for the analysis of longitudinal data developed in this chapter is quite general, these procedures have been illustrated with relatively simple examples. However, for situations in which either the number of time points t, the number of attributes d, or the number of categories $L_1, L_2, \ldots, L_d$ are moderately large, the number of possible multivariate response profiles $r = (L_1 L_2 \ldots L_d)^t$ becomes extremely large. Consequently, the matrices required to implement the GSK procedures directly may be outside the scope of computational feasibility. In addition, for each of the s subpopulations many of the r possible response profiles will not necessarily be observed in the respective samples so that corresponding cell frequencies are zero. Thus, in such cases, specialized computing procedures are required to obtain the estimates of the pertinent functions.

One alternative approach for handling such very large contingency tables in which most of the observed cell frequencies are zero is discussed in Koch *et al.* (1977) and is illustrated in Landis and Koch (1977b). Specifically, this approach permits the same estimators that would need to be obtained from the conceptual multidimensional contingency table to be generated by first forming appropriate indicator variables of the raw data from each subject, and then computing the across-subject arithmetic means. Subsequent to

TABLE 9.10
Estimated Median Age for Successful Performance of Behavioral Task

	Estimated median age	Estimated standard error
Boys	4.00	.25
Girls	1.99	.09

these preliminary steps, the usual matrix operations discussed in the Appendix can then be applied to these indicator variable means to generate the required functions. These alternative computations involving raw data, as well as these involving standard contingency table data, can all be performed via the computer program GENCAT discussed in Landis *et al.* (1976).

Otherwise, several additional potential difficulties associated with the introductory remarks in Section III may arise in the analysis of longitudinal data in studies of human growth and development. First of all, if the response profiles are assumed to be structured (e.g., as specified by certain irreversible growth or learning patterns as discussed in Wohlwill, 1973), some of the π_{ij} will be zero. In such situations, analogous hypotheses to those discussed in the third section that reflect these restrictions imposed by such structures can be taken into account by suitably modifying the definition of the appropriate hypotheses. In particular, the hypotheses pertaining to the first-order marginal probabilities are still appropriate here because their formulation is consistent with the available degrees of freedom. However, the higher-order margins involving joint distributions or measures of association may not be feasible, depending specifically on the nature of the restrictions involved. Secondly, the methods discussed in Koch, Johnson, and Tolley (1972) represent a life-table approach to dealing with the issues involved with subjects who are lost to follow-up. Finally, for a discussion of one approach to the analysis of incomplete data resulting from the failure to measure each subject on each attribute at each time point, see Koch, Imrey, and Reinfurt (1972).

VI. Summary

In this chapter we have proposed an extremely general approach to the analysis of multivariate categorical data associated with longitudinal investigations of human growth and development. For purposes of illustration, two hypothetical data sets were presented to indicate the range of statistical issues of interest in such studies, and the types of functions from corresponding multidimensional contingency tables that can be used to suggest answers to these questions. Within this context, a general methodology for the analysis of categorical data resulting from longitudinal studies was then developed in terms of specific hypotheses. In particular, hypotheses directed at questions pertaining to average differences among subpopulations, attributes, and time points were expressed in terms of constraints on the probabilities associated with first-order marginal distributions of the response profiles. Furthermore, hypotheses directed at relationships among the attributes at a given time point and the extent to which those relationships change across time were formulated in terms of comparisons among joint distributions and in terms of measures of association across time periods.

A general unifying approach to the analysis of multivariate categorical data was recommended to create test statistics for these hypotheses as well as estimators for corresponding model parameters. This procedure can be implemented by constructing the appropriate functions of the observed proportions that are directed at the relationships under investigation by a sequence of matrix operations. Then a weighted least-squares computational algorithm is used to generate linearized minimum modified chi-square statistics as discussed in more detail in the Appendix.

An extensive analysis of each of the two data sets was presented within the context of the hypotheses of interest. In this regard, the matrices required to generate the appropriate functions and the matrices used to compute the test statistics were all specified in detail. Furthermore, the fitting of final smoothed models was illustrated in the second example in terms of an underlying linear logistic model often considered in growth studies. In particular, this modeling permitted the estimation of predicted values for the first-order marginal probabilities, together with their estimated standard errors, even though the analysis was performed on the logit transform scale.

Finally, this chapter concludes with a discussion of certain computational difficulties associated with very large contingency tables, together with other potential difficulties associated with structured response profiles, missing data, and incomplete data.

Acknowledgments

The authors are grateful to Ms. Karen A. Stanecki and Ms. Roberta K. Selin for their competent assistance in the data processing associated with the examples, to Ms. Janice L. Valentine for her careful proofreading of the final manuscript, and to Ms. Linda L. Blakley for her cheerful and conscientious typing of the original manuscript.

Appendix

Let $j = 1, 2, \ldots, r$ index a set of categories that correspond to the r possible response profiles associated with the simultaneous classifications of the subjects on the d attributes. Similarly, let $i = 1, 2, \ldots, s$ index a set of categories that correspond to distinct subpopulations as defined in terms of pertinent independent variables. If samples of size n_i where $i = 1, 2, \ldots, s$ are independently selected from the respective subpopulations, then the resulting data can be summarized in an $(s \times r)$ contingency table as shown in Table 9.11, where n_{ij} denotes the frequency-of-response category j in the sample from the ith subpopulation.

The vector $\mathbf{n}_i$ where $\mathbf{n}_i' = (n_{i1}, n_{i2}, \ldots, n_{ir})$ will be assumed to follow

TABLE 9.11
Observed Contingency Table

Subpopulation	Response profile category				
	1	2	$\cdots$	r	Total
1	n_{11}	n_{12}	$\cdots$	n_{1r}	n_1
2	n_{21}	n_{22}	$\cdots$	n_{2r}	n_2
$\vdots$	$\vdots$	$\vdots$	$\cdots$	$\vdots$	$\vdots$
s	n_{s1}	n_{s2}	$\cdots$	n_{sr}	n_s

the multinomial distribution with parameters n_i and $\pi_i' = (\pi_{i1}, \pi_{i2}, \ldots, \pi_{ir})$, where π_{ij} represents the probability that a randomly selected element from the ith population is classified in the jth response category. Thus, the relevant product multinomial model is

$$\phi = \prod_{i=1}^{s} \left\{ n_i! \prod_{j=1}^{r} [\pi_{ij}^{n_{ij}}/n_{ij}!] \right\} \tag{A.1}$$

with the constraints

$$\sum_{j=1}^{r} \pi_{ij} = 1 \qquad \text{for } i = 1, 2, \ldots, s. \tag{A.2}$$

Let $p_i = (n_i/n_i)$ be the $(r \times 1)$ vector of observed proportions associated with the sample from the ith subpopulation and let p be the $(sr \times 1)$ compound vector defined by $p' = (p_1', p_2', \ldots, p_s')$. Thus, the vector p is the unrestricted maximum likelihood estimator of π where $\pi' = (\pi_1', \pi_2', \ldots, \pi_s')$. A consistent estimator for the covariance matrix of p is given by the $(sr \times sr)$ block diagonal matrix $V(p)$ with the matrices

$$\underset{(r \times r)}{V_i(p_i)} = \frac{1}{n_i} [D_{p_i} - p_i p_i'] \tag{A.3}$$

for $i = 1, 2, \ldots,$ s on the main diagonal, where D_{p_i} is an $(r \times r)$ diagonal matrix with elements of the vector p_i on the main diagonal.

Let $F_1(p), F_2(p), \ldots, F_u(p)$ be a set of u functions of p that pertain to some aspect of the relationship between the distribution of the response profiles and the nature of the subpopulations. Each of these functions is assumed to have continuous partial derivatives through order 2 with respect to the elements of p within an open region containing $\pi = E\{p\}$. If $F \equiv F(p)$ is defined by

$$F' = [F(p)]' = [F_1(p), F_2(p), \ldots, F_u(p)], \tag{A.4}$$

then a consistent estimator for the covariance matrix of F is the $(u \times u)$ matrix

$$V_F = H[V(p)]H' \tag{A.5}$$

where $\mathbf{H} = [d\mathbf{F(x)}/d\mathbf{x} \mid \mathbf{x} = \mathbf{p}]$ is the $(u \times sr)$ matrix of first partial derivatives of the functions $\mathbf{F}$ evaluated at $\mathbf{p}$. In all applications, the functions comprising $\mathbf{F}$ are chosen so that $\mathbf{V_F}$ is asymptotically nonsingular.

The function vector $\mathbf{F}$ is a consistent estimator of $\mathbf{F}(\boldsymbol{\pi})$. Hence, the variation among the elements of $\mathbf{F}(\boldsymbol{\pi})$ can be investigated by fitting linear-regression models by the method of weighted least squares. This phase of the analysis can be characterized by writing

$$E_A\{\mathbf{F}\} \equiv E_A\{\mathbf{F(p)}\} = \mathbf{F}(\boldsymbol{\pi}) = \mathbf{X}\boldsymbol{\beta} \tag{A.6}$$

where $\mathbf{X}$ is a prespecified $(u \times t)$ design (or independent variable) matrix of known coefficients with full rank $t \leq u$, $\boldsymbol{\beta}$ is an unknown $(t \times 1)$ vector of parameters, and "E_A" means "asymptotic expectation."

An appropriate test statistic for the goodness of fit of the model Eq. (A.6) is

$$Q = Q(\mathbf{X}, \mathbf{\mathring{F}}) = (\mathbf{RF})'[\mathbf{RV_FR}']^{-1}\mathbf{RF}, \tag{A.7}$$

where $\mathbf{R}$ is any full rank $[(u - t) \times u]$ matrix orthogonal to $\mathbf{X}$. Here Q is approximately distributed according to the χ^2 distribution with $df = (u - t)$ if the sample sizes $\{n_i\}$ are sufficiently large that the elements of the vector $\mathbf{F}$ have an appropriate multivariate normal distribution as a consequence of Central Limit Theory (CLT). Test statistics such as Q are known as generalized Wald (1943) statistics, and various aspects of their application to a broad range of problems involving the analysis of multivariate categorical data are discussed in Bhapkar and Koch (1968a, 1968b) and Grizzle *et al.* (1969).

However, these test statistics like Eq. (A.7) are obtained in actual practice by using weighted least squares as a computational algorithm, which is justified on the basis of the fact that Q of Eq. (A.7) is identically equal to

$$Q = (\mathbf{F} - \mathbf{Xb})'\mathbf{V_F}^{-1}(\mathbf{F} - \mathbf{Xb}), \tag{A.8}$$

where $\mathbf{b} = (\mathbf{X}'\mathbf{V_F}^{-1}\mathbf{X})^{-1}\mathbf{X}'\mathbf{V_F}^{-1}\mathbf{F}$ is a BAN estimator for $\boldsymbol{\beta}$ based on the linearized modified χ_1^2-statistic of Neyman (1949). In view of this identity demonstrated in Bhapkar (1966), both Q and $\mathbf{b}$ are regarded as having reasonable statistical properties in samples that are sufficiently large for applying CLT to the functions $\mathbf{F}$. As a result, a consistent estimator for the covariance matrix of $\mathbf{b}$ is given by

$$V_b = (\mathbf{X}'\mathbf{V_F}^{-1}X)^{-1}. \tag{A.9}$$

If the model Eq. (A.6) does adequately characterize the vector $\mathbf{F}(\boldsymbol{\pi})$, tests of linear hypotheses pertaining to the parameters $\boldsymbol{\beta}$ can be undertaken by standard multiple-regression procedures. In particular, for a general hypothesis of the form,

$$H_0: \quad \mathbf{C}\boldsymbol{\beta} = 0, \tag{A.10}$$

where C is a known $(c \times t)$ matrix of full rank $c \le t$ and 0 is a $(c \times 1)$ vector of 0's, a suitable test statistic is

$$Q_C = (Cb)'[C(X'V_F^{-1}X)^{-1}C']^{-1}Cb \tag{A.11}$$

which has approximately a χ^2-distribution with $df = c$ in large samples under H_0 in Eq. (A. 10).

In this framework, the test statistic Q_C reflects the amount by which the goodness-of-fit statistic Eq. (A. 8) would increase if the model Eq. (A.6) were simplified (or reduced) by substitutions based on the additional constraints implied by Eq. (A.10). Thus, these methods permit the total variation within $F(\pi)$ to be partitioned into specific sources and hence represent a statistically valid analysis of variance for the corresponding estimator functions F.

Predicted values for $F(\pi)$ based on the model Eq. (A.6) can be calculated from

$$\hat{F} = Xb = X(X'V_F^{-1}X)^{-1}X'V_F^{-1}F. \tag{A.12}$$

Thus, consistent estimators for the variances of the elements of $\hat{F}$ can be obtained from the diagonal elements of

$$V_{\hat{F}} = X(X'V_F^{-1}X)^{-1}X'. \tag{A.13}$$

The predicted values $\hat{F}$ not only have the advantage of characterizing essentially all the important features of the variation in $F(\pi)$, but also represent better estimators than the original function statistics F since they are based on the data from the entire sample as opposed to its component parts. Moreover, they are descriptively advantageous in the sense that they make trends more apparent and permit a clearer interpretation of the relationship between $F(\pi)$ and the variables comprising the columns of X.

Although the formulation of $F(p)$ can be quite general, Grizzle et al. (1969) and Forthofer and Koch (1973) demonstrated that a wide range of problems in categorical data analysis could be considered within the framework of a few specified classes of compounded logarithmic, exponential, and linear functions of the observed proportions. However, these functions are all special cases of a broad class of functions that can be expressed in terms of repeated applications of any sequence of the following matrix operations:

1. Linear transformations of the type

$$F_1(p) = A_1p = a_1, \tag{A.14}$$

where A_1 is a matrix of known constants
2. Logarithmic transformations of the type

$$F_2(p) = \log_e(p) = a_2, \tag{A.15}$$

where $\log_e$ transforms a vector to the corresponding vector of natural logarithms

3. Exponential transformations of the type

$$F_3(p) = \exp(p) = a_3 \qquad (A.16)$$

where **exp** transforms a vector to the corresponding vector of exponential functions; that is, of antilogarithms

Then the linearized Taylor-series-based estimate of the covariance matrix of F_k for $k = 1,2,3$, is given by Eq. (A.5), where the corresponding H_k matrix operator is

$$H_1 = A_1; \qquad (A.17)$$

$$H_2 = D_p^{-1}; \qquad (A.18)$$

$$H_3 = D_{a_3}; \qquad (A.19)$$

where D_y is a diagonal matrix with elements of the vector y on the main diagonal.

The hypotheses involving marginal distributions can all be tested in terms of linear functions of the form given in Eq. (A.14). Furthermore, log-linear functions of the form

$$F(p) = A_2\{\log_e[A_1p]\} \qquad (A.20)$$

can be used to generate logits and log cross-product ratios; whereas compounded functions of the form

$$F(p) = \exp[A_4(\log_e\{A_3[\exp(A_2\{\log_e[A_1p]\})]\})] \qquad (A.21)$$

can be used to generate complex ratio estimates such as Yule's Q statistic or generalized kappa-type statistics. As a result, the linearized Taylor-series-based estimates of the covariance matrices associated with $F(p)$ in Eq. (A.20) and Eq. (A.21) can be obtained by repeated application of the chain rule for matrix differentiation. In particular, let

$$a_1 = A_1p; \qquad (A.22)$$

$$a_2 = \exp\{A_2[\log_e(a_1)]\}; \qquad (A.23)$$

$$a_3 = A_3a_2; \qquad (A.24)$$

$$a_4 = \exp\{A_4[\log_e(a_3)]\}. \qquad (A.25)$$

Then the results in Eqs. (A.17)–(A.19) can be used to provide a consistent estimate of the covariance matrix via Eq. (A.5) for $F(p)$ in Eq. (A.20) by using

$$H = A_2D_{a_1}^{-1}A_1, \qquad (A.26)$$

and for $\mathbf{F}(\mathbf{p})$ in Eq. (A.21) by using

$$\mathbf{H} = \mathbf{D}_{a_4}\mathbf{A}_4\mathbf{D}_{a_3}^{-1}\mathbf{A}_3\mathbf{D}_{a_2}\mathbf{A}_2\mathbf{D}_{a_1}^{-1}\mathbf{A}_1. \tag{A.27}$$

Finally, Koch, Imrey, Freeman, and Tolley (1976) discuss the application of this general approach to implicitly defined functions of $\mathbf{p}$ in the context of estimated parameters from fitted log-linear models. Thus, all aspects of this methodology can be directed at implicit functions that are based on maximum-likelihood estimation equations corresponding to preliminary or intermediate (as opposed to final) models with a priori assumed validity; in other words, models in which the likelihood Eq. (A.1) initially (i.e., prior to any data analysis) satisfies both Eq. (A.2) and certain other constraints analogous to Eq. (A.6).

For purposes of completeness, it should be noted that other statistical procedures for the analysis of categorical data from longitudinal and other types of repeated-measurement experiments are available in the literature. In this regard, Bishop, Fienberg, and Holland (1975, Chapter 8) discuss the application of maximum likelihood methods to test hypotheses of total symmetry and marginal symmetry as well as certain other hypotheses of interest. They also provide a relatively complete literature review of other papers dealing with similar questions, including the early work of Bowker (1948).

Chapter 10

Causal Models in Longitudinal Research: Rationale, Formulation, and Interpretation[1]

DAVID ROGOSA

ABSTRACT

The use of causal models in longitudinal research is discussed with emphasis on their logic and construction. The construction of causal models is explained and illustrated as a two-stage process involving (1) the structural model that specifies the causal relations among the latent variables, and (2) the measurement model that relates these unobserved variables to the observed measures. The investigation of reciprocal causal effects in developmental processes is the focus for the models considered in this chapter. Structural equation models for longitudinal panel data from various empirical studies are developed, and the important causal parameters that represent the reciprocal processes are identified and interpreted. The use of correlations, especially cross-lagged correlations, in these studies to support causal statements is shown to be unsound.

I. Introduction

In this chapter we consider methods, commonly termed *causal models* or *structural equation models,* that are used for making causal inferences from longitudinal data. As a first step, it is useful to distinguish between *explanation* (which implies some form of causal statement) and *description.* A descriptive approach addresses such questions as how and how much,

[1] Portions of this research were supported by grants from the Spencer Foundation to the School of Education, Stanford University, and to the Department of Education, The University of Chicago.

LONGITUDINAL RESEARCH IN THE
STUDY OF BEHAVIOR AND DEVELOPMENT

whereas an explanatory approach treats the question why and thus incorporates causal inference. (See the discussion of description versus explanation in Wold, 1956). For example, measurement of a child's cognitive functioning over time is a description, whereas an investigation of the dependence of cognitive functioning on maternal nurturance and the child's motivation is an example of explanation. Labouvie (1974) concluded that "a good deal of developmental research has been descriptive, rather than explanatory [p. 449]." Descriptive developmental studies often focus on a change in the level of a certain attribute over time. Research strategies such as in Schaie (1965) can be considered descriptive in this context, examining change in a single outcome. An explanatory study examines the relationships between variables in investigating the existence of a causal link. To determine causality the joint change of two or more variables is of primary importance. Causal hypotheses, even those involving the effects of an experimental manipulation of a treatment variable on an outcome, can be expressed in terms of associations among suitably defined variables.

No formal definition of a causal effect is attempted here; a natural and convenient way to discuss causality is to ask whether a change in one variable (the antecedent or causal variable) results in a change in an outcome variable. (This change may be induced through complex mediating influences, and all statements about single variables may be generalized to groups of variables.) This approach leads to a regression framework for describing causal influences, since regression coefficients are the natural measure of the effect on an outcome variable of a specified change in an antecedent variable. Explanation of developmental processes from longitudinal data is the primary focus of this chapter, but the discussion has clear implications for a variety of applications to other content domains.

A. Why Use Longitudinal Data for Causal Inferences?

In a recent review of methodological issues in developmental psychology McCall (1977) termed longitudinal methods "the lifeblood of developmental psychology," criticized developmental psychology for not being sufficiently developmental, and urged that investigators studying development use longitudinal, not cross-sectional, approaches. Cross-sectional designs in which data are collected at a single time point were originally conceived as a practical and appropriate means to study longitudinal change. However, the limitations of cross-sectional data for the study of development as evidenced by the insensitivity of cross-sectional data to the dynamics of growth and change (see, for example, Coleman, 1968; Freeman & Hannan, 1975) and findings of sharp differences between the results of cross-sectional and longitudinal studies (Damon, 1965; Kuhlen, 1963; Labouvie, Bartsch, Nesselroade, & Baltes, 1974) have given considerable impetus to the use of longitudinal designs in developmental research.

Cross-sectional designs confound interindividual growth with interindividual differences in intraindividual growth (Baltes & Nesselroade, 1973) and consequently are not adequate for the study of developmental processes. In cross-sectional analysis it is assumed that interindividual differences in development are stable over time. The measurement of certain individuals at one time period, then, would presumably yield the same results as the measurement of other individuals at the same developmental stages at a different time. Coleman (1968) expressed this as an assumption of equilibrium, that the developmental processes are in a sufficiently stable state that analyses of different cross-sections would yield the same results.

Cross-sectional research incorporates the further assumption that the *inter*individual differences found between age groups can be interpreted as changes that an individual would undergo across time (*intra*individual change). It has been shown, however, that interindividual differences in growth do not adequately measure intraindividual growth, but rather reflect the increasing variability in the rate of growth among individuals (Huston-Stein & Baltes, 1976). Repeated measurements on the same individuals are essential for assessment of individual growth and change.

An important advantage of longitudinal research lies in the possibility of untangling the complex effects of reciprocal causal influences. Research on the reciprocal influences (of mother on child and child on mother) in mother–child dyads (Lewis & Rosenblum, 1974; Rogosa & Ambron, 1976) and on the feedback processes between students' self-concept and academic achievement, discussed in Section IV, exemplifies the study of reciprocal causal influences. For example, in research on self-concept and academic achievement a number of cross-sectional studies established a persistent relationship between measures of these attributes (Purkey, 1970). However, only from longitudinal data can assessments of the strength, balance, and duration of the reciprocal causal influences be made (see Bachman & O'Malley, 1977; Calsyn & Kenny, 1977).

B. Longitudinal Research and Classical Experimental Design and Analysis

Though longitudinal designs hold considerable promise for developmental research for assessing causal effects and studying intraindividual change, problems of implementation and analysis are often severe relative to conventional laboratory experiments. First of all, developmental studies often focus on variables that cannot be effectively controlled or manipulated (i.e., organismic variables). Furthermore, many longitudinal studies are carried out outside controlled laboratory settings where the characteristic features of classical experimentation—control of extraneous influences, manipulation of treatment variables, and formation of equivalent comparison groups—are frequently impossible to implement. Finally, when some of these controls are implemented, the resulting studies are often criticized for deficiencies in external and ecological validity.

For example, Bronfenbrenner (1977) charged that "much of developmental psychology is the science of the strange behavior of children in strange situations with strange adults for the briefest possible periods of time [p. 513]" and called for a new perspective in developmental research termed *experimental ecology*. McCall (1977) argued that the constraints of classical experimental design inhibit the study of important developmental processes, and that when behavior is developing the interpretation of experimental results is often equivocal. From the perspective of life-span psychology, Huston-Stein & Baltes (1976) stated that "most of the traditional, experimental design methods in the psychological sciences are ill-suited for the assessment of long-term chains and distal causes [p. 182]."

Analysis techniques useful in making causal inferences from experimental data are not as useful for the analysis of causal patterns in naturalistic studies. The lack of experimental control in these developmental studies forces a heavier reliance on statistical methods in the assessment of causal effects. In a seminal paper, "Causal inference from observational data," Herman Wold (1956) characterized an essential feature of such methods: "In the absence of experiments the statistical analysis has to be closely coordinated with subject-matter theory both in specifying the causal hypotheses and in testing them against other sources of knowledge [p. 31]."

The assessment of causal effects from nonexperimental data can sometimes be successfully accomplished through use of causal models that incorporate substantive knowledge into the data analysis. The incorporation of substantive knowledge into the analysis of developmental data through the construction of appropriate causal models is illustrated in Sections III and IV. In Section II the heuristic value of causal models for the formulation of explicit statements of the postulated relations among variables is emphasized.

II. Logic of Causal Models

A. What Are Causal Models?

A causal model is an *explicit and quantitative statement* of the postulated causal links between the variables of interest. Through the use of causal models substantive hypotheses are recast in terms of the causal processes assumed to operate among the variables under consideration. The use of causal models forces the researcher to make explicit all causal assumptions in an internally consistent system.

In the formulation of a causal model, the important variables in the developmental process are first identified (e.g., self-esteem, educational attainment, occupational aspiration), and the causal links among these variables over time are specified. On psychological grounds some variables can be said to influence others; in other instances the causal link may be assumed not to exist. The variables to be included in the model and their postulated causal links may be obtained from the theoretical formulation of the problem or from relevant empirical evidence.

Causal models have been discussed under a variety of names in a number of different literatures. We use the technical term *structural equation model* interchangeably with the generic label of *causal model*. *Structural equation model* is the term used most often in econometrics; *path analysis* was formulated by Sewall Wright in genetics and brought over into sociology as path analysis, or as *causal modeling*. Goldberger (1972) provided an interesting history of the parallel but independent historical developments in econometrics and biometrics. Path analysis can be viewed as a special case of these structural equation methods; some serious limitations of path analysis are discussed in Section IV.

The regression equations that compose a structural equation model are termed *structural regression equations*. Systems of structural regression equations, in which each equation represents a causal link between variables, differ from predictive regression equations, which represent empirical associations with no special regard for underlying causal mechanisms. In structural regression, the concern is with the interrelationships of the theoretically important variables, not simply the predictability of one from the others. In structural regression, that mechanism which generates the observations can be characterized in terms of more fundamental parameters. Goldberger (1973) showed that, in general, the coefficients in predictive regression are a mixture of the structural parameters; hence a change in one structural parameter may change all the predictive-regression coefficients. Therefore, the more fundamental structural parameters have the invariance and stability desired of scientific formulations. As Abraham Wald (1940) pointed out, "The knowledge of the structural relationship is essential for constructing any theory in the empirical sciences . . . in deducing laws from observations we have the task of estimating structural relationships [p. 300]." Tukey (1954) concluded: "Almost any causal theory comes sooner or later to deal with structural regression rather than predictive regression [p. 41]."

Once a causal model is constructed, the set of causal links in the model is written as a set of structural regression equations. Estimation of the parameters in the structural regressions (see Chapter 11, this volume) yields estimates of the causal influences between the variables and thus is a determination of how change in one variable in the system would affect the other variables in the system. The results of these analyses depend on the theory that determines the structural equation model. Intuitively, the estimation techiques for these structural equation models decompose the observed association of the variables into direct and indirect effects. We are, in some sense, taking the correlation apart and examining its causal components. However, this decomposition of the observed covariation depends upon the particular causal ordering assumed to be valid by the researcher. The incorporation of relevant substantive knowledge into the regression analysis may be termed *data analysis conditional on a theory*. From the theoretical and psychological conceptualization of the investigation, the patterns of association between the variables are specified. Then the analysis techniques supply estimates of causal parameters from the nonexperimental data. Of course, the number obtained are soundly interpretable only if the substantive specification is adequate.

These causal-modeling techniques cannot prove causality. They may aid in choosing among relevant causal hypotheses by ruling out those not supported by empirical evidence. This is the logic of falsification (Popper, 1972). When theories are expressed as causal models, they are subject to rejection if contradicted by data.

In addition to providing promising statistical tools for the assessment of causal effects in nonexperimental data, causal models potentially have a positive role in bridging gaps between theory and research. A major problem in empirical research is that when theories include ambiguous concepts whose postulated causal relations are not well specified, the resulting research is usually a collection of noncomparable studies that relate only vaguely to the original theory. Two examples are research on Piaget's theory of moral development and research on attachment (Ambron & Rogosa, 1975). In order to guide research, theory should be explicit about the relations of its components—that is, be translatable into empirically justifiable statements—since vague, verbal theories will rarely help to focus research. Many developmental theories are stated ambiguously; consequently, they are often misinterpreted and are difficult for the researcher to support or refute with empirical evidence. (See Phillips & Kelly, 1975, and Suppes, 1973, 1974 for critical discussions of many developmental theories.)

Possibly, the construction of causal models would serve in some cases to alleviate these problems by recasting theoretical formulations as explicit propositions about the causal relations among the variables of interest (Blalock, 1963; Duncan, 1966). Such formulations may lead to productive theory-based research.

B. Spurious Correlation: A Causal Interpretation

A specific problem that illustrates the importance of careful interpretation of the relationships between variables is that of spurious correlation, where the association between two variables is entirely due to the influence of a common factor. In investigating spurious correlation interest lies in whether a relation between two variables (X and Y) disappears when a third variable Z is introduced. The correlation of X and Y is spurious if the association of X and Y is totally due to the causal influence of Z. Spurious correlation is illustrated in Figure 10.1a. To guard against this possibility, the sample partial correlation $r_{XY \cdot Z}$ (the correlation of X and Y with Z partialed out) may be computed. If $r_{XY \cdot Z}$ does not differ markedly from zero, then a spurious relation between X and Y may exist. Alternatively, Z may be a mediating variable in a "true" relationship of X and Y, as illustrated in Figure 10.1b.

Whether an association is spurious or true (from a causal standpoint) cannot be determined on the basis of correlations. Information about the causal ordering of the system of variables, which may often be derived from substantive knowledge, is required.

In Simon's (1954) classic example, a high negative correlation is found between X, the percentage of a group that is married, and Y, the average number of pounds of candy consumed per month per person. Can we conclude that marriage causes a reduction in candy consumption? Variable Z is the average age of members in each of the several groups. However, when age is held constant, the correlation between X and Y disappears. On the basis of common sense the relationship in Figure 10.1a is believed to hold. The correlation between candy consumption and marital status is jointly caused by a variation in age—the relationship is spurious. This is a "common-sense" conclusion, but it depends on the assumption that certain relations are not causal. In this example, the decision between Models (a) and (b) was made by the a priori assumption that the age of a person does not depend upon marital status or candy consumption. Here the answer is obvious, but determining causal ordering and structure is often treacherous, and explicit statements of theory are necessary for the sound interpretation of data.

Although problems with the causal ordering of variables affect all analysis schemes, a number of other characteristics of correlation coefficients make their use to support claims of causation in nonexperimental studies inap-

FIGURE 10.1. **Examples of (a) spurious and (b) true correlation. The partial correlation** $\rho_{XY \cdot Z}$ **will equal zero in the population in both cases. Assumptions about the causal ordering of the variables are necessary to differentiate (a) from (b). (a) The correlation between X and Y is spurious since the association is entirely due to the causal influence of Z. (b) The true association between X and Y is mediated by Z.**

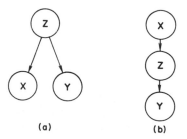
(a)   (b)

propriate and often misleading. Correlation is a descriptive statistic, and it contains no information about the direction of the association. Thus, correlations are not an appropriate basis for causal statements. However, many longitudinal investigations report correlations as evidence of causal relationships. Longitudinal researchers may do well to heed the message of John Tukey (1954), who in an article relating to causal models, argued that ''correlation coefficients are justified in two and only two circumstances, when they are regression coefficients, or when the measurement of one or both variables on a determinate scale is hopeless [p. 39].''

The use of regression coefficients instead of correlations solves some of the problems associated with the stability of reported effects over different samples. As Tukey (1954) noted, ''We are very sure that the correlation cannot remain the same over a wide range of situations, but it is possible that the regression coefficients might [p. 41].'' The regression coefficients that possess the desired stability are those of structural regression equations. In the substantive examples presented in Sections III and IV some of the many pitfalls associated with the use of correlations for causal statements are illustrated.

III. Construction of Causal Models

The construction of a causal model from a previously published developmental study is presented to clarify the preceding discussion. Radin (1971, 1974) investigated antecedents of cognitive development in lower-class children. Radin was primarily interested in the effects of child-rearing practices, in particular those of maternal behavior, on the intellectual development of the child. On the basis of theoretical and empirical studies, Radin hypothesized that maternal nurturance would foster intellectual functioning of the child. Radin also considered evidence that the motivation of the child to achieve is an intervening variable in the process by which maternal behavior influences the child's cognitive functioning.

Radin's overall hypothesis that maternal nurturance would foster the child's intellectual functioning can be represented as a relation between the constructs labeled Maternal Behavior and Cognitive Functioning as depicted in Figure 10.2a. The arrow leading to Cognitive Functioning indicates the hypothesized causal influence of Maternal Behavior on Cognitive Functioning.

The consideration of motivation to achieve as a mediating variable can be incorporated into the relationship described in Figure 10.2a. Figure 10.2b includes the Motivation construct in the postulated causal ordering. Figure 10.2b exhibits the two causal paths by which Maternal Behavior is assumed to influence Cognitive Functioning. The direct path connects Maternal Behavior and Cognitive Functioning, and the indirect path involves the Mo-

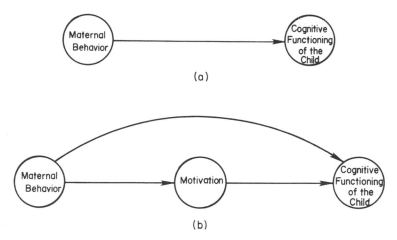

(a)

(b)

FIGURE 10.2. **(a and b) Representations of the causal relationship between maternal behavior and the cognitive functioning of the child. (a) Representation of the hypothesized causal effect of maternal behavior on the cognitive functioning of the child. (b) Representation of the three constructs (unmeasured variables) in the postulated causal ordering.**

tivation construct as an intervening variable. The direct path also includes the influence of any omitted intervening construct, such as identification with the parent.

Figure 10.2b is a representation of the structural model that expresses the assumed relations between the unmeasured or latent variables. Unmeasured or unobserved variables arise when the measurable variables differ from their theoretical counterparts. The unmeasured variables often are theoretical constructs that have implications for determining the relationship between observables. Since theory is most often expressed in terms of constructs and unmeasured variables, the structural model contains a statement of substantive knowledge that is incorporated into the data analysis. Causal models provide the machinery to relate theory and hypotheses expressed in unmeasured constructs to observed variables. The goal is to make causal statements about the unmeasured variables from the observed relations of the indicators.

The measurement model provides the link between the constructs and the indicators. Radin obtained two indicators for each of the constructs shown in Figure 10.2b. The two indicators of Maternal Behavior were measures of warmth and restrictiveness, obtained during a 1-hour observation of interaction between mother and child. The two indicators of Motivation were a subscale of the Pupil Behavioral Inventory (PBI) and a psychologist's rating of the child's motivation while taking the Stanford–Binet Intelligence Scale. For Cognitive Functioning the two indicators used were the Stanford–Binet and the Peabody Picture Vocabulary Test (PPVT).

Figure 10.3 depicts the full causal model, a combination of the structural and measurement models. The symbols $\beta_1, \beta_2, \beta_3$, and $\delta_1-\delta_6$ denote parameters in the model that may be estimated from the data. In Figure 10.3 the e_i represent the part of the observed variable that is not part of the construct it is presumed to measure. The e_i include measurement error and other information irrelevant to the construct. The e_i may be thought of as the unique part of the observed variable. Often the e_i are assumed to be uncorrelated with each other. In Figure 10.3 a correlation between e_4 and e_5 is allowed. This correlation is not assumed to be zero because X_4 and X_5, measures of Motivation and Cognitive Functioning, respectively, are obtained on the same occasion, the administration of the Binet. Consequently, X_4 and X_5 are likely to be related for reasons additional to the presumed relation between Motivation and Cognitive Functioning. The capability to estimate models with correlated errors is an important feature of the estimation techniques developed for these models (see Jöreskog & Sörbom, 1977; and Chapter 11, this volume).

The causal model for Radin's data may be represented by a series of regression equations with the same parameters as in Figure 10.3. The structural model is (intercepts omitted).

$$X_B = \beta_1 X_A + u,$$

$$X_C = \beta_2 X_B + \beta_3 X_A + v.$$

The measurement model is

$$X_1 = \delta_1 X_A + e_1,$$

$$X_2 = \delta_2 X_A + e_2,$$

$$X_3 = \delta_3 X_B + e_3,$$

$$X_4 = \delta_4 X_B + e_4,$$

$$X_5 = \delta_5 X_C + e_5,$$

$$X_6 = \delta_6 X_C + e_6.$$

In this example the parameters β_1, β_2, and β_3, which represent the causal influence among the constructs, are of central interest. The direct influence of Maternal Behavior on Cognitive Functioning is represented by β_3. That is, if β_3 were zero, all influence of Maternal Behavior on Cognitive Functioning would be mediated by motivation. Conversely, if β_3 were large, two interpretations would be plausible: (1) Constructs that were not included in the model, such as identification with the parent, are important mediating variables; (2) Maternal Behavior has a strong direct effect on Cognitive Functioning.

Rogosa, Webb, and Radin (1978) analyzed a number of alternative structural-equation models for Radin's data using the computer program LISREL

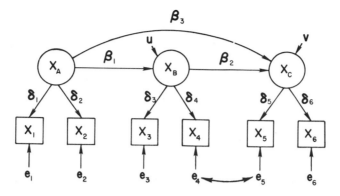

FIGURE 10.3. **Complete causal model for Radin's investigation. Constructs (unmeasured variables): X_A = maternal behavior; X_B = motivation of child; X_C = cognitive functioning of the child. Indicators (measured variables): X_1 = maternal warmth; X_2 = maternal restrictiveness; X_3 = motivation (PBI); X_4 = motivation during Binet; X_5 = Stanford Binet Score; X_6 = PPVT score.**

(Jöreskog & Sörbom, 1978). For a model corresponding to Figure 10.3 an estimate of β_3 of .055 with an estimated standard error of .31 was obtained. The t-ratio of the estimate to its standard error was .18. Thus the data do not contain strong evidence for a direct effect of Maternal Behavior on Cognitive Functioning or for the existence of additional mediating variables. No important association between the errors e_4 and e_5 was detected; the estimate of the covariance of these errors was -1.40 with an estimated standard error of 7.37. The overall fit of this model to the data was assessed by a chi-square statistic with five degrees of freedom that was equal to 8.04.

A formal statistical procedure for assessing the importance of β_3 is to fit a restricted model with β_3 set to zero. The difference of the χ^2 goodness-of-fit statistics for the full and restricted models yields a χ^2 statistic with 1 df for assessing the significance of β_3. For the Radin data, the goodness-of-fit statistic for the restricted model was 8.09. Thus the decrement to the fit of the model by restricting β_3 to be zero was only .05, which is highly nonsignificant.

Radin's original analysis (1971, Table 2) did not produce conclusive results on the role of motivation as a mediating variable. In the original analysis, which relied on partial correlations between the indicators, all of the indicators could not be considered simultaneously. Eight partial correlations, each with a measure of Motivation partialed out, were considered. Causal-model methods can estimate the relationships between the unmeasured variables using all the data at once and yield one numerical summary of the relations between the constructs. Also the examination of partial correlations among the indicators is greatly complicated by the presence of measurement error in the indicators. Measurement error may have a large effect on the magnitude and even alter the sign of a partial correlation (Lord, 1974b). Under reasonable assumptions about the measurement error, it can be shown that examining the relations between the unmeasured constructs does much to offset the effects of measurmement error in the indicators and thus provides a more valid determination of the role of the mediating variable. (Further discussion is contained in Rogosa, Webb, & Radin, 1978.)

The process of selecting the variables to be included in the model and postulating the relationships of the variables and of the residual terms constitutes the *specification* of the model. Mistakes in the specification such as omitting an important causal variable or incorrectly assuming that a causal path does not exist are termed *specification errors*. Duncan (1975a) suggested that specification error ''is quite a useful euphemism for what in blunter language would be called 'using the wrong model'. There are many more wrong models than right ones, so that specification error is very common, though often not recognized and usually not easily recognizable [p. 101].''

The presence of two measures of each construct in the Radin study allows the unique estimation of the parameters in the model depicted in Figure 10.3. This relates to the technical problem of *identification*; a model is identified when all the causal parameters are uniquely estimable from the data. Underidentification results when there is not enough information to estimate certain causal parameters. The reader is referred to Duncan (1975a) for further treatment of specification and identification.

For many constructs used in developmental research a single measure will rarely be sufficient for valid measurement, and thus multiple indicators are important both for the technical concerns with identification and for the substantive problems of valid measurement. Baltes and Nesselroade (1973) argued:

> If one wishes to deal with more abstract concepts, such as patterned change—change in the interrelationships among a variety of measures—then a multivariate approach is necessary. It is from the interrelationships among measures (e.g., covariances), so often ignored in developmental research, that we may eventually extract the raw material that can be efficiently molded into general, but powerful constructs to aid the scientific study of development. A related point is that when research interest centers on change in more molar behavior patterns such as anxiety and aggression, no single variable can serve as a perfect indictor of the target construction. The use of multiple indicators (measures) enables us to form some combination of measures which ''locates'' the construct more precisely [p. 222].

The choice of multiple indicators requires careful planning. A very high intercorrelation of indicators is not always desirable, since it may indicate the presence of redundant information or correlated measurement errors and not necessarily an increase in information or measurement validity.

Detailed discussion of the choice and interpretation of multiple indicators may be found, for example, in Chapters 7 and 8 of Blalock (1974).

IV. Longitudinal Panel Designs

One of the most common and useful designs for longitudinal research is the *longitudinal panel design,* in which the same sample of cases is observed at more than one point in time. Essentially, panel designs are a combination of time-series and cross-sectional designs, with measurements obtained on a cross-section (wave) at each time point. Typically, the number of cases in each wave is considerably greater than the number of waves. Longitudinal panel designs may be profitably employed to study reciprocal causation, using "longitudinal (or intertemporal) variation to disentangle reciprocal causal effects [Hannan & Young, 1977, p. 54]." Schaie (1965) and Baltes (1968b) advocated longitudinal designs similar to longitudinal panels except that a new random sample of cases is drawn at each time point. Clearly, when associations between variables are analyzed, these designs are inappropriate; the same cases are needed at each time point.

A. Two-Wave Panel Designs

The simplest panel design is the two-wave panel, with observations on the same cases recorded at two points in time. Measurement at only two points in time is a less-than-ideal design for a longitudinal study, though two points are certainly much better than one. For example, consider the controversy over regression-toward-the-mean phenomena in developmental research (Baltes & Nesselroade, 1976, Furby, 1973). Baltes and Nesselroade (1976) soundly pointed out that using more than two points in time alleviates almost all potential problems with regression toward the mean since the fluctuations toward the mean will cancel out on the average. With only two points in time a developmental function must pass through the two points exactly. Consequently, the developmental function is greatly affected by the regression toward the mean at Time 2. Other limitations of two-wave designs for investigating reliability and stability are discussed in Wheaton, Muthén, Alwin, and Summers (1977).

In the most popular and widely discussed two-wave design for investigating reciprocal causal influences, two variables are measured at each time point. This design is termed the *two-wave–two-variable* (2W2V) *panel.* The representation of the causal model usually assumed for 2W2V panels is shown in Figure 10.4. Some important restrictions are built into this model to permit estimation and interpretation of the parameters. Most important is the assumption that lagged causation is the sole causal force; simultaneous causation between X_2 and Y_2 is ruled out. Thus, the parameters β_2 and γ_2

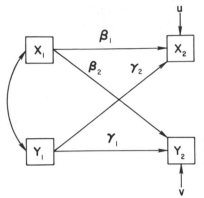

FIGURE 10.4. **Representation of the causal model for 2W2V panel. Assumptions built into this model are no simultaneous causation, measurement without error, and uncorrelated residuals.**

represent the reciprocal causal effects. Also, the residuals (disturbance terms) u and v are assumed to be independent, and the variables must be measured without error. More general models are considered by Duncan (1969b, 1972), who concluded: "No set of 2W2V data will answer a question about direction of causal influence or relative importance of causes except on some set of definite assumptions. If one wishes to avoid assumptions of the type illustrated here, the only recourse is to expand the study design beyond the limits of 2W2V [1969, p. 181]."

The configuration in Figure 10.4 can be represented by the structural-regression equations:

$$X_2 = \beta_1 X_1 + \gamma_2 Y_1 + u,$$

$$Y_2 = \beta_2 X_1 + \gamma_1 Y_1 + v.$$

The parameters β_2 and γ_2 represent the lagged causal effects of X on Y and Y on X and are of central importance in this investigation. The parameters β_1 and γ_1 represent the causal influence of the variable on itself over time and reflect the stability of that attribute over time.

The model represented in Figure 10.4 is less restrictive than is usually recognized. The time between waves might appear to be a very inconvenient quality to deal with. The pictorial representation appears to presume that the interactive influences operate over discrete time intervals; indeed, if the time between observations does not correspond to the actual causal lag, it appears that this panel design may be insensitive to important causal interactions. However, Figure 10.4 can be shown to arise also from a dynamic model in which X and Y adjust continuously to levels of X and Y during the period of observation. Thus, instead of only corresponding to the experimental lag, this panel model represents a more general process, that of causal influences and resulting adjustments that are continuous in time.

A simple two-variable dynamic-change model corresponding to the structural-regression model for the 2W2V panel data is

$$\frac{dX}{dt} = b_0 + b_1 X + c_2 Y$$

$$\frac{dY}{dt} = c_0 + c_1 Y + b_2 X.$$

In this equation b_2 and c_2 represent the influence of X on the rate of change in Y and the influence of Y on the rate of change in X, respectively. The solution of these equations results in equations of the same form as the structural-regression equations. The β_i and γ_i are nonlinear functions of b_i and c_i and of the time between waves (see Coleman, 1968; Freeman & Hannan, 1975). Thomas and Martin (1976) provide an interesting application of dynamic-change models to the analysis of mother–child interaction.

1. Problems with Cross-Lagged Correlations

In the educational and psychological literature, much attention has been given to the method of cross-lagged correlation as a means for inferring the predominant direction of causal influence from nonexperimental panel data. The relevant population correlations in the method of cross-lagged correlations for the 2W2V design are shown in Figure 10.5. The population cross-lagged correlations are $\rho_{X_1 Y_2}$ and $\rho_{Y_1 X_2}$. The sample cross-lagged correlations are $r_{X_1 Y_2}$ and $r_{Y_1 X_2}$. If $r_{X_1 Y_2} > r_{Y_1 X_2}$, the suggested interpretation (Campbell, 1963, and others) is that the predominant causal influence is in the direction of X causing Y. The opposite pattern of cross-lagged correlations reverses the direction of the causal attribution. Usually, an attribution of predominant causal influence is made only when the difference of the sample cross-lagged correlations is statistically significant.

Users of the method of cross-lagged correlations often make enthusiastic claims for the method. For example, Crano (1977) asserted "inferences concerning the preponderant causal relationship operating between two

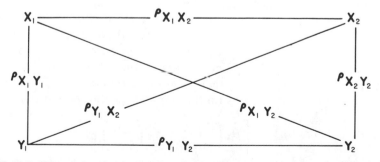

FIGURE 10.5. **The array of population correlations in a 2W2V design relevant to the method of cross-lagged correlation.**

variables would be legitimate, and would enjoy the same logical status as those derived through the use of the experimental method [p. 146].'' Although the cross-lagged procedure has come under sharp attack from some methodologists (Duncan, 1969a; Goldberger, 1971; Heise, 1970), its use is still widely recommended (e.g., Calsyn & Kenny, 1977; Clarke-Stewart, 1973, 1975; Crano, 1974, 1977; Humphreys & Stubbs, 1977; Kenny, 1973, 1975a).

We find serious problems with the logic, technical properties, and implementation of the method of cross-lagged correlation. First, the goal of establishing a preponderant direction of causal influence—identifying a causal ''winner''—seems ill advised. The current recognition that most social and developmental processes are reciprocal, as between mother and child or as between a person's self-concept and achievement, renders this sort of conclusion not very useful. Instead, measures of the strength and duration of the reciprocal relationship and of the individual causal effects are more informative and more directly interpretable.

In addition, the difference of the cross-lagged correlations does not provide unambiguous evidence as to the predominant direction of causal influence. In fact, in many situations the difference of the cross-lagged correlations will indicate a direction of causal predominance opposite to that of the causal structure built into the data. Also, a zero difference of the cross-lagged correlations may be obtained when important causal influences, balanced or unbalanced, are present. Essentially, the method fails because it ignores the causal influence of a variable on itself over time and by its implicit standardization is not sensitive to changes in variability over time. Some analytic results and numerical illustrations are given below; see Rogosa (1978) for additional results and discussion.

ANALYTIC RESULTS

Following the notion of a causal influence previously represented in the 2W2V model in Figure 10.4, β_2 and γ_2 represent the causal influences of X on Y and Y on X, respectively. These parameters represent the change induced in one variable at Time 2 by a change in the other variable at Time 1. To evaluate the usefulness of the cross-lagged correlation procedure, it is informative to examine how the cross-lagged correlations relate to the structural parameters of the model depicted in Figure 10.4. The cross-lagged correlations are a complicated function of these parameters. The difference of the cross lagged correlations (in the population) can be written as

$$\rho_{X_1Y_2} - \rho_{Y_1X_2} = (1 - \rho_{X_1Y_1}^2) \left[\beta_2 \left(\frac{\sigma_{X_1}}{\sigma_{Y_2}} \right) - \gamma_2 \left(\frac{\sigma_{Y_1}}{\sigma_{X_2}} \right) \right]$$
$$+ \rho_{X_1Y_1}(\rho_{Y_1Y_2} - \rho_{X_1X_2}).$$

We assume that $\rho_{X_1 Y_1}$ and the structural parameters are nonnegative, for purposes of discussion.

This expression reveals that the difference of the cross-lagged correlations will diverge from the difference of the structural parameters ($\beta_2 - \gamma_2$) for two reasons: differences in the stabilities of X and Y, represented by $\rho_{X_1 X_2}$ and $\rho_{Y_1 Y_2}$, and differences in the variances of X and Y over time. We examine the effects of each in turn and jointly. We argue that in many research settings it is plausible that the difference of the cross-lagged correlations may not be close in magnitude to or even of the same sign as the difference of the structural parameters. A discrepancy in the sign of these two differences would create the situation in which the conclusion about the preponderant direction of causal influence obtained from the cross-lagged correlation analysis is the opposite of the direction indicated by the difference of the structural parameters. That is, given the underlying structural model, exactly the wrong conclusion as to the preponderant causal influence is indicated by the difference of the cross-lagged correlations.

To examine just the effects of differences in the stabilities of X and Y on the difference of the cross-lagged correlations, we set the variances of X and Y equal to 1. When the difference of the cross-lags is a weighted sum of the difference of the structural parameters and the difference of the stabilities. The cross-lagged technique tends to favor the less stable variable in assigning causal influence. For example, let $\beta_2 = \gamma_2$ and let Y be the more stable variable. Then the difference of the population cross-lags is positive, indicating the conclusion that the predominant causal influence is in the direction of X causes Y, even though the structural parameters are equal. For a numerical example, let the population parameters take on the values $\beta_2 = .3$, $\gamma_2 = .5$, $\rho_{X_1 Y_1} = .6$, $\rho_{X_1 X_2} = .4$, and $\rho_{Y_1 Y_2} = .8$. The cross-lags are $\rho_{X_1 Y_2} = .67$, $\rho_{Y_1 X_2} = .56$, and their difference of .11 would be interpreted as showing that the preponderant direction of causal influence is from X to Y, although the structural parameters are in the opposite direction. For a more extreme example, change β_2 to .1 and γ_2 to .4. Then the difference of the cross-lags is .05, and the causal conclusion based on the cross-lags goes against a 4-to-1 ratio of the structural parameters. Of course, many other numerical illustrations can be constructed. Large differences in stabilities are not uncommon; for example, in research on mother–child interactions, maternal behaviors are often found to be considerably more stable over 6- or 12-month periods than are the behaviors of young children (e.g., Clarke-Stewart, 1973).

The variances of X and Y at Time 2 can also pose problems for the cross-lagged correlation analysis. The cross-lagged correlations tend to favor the variable with the larger product of variances; that is, if $\sigma_{X_1} \sigma_{X_2} > \sigma_{Y_1} \sigma_{Y_2}$, the expression for the difference of the cross-lags is more likely to be positive, even when the stabilities of X and Y are the same.

When the less stable variable also is more variable at Time 2, the lack of stability and the increased variability combine to distort the cross-lagged correlation analysis. For instance, in the first numerical example set the variances of X_1 and Y_1 to 1 and let $\sigma_{X_2} = 2.0$ and $\sigma_{Y_2} = 1.0$. Then the difference of the cross-lags increases to .27, even though the structural parameters are constrained so that Y has the larger causal effect.

An additional problem is the use and interpretation of tests of significance in applications of the method of cross-lagged correlation. A statistically significant difference between the cross-lagged correlations is often used as the basis for assigning the preponderant direction of causal influence with little regard for the size of the sample and the power of the statistical test. For example, Crano, Kenny, and Campbell (1972) find significant differences between cross-lagged correlations of .65 and .67 due to their very large sample size, and interpret many of these very small differences as indicating that intelligence causes later achievement. Other authors have the opposite problem. With small sample sizes, differences between cross-lags are interpreted as if these sample estimates were population values— sampling variation is ignored, and no significance testing is attempted. Interval estimates of the difference of the cross-lagged correlations are more useful and informative.

We should note that Kenny (1975a) qualified many of the strong claims for the method of cross-lagged correlation and offered some appropriate cautions to users of the method. Unfortunately, these cautions are not widely heeded in current practice. In particular, Kenny classified cross-lagged correlation as "largely an exploratory strategy of data analysis" that might be followed by "the estimation of causal parameters of the system by structural equation models [1975a, p. 901]." But from the results presented above, it is certainly possible that the cross-lagged correlations may show little or no difference when a strong causal relation, balanced or unbalanced, is present between the variables under investigation. The method of cross-lagged correlation may well conceal causal relations that merit further investigation and thus is not well-suited to an exploratory function. Estimating the causal parameters of a structural model is a superior strategy for detecting causal relations.

EMPIRICAL EXAMPLES

Important problems with the application of cross-lagged correlations are illustrated in the often-cited investigation of Eron, Huesmann, Lefkowitz, and Walder (1972) of the causal influences of television violence and aggression. The 2W2V design included measures of peer-rated aggression and preference for violent television programs when the subjects were in the third and thirteenth grades. As shown in Figure 10.6, for the 211 boys the sample cross-lagged correlations were .31 and .01, the large correlation being between early TV preference and later aggression. Eron *et al.* (1972)

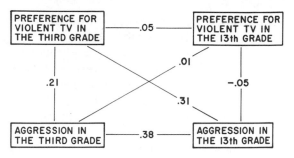

FIGURE 10.6. **The sample correlations in the 2W2V data of Eron, Huesmann, Lefkowitz, and Walder (1972) that were used in the cross-lagged correlation analysis of their data. [Adapted from Eron et al., 1972.]**

proceeded to make a causal inference on the basis of this difference—TV violence causes later aggression. Unfortunately, Eron *et al.* seem to have ignored the most salient feature of their data: Preference for TV violence at Time 2 correlated with nothing at all—.05 with Time 1 preference for TV violence, −.05 with Time 2 aggression, .01 with a Time 2 self-rating of antisocial behavior, and .06 with subscales of the MMPI administered at Time 2.

It appears that the causal conclusion reached by Eron *et al.* (1972) is based on the difficulty of accurate measurement of an adequate variable that represented preference for TV violence at Time 2. That is not to say that their causal conclusion is incorrect; the data simply are not strong enough to make such a conclusion highly convincing. It can be seen from this example that to establish a predominant causal effect for a variable by the use of cross-lagged correlations, it is only necessary to measure that variable poorly at Time 2. It should be pointed out that some of the methodological literature on cross-lagged correlations warns against use of the technique when the within-time, across-variable correlations differ substantially, as occurs in the Eron *et al.* data.

A similar problem is found in one of the major results in Clark-Stewart's (1973) study of mother–child interaction. Her cross-lagged comparison was between the Bayley mental-test score of the child and visual attention of the mother at child ages of 11 and 17 months. The cross-lagged correlations were −.04 and .60; the larger correlation was between maternal attention at Time 1 and mental score at Time 2. Thus, the causal interpretation was that the amount of maternal visual attention influences the child's later intellectual competence.

A problem with this conclusion is that the mental-test score at Time 1 was not related to other major variables in the study. For example, mental test score at Time 1 correlated .00 with maternal attention at Time 1, −.01 with maternal responsiveness to social signals at Time 1, and .13 with infant's positive emotional expression at Time 1. The same correlations with the mental-test score at Time 2 (6 months later) were .60, .50, and .47, respectively. This pattern of strong associations for the later mental-test score and almost no association for the early mental-test score with other infant and maternal variables was seen throughout the data. Possibly, the mental-test scores at 11 and 17 months were not strictly comparable because of the child's development of verbal skills in that time period. This qualitative change in intelligence over time makes causal interpretations difficult.

Atkin, Bray, Davison, Herzberger, Humphreys, and Selzer (1977) presented a complex method for developing cross-lagged correlations when there are many measures of each variable. They reanalyzed the ETS growth data (Hilton, 1969), which has also been analyzed using the framework presented in this chapter by Jöreskog (1970a and Chapter 11, this volume). Atkin *et al.* considered data from two waves, Grades 5 and 11, for the 16 cognitive tests administered in the study. The featured result of their analysis was a comparison of the Listening Test (an aural comprehension test) with an Intellectual Composite formed from the remaining 15 measures. Because the correlation (.73) between Listening at Grade 5 and the Intellectual Composite at Grade 11 was larger than the correlation (.60) between Listening at Grade 11 and the Intellectual Composite at Grade 5, Atkin *et al.* suggested that "individual differences on the measure of aural comprehension are causally related to later intellectual development [1977, p. 947]."

The stabilities of the two variables differed considerably: .86 for the Intellectual Composite and .62 for Listening. Thus, the difference of the cross-lagged correlations may not accurately reflect the relative magnitudes of the underlying structural parameters. Unfortunately, Atkin *et al.* did not report the relevant variances, and thus only standardized versions of the estimates of the structural parameters β_2 and γ_2 can be calculated. This calculation yields a result in conflict with that of Atkin *et al.*—the standardized estimates of β_2 and γ_2 are .20 and .28, respectively, when Listening is identified with X and the Intellectual Composite with Y in Figure 10.4. Thus, if an attribution of preponderant causal effect must be made from these data, it should be opposite from that of Atkin *et al.* At the very least, this conflict in results renders equivocal their causal attributions.

2. Complications in 2W2V Model

As Duncan (1972) sagely observed, it is unreasonable to expect "that in panel analysis the usual obstacles to inference and estimation are suspended for the benefit of the analyst [p. 37]." Two major obstacles are measurement error and specification error. Their consequences for analysis and the consideration of alternative causal models are discussed below in the context of the 2W2V design. This discussion is also applicable to more complex causal models.

MEASUREMENT ERROR

A 2W2V model in which the observed variables are measured with error is shown in Figure 10.7. The causal influences are presumed to be trans-

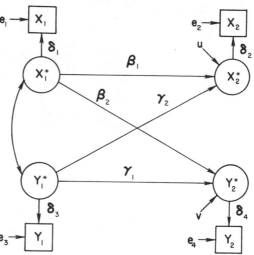

FIGURE 10.7. **Representation of a 2W2V design with measurement error. In addition to the previous assumptions for 2W2V panels the measurement errors (e₁) are assumed uncorrelated. Without additional information, this model is not identified.**

mitted through the unmeasured latent variables X^* and Y^*. Because additional parameters must be included in the model to represent the measurement error, there is no longer enough information in the relations among the observables to estimate the causal parameters relating the latent variables, and the model is underidentified.

In order to identify the model so that the desired causal parameters may be estimated from the data, additional information is necessary. One useful source of additional information would be the reliabilities of X and Y, which could be used to form consistent estimates of the causal parameters. If independent estimates of the reliabilities are not available, the additional information needed to identify the model may be obtained by increasing the number of measures of each variable at each time point (Wiley & Hornik, 1973).

An example of the use of multiple measures or indicators was the Radin (1971, 1974) study discussed in Section III. The presence of two measures of each of the three constructs made possible consistent estimation of the model parameters. In two-wave models, when two measures of X^* and Y^* that satisfy certain assumptions are available at each time point, the causal model is identified. Figure 10.8 illustrates a two-wave, two-variable, two-indicator (2W2V2I) model. The duplicate measures of each latent variable at each time point may be related by various psychometric models, the most general being a congeneric model (Jöreskog, 1973b).

The presence of measurement error is cited by advocates of cross-lagged correlation methods as invalidating the regression-based structural-model analyses (see Kenny, 1975a). This argument is based on the fact that partial regression coefficients are more severely affected by errors of measurement than are first-order correlations. It is true that with only one fallible measure

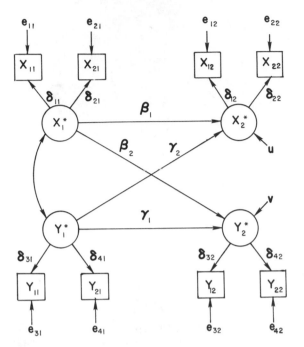

FIGURE 10.8. **A two-wave–two-variable–two-indicator (2W2V2I) model. The duplicate measures of each causal variable allow estimation of the causal parameters, β_1, β_2, γ_1, γ_2.**

of each variable at each time point, it is not possible, in general, to obtain acceptable estimates of the structural parameters, simply because estimation of an underidentified model rarely yields desirable results. The use of additional measures of each variable, as in Figure 10.8, alleviates the difficulties. Thus, we argue that the problem is one of research design; an appropriate research design that incorporates multiple indicators effectively counters the criticisms of the use of structural-model techniques with fallible measures.

Dealing with single, fallible measures or with multiple indicators is often complex in cross-lagged correlation methods. With one fallible measure of each variable, cross-lagged correlation methods employ complicated correction procedures designed to disattenuate the cross-lagged correlations and to control for changes in reliability over time (see Crano *et al.*, 1972; Kenny, 1975a). Because, as we argue, cross-lagged correlations rarely are an appropriate measure of causal influence, it is not clear that even if a proper procedure for correcting the correlations were available, the method would even be as good as estimation of an underidentified structural model, such as Figure 10.7.

When there are multiple, fallible indicators of each variable, the determination of causal influences using cross-lagged correlations increases in complexity. Unlike the structural-regression methods, with cross-lagged correlations no procedure exists for using information from the multiple indicators simultaneously. Each fallible indicator is considered separately in making the cross-lagged comparisons, and measurement error is dealt with without taking advantage of the information availabe from other indicators of the same variable.

With multiple indicators, the number of cross-lagged comparisons obtained from a set of data can become quite large. When there are k waves of data, p indicators of one variable, and q indicators of the other variable, the number of possible cross-lagged comparisons is $pq\binom{k}{2}$. In the Crano *et al.* (1972) investigation of intelligence and achievement, $k = 2$, $p = 12$, $q = 3$, and there are 36 cross-lagged comparisons. (Crano *et al.* also consider cross-lagged comparisons between indicators of the same construct and obtain many more than 36 comparisons.)

SPECIFICATION ERROR

Specification error, as described in Section III, occurs when the postulated causal model is an incorrect representation of the actual (psychological) process. (Measurement error can be considered a special form of specification error.) Clearly, numerous ways exist for model assumptions to be violated; we consider briefly forms of specification error particularly relevant to models for longitudinal panel data. Duncan (1972) presented many examples of specification errors in panel models due to omitted causal influences and correlated errors. Sörbom (1975) discussed detection of correlated errors in panel data by comparison of alternative structural models. Many other plausible forms of specification error in longitudinal panel models are considered in Duncan (1975a) and in Jöreskog and Sörbom (1977).

A commonly considered form of specification error in models for analyzing panel data is the existence of a common factor causing both variables (X and Y). In Figure 10.9 the common factor (Z) is posited as the sole causal factor; the observed scores are related only through this common causal influence. An analysis based on the model in Figure 10.4 when the

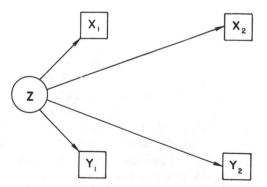

FIGURE 10.9. **An alternative causal structure for the 2W2V design. All the causal influence is carried by the common factor Z.**

model in Figure 10.9 is correct is likely to yield misleading results. This specification error is just a form of spurious correlation as discussed in Section I and depicted in Figure 10.1a. Kenny (1975a) reinterpreted the method of cross-lagged correlation as a technique for ruling out a rival hypothesis of spurious correlation.

Another important and similar form of specification error involves omitted causal variables that influence the Time 2 variables. When these variables are correlated with the Time 1 measures, the assumption that the disturbance terms (u and v) at Time 2 are uncorrelated with the Time 1 variables is violated. Kenny (1975a) claimed that the likely presence of omitted causal variables makes inference from panel data by regression methods "problematic."

Complete specification by the inclusion of all important causal variables is extremely important. However, we take exception to the claim that cross-lagged correlations are immune to the effects of specification error. Consider the relation between the difference of the cross-lagged correlations and the difference of the structural parameters in the simple case where X and Y have equal stabilities and their variances are standardized. The two differences are then proportional, and any specification error that seriously distorts the estimates of the structural parameters will, almost certainly, also seriously distort the difference of the cross-lagged correlations. This argument generalizes to more complex cases.

B. Multiple Wave Panel Designs

In developmental research, more than two waves of observations are often desired, since measurements at additional points in time offer additional information about the developmental processes. The multiplicity of plausible models that can be constructed for 2W2V data (Duncan, 1969b, 1972, 1975b) illustrates the difficulty of making causal inferences from analyses of two-wave panel data. Much less is known about the formulation and analysis of structural models for multiwave panel data; some procedures and problems for the analysis of multiwave panel data are considered in Bielby and Hauser (1977), Hannan, Rubinson, and Warren (1974), Jöreskog and Sörbom (1977), and Wheaton et al. (1977). What is clear from these analyses is that the problems are complex; "there are no stock or universal models for analyzing panel data [Bielby & Hauser, 1977, p. 148]."

A number of empirical studies in which researchers attempted to make causal statements from analyses of multiwave, longitudinal panel data are discussed below. Most of these studies focus on the examination of reciprocal causal effects. To illustrate the potential usefulness of structural-equation models for such analyses, a causal model for the panel data in each of these studies is illustrated, and issues in the analysis of these models are briefly discussed. These models should be viewed with considerable caution; their purpose is primarily to illustrate that through the use of structural equation models substantive questions about causal effects can be explicitly formulated, and the key parameters that represent these causal effects can be identified and interpreted. Measurement models and error specifications have been greatly simplified, and in many cases the number of indicators is probably excessive. An adequate structural regression model for each of these data can be obtained only after a thorough examination and analysis of the properties of the data and of alternative structural regression models for the data.

1. Infant Behavior and Intellectual Development

Crano (1977) reported an analysis of data from the Berkeley Growth Study, which includes longitudinal data on infant behavior and intellectual development. Behavioral and mental-test measures on the original sample of 61 children were collected monthly for the first 15 months of life, at 3-month intervals through 30 months, and at 6-month intervals through 18 years. The Crano analysis concentrated on the span of 10–36 months. As in previous analyses of these data, some grouping of the data was undertaken. Four waves of data were created by grouping into single waves the following three-wave groupings of the time periods: 10–12 months, 13–15 months, 18–24 months, and 27–36 months. Each wave contained a mental-abiliities measure and multiple measures of infant behavior. The four waves are represented as a structural model in Figure 10.10. This model is discussed in detail below.

Crano investigated the causal influences of infant behavior and intelligence over time. He employed the method of cross-lagged correlation to detect a preponderant direction of causal influence. Crano found that "the

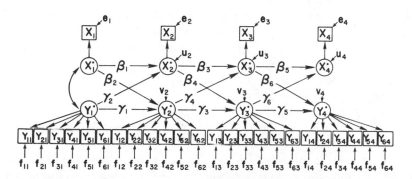

FIGURE 10.10. **A possible model for the data considered by Crano (1977). Parameters for the loadings of indicators on latent variables have been omitted for simplicity. Constructs: X* = infant intelligence; Y* = infant behavior. Indicators: X = mental-test score; Y_1 = activity; Y_2 = responsiveness; Y_3 = speed of movements; Y_4 = degree of strangeness; Y_5 = positive behavior; Y_6 = emotional tone.**

factors underlying mental scores operated as causes of later behavior [1977, p. 147]." With four waves of data, one intelligence measure, and six behavior measures, 36 cross-lagged comparisons of behavior and intelligence were available. After adjusting these correlations for changes in reliability over time, 31 of these comparisons favored the conclusion that intelligence causes later behavior; 7 of these 31 differences were statistically significant.

The reciprocal relation between infant intelligence and infant behavior is of central interest in Crano's analysis. This reciprocal relation over time between these two constructs, which are denoted by X^* and Y^* in Figure 10.10, is the major feature of the structural model component of a causal model for these longitudinal panel data. The parameters of the structural model are the β_i and γ_i ($i = 1,...,6$). Many plausible structural models can be formulated; the one depicted in Figure 10.10 incorporates many important restrictions. The causal influences are assumed to span only one time period in this model; for example, no direct causal influences are postulated on behavior at Time 3 by either intelligence at Time 1 or behavior at Time 1. The causal influences of Time 1 constructs on Time 3 constructs are assumed to be mediated by the Time 2 constructs. Also, autocorrelations of the disturbances (the u_i and v_i) are assumed to be zero.

The measurement model relates X^* and Y^* to the observed indicators of infant intelligence and infant behavior. Figure 10.10 has a rather formidable appearance due primarily to the inclusion of six indicators of infant behavior at each time point. It is not certain that all six are necessary or even desirable; a more cohesive and valid representation of this construct might be obtained by using some subset of these indicators. The parameters of the measurement model are not shown in Figure 10.10. The f_{jk} represent the unique portion of each of the indicators ($j = 1,...,6$) at each point in time ($k = 1,...,3$). Correlations of the f_{jk} within and between time periods are not included in the model depicted in Figure 10.10. However, correlations among the unique portions of the same indicator at different time points are often found to be important features of the data.

With only one indicator of intelligence at each time point, not all parts of a general model for Crano's data are identified. Estimated reliabilities of the mental-abilities measures as in Bayley (1933) provide additional information necessary to identify the model.

Data-analysis procedures for these structural models facilitate model modification on the basis of the fit of alternative models to the data. For example, the usefulness of direct causal influences that span more than one wave of data can be investigated by fitting a model to the data that includes these causal paths and then determining whether these additional causal paths improve the fit of the model to the data. (Technical methods and issues in comparing alternative models are presented in Jöreskog and Sörbom, 1977, 1978; and Sörbom, 1975. See also Chapter 11, this volume.) Other alternative models that allow autocorrelated errors in the indicators could similarly be compared with the model in Figure 10.10. Some measure of predominant causal influences or of the strength of the reciprocal causal relation can be obtained by examining the fit of models that restrict the β_i and/or the γ_i ($i = 2,4,6$) to be zero.

2. Home Environment and Intellectual Development

A longitudinal study of infants' home environments and their intellectual development was reported in a series of papers by Bradley, Caldwell, and Elardo (Bradley & Caldwell, 1976a, 1976b; Elardo, Bradley, & Caldwell, 1975). The authors were primarily interested in the prediction of later mental-test performance by measures of home environment. Elardo *et al.* reported data gathered on 77 normal infants whose mental-test performance was assessed at 6, 12, and 36 months of age, and whose home environment was assessed at 6, 12, and 24 months of age using the Inventory of Home Stimulation. The Inventory of Home Stimulation consists of 45 items organized into six separate subscales.

This longitudinal study can be represented as an incomplete four-wave panel with waves at 6, 12, 24, and 36 months. Mental-test scores are missing at Wave 3, and home environment measures are missing at Wave 4. A continuation of this study reported in Bradley and Caldwell (1976b) adds a fifth-wave measurement of mental ability from the Stanford–Binet at 54 months.

A causal model for these longitudinal data is shown in Figure 10.11. The two latent variables are mental ability and home environment. The structural parameters representing the influence of the home-environment construct

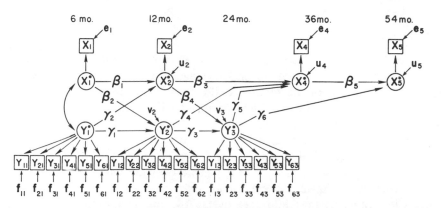

FIGURE 10.11. **A possible model for the data on home environment and intellectual development. Parameters for the loadings of indicators on the latent variables have been omitted for simplicity. Constructs: X* = infant intelligence; Y* = home environment. Indicators: X = mental-test score; Y$_1$ = maternal responsiveness; Y$_2$ = avoidance of restriction; Y$_3$ = organization of environment; Y$_4$ = play materials; Y$_5$ = maternal involvement; Y$_6$ = variety in stimulation.**

on later mental ability are of central interest to the investigators, although they did not frame their analyses in this manner. Also of interest are the reciprocal influences of mental ability on later home environment and the stability of the home-environment measure. Estimation of the causal parameters for home environment over time, and of the loadings of the subscales of the Inventory of Home Stimulation on the latent variable would be useful in interpreting the home-environment measures. Although no correlated errors between subscales within time periods or autocorrelations of individual subscales are built into this particular model, alternative models, incorporating correlated errors may provide better fits to the data. Other model modifications, such as direct causal paths longer than one time period, could also be incorporated. A data analysis based on these possible models would help to explicate the causal influences between home environment and intellectual development and provide a more detailed longitudinal description of the properties of the Inventory of Home Stimulation.

The analyses in Elardo *et al.* (1975) described the prediction of later mental-test scores by the home-environment measures. The most predictable mental-test score was the score on the Stanford–Binet at 36 months. Inspection of the results reveals that when predicting mental-test scores at 36 months, the unit weighting of the subscales to form a total home-environment score is at least as useful as using the data to determine individual subscale weights. As would be expected, the correlation between mental-test scores and home-environment measures increased as the time lag between the two measures decreased. Certainly a relationship between home environment and later intellectual development is supported by these studies. Further analyses may provide more detailed descriptions of the important causal processes.

3. Mother–Child Interaction

Clarke-Stewart (1973) collected data on 36 mother–child dyads over a 9-month period, tracing the children from age 9 months to 18 months. Repeated observations of the mother–child dyads were made both in natural settings (the home) and in a variety of standardized or semistructured (test and laboratory) situations. The longitudinal panel design, measuring both mother and child attributes and behaviors at each wave, is appropriate for untangling the reciprocal causal influences in mother–child interaction.

The portion of the total data that Clarke-Stewart used to make causal inferences (see 1973, pp. 82–91) corresponds to a three-wave longitudinal panel with waves at the child ages of 11, 14, and 17 months. Most of the attempts at causal explanation used data from only the first and third waves. For all causal statements Clarke-Stewart used the method of cross-lagged correlation. One of these 2W2V analyses was discussed in Section III. All three waves of data were involved in a cross-lagged comparison of the causal influences of maternal attention and the child's attachment to the mother. Clarke-Stewart considered the three waves of data as two two-wave pieces. That is, a 2W2V analysis of Waves 1 and 2 and a 2W2V analysis of Waves 2 and 3 were conducted separately using cross-lagged correlations. Unlike the multiple-wave, cross-lagged comparisons of Crano (1977) and Calsyn and Kenny (1977), Clarke-Stewart presented no information on a 2W2V analysis of Waves 1 and 3.

Based on the two sets of cross-lagged correlations, Clarke-Stewart (1973) offered the following interpretation:

> At times 1 and 2 the cross-lagged correlations for infant attachment and maternal attention suggested that maternal attention was causing an increase in infant attachment. From Time 2 to Time 3, however, the cross-lagged correlations implied the opposite: that infant attachment was causing maternal attention. This finding suggests the possibility that, as mother and child search for harmonious, balanced interaction over the course of development, first one then the other assumes the "causal role" [pp. 90–91].

Without a comprehensive analysis of the entire time span (11–17 months) and given the potential of cross-lagged correlations to produce misleading conclusions, this conclusion should be regarded as tentative. In fact, some sets of data can produce this alternating cross-lagged pattern even though the underlying causal structure is not consistent with this interpretation.

A possible causal model for the 3W2V panel is shown in Figure 10.12. This panel model in Figure 10.12 allows doubly lagged causation between Waves 1 and 3 between variables but not within variables. Labouvie (1974) also considered distal and proximal reciprocal causation in a causal model.

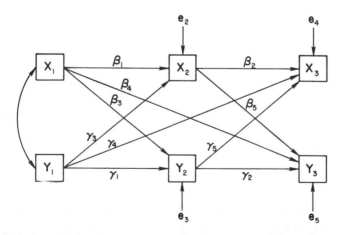

FIGURE 10.12. **A possible model for the 3W2V data of Clarke-Stewart (1973) with the causal parameters and structural-regression equations shown. The X variables are maternal attention to the child and the Y variables are the child's attachment to the mother.** $X_2 = \beta_1 X_1 + \gamma_3 Y_1 + e_2$; $X_3 = \beta_2 X_2 + \gamma_4 Y_1 + \gamma_5 Y_2 + e_4$; $Y_2 = \gamma_1 Y_1 + \beta_3 X_1 + e_3$; $Y_3 = \gamma_2 Y_2 + \beta_4 X_1 + \beta_5 X_2 + e_5$.

This model is not identified unless additional information on the reliabilities of the observation is incorporated into the analysis or the unrealistic assumption of perfect measurement is made. A causal model analysis of these three-wave data is certainly more attractive, since it would use all the data at once. Also, given the problems with the cross-lagged correlations, it might be expected that analyzing all three time periods at once would alter the original conclusions, especially if there were any appreciable direct causal effects between Wave 1 and Wave 3, represented by β_4 and γ_4 in Figure 10.12.

It should be noted that Figure 10.12 is equivalent to a path analysis model and is subject to many of the severe problems of such models. A model based on only the data shown in Figure 10.12 is unlikely to be adequate for assessing causal effects.

4. Self-Concept and Achievement

A reanalysis of data from a five-wave longitudinal panel design that included measures of self-concept and academic achievement was reported by Calsyn and Kenny (1977). The original study included data collected on 556 adolescents over a 5 year span. Data from this five-wave panel were analyzed by the method of cross-lagged correlation in order to investigate the causal influences of academic achievement and self-concept. For the females in the sample, multiple comparisons of the cross-lagged correlations led Calsyn and Kenny to conclude that grade-point average is causally predominant over self-concept of ability. This conclusion was not supported by the data on the males in the study. A causal model for these 5W2V data could be constructed analogous to Figure 10.12. Reliability information for the two measures would be necessary for estimation or assessment of that model.

An interesting complication in the analysis of Calsyn and Kenny was their attempt to test the validity of the self-enhancement model, which predicts that perceived evaluation of others influences self-concept, which in turn influences academic achievement. Measures of the perceived evaluations of teachers, parents, and friends were included in the original study to investigate this model. Using cross-lagged correlations, Calsyn and Kenny found little support for this model. More support was found for a skill-development model in which academic achievement influences both self-concept and perceived evaluation of others. Analyses of alternative causal models for these longitudinal data incorporating the alternative causal orderings may yield useful information about the relative validities of the self-enhancement and skill-development models.

C. Limitations of Path Analysis

Path analysis has been widely used in many areas of social science as a data-analysis method for making causal inferences and assessing causal effects from cross-sectional and longitudinal data. Path analysis is a very special and limited structural equation method in which a measurement model to accommodate multiple, fallible indicators does not exist. Although path analysis does incorporate many of the attractive heuristics of structural equation models, path analysis possesses major shortcomings as a statistical method. Essentially, path analysis is "multiple regression with pictures." We discuss some specific problems below.

Important problems with inferences based on path analyses arise as a result of fallible measurement. In examining structural-equation models we saw that single fallible indicators of constructs in the model often caused the parameters of the relations among the latent variables to be underidentified, as their relations could not be estimated from the data. In fact, the usefulness of multiple measures for overcoming such problems is a major message of this chapter. However, path analysis has very limited ability to take advantage of multiple indicators. In path analysis causal effects are indicated by use of (standardized) partial-regression coefficients for the causal paths among the observed variables that are specified by the model. It is well known that errors of measurement have severe and complex effects on estimates obtained from multiple regressions of observed fallible measures. Thus, these path coefficients are not sound evidence upon which to base causal attributions when measurement is not perfect.

Additional adverse complications are present when multiple fallible measures of the same latent variable are included in a path analysis, such as by using multiple background (exogenous) measures or by incorporating parallel causal paths for endogenous multiple measures. Consider two parallel (in the sense of classical test theory) measures, X_1 and X_2, of the latent variable X^*, we wish to investigate the effect of the variable denoted by X^* on an outcome variable Y. It is well known that an estimate of the slope of interest, β_{YX^*}, obtained from a regression of Y on one of the fallible measures, is biased downward and has expectation $\rho^2\beta_{YX^*}$, where ρ^2 is the reliability of the measures of X^*. However, if both measures were used in an attempt, say, to incorporate multiple measures into a path analysis, the resulting estimates are even less desirable than that above. For the regression equation $Y = \beta_0 + \beta_1 X_1 + \beta_2 X_2 + e$, it is easy to show that $\beta_1 = \beta_2 = \beta_{YX^*}[\rho^2/(1 + \rho^2)]$, and thus each regression estimate (path coefficient) is more severely biased downward than when only a single measure was used. This kind of result generalizes to more complex measurement models and to multiple regression with additional predicators. The point is that including multiple measures in a path analysis will work to distort and probably diminish the causal attribution made to each of the multiple measures.

For example, Weinraub and Lewis (1977) performed a path analysis for data on the reaction of the child to maternal separation. In the path model, mother scores on the Wechsler Adult Intelligence Scale and the Embedded Figures Test, which can be considered as measures of intelligence, were included as exogenous variables. Almost all the predicted causal effects of these variables (Weinraub & Lewis, Figure 1) were not substantiated in the results of their path analysis (Weinraub & Lewis, Figure 2). In addition, multiple measures of the mother–child interaction were incorporated into the path model as endogenous variables in predicting the child's response to maternal absence.

Some of the simple models for longitudinal panel data that have been presented, such as Figure 10.4, are equivalent to path analysis models. Duncan (1969b, 1972) has shown in great detail the problems with making causal attributions from such 2W2V models. Our major motivation in presenting such models was to illustrate the severe problems with cross-lagged correlation; even in the very special situations in which the path-analysis model is adequate, the method of cross-lagged correlation will rarely yield satisfactory results. Also, the simple models serve as a foundation on which to construct more sophisticated and useful models that incorporate multiple waves and multiple measures.

Additional problems more specific to the analysis of longitudinal panel data must also be considered in an assessment of path analysis. Even with perfect measurement of the variables in the model, error structures commonly seen in longitudinal data cause serious problems for ordinary least squares (OLS), the usual estimation method employed for the multiple-regression equations that are derived from a path model. Path-analysis models for longitudinal panel data frequently incorporate lagged regression equations; that is, regression equations in which one of the predictor variables is an earlier measure of the outcome variable. For example, Bachman and O'Malley (1977) report a path analysis of longitudinal-panel data on self-esteem and educational and occupational attainment that included measures of self-esteem during high school and 5 years after high school. OLS is not adequate for estimating lagged regression models (e.g., Hannan & Young, 1977), especially when reciprocal influences such as those between self-esteem and attainment are presumed to exist. Hannan and Young (1977) discuss various alternative estimators for lagged and reciprocal regression models.

We arrive at a negative assessment of the value of path analysis for detecting causal influences because of some important limitations of the method; however, we recognize that the contribution of path analysis to the evolution and use of causal models has been considerable. With the availability of more powerful modeling and analysis strategies, path analysis should be supplanted. But this is certainly not to say that no difficulties exist with the use and interpretation of structural equation methods.

V. Further Issues

So far we have considered the construction and analysis of causal models for data arising from various longitudinal panel designs. Some alternative techniques for the analysis of such data have been compared with the estimation of the appropriate structural models. A number of unresolved and important issues have not been dealt with in the previous discussion. Some topics of current and future methodological interest are discussed below. We hope that other issues, such as the proper design, analysis, and interpretation of longitudinal panels incorporating many background variables, will receive extended treatment in future methodological work.

A. Comparing Nonequivalent Groups

The pretest–posttest design employed in much of educational research and evaluation is a simple longitudinal design, with two waves of measurement on one variable. Often this design is used to compare two or more groups given alternative (educational) treatments. These groups may be formed by random assignment of cases to groups or by nonrandom, often uncontrolled, mechanisms such as self-selection. In the latter case the groups are nonequivalent. Various statistical adjustments and techniques have been proposed for the comparison of nonequivalent groups. Estimation of the effect of a treatment is the usual purpose of such a comparison. The following discussion of these techniques in the context of models for data from two-wave longitudinal panels emphasizes the important role of complete model specification.

We denote the pretest (the measure at Time 1) by X_1 and the posttest (the measure at Time 2) by X_2. We define a dummy variable, T, to indicate group membership. For two groups, Group A and Group B, $T = 1$ for members of Group A, and $T = 0$ for members of Group B. Since a measure of T for each person at each time point is available (albeit the same value at both times), a 2W2V design can be constructed using measures of X and T at each of the two waves. Figure 10.13 illustrates this 2W2V design. When Groups A and B are formed by random assignment, X_1 and T are uncorrelated in the population. When the groups are nonequivalent, X and T are correlated at Time 1. This correlation between X_1 and T necessitates statistical adjustments for the initial nonequivalence of the groups.

Some of the most widely discussed methods proposed for analyzing data from nonequivalent groups can be obtained by applying the analysis meth-

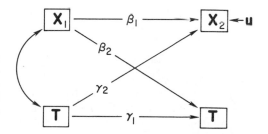

FIGURE 10.13. **A 2W2V model for a pretest–posttest design with nonequivalent groups.** X_1 and X_2 are pretest and posttest, respectively, and the dummy variable T indicates group membership.

ods discussed in this chapter to this 2W2V design. A comparison of the structural parameters of the model in Figure 10.13 is equivalent to the analysis of covariance (ANCOVA) with X_1 as the covariate. The regression model for this ANCOVA can be written in term of the structural parameters in Figure 10.13:

$$X_2 = \mu + \gamma_2 T + \beta_1 X_1 + u.$$

Since $\gamma_2 = \beta_{X_2 T \cdot X_1}$, an estimate of the parameter γ_2 is an estimate of the treatment effect defined by ANCOVA. The usual ANCOVA null hypothesis can be written as $H_0: \beta_{X_2 T \cdot X_1} = 0$. Since β_2 is the regression parameter $\beta_{TX_1 \cdot T}$, by the definition of a partial-regression coefficient, β_2 is identically zero. (The least-squares estimate of β_2 is also zero in the sample). Thus, a test of the equality of the structural parameters ($H_0: \gamma_2 = \beta_2$) is equivalent to a test of the ANCOVA null hypothesis. Comparing the estimates of γ_2 and β_2 is the same as comparing the ANCOVA estimate of the treatment effect with zero.

The equivalences of the structural-model estimates with ANCOVA procedures extend to analyses with fallible covariates. Since the pretest X_1 is often acknowledged to be a fallible measure of initial ability, it is necessary to use duplicate measures of initial ability (as in Figure 10.8) or to correct for the unreliability of X_1 (see Figure 10.7). Comparing the structural parameters in these models, which allow fallible measurement, is equivalent to ANCOVA procedures devised for dealing with measurment errors. Duplicate pretest measures were considered in Lord (1960), and reliability corrections were investigated in Porter (1967).

An analysis of the 2W2V design in Figure 10.13 using the method of cross-lagged correlation yields other methods proposed for analyzing data from nonequivalent groups. In Figure 10.13, the null hypothesis for the equality of the cross-lagged correlations is $H_0: \rho_{X_1 T} = \rho_{X_2 T}$. This null hypothesis is identical to that of standarized change-score analysis proposed by Kenny (1975b).

Standardized change score analysis is also closely related to the ANCOVA correction procedure proposed by Campbell and Erlebacher (1970). Their common-factor correction involves a reliability correction of the ANCOVA pooled-within slope using the correlation of X_1 and X_2. The Campbell–Erlebacher null hypothesis is also identical to that of standardized change scores.

Kenny (1975b) argued for the use of standardized change scores when a fan-spread model of growth is appropriate. The fan-spread model predicts that the mean difference between Groups A and B increases at the same rate as the pooled within-group standard deviation of X. Bryk and Weisberg (1977) demonstrated that, when a very special fan-spread model of growth is satisfied, the use of standardized change scores is justified and that ANCOVA also is an appropriate method of analysis. For more general models of growth, Bryk and Weisberg found serious problems with standardized change scores and with other linear-model adjustment techniques. Bryk and Weisberg also strongly recommended use of multiwave designs for assessment of treatment effects.

Cronbach, Rogosa, Floden, and Price (1977) presented a model for quasi-experimental data that emphasized the nonrandom group-assignment process and specification of the within-group models for the outcome variable. Cronbach *et al.* considered a selection variable D, composed of various initial characteristics of the cases, which has the property that membership in Group A or Group B is a probabilistic function of D. When a direct influence of D and X_2 exists ($\rho_{X_2 D \cdot X_1 T} \neq 0$), ANCOVA with X_1 as the covariate does not adequately adjust for the initial nonequivalence of the groups. Cronbach *et al.* expressed the bias resulting from the ANCOVA adjustment as a function of $\rho_{X_2 D \cdot X_1}$. The model in Figure 10.13 is not correctly specified when D has a direct causal influence on X_2, since an important causal influence on X_2 has been omitted from the model. An analysis based on the misspecified model will not yield adequate estimates of the structural parameters. Complete specification of either the within-group models for outcome or the between-groups model of the group-assignment process is necessary to form adequate adjustments for the initial nonequivalence of the groups.

Sörbom (1978) applied structural models to the comparison of nonequivalent groups, incorporating model-modification techniques and general measurement models. Unless the model is completely specified with respect to the selection mechanisms that formed the nonequivalent groups or with respect to the within-group model for outcome, proper assessment of the effect of the treatment using Sörbom's method is very unlikely.

B. Causal Lag and Distal Causation

The duration of direct causal influences within and between variables is a central research question in the design, analysis, and interpretation of longitudinal research. The temporal lag between repeated measurements or waves is a crucial element in the design of a longitudinal study. Unfortunately, developmental theories that would be the best guides to the appropriate temporal spacing of measurements offer little guidance in most situations. As a result, as Kenny (1975a) noted: "Normally the lag between measurements is chosen because of convenience not theory, since theory rarely specifies the exact length of the causal lag [p. 894]." The appropriate temporal spacing of measurements certainly depends on the substantive process under scrutiny. A secondary consideration is the correspondence or lack of correspondence between chronological time and psychological time in the particular developmental process. Lack of sensitivity to important developmental change and uneconomical repetition of measurements are two possible consequences of inappropriate timing and spacing of measurements in a longitudinal study.

If theory cannot aid in the resolution of these design questions, can empirical determinations of the proper temporal spacing of measurements be made? No empirical or technical criteria exist for determining the adequacy of a longitudinal design in a specific research setting. However, it is possible that the comparison and modification of alternative causal models for multiwave designs may yield useful information. The majority of structural models for longitudinal panel data postulate single-period causal lags or equal lags across multiple waves. Exceptions are the 3W2V model of Hannan *et al.* (1974), the discussion in Labouvie (1974), and some models discussed in this chapter. An empirical determination of the duration of direct causal influences for a particular psychological process would be important information for the design of future longitudinal research in that area.

The benefits of empirical determinations of appropriate causal lags may extend far beyond improvements in the design of longitudinal studies. In some research areas the empirical determination of the causal lag of the psychological process may be the most important substantive knowledge obtained from a program of longitudinal research. The structure and duration of an interactive process is often of great interest. In other contexts information on causal lags may be the first step in building a knowledge base that later will include empirical determinations of the magnitude of causal effects. Also, the correlations of measurement errors (uniquenesses) over time, sometimes considered a nuisance in analyses, may yield useful psychometric information on the measurement instruments employed in the study. These considerations also apply to longitudinal microanalyses of interactive processes, which have not been explicitly discussed, and to interactive models for these data such as those formulated by Thomas and Martin (1976).

C. Stength of Reciprocal Effects

Despite the extended discussion of reciprocal causal effects and of their assessment from longitudinal data, no measure of the strength of a reciprocal causal relation has been presented. In some substantive areas, the strength of the reciprocal relations between variables is of major interest. For example, in developmental research the concept of attachment, commonly viewed as the strength of the mother–child bond, can be interpreted in the context of the reciprocal causal relation between mother and child behaviors (Rogosa & Ambron, 1976). The strength (or secureness) of the attachment could be assessed by estimating the strength of the reciprocal relation between mother and child behaviors using data from a longitudinal panel design.

For data from a 2W2V design, a number of descriptive measures appear to be plausible measures of the strength of a reciprocal relation. The synchronous (within-time, between-variable) correlations, perhaps appropriately averaged, provide one measure of the strength of the relation between the variables. The magnitudes of the cross-lagged correlations provide another measure.

An alternative to these descriptive measures is based on the structural model for 2W2V data. The full model for 2W2V data is shown in Figure 10.4. The importance of the reciprocal relation between the two variables in fitting a model to the data could be assessed by comparing the fit to the data of the model in Figure 10.4 with the fit to the same data of a restricted model in which β_2 and γ_2 are constrained to be zero. According to this restricted model, associations between X and Y at both time points result from their background correlation; no direct causal influences are postulated. A relative measure of the strength of the reciprocal causation is the relative incremental lack of fit of the restricted model to the 2W2V data. That is, the full and restricted models are fitted to the data, and the difference of the goodness of fit (usually assessed by a chi-square statistic as in Jöreskog & Sörbom, 1977) of these alternative models is compared with the fit of the full model.

This method for assessing the strength of a reciprocal relation is consistent with the strategy, emphasized in this chapter, of fitting alternative structural models, resulting from the inclusion or omission of different model components, to longitudinal data. Methodological work is needed to determine the most useful measure of the strength of a reciprocal relation and to evaluate its properties. The proposed comparison of full and restricted models is possibly a more appropriate test of the null hypothesis of spuriousness described by Kenny (1975a) than the cross-lagged correlation analysis that Kenny advocated. Note that even when $\beta_2 = \gamma_2 = 0$ the difference of the cross-lagged correlations may be large if the stabilities of X and Y differ appreciably.

Generalizations of the proposed method to multiwave studies are straightforward. In some applications, it may be profitable to assess the strength of the reciprocal relation in subsets of the full multiwave design, as the strength of the reciprocal relation may not be constant over the entire time period. Other generalizations of the method, such as to longitudinal designs with multiple, fallible indicators, are also feasible.

D. Cohort Effects

Cohort effects have received considerable attention in the design and analysis of research on developmental and life-span trends. Consideration of cohort effects as in Schaie (1965) and Nesselroade and Baltes (1974) is also important in longitudinal studies that focus on associations among variables. The framework for this discussion of cohort effects is that members of the same cohort are more alike in relevant dimensions than are members of different cohorts. A useful analogy is to educational research on classroom learning where members of the same class have shared educational experiences and thus are more similar in important ways than are members of different classes (Cronbach & Webb, 1975).

In many instances, a data analysis conducted within cohorts and between cohorts may be very informative. The relations among variables over all cases (cohort membership ignored) within and between waves can be decomposed into within-cohort and between-cohort relations. Mathematical expressions for this kind of decomposition are well known in the literature on data aggregation and multilevel data analysis (e.g., Hannan & Burstein, 1974). Relations between overall analyses, which ignore cohort membership, and within-cohort analyses can be interpreted using these results. If substantial cohort effects exist, an overall analysis will confound them with other developmental effects; consequently, separate between- and within-cohort analyses are necessary for proper interpretation of the data.

E. Are We Ready for (Sound) Causal Inference?

Trying to answer a causal question from a set of data is asking a lot from those data. To satisfy the assumptions of the methods considered for making causal inferences from longitudinal data, high-quality data are necessary. Even then, some plausible methods of analysis may conceal more than they reveal. For the structural–causal models considered in this chapter the requirements are that the right variables be measured well. At times, the discussion in this chapter has proceeded as if ideal data were readily available. To measure, without error or with multiple indicators, all the relevant causal influences is a considerable task. Often the state of theoretical and empirical knowledge in a substantive area is not sufficiently advanced that all the relevant causal variables have been identified or that sufficient measurement techniques have been developed.

To avoid specification errors in models for longitudinal data, the simple longitudinal panel designs considered in this chapter may not be adequate. The incorporation of additional background and causal variables into the design and analysis may be necessary. Further complications in the specification of models for longitudinal panel data arise from assumptions of descriptive and explanatory continuity (see Huston-Stein & Baltes, 1976). Descriptive continuity implies that the latent variables that are measured at different time points are qualitatively the same across time. This may be a minimal assumption for making sound causal interpretations from longitudinal data. The presence of explanatory discontinuity would require different causal structures in some parts of the longitudinal model to represent adequately the psychological process in which the mediating processes and important behavioral antecedents are not constant over time.

The problems of measurement and specification are not insurmountable. But causal attribution is not an automatic process; useful causal conclusions are the product of careful thought, high-quality data, and sound data analysis. The causal models that have been presented have the attractive feature of incorporating substantive knowledge into the analysis of data and of facilitating model modification on the basis of the fit of alternative models to the data. However, in some substantive areas, more knowledge than is now available will be required for productive model building analysis. In other areas the proper and positive use of these methods in longitudinal research may be possible at the present time.

VI. Summary

This chapter has involved consideration of some methods for making causal statements in developmental research. Specific applications focused on the investigation of reciprocal causal effects in developmental processes. In the study of development and growth, longitudinal designs should be used. Cross-sectional designs will give conflicting (and misleading) evidence over replications, and can yield little information on the causal dynamics of development. For reasons of practical necessity and ecological validity the longitudinal designs will often be nonexperimental and naturalistic.

The importance of underlying models in problem formulation and in data analysis in longitudinal research is stressed. Additional knowledge from substantive theory and empirical evidence may be profitably incorporated into the analysis of data from these longitudinal designs through the formulation of causal models.

Causal models are presented as an attractive vehicle for the formulation of well-specified hypotheses in an empirically testable form. The construction of causal models is a two-stage procedure involving the structural model, which specifies the relations between the important constructs, and the measurement model, which relates unobserved constructs to their observable measures. The construction of a causal model from a substantive study illustrates the usefulness of multiple measures of constructs in the estimation of causal effects.

Longitudinal panel designs combine features of cross-sectional and time-series designs in that waves of cross sections, containing the same sampling units, are measured at two or more time points. The applicability of longitudinal designs to the study of reciprocal causal effects is emphasized. The two-wave–two-variable (2W2V) design has been widely used in investigations of reciprocal causal relations. A formulation of the 2W2V design as a causal model reveals that highly restrictive assumptions are necessary for estimation of causal influences. The popular method of cross-lagged correlation is shown to be undesirable and often misleading; direct estimation of the relevant causal parameters is preferable. Problems in measurement and model specification are considered for analyses based on structural models and on cross-lagged correlations, and some common forms of these two problems are illustrated for the 2W2V design.

The more powerful multiwave panel designs are described by formulating causal models for data from previously published longitudinal studies. The usefulness of alternative causal models and subsequent model modification in analyses of longitudinal panel data is stressed. Also, some serious limitations of the widely used method of path analysis, which is a special case of these structural equation models, are discussed.

Some unsolved methodological problems in the design and analysis of longitudinal research are discussed in the context of causal models for longitudinal panel data. Some speculations are offered for problems involving the comparison of nonequivalent groups, the detection of appropriate causal lags, the measurement of the strength of reciprocal effects, and the interpretation of cohort effects.

Acknowledgment

I am grateful to David Brandt, Frank Capell, Marco Martinez, Linda Martinson, Noreen Webb, and Michelle Zimowski for their comments and insights; the remaining problems are the responsibility of the author.

Chapter 11

Statistical Estimation of Structural Models in Longitudinal–Developmental Investigations

KARL G. JÖRESKOG

ABSTRACT

This chapter deals with statistical methodological problems in the analysis of data from large longitudinal studies in which the same or similar quantitative measurements have been obtained at two or more occasions, possibly from several different groups of people. Several models are developed for a wide range of applications for psychological and educational measurements. The problems of model specification, statistical identification, estimation and testing are discussed. In particular, the chapter focuses on the following problems: (1) the estimation of growth curves under autoregressive models; (2) the treatment of measurement errors in observed variables; and (3) the scaling of latent variables. Several examples are given illustrating the assessment of fit of a model and data-analytic strategies for model modification.

I. Introduction

The characteristic feature of a longitudinal research design is that the same measurements are obtained from the same people at two or more occasions. The purpose of a longitudinal or panel study is to assess the changes that occur between the occasions and to attribute these changes to certain background characteristics and events existing or occurring before the first occasion and/or to various treatments and developments that occur after the first occasion. A schematic illustration of a two-wave longitudinal design is given in Figure 11.1. Earlier chapters of this volume have dealt

303

LONGITUDINAL RESEARCH IN THE
STUDY OF BEHAVIOR AND DEVELOPMENT

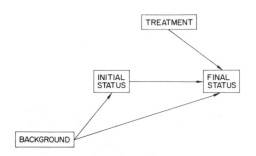

FIGURE 11.1. **Schematic representation of a two-wave longitudinal design.**

with the conceptual and substantive issues and with the logic of causal model building in longitudinal research in developmental psychology and education. Other chapters have dealt with specific methodological problems. Wiley and Harnischfeger (1973) have given an account of the conceptual issues in the attribution of change in educational studies. In the sociological literature there have been a number of articles concerned with the specification of models incorporating causation and measurement errors and the analysis of data from panel studies (see, e.g., Bohrnstedt, 1969; Duncan, 1969a, 1972, 1975b; Heise, 1969, 1970). Other papers dealing with methodological problems are Lord (1963), Thorndike (1966), Härnqvist (1968), Cronbach and Furby (1970), and Bergman (1971). Complex models involving multiple measurements and/or several occasions have been considered by Harris (1963a), Jöreskog (1970a), Corballis and Traub (1970), Nesselroade (1972), Corballis (1973), Bentler (1973), Frederiksen (1974), Jöreskog and Sörbom (1976, 1977), and Olsson and Bergman (1977).

In this chapter we consider several models suitable for analyzing longitudinal data and deal with problems of model specification and statistical identification, estimation, and testing. The general setup is that of a longitudinal study where the same or similar quantitative measurements have been obtained at two or more occasions, possibly from several different groups of people. The models cover a wide range of applications and are relevant for psychological and educational measurements as well as for social and socioeconomic measurements.

Section III considers the measurement and assessment of change at the group level. It deals with the estimation of growth curves describing the means of the variables as functions of time. This section also considers various autoregressive or first-order Markov models that occur naturally in repeated measurements. In this section we treat the variables as error-free.

One of the most difficult problems for social scientists, when it comes to the formulation of a causal model, arises because many of the concepts and constructs that they want to work with are not directly measurable (see, e.g., Duncan, 1975a; Goldberger, 1972; Heise, 1975; and Torgerson, 1958, Chapter 1). Although such hypothetical concepts and constructs, or *latent variables,* as we shall call them, cannot be directly measured, a number of variables can be used to measure various aspects of these latent variables more or less accurately. Thus, although the latent variables cannot be directly observed, they have operational implications for relationships among observed variables. We may regard the observed variables as indicators of the latent variables. Each indicator has a relationship with the latent variable, but if we take one indicator alone to measure the latent variable, we obtain a biased measurement. By using several indicators of each latent variable we get a better measurement of the latent variable.

Another reason for using latent variables in behavioral and socioeconomic studies is that most of the measurements employed contain sizable errors of measurement (observational errors) that, if not taken into account, can cause severe bias in the results. Errors of measurement arise because of imperfection in the various measurement instruments (questionnaires, tests, etc.), that are used to measure such abstractions as people's behavior, attitudes, feelings, and motivations. Even if we could construct valid measurements of these, it is usually impossible to obtain perfectly reliable variables. Special care must be taken to obtain measurements that really measure the latent traits or hypothetical constructs that one is interested in measuring. Various models with latent variables for two-wave and multiwave situations are considered in Sections IV and V.

A common experience in two-wave longitudinal studies is that the initial status is the best determinant or predictor of the final status (see, e.g., Lord, 1963). Therefore, if one is interested in attributing change to certain background variables, one must find some way of effectively eliminating the initial status from the final status. This has been taken to mean that one should study difference scores (final scores minus initial scores). However, this is not necessary; the important thing is that both background variables and initial measures be included in the model as determinants of final measures. In multiwave studies one can determine the effect of the background variables on the dependent variable at various points in time. Most of the models introduced in Sections IV and V are considered both with and without background variables.

Often it is not possible, or even desirable, to specify the model completely, since there may be other models that are equally plausible. In such a situation it is necessary to have a technique of analysis that will give information about which of a number of alternative models is (are) the most reasonable. Also, if there is sufficient evidence to reject a given model because of poor fit to the data, the technique should be such as to suggest which part of the model is causing the poor fit. Several examples will be given illustrating the assessment of fit of a model and strategies for model modification.

In presenting the various models it is convenient to use a path diagram. In this path diagram observed variables are enclosed in squares, whereas latent variables are enclosed in circles. Residuals (errors in equations) and errors of measurements are included in the diagram but are not enclosed. A one-way arrow pointing from one variable x to another variable y indicates a possible direct causal influence of x on y, whereas a curved two-way arrow between x and y indicates that x and y may correlate without any causal interpretation of this correlation being given. It is convenient to write the coefficient associated with each arrow in the path diagram. When the coefficient is omitted it means that it is 1. For one-way arrows such coefficients will be (partial) regression coefficients (path coefficients) and for two-way arrows they will be covariances. In the special case when all observed and latent variables are standardized, these coefficients will be correlations. With these conventions it is possible to write down the model equations from the path diagram. In order to define the model completely it is necessary only to specify the assumptions about the origin and unit of measurement of the variables involved and the distributional assumptions, if any.

II. Computer Programs

All the models considered in this chapter may be estimated by means of three computer programs: ACOVSM by Jöreskog, van Thillo, and Gruvaeus (1970); LISREL by Jöreskog and Sörbom (1978); and COFAMM by Sörbom and Jöreskog (1976). The general models on which these programs are based are described briefly here for future reference. For each model introduced in later sections of this chapter it will be shown how this is a special case of one of the models presented here.

A. ACOVSM

The ACOVSM model considers a data matrix $\mathbf{X}(N \times p)$ of N observations on p variables and assumes that the rows of $\mathbf{X}$ are independently distributed, each having a multivariate normal distribution with the same variance–covariance matrix $\mathbf{\Sigma}$. It is assumed that

$$E(\mathbf{X}) = \mathbf{A}\mathbf{\Xi}\mathbf{P}, \tag{1}$$

where $\mathbf{A}(N \times g) = (a_{\alpha s})$ and $\mathbf{P}(h \times p) = (p_{ti})$ are known matrices of ranks g and h, respectively, $g \leq N$, $h \leq p$, and $\mathbf{\Xi}(g \times h) = (\xi_{st})$ is a matrix of parameters; and that $\mathbf{\Sigma}$ has the form

$$\mathbf{\Sigma} = \mathbf{B}(\mathbf{\Lambda}\mathbf{\Phi}\mathbf{\Lambda}' + \mathbf{\Psi}^2)\mathbf{B}' + \mathbf{\Theta}^2, \tag{2}$$

where the matrices $\mathbf{B}(p \times q) = (\beta_{ik})$, $\mathbf{\Lambda}(q \times r) = (\lambda_{km})$, the symmetric matrix $\mathbf{\Phi}(r \times r) = (\phi_{mn})$, and the diagonal matrices $\mathbf{\Psi}(q \times q) = (\delta_{kl}\psi_k)$ and $\mathbf{\Theta}(p \times p) = (\delta_{ij}\theta_i)$ are parameter matrices; δ_{ij} denotes the Kronecker delta, which is 1 if $i = j$ and 0 otherwise.

Thus, the general model is one where means, variances, and covariances are structured in terms of other sets of parameters that are to be estimated. In any application of this model, p, N, and $\mathbf{X}$ will be given by the data, and g, h, q, r, $\mathbf{A}$, and $\mathbf{P}$ will be given by the particular application. In the special case when both Ξ and Σ are unconstrained, one may test a sequence of linear hypotheses of the form

$$\mathbf{C}\Xi\mathbf{D} = 0, \tag{3}$$

where $\mathbf{C}(s \times g)$ and $\mathbf{D}(h \times t)$ are given matrices of ranks s and t, respectively.

For further information about the ACOVSM model and its uses see Jöreskog (1970c, 1973b).

B. LISREL

The LISREL model considers random vectors $\boldsymbol{\eta}' = (\eta_1, \eta_2, \ldots, \eta_m)$ and $\boldsymbol{\xi}' = (\xi_1, \xi_2, \ldots, \xi_n)$ of latent dependent and independent variables, respectively, and the following system of linear structural relations

$$\mathbf{B}\boldsymbol{\eta} = \boldsymbol{\Gamma}\boldsymbol{\xi} + \boldsymbol{\zeta} \tag{4}$$

where $\mathbf{B}(m \times m)$ and $\boldsymbol{\Gamma}(m \times n)$ are coefficient matrices and $\boldsymbol{\zeta}' = (\zeta_1, \zeta_2, \ldots, \zeta_m)$ is a random vector of residuals (errors in equations, random disturbance terms). Without loss of generality it may be assumed that $E(\boldsymbol{\eta}) = E(\boldsymbol{\zeta}) = 0$ and $\mathbf{E}(\boldsymbol{\xi}) = \mathbf{0}$. It is furthermore assumed that $\boldsymbol{\zeta}$ is uncorrelated with $\boldsymbol{\xi}$ and that $\mathbf{B}$ is nonsingular.

The vectors $\boldsymbol{\eta}$ and $\boldsymbol{\xi}$ are not observed but instead vectors $\mathbf{y}' = (y_1, y_2, \ldots, y_p)$ and $\mathbf{x}' = (x_1, x_2, \ldots, x_q)$ are observed, such that

$$\mathbf{y} = \boldsymbol{\Lambda}_y\boldsymbol{\eta} + \boldsymbol{\epsilon}, \tag{5}$$

$$\mathbf{x} = \boldsymbol{\Lambda}_x\boldsymbol{\xi} + \boldsymbol{\delta}, \tag{6}$$

where $\boldsymbol{\epsilon}$ and $\boldsymbol{\delta}$ are vectors of errors of measurement in $\mathbf{y}$ and $\mathbf{x}$, respectively. Both $\mathbf{y}$ and $\mathbf{x}$ are assumed to be measured as deviations from their means. The matrices $\boldsymbol{\Lambda}_y(p \times m)$ and $\boldsymbol{\Lambda}_x(q \times n)$ are regression matrices of $\mathbf{y}$ on $\boldsymbol{\eta}$ and of $\mathbf{x}$ on $\boldsymbol{\xi}$, respectively. It is convenient to refer to $\mathbf{y}$ and $\mathbf{x}$ as the observed variables and $\boldsymbol{\eta}$ and $\boldsymbol{\xi}$ as the latent variables. The errors of measurement are assumed to be uncorrelated with the latent variables.

Let $\boldsymbol{\Phi}(n \times n)$ and $\boldsymbol{\Psi}(m \times m)$ be the covariance matrices of $\boldsymbol{\xi}$ and $\boldsymbol{\zeta}$, respectively, and let $\boldsymbol{\Theta}_\epsilon$ and $\boldsymbol{\Theta}_\delta$ be the covariance matrices of $\boldsymbol{\epsilon}$ and $\boldsymbol{\delta}$, respectively. Then it follows, from the above assumption, that the covariance matrix $\boldsymbol{\Sigma}[(p + q) \times (p + q)]$ of $\mathbf{z} = (\mathbf{y}', \mathbf{x}')'$ is

$$\boldsymbol{\Sigma} = \begin{bmatrix} \boldsymbol{\Lambda}_y(\mathbf{B}^{-1}\boldsymbol{\Gamma}\boldsymbol{\Phi}\boldsymbol{\Gamma}'\mathbf{B}'^{-1} + \mathbf{B}^{-1}\boldsymbol{\Psi}\mathbf{B}'^{-1})\boldsymbol{\Lambda}_y' + \boldsymbol{\Theta}_\epsilon & \boldsymbol{\Lambda}_y\mathbf{B}^{-1}\boldsymbol{\Gamma}\boldsymbol{\Phi}\boldsymbol{\Lambda}_x' \\ \boldsymbol{\Lambda}_x\boldsymbol{\Phi}\boldsymbol{\Gamma}'\mathbf{B}'^{-1}\boldsymbol{\Lambda}_y' & \boldsymbol{\Lambda}_x\boldsymbol{\Phi}\boldsymbol{\Lambda}_x' + \boldsymbol{\Theta}_\delta \end{bmatrix} \tag{7}$$

The elements of $\boldsymbol{\Sigma}$ are functions of the elements of $\boldsymbol{\Lambda}_y$, $\boldsymbol{\Lambda}_x$, $\mathbf{B}$, $\boldsymbol{\Gamma}$, $\boldsymbol{\Phi}$, $\boldsymbol{\Theta}_\delta$

and Θ_ϵ. In applications some of these elements are fixed and equal to assigned values. In particular, this is so for elements in Λ_y, Λ_x, **B**, and Γ. There is no requirement that $m < p$, $n < q$ and that Θ_ϵ and Θ_δ be diagonal as in traditional factor analysis. The only requirement is that Σ in Eq. (7) be nonsingular and that the model be identified (see the section on identification of parameters).

There are several options available to the user to choose various special cases of the general model. Probably the most important of these options is the "no x" option; that is, the specification of a model in which there is no **x**. Then, the whole equation (6) is missing, so there are no δ, Λ_x, and Θ_δ. In this case, the only vector of observed variables is **y** and the covariance matrix of **y**, $\Sigma\ (p \times p\ )$ is

$$\Sigma = \Lambda_y(\mathbf{B}^{-1}\Gamma\Phi\Gamma'\mathbf{B}'^{-1} + \mathbf{B}^{-1}\Psi\mathbf{B}'^{-1})\ \Lambda_y + \Theta_\epsilon \tag{8}$$

The only parameter matrices are Λ_y, **B**, Γ, Φ, Ψ, and Θ_ϵ.

The measurement model part of the general model, as given by Eq. (5) and Eq. (6), specifies how the latent variables are measured in terms of the observed variables. This is used to describe the measurement properties (reliabilities and validities) of the observed variables. *The structural-equation model part* of the general model, as given by Eq. (4), specifies the causal relationships assumed to hold among the latent variables. This is used to describe and assess the causal effects and to estimate the amount of unexplained variance in the dependent variables. In order to assess the causal effects it is necessary that the units of measurement in the latent variables be defined in a natural way. This can often be done by specifying the unit of measurement to be the same as in one of the observed variables. For further information about LISREL and its uses, see Jöreskog (1973a, 1977) and Jöreskog and Sörbom (1976, 1977, 1978).

C. COFAMM

The COFAMM model assumes that we have measurements from several independent groups of individuals, possibly with different mean vectors and covariance matrices. It is assumed that p variables have been measured in a random sample of individuals from each population.

Let $\mathbf{z}_g$ be a vector of order p, representing the measurements obtained in group g, $g = 1, 2, \ldots, G$. We regard $\mathbf{z}_g$ as a random vector with mean vector $\boldsymbol{\mu}_g$ and covariance matrix Σ_g. It is assumed that a factor-analysis model holds in each population so that $\mathbf{z}_g$ can be accounted for by k common factors $\mathbf{f}_g$ and p unique factors or residuals $\mathbf{e}_g$, as

$$\mathbf{z}_g = \boldsymbol{\nu}_g + \Lambda_g\mathbf{f}_g + \mathbf{e}_g, \tag{9}$$

where $\boldsymbol{\nu}_g$ is a $p \times 1$ vector of location parameters and Λ_g a $p \times k$ parameter matrix of factor loadings. It is assumed that $E(\mathbf{e}_g) = \mathbf{0}$ and $E(\mathbf{f}_g) = \boldsymbol{\theta}_g$, a k × 1 parameter vector and that $\mathbf{e}_g$ and $\mathbf{f}_g$ are uncorrelated. These assumptions imply that the mean vector $\boldsymbol{\mu}_g$ of $\mathbf{z}_g$ is

$$\boldsymbol{\mu}_g = \boldsymbol{\nu}_g + \boldsymbol{\Lambda}_g \boldsymbol{\theta}_g \tag{10}$$

and that the covariance matrix $\boldsymbol{\Sigma}_g$ of $\mathbf{z}_g$ is

$$\boldsymbol{\Sigma}_g = \boldsymbol{\Lambda}_g \boldsymbol{\Phi}_g \boldsymbol{\Lambda}_g{}' + \boldsymbol{\Psi}_g \tag{11}$$

where $\boldsymbol{\Phi}_g$ is the covariance matrix of $\mathbf{f}_g$ and $\boldsymbol{\Psi}_g$ is the covariance matrix of $\mathbf{e}_g$.

Concerning the specification of parameters $\boldsymbol{\nu}_g$ and $\boldsymbol{\Lambda}_g$ there are several options. The most important of these is the specification of invariance over groups; that is,

$$\boldsymbol{\nu}_1 = \boldsymbol{\nu}_2 = \cdots = \boldsymbol{\nu}_G$$

$$\boldsymbol{\Lambda}_1 = \boldsymbol{\Lambda}_2 = \cdots = \boldsymbol{\Lambda}_G.$$

This makes it possible to estimate the $\boldsymbol{\theta}_g$, $g = 1, 2, \ldots, G$ on a common scale. For further information about COFAMM and its uses, see Jöreskog (1971), Sörbom (1974), and Sörbom and Jöreskog (1976).

D. Fixed, Free, and Constrained Parameters

In all three models and computer programs, some elements of any parameter matrix may be fixed and equal to assigned values. For the remaining nonfixed elements of the parameter matrices one or more subsets may have identical but unknown values. Thus each element in any parameter matrix may be

1. *A fixed parameter* that has been assigned a given value
2. *A constrained parameter* that is unknown but equal to one or more other parameters
3. *A free parameter* that is unknown and not constrained to be equal to any other parameter

This results in great generality and flexibility in that many different kinds of models may be handled. The three models and the programs cover a wide range of applications in the behavioral and social sciences.

E. Identification of Parameters

The general models described here and those that will be considered in later sections of this chapter are all of the following form. The distribution of the observed variables is multivariate with mean vector $\boldsymbol{\mu}(\boldsymbol{\theta})$ and cov-

ariance matrix $\Sigma(\boldsymbol{\theta})$ both being functions of parameters $\boldsymbol{\theta}' = (\theta_1,$
$\theta_2, \ldots, \theta_s)$, which are to be estimated from data. It is assumed that the
distribution of the observed variables is sufficiently well described by the
moments of first and second order—that is, by the mean vector $\boldsymbol{\mu}$ and the
covariance matrix Σ—that information about $\boldsymbol{\theta}$ contained in moments of
higher order than the second may be ignored. In particular, this will hold
if the distribution is multivariate normal.

In general the parameters in $\boldsymbol{\theta}$ may be of three kinds:

1. Those that are involved in both $\boldsymbol{\mu}$ and Σ
2. Those that are involved in $\boldsymbol{\mu}$ only
3. Those that are involved in Σ only

Let $\boldsymbol{\theta}_1$, $\boldsymbol{\theta}_2$, and $\boldsymbol{\theta}_3$ be vectors with these three types of parameters, so
that $\boldsymbol{\theta}' = (\boldsymbol{\theta}_1', \boldsymbol{\theta}_2', \boldsymbol{\theta}_3')$. A special case is when $\boldsymbol{\theta}_1$ is empty as in ACOVSM
and LISREL. A further special case is when $\boldsymbol{\theta}_1$ is empty and the transfor-
mation $\boldsymbol{\mu}(\boldsymbol{\theta}_2)$ is one to one as in LISREL. Then the mean vector $\boldsymbol{\mu}$ is
unconstrained and the only restriction is on Σ. Another special case is when
$\boldsymbol{\theta}_1$ is empty and the transformation $\Sigma(\boldsymbol{\theta}_3)$ is one to one. Then Σ is unconstrained and the only restriction is on $\boldsymbol{\mu}$.

Before an attempt is made to estimate the parameters $\boldsymbol{\theta}$, the identification
problem must be resolved. The model is said to be identified if $\boldsymbol{\theta}_1 \neq \boldsymbol{\theta}_2$
implies that $[\boldsymbol{\mu}(\boldsymbol{\theta}_1), \Sigma(\boldsymbol{\theta}_1)] \neq [\boldsymbol{\mu}(\boldsymbol{\theta}_2), \Sigma(\boldsymbol{\theta}_2)]$; that is, if $(\boldsymbol{\mu}, \Sigma)$ is generated
by one and only one $\boldsymbol{\theta}$. However, even if the whole model is not identified,
some parameters in $\boldsymbol{\theta}$ can still be identified. Consider the set Θ of all $\boldsymbol{\theta}$
generating the same $(\boldsymbol{\mu}, \Sigma)$. If a parameter θ_i has the same value in all
vectors $\boldsymbol{\theta} \in \Theta$ then θ_i is said to be identified. For parameters that are
identified it is usually possible to find consistent estimators. If a model is
not completely identified, restrictions must be imposed on $\boldsymbol{\theta}$ to make it so.
If a parameter is not identified, it is not possible to find a consistent
estimator of it.

Identifiability depends on the choice of model and on the specification of
fixed, constrained, and free parameters. To examine the identification problem, consider the model equations in the form

$$\mu_i = f_i(\boldsymbol{\theta}),$$

$$\sigma_{jk} = g_{jk}(\boldsymbol{\theta}), \qquad j \leq k, \tag{12}$$

where f_i and g_{jk} are continuous nonlinear functions of $\boldsymbol{\theta}$. If, for given $\boldsymbol{\mu}$
and Σ, a parameter θ can be determined from $\boldsymbol{\mu}$ and Σ, this parameter is
identified; otherwise it is not. Often some parameters can be determined
from Σ and/or $\boldsymbol{\mu}$ in different ways. This gives rise to overidentifying conditions on Σ and/or $\boldsymbol{\mu}$ that must hold if the model is true. The solution of
Eq. (12) is often complicated and tedious, and explicit solutions for all θ's
seldom exist. It is sometimes difficult to determine whether or not a param-

eter is identified and whether or not the whole model is identified. Fortunately, however, there is one way in which the computer program checks the identification status of the model. At the starting point of the iterations, the program computes the *information matrix* (see, e.g., Silvey, 1970) for all the independent unknown parameters. If this matrix is positive definite, the model is identified. On the other hand, if the information matrix is singular, the model is not identified. If the information matrix is inverted by the square root method and the nth pivotal element is zero or negative, this is an indication that the nth parameter is not identified.

F. Estimation and Testing of the Models

Once the model has been specified to be of the form suitable for any of the three programs—ACOVSM, LISREL, or COFAMM—these programs may be used to estimate the model from data. This is done by fitting $\mu(\theta)$ and $\Sigma(\theta)$ to the corresponding sample estimates $\bar{z}$, the sample mean vector, and S, the sample covariance matrix. The fitting function is

$$F = N[\log|\Sigma| + \text{tr}(S\Sigma^{-1}) + (\bar{z} - \mu)'\Sigma^{-1}(\bar{z} - \mu) - \log|S| - p]$$

where p is the number of observed variables. F is minimized with respect to θ. This gives maximum-likelihood estimates if the distribution of the observed variables is multivariate normal. Standard errors may be obtained for each estimated parameter by computing the inverse of the information matrix at the minimum of F.

The minimum value of F provides a χ^2-goodness-of-fit measure of how well the model fits the data. This may be regarded as a large sample χ^2 test of the specified model against the most general alternative model that both μ and Σ are unconstrained. The degrees of freedom for this test are $(\frac{1}{2})p$ $(p + 3) - s$, where p is the number of observed variables and s is the total number of independent parameters estimated under the model. If μ is unconstrained, the degrees of freedom are $(\frac{1}{2})p(p + 1) - s$.

Suppose H_0 represents one model under given specifications of fixed, free, and constrained parameters. Then it is possible, in large samples, to test the model H_0 against any more general model H_1, by estimating each of them separately and comparing their χ^2 goodness-of-fit values. The difference in χ^2 is asymptotically a χ^2 with degrees of freedom equal to the corresponding difference in degrees of freedom. In many situations, it is possible to set up a sequence of hypotheses such that each one is a special case of the preceding and to test these hypotheses sequentially.

In a more exploratory situation the χ^2-goodness-of-fit-values can be used as follows. If a value of χ^2 is obtained, which is large compared with the number of degrees of freedom, the fit may be examined by an inspection of the magnitudes of the first derivatives of F with respect to the fixed parameters. Often such an inspection of the results of analysis will suggest ways to relax the model somewhat by introducing more parameters. The new model usually yields a smaller χ^2. A drop in χ^2 that is large compared with the difference in degrees of freedom indicates that the changes made in the model represent a real improvement. On the other hand, a drop in χ^2 close to the difference in the number of degrees of freedom indicates that the improvement in fit is obtained by "capitalizing on chance," and the added parameters may not have real significance and meaning.

III. Estimation of Growth Curves

A. One Variable over Time

Consider one variable y being measured on N individuals at T points in time $t_1, t_2, \ldots, t_T$. The raw data takes the form of a data matrix $\mathbf{Y}$ of order $N \times T$:

$$
\begin{bmatrix}
y_{11}, y_{12}, \ldots, y_{1T} \\
y_{21}, y_{22}, \ldots, y_{2T} \\
\vdots \\
y_{N1}, y_{N2}, \ldots, y_{NT}
\end{bmatrix},
$$

where y_{ij} is the observed measurement of individual i at time t_j. We assume that the rows of $\mathbf{Y}$ are independently distributed with the same covariance matrix $\mathbf{\Sigma}$. Also, the mean vectors of the rows are assumed to be the same, namely

$$
\boldsymbol{\mu}' = (\mu_1, \mu_2, \ldots, \mu_T)
$$

However, in this section, the mean values are not regarded as free parameters, but instead we focus attention on the mean μ_t as a function of t. This gives a growth curve describing how the population mean of y changes over time.

We consider polynomial growth curves of the form

$$
\mu_t = \xi_0 + \xi_1 t + \xi_2 t^2 + \cdots + \xi_h t^h, \tag{13}
$$

although other mathematical forms may also be considered. The degree of the polynomial h is assumed to be less than or equal to $T - 1$. When $h < T - 1$, the mean vector $\boldsymbol{\mu}$ is constrained and there is not a one-to-one correspondence between $\mu_1, \mu_2, \ldots, \mu_T$ and the polynomial coefficients $\xi_0, \xi_1, \ldots, \xi_h$. In this section we consider the estimation of these polynomial coefficients.

Let $\xi' = (\xi_0, \xi_1, \ldots, \xi_h)$ and let

$$\mathbf{P} = \begin{bmatrix} 1 & 1 & \cdots & 1 \\ t_1 & t_2 & \cdots & t_T \\ t_1^2 & t_2^2 & \cdots & t_T^2 \\ \vdots & \vdots & & \vdots \\ t_1^h & t_2^h & \cdots & t_T^h \end{bmatrix}.$$

Then the statistical model for the data matrix is

$$E(\mathbf{Y}) = \mathbf{j}\xi'\mathbf{P},$$

where $\mathbf{j}$ is a column vector of order N with all elements equal to 1. If the time points are equidistant, it is convenient to use the $h + 1$ first-orthogonal polynomials of order T as rows of $\mathbf{P}$ (see, e.g., Kendall & Stuart, 1961).

When the rows of $\mathbf{Y}$ have a multinormal distribution, the vector of polynomial coefficients ξ may be estimated by the maximum-likelihood method. The maximum-likelihood estimate of ξ is

$$\hat{\xi} = (\mathbf{P}\mathbf{S}^{-1}\mathbf{P}')^{-1}\mathbf{P}\mathbf{S}^{-1}\bar{\mathbf{y}}, \tag{14}$$

where $\bar{\mathbf{y}}$ is the sample mean vector and $\mathbf{S}$ is the sample covariance matrix computed from $\mathbf{Y}$.

The above result generalizes easily to the case of several groups of individuals with possibly different mean vectors. Suppose, for example, that there are two groups with n_1 and n_2 individuals in each group. Let the first n_1 rows of $\mathbf{Y}$ be the measurements on individuals in Group 1 and let the last n_2 rows be the measurements on individuals in Group 2. The growth curves for the two groups may differ, so we assume that there are two distinct growth curves to be estimated; that is,

$$E(y_{it}^{(g)}) = \xi_0^{(g)} + \xi_1^{(g)}t + \cdots + \xi_h^{(g)}t^h, \qquad g = 1, 2$$

or in compact form

$$E(\mathbf{Y}) = \mathbf{A}\boldsymbol{\Xi}\mathbf{P}, \tag{15}$$

where

$$\mathbf{A}' = \begin{bmatrix} 1 & 1 & \cdots & 1 & 0 & 0 & \cdots & 0 \\ 0 & 0 & \cdots & 0 & 1 & 1 & \cdots & 1 \end{bmatrix}$$

and

$$\boldsymbol{\Xi} = \begin{bmatrix} \xi_0^{(1)} & \xi_1^{(1)} & \cdots & \xi_h^{(1)} \\ \xi_0^{(2)} & \xi_1^{(2)} & \cdots & \xi_h^{(2)} \end{bmatrix}.$$

Let $\mathbf{U} = (1/N)\mathbf{A}'\mathbf{A}$, $\mathbf{V} = (1/N)\mathbf{A}'\mathbf{Y}$, and $\mathbf{W} = (1/N)\mathbf{Y}'\mathbf{Y}$. Then

$$\mathbf{S} = \mathbf{W} - \mathbf{V}'\mathbf{U}^{-1}\mathbf{V} \tag{16}$$

is the pooled-within-groups covariance matrix and the maximum-likelihood estimate of Ξ is (see Khatri, 1966)

$$\hat{\Xi} = \mathbf{U}^{-1}\mathbf{V}\mathbf{S}^{-1}\mathbf{P}'(\mathbf{P}\mathbf{S}^{-1}\mathbf{P}')^{-1} \tag{17}$$

In general, if there are g independent groups of observations with n_s observations in the sth group, $n_1 + n_2 + \cdots + n_g = N$, the model is still in the form of Eq. (15), where $\mathbf{A}$ is of order $N \times g$ and has n_1 rows $(1, 0, \ldots, 0)$, n_2 rows $(0, 1, \ldots, 0)$, $\ldots$, and n_g rows $(0, 0, \ldots, 1)$. Furthermore,

$$\Xi = \begin{bmatrix} \xi_0^{(1)} & \xi_1^{(1)} & \cdots & \xi_h^{(1)} \\ \xi_0^{(2)} & \xi_1^{(2)} & \cdots & \xi_h^{(2)} \\ \vdots & \vdots & & \vdots \\ \xi_0^{(g)} & \xi_1^{(g)} & & \xi_h^{(g)} \end{bmatrix}$$

and $\mathbf{P}$ is as before. The sth row of Ξ consists of the polynomial coefficients for group s. The growth curves are assumed to have the same degree h for all groups. Even in the general case, the result is given by Eq. (17), where $\mathbf{U}$, $\mathbf{V}$, and $\mathbf{S}$ are defined as before.

For practical purposes the maximum-likelihood estimate of Ξ may be obtained by means of the computer program ACOVSM (as described in the preceding section). With this program one can also test linear hypotheses on Ξ of the form

$$\mathbf{C}\Xi\mathbf{D} = \mathbf{0}$$

where $\mathbf{C}(u \times g)$ and $\mathbf{D}(h \times v)$ are given matrices of ranks u and v, respectively. In particular, one can test the hypothesis that certain coefficients in one or more growth curves are zero and the hypothesis that certain groups have the same or parallel growth curves. One can also restrict elements of Ξ to zero in advance. Thus, with the ACOVSM program it is not necessary to assume that all groups have growth curves of the same degree. In this case, of course, $\hat{\Xi}$ is no longer given by Eq. (17) but can still be easily computed subject to the zero a priori restrictions.

As an illustration, consider the data in Table 11.1 taken from Potthoff and Roy (1964). The data are from a dental study in which the distance, in millimeters, from the center of the pituitary to the pteryomaxillary tissue was measured on each of 11 girls and 16 boys at ages 8, 10, 12, and 14. The data matrix has 27 rows and 4 columns, the first 11 rows representing the girls and the last 16 rows representing the boys.

The following two questions may be asked:

1. Should the growth curves be represented by second-degree polynomials or are linear equations adequate?
2. Should two separate growth curves be used for boys and girls, or do both have the same growth curve?

TABLE 11.1
Dental Measurements (mm) on Eleven Girls and Sixteen Boys at Four Different Ages[a]

	Girls (age in years)					Boys (age in years)			
Individual	8	10	12	14	Individual	8	10	12	14
1	21	20	21.5	23	1	26	25	29	31
2	21	21.5	24	25.5	2	21.5	22.5	23	26.5
3	20.5	24	24.5	26	3	23	22.5	24	27.5
4	23.5	24.5	25	26.5	4	25.5	27.5	26.5	27
5	21.5	23	22.5	23.5	5	20	23.5	22.5	26
6	20	21	21	22.5	6	24.5	25.5	27	28.5
7	21.5	22.5	23	25	7	22	22	24.5	26.5
8	23	23	23.5	24	8	24	21.5	24.5	25.5
9	20	21	22	21.5	9	23	20.5	31	26
10	16.5	19	19	19.5	10	27.5	28	31	31.5
11	24.5	25	28	28	11	23	23	23.5	25
					12	21.5	23.5	24	28
					13	17	24.5	26	29.5
					14	22.5	25.5	25.5	26
					15	23	24.5	26	30
					16	22	21.5	23.5	25
Mean	21.18	22.23	23.09	24.09	Mean	22.87	23.81	25.72	27.47

[a] Data from Potthoff & Roy (1964, Table 1.)

To answer these questions we set up a model as in Eq. (15) with $N = 27$, $T = 4$, and $g = 2$ and $h = 2$, with $\mathbf{A}$, a matrix of order $N \times 2$ with the first 11 rows equal to $(1, 0)$ and the last 16 rows equal to $(0, 1)$ and with

$$\Xi = \begin{bmatrix} \xi_0^{(G)} & \xi_1^{(G)} & \xi_2^{(G)} \\ \xi_0^{(B)} & \xi_1^{(B)} & \xi_2^{(B)} \end{bmatrix}$$

Since the time points are equidistant, we take the rows of $\mathbf{P}$ as the first three orthogonal polynomials of Order 4; that is,

$$\mathbf{P} = \begin{bmatrix} 1 & 1 & 1 & 1 \\ -3 & -1 & 1 & 3 \\ 9 & 1 & 1 & 9 \end{bmatrix}$$

The maximum likelihood estimate of Ξ is

$$\hat{\Xi} = \begin{bmatrix} 22.704 & 0.479 & -0.003 \\ 24.631 & 0.788 & 0.050 \end{bmatrix}$$

To examine Question (1) we test the hypothesis $\xi_2^{(G)} = \xi_2^{(B)} = 0$. This can be done by choosing

$$\mathbf{C} = \begin{pmatrix} 1 & 0 \\ 0 & 1 \end{pmatrix} \qquad \mathbf{D} = \begin{pmatrix} 0 \\ 0 \\ 1 \end{pmatrix}$$

The test statistic can be transformed to an F distribution (see Pottoff & Roy, 1964). In this case one obtains an $F = 1.19$ with 2 and 24 df. This indicates that the hypothesis cannot be rejected. We may therefore regard the growth curves as linear rather than quadratic.

We now modify the model and take Ξ as

$$\Xi = \begin{bmatrix} \xi_0^{(G)} & \xi_1^{(G)} \\ \xi_0^{(B)} & \xi_1^{(B)} \end{bmatrix}$$

and $\mathbf{P}$ with only two rows instead of three. The maximum likelihood estimate of Ξ is now

$$\hat{\Xi} = \begin{bmatrix} 22.689 & 0.477 \\ 24.923 & 0.826 \end{bmatrix}$$

To examine Question (2) we set up the hypothesis $\xi_0^{(G)} = \xi_0^{(B)}$, $\xi_1^{(G)} = \xi_1^{(B)}$. This corresponds to choosing

$$\mathbf{C} = [1, -1], \qquad \mathbf{D} = \begin{pmatrix} 1 & 0 \\ 0 & 1 \end{pmatrix}$$

Also, in this case, the test statistic can be transformed to an F distribution. The test gives $F = 6.44$ with 2 and 22 df, suggesting that the hypothesis should be rejected. Boys and girls have different growth curves.

B. An Autoregressive Model for One Variable over Time

The development in the previous subsection did not take the covariance structure in Σ into account. However, the growth curves can be estimated more efficiently and the tests will be more powerful if the covariance structure, which arises naturally in repeated measurements, is taken into account. This covariance structure very often has an autoregressive nature. Therefore, in this subsection, we focus attention on the deviation $e_t = y_t - \mu_t$ of y_t from its mean value μ_t on the growth curve and consider various autoregressive models for this.

The first-order autoregressive model is

$$e_t = \beta_t e_{t-1} + z_t, \qquad t = 2, 3, \ldots, T, \tag{18}$$

where the residual z_t is uncorrelated with e_{t-1}. It is also assumed that z_2, z_3, ..., z_T are all uncorrelated. A path diagram of this model is shown in Figure 11.2 for the case of $T = 4$.

It is readily verified that

$$\mathrm{Cov}(y_t, y_{t-1}) = E(e_t, e_{t-1}) = \beta_t \sigma_{t-1}^2,$$

where

$$\sigma_{t-1}^2 = \mathrm{Var}(y_{t-1}) = E(e_{t-1}^2),$$

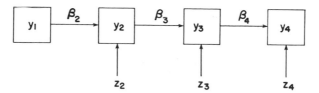

FIGURE 11.2. **An autoregressive model for one variable over time.**

and that

$$\text{Cov}(y_t, y_{t-k}) = \beta_t \beta_{t-1} \cdots \beta_{t-k+1} \sigma_{t-k}^2, \qquad k = 1, 2, \ldots$$

where

$$\sigma_{t-k}^2 = \text{Var}(y_{t-k}).$$

Hence, the covariance matrix of y is (in the case of $T = 4$)

$$\Sigma = \begin{bmatrix} \sigma_1^2 & & & \\ \beta_2\sigma_1^2 & \sigma_2^2 & & \\ \beta_3\beta_2\sigma_1^2 & \beta_3\sigma_2^2 & \sigma_3^2 & \\ \beta_4\beta_3\beta_2\sigma_1^2 & \beta_4\beta_3\sigma_2^2 & \beta_4\sigma_3^2 & \sigma_4^2 \end{bmatrix} \tag{19}$$

From Eq. (18) it is seen that Σ is constrained; its 10 variances and covariances are functions of only seven parameters. Since the variances are free parameters, it is the 6 covariances that are functions of the three parameters β_2, β_3, and β_4. In the general case there are $(\frac{1}{2})T(T + 1)$ variances and covariances in Σ and $2T - 1$ free parameters.

The correlation matrix corresponding to Eq. (19) is

$$\begin{bmatrix} 1 & & & \\ \rho_2 & 1 & & \\ \rho_2\rho_3 & \rho_3 & 1 & \\ \rho_2\rho_3\rho_4 & \rho_3\rho_4 & \rho_4 & 1 \end{bmatrix}, \tag{20}$$

where $\rho_i = \beta_i(\sigma_{i-1}/\sigma_i)$. There are only $T - 1$ independent correlations, namely those just below (or above) the main diagonal, and the other correlations are products of these. For example,

$$\rho_{ji} = \prod_{k=i+1}^{k=j} \rho_k \qquad (i < j). \tag{21}$$

It is seen that the correlations fall off as one moves away from the main diagonal, a phenomenon usually found to occur empirically. The partial correlation $\rho_{ik \cdot j}$ is zero, whenever $i < j < k$. This is readily verified since $\rho_{ik} - \rho_{ij}\rho_{jk} = 0$ by virtue of Eq. (21). Higher-order partial correlations, with two or more intermediate variables held constant, also vanish. It follows that in the regression

$$y_t = \beta_{t1}y_1 + \beta_{t2}y_2 + \cdots + \beta_{t,t-1}y_{t-1} + z_t \qquad (22)$$

of y_t on all preceding variables, the only regression coefficient that can be nonzero is $\beta_{t,t-1} = \beta_t$. For the prediction of y_t, only the immediate neighbor y_{t-1} is useful. The effects of $y_{t-2}, y_{t-3}, \ldots, y_1$ on y_t are only indirect via y_{t-1}.

If the growth-curve specification in Eq. (15) is ignored so that the mean vector $\boldsymbol{\mu}$ is unconstrained, this model can be estimated very easily. Under multinormality, the maximum-likelihood estimate of β_t is just the ordinary least-squares estimate one obtains by estimating each regression equation in Eq. (18) separately, namely

$$\hat{\beta}_t = s_{t-1,t}/s_{t-1,t-1},$$

where the s_{ij} are elements of S in Eq. (16). The residual variance, $\mathrm{Var}(z_t)$, is estimated as

$$\mathrm{Var}(z_t) = s_{tt} - \hat{\beta}_t^2 s_{t-1,t-1}.$$

The estimation of the growth curves and the β's simultaneously is not so easy. This may be done numerically by means of the ACOVSM program. We now show that the Σ in Eq. (19) is indeed of the form required by that program. To do so we define $z_1 \equiv e_1$ and write Eqs. (18) as (in the case of $T = 4$)

$$\begin{pmatrix} e_1 \\ e_2 \\ e_3 \\ e_4 \end{pmatrix} = \begin{bmatrix} 1 & 0 & 0 & 0 \\ \beta_2 & 1 & 0 & 0 \\ \beta_2\beta_3 & \beta_3 & 1 & 0 \\ \beta_2\beta_3\beta_4 & \beta_3\beta_4 & \beta_4 & 1 \end{bmatrix} \begin{pmatrix} z_1 \\ z_2 \\ z_3 \\ z_4 \end{pmatrix}. \qquad (23)$$

Let $\kappa_i = \beta_2\beta_3\cdots\beta_i$ for $i = 2, 3, \ldots, T$. Then if all $\beta_i \neq 0$, there is a one-to-one correspondence between $\kappa_2, \kappa_3, \ldots, \kappa_T$ and $\beta_2, \beta_3, \ldots, \beta_T$ and $\beta_i = \kappa_i/\kappa_{i-1}$. The matrix in Eq. (23) is

$$\begin{bmatrix} 1 & 0 & 0 & 0 \\ \kappa_2 & 1 & 0 & 0 \\ \kappa_3 & \kappa_3/\kappa_2 & 1 & 0 \\ \kappa_4 & \kappa_4/\kappa_2 & \kappa_4/\kappa_3 & 1 \end{bmatrix} = \mathbf{D}_\kappa \mathbf{T} \mathbf{D}_\kappa^{-1},$$

where $\mathbf{D}_\kappa = \mathrm{diag}(1, \kappa_2, \kappa_3, \kappa_4)$ and

$$\mathbf{T} = \begin{bmatrix} 1 & 0 & 0 & 0 \\ 1 & 1 & 0 & 0 \\ 1 & 1 & 1 & 0 \\ 1 & 1 & 1 & 1 \end{bmatrix}$$

Hence, Eq. (23) can be written

$$\mathbf{e} = \mathbf{D}_\kappa \mathbf{T} \mathbf{D}_\kappa^{-1} \mathbf{z}$$

$$= \mathbf{D}_\kappa \mathbf{T} \mathbf{z}^*,$$

with covariance matrix

$$\Sigma = D_\kappa T \Psi^* T' D_\kappa, \tag{24}$$

where Ψ^* is the diagonal covariance matrix of $z^* = D_\kappa^{-1} z$. The $2T - 1$ parameters $\kappa_2, \kappa_3, \ldots, \kappa_T, \psi_{11}^*, \psi_{22}^*, \ldots, \psi_{TT}^*$ are in a one-to-one correspondence with the original parameters $\beta_2, \beta_3, \ldots, \beta_T, \sigma_{11}, \sigma_{22}, \ldots, \sigma_{TT}$. Equation (24) is in the form of Eq. (2). The whole model is defined by Eq. (15) and Eq. (24). The ACOVSM program gives estimates of the growth-curve polynomial coefficients as well as $\beta_2, \beta_3, \ldots, \beta_T, \sigma_{11}, \sigma_{22}, \ldots, \sigma_{TT}$. The program also gives a χ^2-goodness-of-fit-measure for assessing the fit of the overall model. This χ^2-measure may be divided into two components measuring the fit of the growth-curve model Eq. (15) and the covariance-structure model Eq. (24) separately.

C. Growth Curves for Several Variables Simultaneously

The model of the preceding subsection will now be generalized to the case of several variables at each occasion. We still assume that the observed variables are measured without errors. The case of measurement errors in the dependent variables will be considered in later sections. An example of the type of model to be considered is shown in Figure 11.3. Here there are three variables for all t and, as before, we illustrate with $T = 4$ occasions.

The growth-curve specification for the model in Figure 11.3 is as follows. For an arbitrary individual we arrange his observed scores so that his scores at the first occasion come first, then his scores at the second occasion, etc. With two scores at each occasion:

$$y_{11}, y_{12}, y_{21}, y_{22}, y_{31}, y_{32}, y_{41}, y_{42},$$

where y_{tj} is the score on variable j at occasion t. The growth curve for variable j is assumed to be, say,

$$E(y_{tj}) = \xi_{j0} + \xi_{j1}t + \xi_{j2}t^2. \tag{25}$$

As before, the model is given in matrix form by Eq. (15), where

$$\Xi(1 \times 6) = (\xi_{10}, \xi_{11}, \xi_{12}, \xi_{20}, \xi_{21}, \xi_{22},)$$

and

$$P(6 \times 8) = \begin{bmatrix} 1 & 0 & 1 & 0 & 1 & 0 & 1 & 0 \\ t_1 & 0 & t_2 & 0 & t_3 & 0 & t_4 & 0 \\ t_1^2 & 0 & t_2^2 & 0 & t_3^2 & 0 & t_4^2 & 0 \\ 0 & 1 & 0 & 1 & 0 & 1 & 0 & 1 \\ 0 & t_1 & 0 & t_2 & 0 & t_3 & 0 & t_4 \\ 0 & t_1^2 & 0 & t_2^2 & 0 & t_3^2 & 0 & t_4^2 \end{bmatrix}$$

The matrix A is a column vector of order N with all elements equal to 1. If

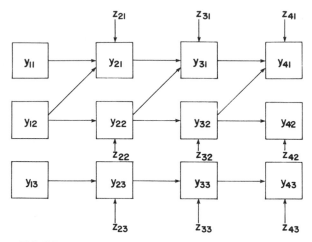

FIGURE 11.3. **A multivariate autoregressive model.**

there are g groups of observations, there will be g rows in Ξ and the matrix **A** will be as described in the earlier section on one variable.

Without constraints on the covariance matrix Σ and with no a priori zero restrictions on Ξ, this model can be estimated as in that previous section. The maximum-likelihood estimate of Ξ is given by Eq. (17).

D. Multivariate Autoregressive Models

We now consider a multivariate autoregressive model that is a direct generalization of the univariate autoregressive model discussed earlier. This autoregressive model is

$$\mathbf{y}_t = \mathbf{B}_t \mathbf{y}_{t-1} + \mathbf{z}_t, \qquad t = 2, 3, \ldots, T, \tag{26}$$

with the y's measured as deviations from their means. For the model in Figure 11.3, each matrix $\mathbf{B}_t$ will be of the form

$$\mathbf{B}_t = \begin{bmatrix} \beta_{11}^{(t)} & \beta_{12}^{(t)} & 0 \\ 0 & \beta_{22}^{(t)} & 0 \\ 0 & 0 & \beta_{33}^{(t)} \end{bmatrix} \tag{27}$$

The residuals in $\mathbf{z}_t$ are assumed to be uncorrelated across time but may be contemporaneously correlated; that is, $E(\mathbf{z}_t \mathbf{z}_s') = 0$ for $s \neq t$. The covariance matrix $E(\mathbf{z}_t \mathbf{z}_t')$ is denoted Φ_t. If the mean vectors $\boldsymbol{\mu}_t$ and the matrices $\mathbf{B}_t$ are unconstrained, this model may be estimated directly by estimating each regression in Eq. (26) separately. Let

$$S = \begin{bmatrix} S_{11} & S_{12} & \cdots & S_{1T} \\ S_{21} & S_{22} & \cdots & S_{2T} \\ \vdots & & & \\ S_{T1} & S_{T2} & \cdots & S_{TT} \end{bmatrix}$$

be the sample covariance matrix of $y' = (y_1', y_2', \ldots, y_t')$, where S_{st} is the covariance matrix between y_t and y_s. Then the maximum-likelihood estimates are

$$\hat{B}_t = S_{t,t-1}S_{t-1,t-1}^{-1}$$

and

$$\hat{\Psi}_t = S_{tt} - S_{t,t-1}S_{t-1,t-1}^{-1}S_{t-1,t}.$$

If the matrices B_t have fixed zero elements as in Eq. (27), the model may be estimated by means of the LISREL program as described earlier. LISREL can estimate the covariance structure but not the growth-curves specification for the means. When the latter are included in the model together with the multivariate autoregressive model, the estimation problem is complicated; there does not seem to be any general program available to handle this estimation. When all B_t are diagonal, ACOVSM may be used in the same way as for the univariate autoregressive model.

IV. Two-Wave Models

A. Two-Wave–Two-Variable Models

In the previous section all the variables were assumed to be measured without error. Measurement errors in the variables were not taken into account in the models that focused directly on relationships between the observed variables. In this and the next section we assume that all the observed variables contain errors of measurement and focus on the relationships among the true or latent variables. In doing so we shall ignore any structure on the mean vector and simply assume this to be unconstrained. We may therefore take all variables to be measured in deviations from their means.

We begin with the simple model shown in Figure 11.4, where two variables are measured at two occasions. We assume that the two variables measure the same latent variable η; that is, y_{11} and y_{12} measure η_1 on the first occasion and y_{21} and y_{22} measure η_2 on the second occasion. We are interested in the relationship between η_1 and η_2 expressed in the structural

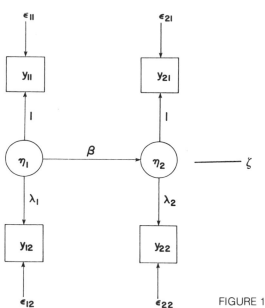

FIGURE 11.4. **A two-wave–two-variable model.**

equation

$$\eta_2 = \beta\eta_1 + \zeta, \tag{28}$$

the regression of η_2 on η_1. In particular, we are interested in whether $\beta = 1$ and ζ is small; that is, whether the same latent variables are measured on both occasions.

The measurement-model part of the model may be written as

$$\begin{pmatrix} y_{11} \\ y_{12} \\ y_{21} \\ y_{22} \end{pmatrix} = \begin{bmatrix} 1 & 0 \\ \lambda_1 & 0 \\ 0 & 1 \\ 0 & \lambda_2 \end{bmatrix} \begin{pmatrix} \eta_1 \\ \eta_2 \end{pmatrix} + \begin{pmatrix} \epsilon_{11} \\ \epsilon_{12} \\ \epsilon_{21} \\ \epsilon_{22} \end{pmatrix}, \tag{29}$$

where it is assumed that η_1 and η_2 are measured in the same metric as y_{11} and y_{21}, respectively. This model is a special case of the general LISREL model with no x. In terms of LISREL, Eq. (28) may be interpreted, in accordance with Eq. (4), as

$$\begin{pmatrix} 1 & 0 \\ -\beta & 1 \end{pmatrix} \begin{pmatrix} \eta_1 \\ \eta_2 \end{pmatrix} = \begin{pmatrix} \zeta_1 \\ \zeta_2 \end{pmatrix},$$

where $\zeta_1 = \eta_1$ and $\zeta_2 = \zeta$. Let $\boldsymbol{\Phi}$ be the covariance matrix of (η_1, η_2) and let $\boldsymbol{\Theta}$ be the covariance matrix of $(\epsilon_{11}, \epsilon_{12}, \epsilon_{21}, \epsilon_{22})$. If all the ϵ's are uncorrelated so that Θ is diagonal, the covariance matrix of $(y_{11}, y_{12}, y_{21}, y_{22})$ is

$$\Sigma = \begin{pmatrix} \phi_{11} + \theta_{11} \\ \lambda_1\phi_{11} & \lambda_1{}^2\phi_{11} + \theta_{22} \\ \phi_{21} & \lambda_1\phi_{21} & \phi_{22} + \theta_{33} \\ \lambda_2\phi_{21} & \lambda_1\lambda_2\phi_{21} & \lambda_2\phi_{22} & \lambda_2{}^2\phi_{22} + \theta_{44} \end{pmatrix},$$

Σ has 10 variances and covariances that are functions of nine parameters. The model has one degree of freedom.

Often when the same variables are used repeatedly, there is a tendency for the corresponding errors (the ϵ's) to correlate over time (see preceding sections on autoregressive models) because of memory and other retest effects. Hence, there is a need to generalize the preceding model to allow for correlations between ϵ_{11} and ϵ_{21} and also between ϵ_{12} and ϵ_{22}. This means that there will be two nonzero covariances θ_{31} and θ_{42} in Θ. This model is shown in Figure 11.5. The covariance matrix of the observed variables will now be

$$\Sigma = \begin{bmatrix} \phi_{11} + \theta_{11} \\ \lambda_1\phi_{11} & \lambda_1{}^2\phi_{11} + \theta_{22} \\ \phi_{21} + \theta_{31} & \lambda_1\phi_{21} & \phi_{22} + \theta_{33} \\ \lambda_2\phi_{21} & \lambda_1\lambda_2\phi_{21} + \theta_{42} & \lambda_2\phi_{22} & \lambda_2{}^2\phi_{22} + \theta_{44} \end{bmatrix}.$$

This Σ has its 10 independent elements expressed in terms of 11 parameters. Hence, it is clear that the model is not identified. In fact, none of the 11 parameters are identified without further restrictions. The loading λ_1 and λ_2 may be multiplied by a constant and the ϕ's divided by the same constant. This does not change σ_{21}, σ_{32}, σ_{41}, and σ_{43}. The change in the other σ's may be compensated by adjusting the θ's additively. Hence, to make the model identified one must fix one λ or one ϕ at a nonzero value or one θ at some arbitrary value. However, the *correlation* between η_1 and η_2 is identified without any restrictions, since

$$\text{Corr}(\eta_1, \eta_2) = [\phi_{21}^2/\phi_{11}\phi_{22}]^{1/2}$$

$$= [(\sigma_{32}\sigma_{41})/(\sigma_{21}\sigma_{43})]^{1/2}$$

This model may therefore be used to estimate this correlation coefficient and to test whether this is 1. The maximum-likelihood estimate of the correlation coefficient is $[(s_{32}s_{41})/(s_{21}s_{43})]^{1/2}$. To make further use of the model it is necessary to make some assumption about the nature of the variables. For example, if it can be assumed that the two variables at each occasion are τ-equivalent (see, e.g., Lord & Novick, 1968) we can set both λ_1 and λ_2 equal to 1. Then the model can be estimated and tested with one degree of freedom.

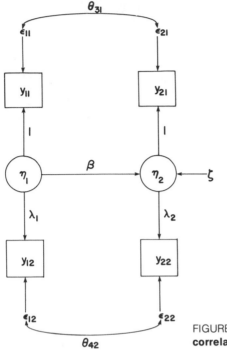

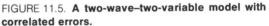

FIGURE 11.5. **A two-wave–two-variable model with correlated errors.**

B. Two-Wave–Two-Variable Models with Background Variables

The model of the previous subsection may be used for the measurement of change between two occasions. However, in many longitudinal studies the objective is not only to measure change but also to attribute or relate change to certain characteristics and events. Such studies must include not only pre- and postmeasures but also various background variables believed to influence change. The background variables may be socioeconomic variables or other characteristics differentiating the individuals prior to the pretest occasion.

Consider the model shown in Figure 11.6. The background variable is denoted x. The main purpose of the model is to separate the direct effect of η_1 on η_2 by eliminating the effect of x.

The measurement model for **y** is the same as in Eq. (29) but now the structural equations are

$$\begin{pmatrix} 1 & 0 \\ \beta & 1 \end{pmatrix} \begin{pmatrix} \eta_1 \\ \eta_2 \end{pmatrix} = \begin{pmatrix} \gamma_1 \\ \gamma_2 \end{pmatrix} x + \begin{pmatrix} \zeta_1 \\ \zeta_2 \end{pmatrix}. \tag{30}$$

The Λ_x in Eq. (6) is a 1×1 matrix with element one and $\delta = 0$.

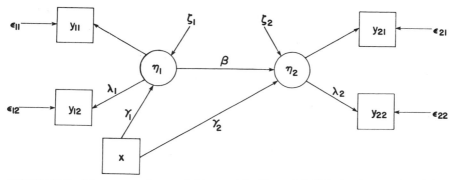

FIGURE 11.6. **A two-wave–two-variable model with an infallible background variable.**

The reduced form of Eq. (30) is

$$\eta_1 = \gamma_1 x + \zeta_1$$

$$\eta_2 = (\gamma_2 - \beta\gamma_1)x + (\zeta_2 - \beta\zeta_1)$$

$$= \pi x + v, \text{ say.}$$

As before, we assume that the measurement errors ϵ_{11}, ϵ_{12}, ϵ_{21}, and ϵ_{22} have zero means and are mutually uncorrelated and uncorrelated with η_1 and η_2. Furthermore, we assume that the residuals ζ_1 and ζ_2 have zero means and are uncorrelated. The variances of ζ_1 and ζ_2 are denoted $\psi_{11} = \text{Var}(\zeta_1)$, $\psi_{22} = \text{Var}(\zeta_2)$.

Let us first consider the identification problem. We have five observed variables, y_{11}, y_{12}, y_{21}, y_{22}, and x, with 15 variances and covariances. The model has the following 12 parameters to be estimated: λ_1, λ_2, β, γ_1, γ_2, $\phi = \text{Var}(x)$, ψ_{11}, ψ_{22}, and θ_{ii}, $i = 1, 2, 3, 4$. We have

$$\text{Cov}(y_{11}, x) = \text{Cov}(\eta_1, x) \quad = \gamma_1\phi$$

$$\text{Cov}(y_{12}, x) = \lambda_1 \text{Cov}(\eta_1, x) = \lambda_1\gamma_1\phi$$

$$\text{Cov}(y_{21}, x) = \text{Cov}(\eta_2, x) \quad = \pi\phi$$

$$\text{Cov}(y_{22}, x) = \lambda_2 \text{Cov}(\eta_2, x) = \lambda_2\pi\phi.$$

Since $\phi = \text{Var}(x)$ is identified, these equations determine γ_1, λ_1, π, and λ_2, respectively. Furthermore,

$$\text{Cov}(y_{11}, y_{12}) = \lambda_1 \text{Var}(\eta_1) = \lambda_1(\gamma_1^2\phi + \psi_{11}),$$

which determines ψ_{11}, and

$$\text{Cov}(y_{21}, y_{22}) = \lambda_2 \text{Var}(\eta_2) = \lambda_2[\pi^2\phi + \text{Var}(v)],$$

which determines

$$\text{Var}(v) = \psi_{22} + \beta^2\psi_{11}. \tag{31}$$

For given λ_1, λ_2, γ_1, π, ϕ, and ψ_{11}, any one of the four equations

$$\text{Cov}(y_{11}, y_{21}) = \gamma_1 \pi \phi - \beta \psi_{11}, \tag{32}$$

$$\text{Cov}(y_{11}, y_{22}) = \lambda_2(\gamma_1 \pi \phi - \beta \psi_{11}), \tag{33}$$

$$\text{Cov}(y_{12}, y_{21}) = \lambda_1(\gamma_1 \pi \phi - \beta \psi_{11}), \tag{34}$$

$$\text{Cov}(y_{12}, y_{22}) = \lambda_1 \lambda_2(\gamma_1 \pi \phi - \beta \psi_{11}), \tag{35}$$

determines β. Then, with β determined, $\gamma_2 = \pi + \beta \gamma_1$ and ψ_{22} is obtained from Eq. (31). The error variances θ_{ii} are determined from σ_{ii}, $i = 1, 2, 3, 4$. Hence, it is clear that the whole model is identified and has three independent restrictions on Σ.

Now suppose that x cannot be measured without error and write

$$x = \xi + \delta,$$

where ξ is the true score and δ the measurement error, the latter assumed to have zero mean and to be uncorrelated with ξ and everything else. We shall consider two cases, namely the following: (1) x has a known reliability $\rho_{xx} = \sigma_\xi^2/\sigma_x^2$; and (2) ξ is measured by two congeneric background variables x_1 and x_2. Case (1) is shown in Figure 11.7.

In Case (1), the above equations are the same except that ϕ is replaced by σ_ξ^2. Since $\sigma_\xi^2 = \rho_{xx}\phi$ where ρ_{xx} is known and ϕ is identified, all the other parameters will be determined as before.

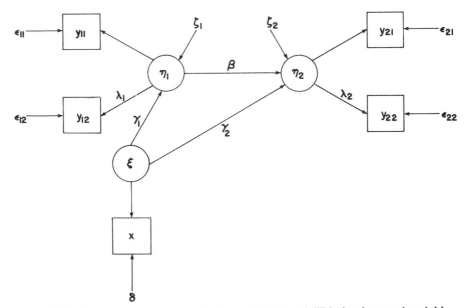

FIGURE 11.7. **A two-wave–two-variable model with a fallible background variable.**

Next suppose the errors ϵ_{11} and ϵ_{21} and also ϵ_{12} and ϵ_{22} are correlated as in the preceding subsection. Such a model is shown in Figure 11.8. Then θ_{31} will be added to the right side of Eq. (32) and θ_{42} will be added to the right side of Eq. (35). Equations (33) and (34) still determine β for given λ_1, λ_2, γ_1, π, ϕ, and ψ_{11} and θ_{31} and θ_{42} are then determined by Eqs. (32) and (35), respectively. Hence, this model has one overidentifying restriction.

Case (2) is shown in Figure 11.9. Here we write

$$x_1 = \xi + \delta_1$$

$$x_2 = \lambda_3 \xi + \delta_2$$

where λ_3 is a parameter to be determined and δ_1 and δ_2 are uncorrelated measurement errors, uncorrelated with ξ and the other latent variables. The other equations are as before except that x is replaced by ξ. We then have three more parameters than before, namely λ_3, $\sigma_{\delta_1}^2$ and $\sigma_{\delta_2}^2$. The parameter $\sigma_\xi^2 = \mathrm{Var}(\xi)$ replaces $\phi = \sigma_x^2 = \mathrm{Var}(x)$. On the other hand, we have now six more manifest parameters, so that the model has 6 degrees of freedom

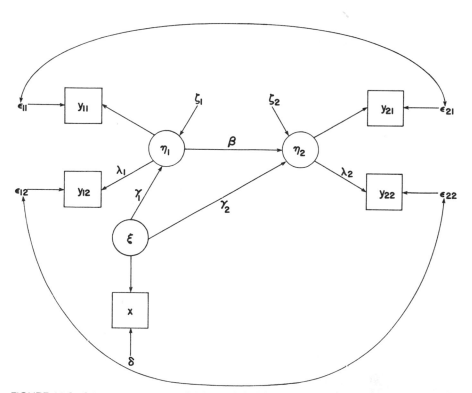

FIGURE 11.8. **A two-wave–two-variable model with correlated errors and a fallible background variable.**

with $\theta_{31} = \theta_{42} = 0$ and 4 degrees of freedom with these covariances included as parameters.

The parameter λ_3 is identified with three overidentifying restrictions since

$$\text{Cov}(x_2, w)/\text{Cov}(x_1, w) = \lambda_3,$$

for $w = y_{11}, y_{12}, y_{21}$, and y_{22}. All the other parameters are determined as before.

The simple models in Figure 11.6–11.9 have deliberately been chosen to explicate the principal points. The models can easily be generalized in two ways. Firstly, the number of pre- and postmeasures y can be more than two. Secondly, we could also have several background variables with a factor structure. We now give two examples of models of this kind.

C. The Stability of Alienation

For the first example we draw on ideas and data in Wheaton, Muthén, Alwin, and Summers (1977). Their study was concerned with the stability over time of attitudes such as alienation and its relation to background variables such as education and occupation. Data on attitude scales were collected from 932 persons in two rural regions in Illinois at three points in time: 1966, 1967, and 1971. (See Summers, Hough, Scott, & Folse, 1969, for further description of the research setting.) The variables we use for the present illustration are the *Anomia* subscale and the *Powerlessness* sub-

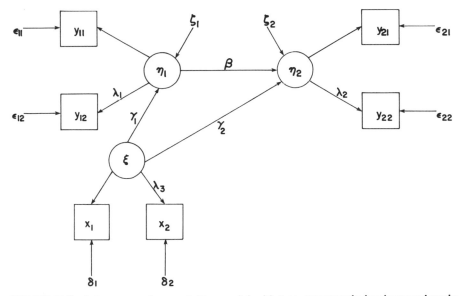

FIGURE 11.9. **A two-wave–two-variable model with two congeneric background variables.**

scale, taken to be indicators of *Alienation*. We use these subscales from 1967 and 1971 only. The background variables are the respondent's education (years of schooling completed) and Duncan's Socioeconomic Index (SEI). These are taken to be indicators of the respondent's socioeconomic status (SES). We analyze these variables under three different models, as shown in Figure 11.10a–c, none of which correspond to that of Wheaton *et al.* (1977). The data are given in Table 11.2.

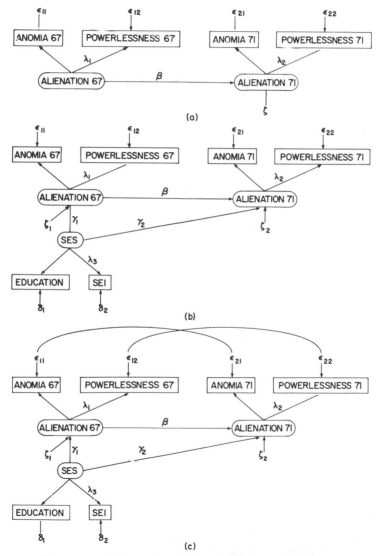

FIGURE 11.10. **Models for study of stability of alienation.**

TABLE 11.2
Covariance Matrix for the Models of Figure 11.10 (N = 932)

Y_1	11.834					
Y_2	6.947	9.364				
Y_3	6.819	5.091	12.532			
Y_4	4.783	5.028	7.495	9.986		
X_1	− 3.839	− 3.889	− 3.841	− 3.625	9.610	
X_2	−21.899	−18.831	−21.748	−18.775	35.522	450.288

The maximum-likelihood estimates of the parameters of the models are given in Table 11.3. The main aim of the Wheaton *et al.* study was to estimate the stability of alienation over time, which is reflected in the parameter β, or in the correlation between Alienation 71 and Alienation 67. As can be seen from Table 11.3 we obtain an estimate of β that is biased upward if we use a model that does not take SES into account. The influence of SES on Alienation at the two occasions is significant (see Figure 11.10b). The coefficient for 1967, γ_1, is −.614 with a standard error of .056; for 1971, γ_2, it is −.174 with a standard error equal to .054. The negative signs

TABLE 11.3
Maximum-Likelihood Estimates for the Models in Figure 11.10 a–c

	Model in Figure 11.10a	Model in Figure 11.10b	Model in Figure 11.10c
λ_1	.815 (.040)[a]	.888 (.041)	.979 (.062)
λ_2	.847 (.042)	.849 (.040)	.922 (.059)
λ_3	—	5.331 (.430)	5.221 (.422)
β	.789 (.044)	.705 (.054)	.607 (.051)
γ_1	—	−.614 (.056)	−.575 (.056)
γ_2	—	−.174 (.054)	−.227 (.052)
ψ_{11}	—	5.307 (.473)	4.847 (.468)
ψ_{22}	4.085 (.432)	3.742 (.388)	4.089 (.405)
ϕ	—	6.663 (.641)	6.803 (.650)
σ_{δ_1}	—	1.717 (.145)	1.675 (.151)
σ_{δ_2}	—	16.153 (.565)	16.273 (.558)
$\sigma_{\epsilon_{11}}$	1.906 (.097)	2.004 (.086)	2.176 (.104)
$\sigma_{\epsilon_{12}}$	1.865 (.077)	1.786 (.076)	1.602 (.126)
$\sigma_{\epsilon_{21}}$	1.827 (.109)	1.923 (.097)	2.098 (.123)
$\sigma_{\epsilon_{22}}$	1.969 (.077)	1.904 (.077)	1.754 (.124)
corr(ϵ_{11}, ϵ_{21})	—	—	.356 (.047)
corr(ϵ_{12}, ϵ_{22})	—	—	.121 (.082)
χ^2	61.155	71.544	4.770
df	1	6	4

[a] The standard errors of the estimates are given within parentheses.

of the SES coefficients γ_1 and γ_2 indicate that for high socioeconomic status the alienation is low and vice versa. However, the overall fit of the Model in Figure 11.10b is not acceptable; χ^2 with 6 df equals 71.544. Since the same scales are used on both occasions, it seems reasonable to assume that if the influence of the true score (i.e., Alienation) is removed from the measured variables (i.e., Anomia and Powerlessness), there might still be some correlation left between the same measures at the two occasions. Thus, the model in Figure 11.10c is intuitively more plausible. As can be seen from Table 11.3, the inclusion of these error correlations results in a model with an acceptable overall fit.

D. An Analysis of Verbal and Quantitative Ability

For the second illustration we use some longitudinal data from a large growth study conducted at the Educational Testing Service (Anderson & Maier, 1963; Hilton, 1969). In this study, a nationwide sample of fifth graders was tested in 1961 and then again in 1963, 1965, and 1967 as seventh, ninth, and eleventh graders, respectively. The test scores include the verbal (SCATV) and quantitative (SCATQ) parts of the SCAT (Scholastic Aptitude Test) and achievement tests in mathematics (MATH), science (SCI), social studies (SS), reading (READ), listening (LIST), and writing (WRIT). The examinees for which complete data were available for all the grades, 5, 7, 9 and 11, were divided into four groups according to sex and whether or not they were in the academic curriculum in Grade 12. The four groups and their sample sizes are as follows:

Boys academic (BA):	$N = 373$
Boys nonacademic (BNA):	$N = 249$
Girls academic (GA):	$N = 383$
Girls nonacademic (GNA):	$N = 387$

Scores on each test have been scaled so that the unit of measurement is approximately the same at all occasions. All analyses reported here are based on information provided by the means, standard deviations, and intercorrelations of the 32 variables (8 tests at 4 occasions) for the four groups.

In this example we use the six tests MATH, SCI, SS, READ, SCATV, SCATQ in Grades 7 and 9 only and only for the group GA. In later sections we use data from other grades and groups as well. Earlier studies (Jöreskog, 1970a) suggest that these tests measure two oblique factors that may reasonably be interpreted as a verbal (V) and a quantitative (Q) factor. We set up the model in Figure 11.11, which represents a model for the measurement of change in verbal and quantitative ability between Grades 7 and 9. Since

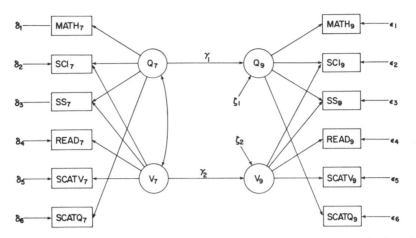

FIGURE 11.11. **Model for the measurement of change in verbal and quantitative ability between Grades 7 and 9.**

there are no background variables in this model, we may for estimation purposes treat the pretests as the independent variables. Hence we use the notation x for these. Note that the model includes the following features:

1. On each occasion the factor pattern is postulated to be restricted in the following way: MATH and SCATQ are pure measures of Q. READ and SCATV are pure measures of V. SCI and SS are composite measures of V and Q. This implies that there are four zero loadings in both Λ_x and Λ_y. To fix the scales for V and Q we assume that they are measured in the same units as SCATV and SCATQ, respectively. This means that there is a fixed 1 in each column of Λ_x and Λ_y.

2. It is postulated that Q_7 affects Q_9 only and not V_9, and similarly for V_7. This means that there are two zero coefficients in Γ. Furthermore, we postulate that the residuals ζ_1 and ζ_2 are uncorrelated, which means that, whatever remains in Q_9 and V_9 after Q_7 and V_7 are accounted for is uncorrelated with everything else.

3. The errors or unique factors in δ and ϵ are assumed to be uncorrelated both within and between occasions.

The maximum-likelihood estimates are given in Table 11.4. The rather low loadings of SCI and SS on Q at both occasions may seem a little surprising. However, an inspection of the items in tests SCI and SS reveals that these are mostly verbal problems concerned with logical reasoning in contrast to the items in SCATQ, which are mostly numerical items measuring the ability to work with numbers. The small residual variance 1.85 of ζ_2 means that V_9 can be predicted almost perfectly from V_7. This is not quite so for Q since we here have a residual variance of 18.49. However, this may be due to the more rapid increase in variance of Q from Grade 7 to 9, which is manifested in the increase in variances, which is $143.54 - 103.87 = 39.67$ for Q and $117.15 - 115.41 = 1.74$ for V.

There is a reason not to look at each number in Table 11.4 too seriously, and this is the poor overall fit of the model as evidenced by the χ^2-value of 217.79 with 47 df. We shall therefore investigate the reason for this poor fit and demonstrate that LISREL may be used not only to assess or measure the goodness-of-fit of a model but also to detect the parts of the model where the fit is poor. Taking the more fundamental assumptions of linearity

TABLE 11.4

Maximum-Likelihood Estimates (LISREL) for the Model of Figure 11.11[a]

$$\hat{\Lambda}_x = \begin{bmatrix} Q_7 & V_7 \\ .97 & .^b \\ .20 & .52 \\ .25 & .84 \\ 0.^b & 1.21 \\ 0.^b & 1^b \\ 1^b & 0^b \end{bmatrix} \quad \begin{array}{ll} & \theta_\delta \\ \mathrm{MATH}_7 & 5.68 \\ \mathrm{SCI}_7 & 5.49 \\ \mathrm{SS}_3 & 6.61 \\ \mathrm{READ}_7 & 6.80 \\ \mathrm{SCATV}_7 & 4.44 \\ \mathrm{SCATQ}_7 & 7.10 \end{array}$$

$$\hat{\Lambda}_x = \begin{bmatrix} Q_9 & V_9 \\ .88 & 0^b \\ .24 & .64 \\ .36 & .69 \\ 0.^b & .95 \\ 0.^b & 1^b \\ 1^b & 0.^b \end{bmatrix} \quad \begin{array}{ll} & \theta_\varepsilon \\ \mathrm{MATH}_9 & 4.80 \\ \mathrm{SCI}_9 & 6.57 \\ \mathrm{SS}_9 & 7.24 \\ \mathrm{READ}_9 & 6.49 \\ \mathrm{SCATV}_9 & 4.47 \\ \mathrm{SCATQ}_9 & 8.23 \end{array}$$

$$\hat{\Gamma} = \begin{pmatrix} Q_7 & V_7 \\ 1.10 & 0^b \\ 0^b & 1.00 \end{pmatrix} \quad \begin{array}{l} Q_9 \\ V_9 \end{array}$$

$$\hat{\Phi} = \begin{pmatrix} Q_7 & V_7 \\ 103.87 & 92.58 \\ 92.58 & 115.41 \end{pmatrix} \quad \begin{array}{l} Q_7 \\ V_7 \end{array}$$

$$\hat{\Psi} = \begin{pmatrix} \zeta_1 & \zeta_2 \\ 18.49 & 0^b \\ 0^b & 1.85 \end{pmatrix} \quad \begin{array}{l} \zeta_1 \\ \zeta_2 \end{array}$$

$$\hat{\Omega} = \begin{pmatrix} Q_9 & V_9 \\ 143.54 & 101.54 \\ 101.54 & 117.15 \end{pmatrix} \quad \begin{array}{l} Q_9 \\ V_9 \end{array}$$

$\chi^2 = 217.79$ with $df = 47$

[a] Group: GA (Girls Academic), $N = 383$.
[b] The value of this parameter was specified by the model.

and multinormality for granted, lack of fit of the model in Figure 11.11 may be due to the fact that one or more of the Postulates 1, 2, or 3 is not reasonable. We shall therefore investigate each of these separately.

To investigate (1), we set up a factor analysis of the pre- and posttests separately, assuming the postulated two-factor structure. This gives $\chi^2 = 17.64$ for the pretests and $\chi^2 = 2.62$ for the posttests, both with 10 degrees of freedom. Although the fit is not quite acceptable in Grade 7, we take the postulated factor structure to hold for both the pre- and posttests. So we must continue to look for lack of fit due to Postulate (2) or (3).

Postulate 2 is concerned with the interrelationships between the four factors Q_7, V_7, Q_9, and V_9. The most general assumption is that these four factors are freely intercorrelated, and this is equivalent to a LISREL model with all four coefficients in Γ free and with Ψ free as a full symmetric matrix. Hence, it is clear that the assumption made in (2) is the intersection of the two hypotheses "Γ is diagonal" and "Ψ is diagonal." It is therefore useful to test each of the four possible hypotheses. The results of these analyses may be presented in a 2×2 table as in Table 11.5. The row marginals of the table represent χ^2-values with one degree of freedom for testing the hypothesis that Ψ is diagonal. It is seen that this hypothesis may be rejected. The column marginals represent χ^2-values with 2 df for testing the hypothesis that Γ is diagonal. This hypothesis seems quite reasonable. From these analyses it is clear that "Γ diagonal and Ψ free" is the most reasonable assumption to retain. The overall fit of this model is $\chi^2 = 196.4$ with 46 df. Since this is still too large, we must continue to investigate Postulate 3.

The assumption in Postulate 3 is that the unique factors in δ and ϵ are uncorrelated both within and between sets. That they are uncorrelated within sets should not be questioned, since we have already found that the postulated factor-analysis model holds for both pre- and posttest. That they are uncorrelated between sets, however, is more questionable because of specific factors in each test. This means that the unique factors for corresponding tests should be allowed to correlate. To account for such correlations, Jöreskog (1970a) introduced so-called *test-specific factors*; that is, factors that do not contribute to correlations between tests within occasions

TABLE 11.5
Test of Assumptions (2) for the Model in Figure 10.11[a]

	Ψ diagonal	Ψ free	
Γ diagonal	$\chi^2_{47} = 217.8$	$\chi^2_{46} = 196.4$	$\chi_1^2 = 21.4$
Γ free	$\chi^2_{45} = 216.8$	$\chi^2_{44} = 193.7$	$\chi_1^2 = 23.1$
	$\chi_2^2 = 1.0$	$\chi_2^2 = 2.7$	

[a] Group: GA (Girls Academic), $N = 383$.

but between the *same* tests at different occasions. In this case, when there are only two occasions, it is not possible to define (identify) test-specific factors; we can merely introduce correlations between unique factors for corresponding pre- and posttests.

The model in Figure 11.11 is therefore modified as in Figure 11.12. This revised model can also be estimated with the LISREL program. The analysis of the revised model gives the results shown in Table 11.6, which also gives standard errors of the estimated parameters. It is seen that all the estimated parameters are significantly different from zero. The test of over-

TABLE 11.6

Maximum-Likelihood Estimates (LISREL) for the Model of Figure 11.12[a]

$$\hat{\Lambda}_x = \begin{bmatrix} 1.01\ (.05)^b & 0^c \\ .13\ (.07) & .60\ (.07) \\ .12\ (.09) & .98\ (.09) \\ 0^c & 1.24\ (.05) \\ 0^c & 1^c \\ 1.^c & 0^c \end{bmatrix} \begin{array}{l} \text{MATH}_7 \\ \text{SCI}_7 \\ \text{SS}_7 \\ \text{READ}_7 \\ \text{SCATV}_7 \\ \text{SCATQ}_7 \end{array}$$

with column headings $Q_7 \quad V_7$

$$\hat{\Lambda}_y = \begin{bmatrix} .93\ (.05) & 0^c \\ .13\ (.07) & .77\ (0.08) \\ .25\ (.08) & .82\ (0.08) \\ 0^c & .98\ (0.04) \\ 0^c & 1^c \\ 1^c & 0^c \end{bmatrix} \begin{array}{l} \text{MATH}_9 \\ \text{SCI}_9 \\ \text{SS}_9 \\ \text{READ}_9 \\ \text{SCATV}_9 \\ \text{SCATQ}_9 \end{array}$$

with column headings $Q_9 \quad V_9$

$$\Gamma = \begin{pmatrix} 1.06\ (.05) & 0.^c \\ 0^c & 0.98\ (.03) \end{pmatrix} \begin{array}{l} Q_9 \\ V_9 \end{array}$$

with column headings $Q_7 \quad V_7$

$$\hat{\Phi} = \begin{pmatrix} 100.57\ (10.86) & 90.53\ (8.46) \\ 90.53\ (8.46) & 110.45\ (9.74) \end{pmatrix} \begin{array}{l} Q_7 \\ V_7 \end{array}$$

with column headings $Q_7 \quad V_7$

$$\hat{\Psi} = \begin{pmatrix} 22.63\ (4.41) & 8.42\ (1.73) \\ 8.42\ (1.73) & 6.94\ (1.58) \end{pmatrix} \begin{array}{l} \xi_1 \\ \xi_2 \end{array}$$

with column headings F $\quad \xi_1 \quad \xi_2$

$$\hat{\Omega} = \begin{pmatrix} 136.52 & 102.62 \\ 102.62 & 112.53 \end{pmatrix} \begin{array}{l} Q_9 \\ V_9 \end{array}$$

with column headings $Q_9 \quad V_9$

$\chi^2 = 65.63$ with $df = 40$

[a] Group: GA [Girls Academic], $N = 383$.
[b] Standard errors in parentheses.
[c] The value of this parameter was specified by the model.

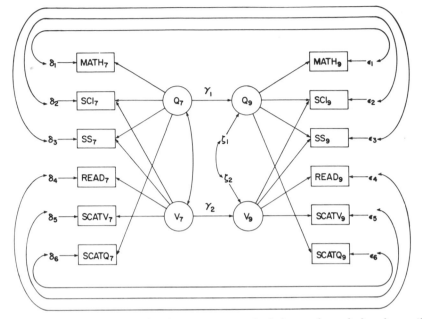

FIGURE 11.12. **Revised model for the measurement of change in verbal and quantitative ability between Grades 7 and 9.**

all goodness of fit gives $\chi^2 = 65.63$ with 40 df. This represents a reasonably good fit of the model to the data. An approximate test of the hypothesis that the unique factors are uncorrelated between occasions is obtained as $\chi^2 = 196.4 - 65.6 = 130.8$ with 6 df so that it is clear that this hypothesis is quite unreasonable. The variances, covariances, and correlations of the unique factors are given in Table 11.7. A comparison of the covariances with their standard errors reveals that all covariances except possibly the one between δ_1 and ϵ_1 are significantly nonzero.

TABLE 11.7
Variances, Covariances, and Correlations for the Unique Factors in Table 11.6 (Figure 11.12)

i	$\mathrm{Var}(\delta_i)$	$\mathrm{Var}(\epsilon_i)$	$\mathrm{Cov}(\delta_i\epsilon_i)$	$\mathrm{Corr}(\delta_i\epsilon_i)$
1	27.75 (3.78)[a]	17.67 (3.88)	−3.47 (2.78)	.157
2	29.59 (2.37)	41.15 (3.38)	9.60 (2.10)	.275
3	40.27 (3.60)	50.89 (4.21)	6.15 (2.82)	.136
4	44.21 (4.25)	40.34 (3.59)	7.52 (2.89)	.178
5	24.37 (2.47)	24.84 (2.60)	12.04 (2.05)	.489
6	54.28 (4.87)	74.53 (6.73)	22.84 (4.40)	.359

[a] Standard errors in parentheses.

E. Comparison of Change between Groups

In many longitudinal studies both pretests and posttests are administered to several groups of individuals and one is interested in comparing the change in various quantities between the different groups. Such groups may be, for example, groups having different socioeconomic backgrounds, groups having obtained different amounts of schooling or training either prior to the pretest occasion or between the two occasions, or groups having obtained different treatments between the two occasions. When we have several groups, it is natural to assume that the distributions of the latent variables are different for the different groups. Sörbom (1974) has developed a model in which the mean vector as well as the covariance matrix of the latent variables may vary from group to group. The structural equations will therefore be different for different groups. On the other hand, the matrix Λ, which describes the relationships between the observed test scores and the latent variables, is considered an attribute of the observed variables and is therefore assumed to be the same for all groups.

It is assumed that observations from different groups are independent. For a "random" examinee from group g we write his observed scores, using the notation in Eq. (9)

$$\mathbf{z}_g = \boldsymbol{\nu} + \Lambda \mathbf{f}_g + \mathbf{e}_g. \tag{36}$$

Note that both $\boldsymbol{\nu}$ and Λ are the same for all groups. The constant vector $\boldsymbol{\nu}$ represents the origin or level of the tests in the sense that when $\mathbf{f}_g = 0$ then $E(\mathbf{z}_g) = \boldsymbol{\nu}$ for all groups. This is considered an attribute of the tests and the scoring procedure. Let the mean vector of $\mathbf{f}_g$ be denoted $\boldsymbol{\theta}_g$. Then the mean vector $\boldsymbol{\mu}_g$ of $\mathbf{z}_g$ is [cf. Eq. (10)]

$$\boldsymbol{\mu}_g = \boldsymbol{\nu} + \Lambda \boldsymbol{\theta}_g \tag{37}$$

and the covariance matrix is (cf. Eq. [11])

$$\boldsymbol{\Sigma}_g = \Lambda \boldsymbol{\Phi}_g \Lambda' + \boldsymbol{\Psi}_g \tag{38}$$

where $\boldsymbol{\Phi}_g$ is the covariance matrix of $\mathbf{f}_g$ and $\boldsymbol{\Psi}_g$ the covariance matrix of $\mathbf{e}_g$.

There are two fundamental indeterminacies in Eqs. (37) and (38). Every factor in $\mathbf{f}_g$ may be subjected to an arbitrary linear transformation that may be different for different factors but the same for all individuals in all groups. The effect of such transformations may be compensated for by adding a constant vector to $\boldsymbol{\nu}$ and by a scaling of the columns of Λ, in such a way that both $\boldsymbol{\mu}_g$ and $\boldsymbol{\Sigma}_g$ are unchanged for all groups. This indeterminacy means that both the origin and the scale for the factors are arbitrary. These may therefore be chosen arbitrarily, but must be the same for all groups. It is convenient to fix the origins and the scales by choosing the vector $\boldsymbol{\theta}$ equal to $\mathbf{0}$ for one group and by choosing a 1 in each column of Λ.

Models of this kind may be estimated by means of the COFAMM program described earlier. This gives maximum-likelihood estimates of the common ν and Λ and of the mean vector θ_g and covariance matrix Φ_g as well as the covariance matrix Ψ_g of the unique factors for each group. One may postulate almost any pattern in Λ, Φ_g, and Ψ_g and any degree of invariance between groups. For example, one may postulate that Ψ_g and some part of Φ_g are invariant over groups.

F. Comparison of Change in Verbal Ability between Groups

To illustrate the method of the preceding subsection we make use of the data introduced in the section on verbal and quantitative ability. This time we use the data for all the four groups, but we use a somewhat simpler model than that of Figures 11.11 and 11.12. We shall use scores on the reading and writing achievement tests in Grades 7 and 9 only. The model is shown in Figure 11.13. Here we are mainly concerned with the comparison of the differences in mean changes and in the regression lines of V_9 on V_7. The regression of V_9 on V_7 in group g is

$$V_9 = \alpha_g + \gamma_g V_7 + \zeta,$$

where

$$\gamma_g = \sigma_{\eta\xi g}/\sigma_{\xi g}^2,$$

$$\alpha_g = \theta_{\eta g} - \gamma_g \theta_{\xi g}.$$

The maximum-likelihood solution is given in Table 11.8. If one takes the intercepts $\hat{\alpha}_g$ as relative measures of change, remembering that the scale is chosen such that α_g is zero for group BA, one finds that group GA has increased their verbal ability most, followed by groups BA, GNA, and BNA, in that order. However, this is not the whole story. For since the slope of the regression lines also differs between groups, one should take this also into account when interpreting the data. Probably the best way of looking at the results is to use the estimates $\hat{\theta}_g$ and $\hat{\Phi}_g$ to draw contour ellipses for each group as in Figure 11.14. With this kind of plot one can fix a given true pretest score and find the likely range of true posttest score for the various groups. For example, at $\xi = -15$, approximate 95% confidence

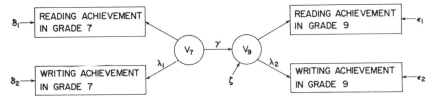

FIGURE 11.13. **Model for comparison of change in verbal ability between groups.**

TABLE 11.8

Maximum-Likelihood Estimates for the Model of Figure 11.13: Simultaneous Analysis for all Four Groups[a]

$$
\Lambda = \begin{pmatrix} 1.00^b & 0^b \\ .95 & 0^b \\ 0^b & 1.00^b \\ 0^b & 1.12 \end{pmatrix} \qquad \nu = \begin{pmatrix} 274.93 \\ 269.76 \\ 286.83 \\ 283.35 \end{pmatrix}
$$

g	$\hat{\sigma}_{\xi g}$	$\hat{\sigma}_{\eta\xi g}$	$\hat{\sigma}_{\eta g}$	$\hat{\gamma}_g$
BA	219.46	171.48	156.97	0.78
BNA	142.35	139.53	166.55	0.98
GA	186.65	143.57	121.49	0.77
GNA	195.17	160.24	163.38	0.82

g	$\theta_{\xi g}$	$\theta_{\eta g}$	α_g
BA	0^b	0^b	0^b
BNA	-16.881	-18.108	-1.56
GA	5.949	5.140	.56
GNA	-9.298	-8.061	$-.43$

[a] Groups: BA (Boys academic), $N = 373$; GA (Girls academic), $N = 383$; BNA (Boys nonacademic), $N = 249$; GNA (Girls nonacademic), $N = 387$.

[b] The value of this parameter was specified by the model.

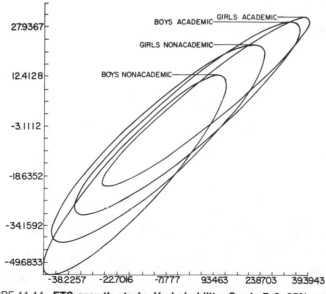

FIGURE 11.14. **ETS growth study: Verbal ability, Grade 7–9. 95% regions.**

intervals for η are

$$
\begin{aligned}
\text{GA:} &\ -17.32 \le \eta \le -4.63, \\
\text{BA:} &\ -22.40 \le \eta \le -1.038, \\
\text{GNA:} &\ -26.36 \le \eta \le -.87, \\
\text{BNA:} &\ -29.60 \le \eta \le -2.93.
\end{aligned}
$$

At $\xi = 10$ these confidence intervals show a different pattern:

$$
\begin{aligned}
\text{GA:} &\quad 0.18 \le \eta \le 16.34 \\
\text{BA:} &\ -3.46 \le \eta \le 19.09 \\
\text{GNA:} &\ -3.62 \le \eta \le 19.18 \\
\text{BNA:} &\quad 3.02 \le \eta \le 13.46
\end{aligned}
$$

V. Multiwave Models

A. Multiwave–One-Variable Models

Suppose one fallible measure y is administered repeatedly to the same group of people. An appropriate model for this situation is shown in Figure 11.15 in the case of four occasions. In the following we discuss all models in terms of four occasions; the generalization to an arbitrary number of occasions will be obvious at all stages. Such models have been termed simplex models by Guttman (1954) to designate the typical pattern of inter-correlations they give rise to. Anderson (1960) formulated this model in terms of various stochastic processes and treated the identification problem, and Jöreskog (1970b) treated the estimation problem. An application to the measurement of academic growth has been given by Werts, Linn, and

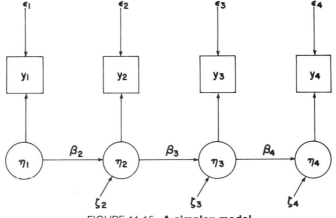

FIGURE 11.15. **A simplex model.**

Jöreskog (1977), and applications to sociological panel analysis have been discussed by Heise (1969), Wiley and Wiley (1970), and Werts, Jöreskog, and Linn (1971).

The unit of measurement in the factors η_i may be chosen to be the same as in y_i, $i = 1, 2, 3, 4$. The equations defining the model, then, are taking all variables as deviations from their mean,

$$y_i = \eta_i + \epsilon_i, \qquad i = 1, 2, 3, 4, \tag{39}$$

$$\eta_i = \beta_i \eta_{i-1} + \zeta_i, \qquad i = 2, 3, 4, \tag{40}$$

where the ϵ_i are uncorrelated among themselves and uncorrelated with all the η_i and where ζ_{i+1} is uncorrelated with η_i, $i = 1, 2, 3$. The parameters of the model are $\phi_i = \text{Var}(\eta_i)$, $\theta_{ii} = \text{Var}(\epsilon_i)$, $i = 1, 2, 3, 4$ and $\beta_2, \beta_3, \beta_4$. (We use ϕ to denote the variances of the dependent variables. Since there are no independent variables, there should be no confusion.) The residual variance $\text{Var}(\zeta_{i+1})$ is a function of ϕ_{i+1}, ϕ_i and β_{i+1}, namely $\text{Var}(\zeta_{i+1}) = \phi_{i+1} - \beta_{i+1}^2 \phi_i$, $i = 1, 2, 3$. The covariance matrix of y_1, y_2, y_3, and y_4 is

$$\Sigma = \begin{bmatrix} \phi_1 + \theta_{11} & & & \\ \beta_2 \phi_1 & \phi_2 + \theta_{22} & & \\ \beta_2 \beta_3 \phi_1 & \beta_3 \phi_2 & \phi_3 + \theta_{33} & \\ \beta_2 \beta_3 \beta_4 \phi_1 & \beta_3 \beta_4 \phi_2 & \beta_4 \phi_3 & \phi_4 + \theta_{44} \end{bmatrix} \tag{41}$$

It is seen from Eq. (41) that although the product $\beta_2 \phi_1 = \sigma_{21}$ is identified, β_2 and ϕ_1 are not separately identified. The product $\beta_2 \phi_1$ is involved in the off-diagonal elements in the first column (and row) only. We can multiply β_2 by a constant and divide ϕ_1 by the same constant without changing the product. The change induced by ϕ_1 in σ_{11} can be absorbed in θ_{11} in such a way that σ_{11} remains unchanged. Hence $\theta_{11} = \text{Var}(\epsilon_1)$ is not identified. For η_2 and η_3 we have

$$\phi_2 = \sigma_{32} \sigma_{21} / \sigma_{31},$$

$$\phi_3 = \sigma_{43} \sigma_{32} / \sigma_{42}$$

so that ϕ_2 and ϕ_3, and hence also θ_{22} and θ_{33}, are identified. With ϕ_2 and ϕ_3 identified, β_3 and β_4 are identified by σ_{32} and σ_{43}. The middle coefficient, β_3, is overidentified since

$$\beta_3 \phi_2 = \sigma_{31} \sigma_{42} / \sigma_{41} = \sigma_{32}.$$

Since both ϕ_4 and θ_{44} are involved in σ_{44} only, these are not identified, but their sum, σ_{44}, is.

This analysis of the identification problem shows that for the "inner" variables y_2 and y_3, ϕ_2, ϕ_3, θ_{22}, θ_{33}, and β_3 are identified, whereas there is an indeterminacy associated with each of the "outer" variables y_1 and y_4. To eliminate these indeterminancies, one of the parameters ϕ_1, θ_{11}, or

β_2 must be specified and one of the parameters ϕ_4 or θ_{44} must also be specified. Hence there are only nine independent parameters, and the model has 1 df. In the general case of $T \geq 4$ occasions there will be $3T - 3$ free parameters and the degrees of freedom are $(\frac{1}{2})T(T + 1) - (3T - 3)$.

The estimation problem associated with the simplex model is a straight-forward application of the LISREL program using the option of "no x." The LISREL equations are

$$\begin{pmatrix} y_1 \\ y_2 \\ y_3 \\ y_4 \end{pmatrix} = \begin{bmatrix} 1 & 0 & 0 & 0 \\ 0 & 1 & 0 & 0 \\ 0 & 0 & 1 & 0 \\ 0 & 0 & 0 & 1 \end{bmatrix} \begin{bmatrix} \eta_1 \\ \eta_2 \\ \eta_3 \\ \eta_4 \end{bmatrix} + \begin{pmatrix} 0 \\ \epsilon_2 \\ \epsilon_3 \\ 0 \end{pmatrix}, \tag{42}$$

$$\begin{bmatrix} 1 & 0 & 0 & 0 \\ -\beta_2 & 1 & 0 & 0 \\ 0 & -\beta_3 & 1 & 0 \\ 0 & 0 & -\beta_4 & 1 \end{bmatrix} \begin{pmatrix} \eta_1 \\ \eta_2 \\ \eta_3 \\ \eta_4 \end{pmatrix} = \begin{pmatrix} \zeta_1 \\ \zeta_2 \\ \zeta_3 \\ \zeta_4 \end{pmatrix}. \tag{43}$$

In Eq. (42) we have taken $\epsilon_1 = \epsilon_4 = 0$ to eliminate the indeterminacies, and in Eq. (43) we have defined ζ_1 as η_1. In LISREL it is inconvenient to treat $\phi_i = \mathrm{Var}(\eta_i)$, $i = 1, 2, 3, 4$ as free parameters, so instead of $\phi_i = \mathrm{Var}(\eta_i)$, $i = 1, 2, 3, 4$, we take $\psi_i = \mathrm{Var}(\zeta_i)$, $i = 1, 2, 3, 4$ as free parameters. It is easily realized that the ϕ_i and the ψ_i, $i = 1, 2, 3, 4$ are in a one-to-one correspondence. So the parameter matrices in LISREL are

$$\Lambda_y = \mathbf{I}, \qquad \mathbf{B} \text{ as in (43)},$$

$$\Psi = \mathrm{diag}(\psi_1, \psi_2, \psi_3, \psi_4)$$

and

$$\Theta_\epsilon = \mathrm{diag}(0, \sigma_{\epsilon_2}^2, \sigma_{\epsilon_3}^2, 0).$$

B. Multiwave–Two-Variable Models

The direct generalization of the model in Figure 11.15 to the case of four occasions is shown in Figure 11.16.

With $\mathbf{x}' = (x_1, x_2, x_3, x_4)$, $\mathbf{y}' = (y_1, y_2, y_3, y_4)$, the model is

$$\mathbf{x} = \boldsymbol{\eta} + \boldsymbol{\delta}, \tag{44}$$

$$\mathbf{y} = \mathbf{D}_\lambda \boldsymbol{\eta} + \boldsymbol{\epsilon} \tag{45}$$

where $\mathbf{D}_\lambda = \mathrm{diag}(\lambda_1, \lambda_2, \lambda_3, \lambda_4)$. The covariance matrix of $\mathbf{z} = (\mathbf{x}', \mathbf{y}')'$ is

$$\Sigma = \begin{pmatrix} \Sigma_{xx} & \Sigma_{xy} \\ \Sigma_{yx} & \Sigma_{yy} \end{pmatrix},$$

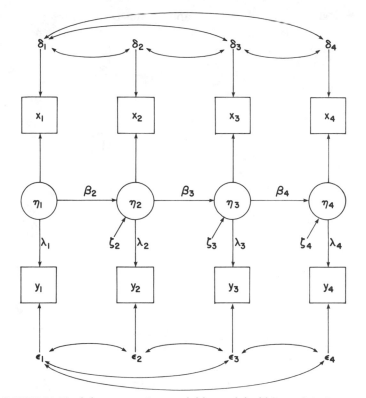

FIGURE 11.16. **A four-wave–two-variable model with correlated errors.**

with

$$\Sigma_{xx} = \Phi + \Theta_\delta,$$

$$\Sigma_{yx} = D_\lambda \Phi,$$

$$\Sigma_{yy} = D_\lambda \Phi D_\lambda + \Theta_\epsilon,$$

where Φ, Θ_δ, and Θ_ϵ are the covariance matrices of η, δ, and ϵ, respectively. It is seen that D_λ may be multiplied by a nonzero constant Φ divided by the same constant, and with Θ_δ and Θ_ϵ properly adjusted, Σ will not change. Hence, the model is not identified. One restriction is needed to make it identified, but there does not seem to be any meaningful way to choose such a restriction. We shall therefore consider two other models that are both identified (see Jöreskog & Sörbom, 1977). These models represent different specification of the correlation structures for the errors in δ and ϵ as follows:

MODEL A: *The errors are uncorrelated.*
MODEL B: *The errors have one common factor.*

Model A is shown in Figure 11.17 and Model B in Figure 11.18. In both models the covariance matrix $\mathbf{\Phi}$ of η is restricted to be generated by a simplex or first-order autoregressive model; that is,

$$\eta_i = \beta_i \eta_{i-1} + \zeta_i, \, i = 2, 3, 4$$

This implies that

$$\mathbf{\Phi} = \begin{bmatrix} \phi_1 & & & \\ \beta_2\phi_1 & \phi_2 & & \\ \beta_2\beta_3\phi_1 & \beta_3\phi_2 & \phi_3 & \\ \beta_2\beta_3\beta_4\phi_1 & \beta_3\beta_4\phi_2 & \beta_4\phi_3 & \phi_4 \end{bmatrix}, \tag{46}$$

where, as before, $\phi_i = \mathrm{Var}(\eta_i)$, $i = 1, 2, 3, 4$. We now consider the LISREL specification of each of these models. In both models we treat both x and y as dependent variables and use the "no-x" option.

1. Model A

The LISREL specification is straightforward:

$$\begin{pmatrix} \mathbf{x} \\ \mathbf{y} \end{pmatrix} = \begin{pmatrix} \mathbf{I} \\ \mathbf{D}_\lambda \end{pmatrix} \eta + \boldsymbol{\epsilon}, \tag{47}$$

and Eq. (43). As before, LISREL treats $\psi_i = \mathrm{Var}(\zeta_i)$ as primary parameters

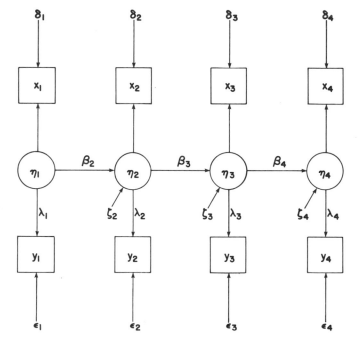

FIGURE 11.17. **A four-wave–two-variable model with uncorrelated errors (Model A).**

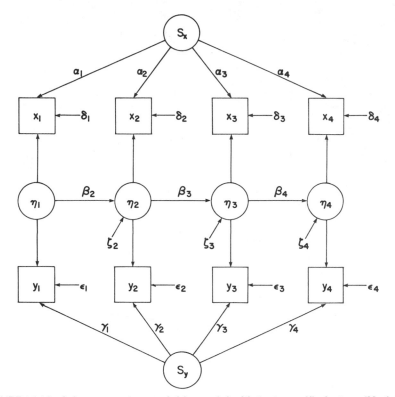

FIGURE 11.18. **A four-wave–two-variable model with test-specific factors (Model B).**

rather than $\phi_i = \text{Var}(\eta_i)$, but estimates of ϕ_i are obtained as a byproduct. The one-to-one relationships between ϕ_i and ψ_i, $i = 1, 2, 3, 4$, are

$$\phi_1 = \psi_1$$
$$\phi_i = \psi_i + \beta_i^2 \phi_{i-1}, \qquad i = 2, 3, 4.$$

The covariance matrix $\mathbf{\Theta}_\epsilon$ of ϵ is diagonal.

2. Model B

Model B assumes that the correlations between the errors δ and ϵ in Figure 11.16 are accounted for by one common factor. These common factors s_x and s_y are *test-specific* factors in contrast to the factors η_1, η_2, η_3, and η_4, which are *occasion-specific* factors in the terminology of Jöreskog (1970a). The test-specific factors s_x and s_y are assumed to be uncorrelated and uncorrelated with η, δ, and ϵ.

The equations for Model B are

$$x = \eta + \alpha s_x + \delta,$$

$$y = D_\lambda \eta + \gamma s_y + \epsilon,$$

where α and γ are factor loadings relating the observed variables x and y to the test-specific factors s_x and s_y, respectively. The factors s_x and s_y are scaled to unit variance, for convenience.

Model A is a special case of Model B, namely when both α and γ are zero. The hypothesis $\alpha = 0$ and $\gamma = 0$ may be tested with eight degrees of freedom.

The LISREL parameter matrices are specified as

$$\Lambda_y = \begin{bmatrix} 1 & 0 & 0 & 0 & \alpha_1 & 0 \\ 0 & 1 & 0 & 0 & \alpha_2 & 0 \\ 0 & 0 & 1 & 0 & \alpha_3 & 0 \\ 0 & 0 & 0 & 1 & \alpha_4 & 0 \\ \lambda_1 & 0 & 0 & 0 & 0 & \gamma_1 \\ 0 & \lambda_2 & 0 & 0 & 0 & \gamma_2 \\ 0 & 0 & \lambda_3 & 0 & 0 & \gamma_3 \\ 0 & 0 & 0 & \lambda_4 & 0 & \gamma_4 \end{bmatrix},$$

$$B = \begin{bmatrix} 1 & 0 & 0 & 0 & 0 & 0 \\ -\beta_2 & 1 & 0 & 0 & 0 & 0 \\ 0 & -\beta_3 & 1 & 0 & 0 & 0 \\ 0 & 0 & -\beta_4 & 1 & 0 & 0 \\ 0 & 0 & 0 & 0 & 1 & 0 \\ 0 & 0 & 0 & 0 & 0 & 1 \end{bmatrix},$$

$$\Psi = \text{diag}(\psi_1, \psi_2, \psi_3, \psi_4, 1, 1),$$

where, as before, $\psi_i = \text{Var}(\zeta_i)$, $i = 1, 2, 3, 4$, and Θ_δ and Θ_ϵ are diagonal as before.

C. Estimation of Four-Wave Models for MATH and SCATQ

To illustrate the models of the previous subsection we use the data on the variables MATH and SCATQ from all four occasions. The maximum-likelihood estimates of the various parameters are shown in Table 11.9 along with χ^2-goodness-of-fit-values and corresponding degrees of freedom. It is seen that Model A is clearly rejected in favor of Model B. The parameters listed in Table 11.9 are those that come out of the LISREL program and that are used to maximize the likelihood function. Some of these may be very difficult to interpret in a meaningful way. However, from these estimates one can compute various other parameters that are more easily

TABLE 11.9
**Maximum-Likelihood Estimates for Models
A and B with x = MATH and y = SCATQ**[a]

Parameter estimate	Model A	Model B
$\hat{\lambda}_1$	.88	.85
$\hat{\lambda}_2$	1.13	1.06
$\hat{\lambda}_3$	1.23	1.14
$\hat{\lambda}_4$	1.31	1.21
$\hat{\beta}_2$	1.22	1.22
$\hat{\beta}_3$	1.01	1.00
$\hat{\beta}_4$	1.06	1.05
$\hat{\sigma}^2_{\zeta_1}$	55.25	57.31
$\hat{\sigma}^2_{\zeta_2}$	9.28	10.93
$\hat{\sigma}^2_{\zeta_3}$	10.29	13.74
$\hat{\sigma}^2_{\zeta_4}$	2.37	5.79
$\hat{\sigma}_{\delta_1}$	6.19	5.94
$\hat{\sigma}_{\delta_2}$	6.20	5.84
$\hat{\sigma}_{\delta_3}$	5.77	2.29
$\hat{\sigma}_{\delta_4}$	7.55	6.83
$\hat{\sigma}_{\epsilon_1}$	4.53	4.47
$\hat{\sigma}_{\epsilon_2}$	6.18	5.83
$\hat{\sigma}_{\epsilon_3}$	7.40	6.87
$\hat{\sigma}_{\epsilon_4}$	7.14	6.51
χ	72.49	23.18
df	17	9

Additional parameters for Model B	
$\hat{\alpha}_1 = .97$	$\hat{\gamma}_1 = 1.48$
$\hat{\alpha}_2 = .26$	$\hat{\gamma}_2 = 3.51$
$\hat{\alpha}_3 = 4.59$	$\hat{\gamma}_3 = 4.66$
$\hat{\alpha}_4 = -.92$	$\hat{\gamma}_4 = 4.90$

[a] Group: GA (Girls Academic), $N = 383$.

interpreted. Table 11.10 gives the estimates of the factor variances and the squared correlations R_i^2 between η_i and η_{i-1} for Model B, and Table 11.11 gives the covariance matrices of the errors $\epsilon^* = y - D_x\eta$ and $\delta^* = x - \eta$; that is, the partial covariance matrices of y and x after elimination of η. Table 11.12 gives the corresponding correlation matrices.

From Table 11.10 it is seen that the squared correlations R_i^2 are quite high. There is a very high stability of the quantitative factor over time. This is also indicated by the stability of the β-coefficients in Table 11.9. Table 11.11 reveals that covariation among the errors is present for the SCATQ tests to a larger extent than for the MATH tests. Table 11.12 shows that the correlations among the ϵ^*'s are in general higher than those among the δ^*'s. The latter are indeed very small. Hence, the model accounts for the

TABLE 11.10
Factor Variances and Squared Correlations for Model B

$\sigma^2_{\eta i}$	R_i^2
57.31	—
96.23	.886
109.97	.875
127.03	.954

TABLE 11.11
Covariance Matrices of ϵ^* and δ^* for Model B

$$\epsilon^* = \begin{pmatrix} 22.17 & & & \\ 5.19 & 46.31 & & \\ 6.90 & 16.36 & 68.91 & \\ 7.25 & 17.20 & 22.83 & 66.39 \end{pmatrix}$$

$$\delta^* = \begin{pmatrix} 36.22 & & & \\ .25 & 34.17 & & \\ 4.45 & 1.19 & 26.31 & \\ -.89 & -.24 & -4.22 & 47.49 \end{pmatrix}$$

TABLE 11.12
Correlation Matrices of ϵ^* and δ^* for Model B

$$\epsilon^* = \begin{pmatrix} 1.00 & & & \\ .16 & 1.00 & & \\ .18 & .29 & 1.00 & \\ .19 & .31 & .34 & 1.00 \end{pmatrix}$$

$$\delta^* = \begin{pmatrix} 1.00 & & & \\ .01 & 1.00 & & \\ .14 & .04 & 1.00 & \\ -.02 & -.01 & -.12 & 1.00 \end{pmatrix}$$

intercorrelations among the MATH tests much better than the intercorrelations among the SCATQ tests.

D. Multiwave–Two-Variable Models with Background Variables

Although the multiwave–two-variable model with freely intercorrelated errors between occasions is not identified, it becomes so as soon as one or more background variables are included. For the case $T = 2$ this was demonstrated in the section on two-wave–two variable models. A model with $T = 4$ and two congeneric background variables x_1 and x_2 may be specified as follows. The structural equations are

$$
\begin{bmatrix}
1 & 0 & 0 & 0 \\
-\beta_2 & 1 & 0 & 0 \\
0 & -\beta_3 & 1 & 0 \\
0 & 0 & -\beta_4 & 1
\end{bmatrix}
\begin{pmatrix}
\eta_1 \\ \eta_2 \\ \eta_3 \\ \eta_4
\end{pmatrix}
=
\begin{pmatrix}
\gamma_1 \\ \gamma_2 \\ \gamma_3 \\ \gamma_4
\end{pmatrix}
\xi +
\begin{pmatrix}
\zeta_1 \\ \zeta_2 \\ \zeta_3 \\ \zeta_4
\end{pmatrix}. \tag{48}
$$

The measurement model for x_1 and x_2 is

$$
\begin{pmatrix} x_1 \\ x_2 \end{pmatrix} = \begin{pmatrix} 1 \\ \lambda_x \end{pmatrix} \xi + \begin{pmatrix} \delta_1 \\ \delta_2 \end{pmatrix}, \tag{49}
$$

and the measurement model for $\mathbf{y}$ is the same as in Eq. (47). The coefficient γ_t measures the direct effect of ξ on η_t and is expected to decrease as t increases. In Eq. (49) we have taken ξ to be measured in the same units as x_1. If there is only one background variable x, Eq. (49) is replaced by $x = \xi$; that is, we take $\lambda = 1$ and $\delta = 0$.

E. A General Model for Analysis of Longitudinal Data

In concluding this section we develop a general model for analysis of longitudinal data. All the models considered in the other sections of this chapter are special cases of this general model.

Suppose that several variables are measured at T points in time: t_1, $t_2, \ldots, t_T$, not necessarily equidistant, where time is measured from an arbitrary origin and with an arbitrary unit of measurement. Let p_t dependent variables be measured at occasion t, where t may be $t_1, t_2, \ldots,$ or t_T, and let $\mathbf{y}_t' = (y_{1t}, y_{2t}, \ldots, y_{p_t t})$ be a vector of these p_t variables. Neither the number of variables nor the variables themselves need to be the same at all occasions, although in most applications they will be so. At each occasion it is assumed that $\mathbf{y}_t$ has a common factor structure with m_t correlated common factors $\boldsymbol{\eta}_t' = (\eta_{1t}, \eta_{2t}, \ldots, \eta_{m_t t})$, so that

$$
\mathbf{y}_t = \boldsymbol{\mu}_t + \boldsymbol{\Lambda}_{yt}\boldsymbol{\eta}_t + \boldsymbol{\epsilon}_t, \tag{50}
$$

where $\boldsymbol{\mu}_t$ is the mean vector of $\mathbf{y}_t$, $\boldsymbol{\epsilon}_t$ is a vector of unique factors, and $\boldsymbol{\Lambda}_{yt}$ is a matrix of order $p_t \times m_t$ of factor loadings.

In addition to the dependent variables $\mathbf{y}_t$, we assume that q independent variables $\mathbf{x}' = (x_1, x_2, \ldots, x_q)$ are measured representing characteristics and conditions existing before the first occasion and assumed to influence the dependent variables $\mathbf{y}_t$. We assume that $\mathbf{x}$ also has a factor structure with common factors $\xi' = (\xi_1, \xi_2, \ldots, \xi_n)$ so that

$$x = \nu + \Lambda_x + \delta \tag{51}$$

where ν is the mean vector of x, δ the vector of unique factors and Λ_x the matrix of factor loadings of order $q \times n$.

The structural equations connecting the η's and ξ are assumed to be

$$\eta_1 = A_1\xi + \zeta_1 \tag{52}$$

$$\eta_t = A_t\xi + B_t\eta_{t-1} + \zeta_t, \tag{53}$$

where A_t is a regression matrix of order $m_t \times n$ and B_t is a regression matrix of order $m_t \times m_{t-1}$. The vectors $\zeta_t' = (\zeta_{1t}, \zeta_{2t}, \ldots, \zeta_{m_t})$ are vectors of residuals assumed to be correlated within occasions but uncorrelated between occasions. As before, t may be $t_1, t_2, \ldots, t_T$ and if $t = t_i$, then $t - 1$ is t_{i-1}.

Equations (50)–(53) constitute the basic general model considered in this chapter. A special case of this model is when there are no independent variables x. Then Eq. (51) is no longer included in the model and Eqs. (52) and (53) are replaced by the single equation

$$\eta_t = B_t\eta_{t-1} + \zeta_t. \tag{54}$$

Equation (50) may be written more compactly as (here illustrated with $T = 4$ occasions),

$$\begin{pmatrix} y_1 \\ y_2 \\ y_3 \\ y_4 \end{pmatrix} = \begin{pmatrix} \mu_1 \\ \mu_2 \\ \mu_3 \\ \mu_4 \end{pmatrix} + \begin{pmatrix} \Lambda_{y1} & 0 & 0 & 0 \\ 0 & \Lambda_{y2} & 0 & 0 \\ 0 & 0 & \Lambda_{y3} & 0 \\ 0 & 0 & 0 & \Lambda_{y4} \end{pmatrix} \begin{pmatrix} \eta_1 \\ \eta_2 \\ \eta_3 \\ \eta_4 \end{pmatrix} + \begin{pmatrix} \epsilon_1 \\ \epsilon_2 \\ \epsilon_3 \\ \epsilon_4 \end{pmatrix} \tag{55}$$

and Eqs. (52) and (53) may be combined and written as (in the case of $T = 4$ occasions)

$$\begin{bmatrix} I & 0 & 0 & 0 \\ -B_2 & I & 0 & 0 \\ 0 & -B_3 & 0 & 0 \\ 0 & 0 & -B_4 & 0 \end{bmatrix} \begin{pmatrix} \eta_1 \\ \eta_2 \\ \eta_3 \\ \eta_4 \end{pmatrix} = \begin{pmatrix} A_1 \\ A_2 \\ A_3 \\ A_4 \end{pmatrix} \xi + \begin{pmatrix} \zeta_1 \\ \zeta_2 \\ \zeta_3 \\ \zeta_4 \end{pmatrix} \tag{56}$$

This shows that the model is a LISREL model with

$$y = \mu + \Lambda_y\eta + \epsilon, \tag{57}$$

$$x = \nu + \Lambda_x\xi + \delta, \tag{58}$$

$$B\eta = \Gamma\xi + \zeta, \tag{59}$$

with Λ_y of order $p \times m$, B of order $m \times m$ and Γ of order $m \times n$, where $p = p_{t_1} + p_{t_2} + \cdots + p_{t_T}$ and $m = m_{t_1} + m_{t_2} + \cdots + m_{t_T}$. In the special case when there is no x, Eq. (58) is omitted and Eq. (59) should be interpreted as $\mathbf{B}\boldsymbol{\eta} = \boldsymbol{\zeta}$. Each of the matrices Λ_x, $\mathbf{B}$, $\boldsymbol{\Gamma}$, and Λ_{yt}, $t = 1, 2, \ldots, T$ may contain fixed, free, and constrained parameters as in Section II.D.

VI. Summary

In this chapter we have developed several models suitable for analyzing longitudinal data and considered the statistical problems of model specification, identification, estimation, and testing. Almost all of the models may be estimated and tested using three computer programs, ACOVSM, LISREL, and COFAMM, which are described briefly in Section II.

Section III deals with the estimation of polynomial growth curves describing the means of response variables as functions of time. The growth curves may be estimated for several variables and for several groups of individuals simultaneously, and various hypotheses may be tested such that (1) the growth curve has a specified degree; (2) the growth curves are identical or parallel for several variables and/or groups. The estimation of growth curves when the response variables are autoregressive is also considered. If the autoregressive model holds, the growth curves can be estimated more efficiently and the tests will be more powerful.

Sections IV and V deal with models involving latent variables or hypothetical constructs and the related problem of measurement errors in the observed variables. The kernel in these models is a set of linear structural relationships among latent variables that are not directly observed but observed by means of two or more indicators. We consider models with or without background variables. Section IV deals with two-wave models and Section V with multiwave models. In subsections IV. E–F, we consider the comparison of change between groups under the assumption that certain characteristics of the response variables are invariant over groups of people.

For most of the models in Sections IV and V we consider the identification problem. The estimation problem is considered in the sense that we show how to specify the model for one of the three computer programs described in Section II. For some of the models, the estimation and testing are illustrated by some data.

References

Achenbach, T. M. *Research in developmental psychology: Concepts, strategies, methods.* New York: Free Press, 1978.

Ambron, S. R., & Rogosa, D. R. Structural equation models and causal inference in child development research. Paper presented at the American Educational Research Association Convention, Washington, D.C., April 1975.

Andersen, E. B., & Madsen, M. Estimating the parameters of the latent population distribution. (Institute of Statistics Research Report No. 35). Univ. of Copenhagen, 1976.

Anderson, J. E. The methods of child psychology. In C. Murchison (Ed.), *A handbook of child psychology.* Worcester, Massachusetts: Clark Univ. Press, 1931.

Anderson, R. L., & Bancroft, T. A. *Statistical theory in research.* New York: McGraw-Hill, 1952.

Anderson, S. B., & Maier, M. H. 34,000 pupils and how they grew. *Journal of Teacher Education,* 1963, *14,* 212–216.

Anderson, T. W. *An introduction to multivariate statistical analysis.* New York: Wiley, 1958.

Anderson, T. W. Some stochastic process models for intelligence test scores. In K. J. Arrow, S. Karlin, & P. Suppes (Eds.), *Mathematical methods in the social sciences, 1959.* Stanford, California: Stanford Univ. Press, 1960.

Anderson, T. W. *Statistical analysis of time series.* New York: Wiley, 1971.

Atkin, R., Bray, R., Davison, M., Herzberger, S., Humphreys, L., & Selzer, U. Cross-lagged panel analysis of sixteen cognitive measures at four grade levels. *Child Development,* 1977, *48,* 944–952.

Ausubel, D., & Sullivan, E. *Theories and problems of child development.* New York: Grune & Stratton, 1970.

Bachman, J. G., & O'Malley, P. M. Self-esteem in young men: A longitudinal analysis of the impact of educational and occupational attainment. *Journal of Personality and Social Psychology,* 1977, *35,* 365–380.

Baer, D. M. An age-irrelevant concept of development. *Merrill-Palmer Quarterly,* 1970, *16,* 238–246.

Baer, D. M. The control of developmental process: Why wait? In J. R. Nesselroade & H. W. Reese (Eds.), *Life-span developmental psychology: Methodological issues.* New York: Academic Press, 1973.

Baer, D. M. The organism as host. *Human Development,* 1976, *19,* 87–98.

Baldwin, B. T. Physical growth and school progress. *U.S. Bureau of Education* (Bulletin No. 10), 1914 (Whole No. 581).

Baldwin, B. T. *The physical growth of children from birth to maturity.* Studies in child welfare, vol. 1. Iowa City: Univ. of Iowa, 1921.

Baltes, M. M., & Baltes, P. B. The ecopsychological relativity and plasticity of psychological aging: Convergent perspectives of cohort effects and operant psychology. *Zeitschrift für Experimentelle und Angewandte Psychologie,* 1977, *24,* 179–197.

Baltes, P. B. Sequenzmodelle zum Studium von Altersprozessen: Querschnitts- und Längsschnittsequenzen. In F. Merz (Ed.), *Bericht über den 25. Kongress der Deutschen Gesellschaft für Psychologie in Münster 1966.* Göttingen: Hogrefe, 1967.

Baltes, P. B. The logical status of age as an experimental variable: Comments on some methodological issues. In K. W. Schaie (Ed.), *Theory and methods of research on aging.* Morgantown, West Virginia: West Virginia Univ. Library, 1968. (a)

Baltes, P. B. Longitudinal and cross-sectional sequences in the study of age and generation effects. *Human Development,* 1968, *11,* 145–171. (b)

Baltes, P. B. Prototypical paradigms and questions in life-span research on development and aging. *Gerontologist,* 1973, *13,* 458–467.

Baltes, P. B. Life-span developmental psychology: Some converging observations on history and theory. In P. B. Baltes & O. G. Brim, Jr. (Eds.), *Life-span development and behavior* (Vol. 2). New York: Academic Press, 1979.

Baltes, P. B., Baltes, M. M., & Reinert, G. The relationship between time of measurement and age in cognitive development of children: An application of cross-sectional sequences. *Human Development,* 1970, *13,* 258–268.

Baltes, P. B., & Cornelius, S. W. The status of dialectics in developmental psychology: Theoretical orientation versus scientific method. In N. Datan & H. W. Reese (Eds.), *Life-span developmental psychology: Dialectical perspectives on experimental research.* New York: Academic Press, 1977.

Baltes, P. B., Cornelius, S. W., & Nesselroade, J. R. Cohort effects in behavioral development: Theoretical and methodological perspectives. In W. A. Collins (Ed.), *Minnesota symposia on child psychology* (Vol. 11). Hillsdale, New Jersey: Erlbaum, 1978.

Baltes, P. B., & Goulet, L. R. Exploration of developmental variables by manipulation and simulation of age differences in behavior. *Human Development,* 1971, *14,* 149–170.

Baltes, P. B., & Nesselroade, J. R. Multivariate longitudinal and cross-sectional sequences for analyzing ontogenetic and generational change: A methodological note. *Developmental Psychology,* 1970, *2,* 163–168.

Baltes, P. B., & Nesselroade, J. R. Cultural change and adolescent personality development. *Developmental Psychology,* 1972, *7,* 244–256.

Baltes, P. B., & Nesselroade, J. R. The developmental analysis of individual differences on multiple measures. In. J. R. Nesselroade & H. W. Reese (Eds.), *Life-span developmental psychology; Methodological issues.* New York: Academic Press, 1973.

Baltes, P. B., & Nesselroade, J. R. A developmentalist's view of regression toward the mean: A largely irrelevant issue in the study of developmental change? Unpublished manuscript, Penn. State Univ., 1976.

Baltes, P. B., Nesselroade, J. R., Schaie, K. W., & Labouvie, E. W. On the dilemma of regression effects in examining ability-level-related differentials in ontogenetic patterns of intelligence. *Developmental Psychology,* 1972, *6,* 78–84.

Baltes, P. B., Reese, H. W., & Lipsitt, L. P. Life-span developmental psychology. *Annual Review of Psychology,* 1980, *31.*

Baltes, P. B., Reese, H. W., & Nesselroade, J. R. Life-span developmental psychology: Introduction to research methods. Monterey, California: Brooks/Cole, 1977.

Baltes, P. B., & Reinert, G. Cohort effects in cognitive development of children as revealed by cross-sectional sequences. *Developmental Psychology,* 1969, *1,* 169–177.

Baltes, P. B., & Schaie, K. W. On the plasticity of intelligence in adulthood and old age: Where Horn and Donaldson fail. *American Psychologist,* 1976, *31,* 720–725.

Baltes, P. B., & Willis, S. L. Toward psychological theories of aging and development. In J. E. Birren & K. W. Schaie (Eds.), *Handbook of the psychology of aging.* New York: Van Nostrand-Reinhold, 1977.

Baltes, P. B., & Willis, S. L. The critical importance of appropriate methodology in the study of aging: The sample case of psychometric intelligence. In F. Hoffmeister & C. C. Mueller (Eds.), *Brain function in old age.* New York: Springer, 1979. (a)

Baltes, P. B., & Willis, S. L. Life-span developmental psychology, cognition, and social policy. In M. W. Riley (Ed.), *Aging from birth to death.* Boulder, Colorado: Westview Press, 1979. (b)

Bandura, A. *Principles of behavior modification.* New York: Holt, 1969.

Bandura, A. *Social learning theory.* New York: General Learning Press, 1971.

Bandura, A. *Social learning theory.* Englewood Cliffs, New Jersey: Prentice-Hall, 1977.

Bargmann, R. E. *A study of independence and dependence in multivariate normal analysis.* (Mimeo Series No. 186). Chapel Hill: Univ. of North Carolina, Institute of Statistics, 1957.

Bayley, N. Mental growth during the first three years: A developmental study of 61 children by repeated tests. *Genetic Psychology Monographs,* 1933, *14,* 1–92.

Bayley, N. Research in child development: A longitudinal perspective. *Merrill-Palmer Quarterly,* 1965, *11,* 183–208.

Bell, R. Q. Convergence: An accelerated longitudinal approach. *Child Development,* 1953, *24,* 145–152.

Bell, R. Q. An experimental test of the accelerated longitudinal approach. *Child Development,* 1954, *25,* 281–286.

Bell. R. Q., & Hertz, T. W. Toward more comparability and generalizability of developmental research. *Child Development,* 1976, *47,* 6–13.

Bengtson, V. L., & Black, K. D. Intergenerational relations and continuities in socialization. In P. B. Baltes & K. W. Schaie (Eds.), *Life-span developmental psychology: Personality and socialization.* New York: Academic Press, 1973.

Bengtson, V. L., & Cutler, N. E. Generations and intergenerational relations: Perspectives on age groups and social change. In R. Binstock & E. Shanas (Eds.), *Handbook of aging and the social sciences.* New York: Van Nostrand-Reinhold, 1976.

Bengtson, V. L., & Laufer, R. S. (Eds.). Youth, generations, and social change. *Journal of Social Issues,* 1974, *30,* 2–3.

Bentler, P. M. Assessment of developmental factor change at the individual and group level. In J. R. Nesselroade & H. W. Reese (Eds.), *Life-span developmental psychology: Methodological issues.* New York: Academic Press, 1973.

Bentler, P. M. The interdependence of theory, methodology, and empirical data: Causal modeling as an approach to construct validation. In D. B. Kandel (Ed.), *Longitudinal research on drug use.* New York: Wiley, 1978.

Bentler, P. M., Lettieri, D. J., & Austin, G. A. (Eds.). *Data analysis strategies and designs for substance abuse research.* Rockville, Maryland: Nat. Inst. on Drug Abuse, 1976.

Bereiter, C. Some persisting dilemmas in the measurement of change. In C. W. Harris (Ed.), *Problems in measuring change.* Madison, Wisconsin: Univ. of Wisconsin Press, 1963.

Bergman, L. R. *Some univariate models in studying change.* (Reports from the Psychological Laboratories, [Suppl. 10]). Stockholm: Univ. Of Stockholm, 1971.

Berkson, J. Application of the logistic function to bioassay. *Journal of the American Statistical Association,* 1944, *39,* 357–365.

Berkson, J. A statistically precise and relatively simple method of estimating the bioassay with quantal response based on the logistic function. *Journal of the American Statistical Association*, 1953, *48*, 565–599.

Berkson, J. Maximum likelihood and minimum χ^2 estimates of the logistic function. *Journal of the American Statistical Association*, 1955, *50*, 130–162.

Bhapkar, V. P. A note on the equivalence of two test criteria for hypotheses in categorical data. *Journal of the American Statistical Association*, 1966, *61*, 228–235.

Bhapkar, V. P., & Koch, G. G. Hypotheses of "no interaction" in multidimensional contingency tables. *Technometrics*, 1968, *10*, 107–123. (a)

Bhapkar, V. P., & Koch, G. G. On the hypotheses of "no interaction" in multidimensional contingency tables. *Biometrics*, 1968, *24*, 567–594. (b)

Bielby, W. T., & Hauser, R. M. Structural equation models. *Annual Review of Sociology*, 1977, *3*, 137–161.

Birren, J. E. Principles of research on aging. In J. E. Birren (Ed.) *Handbook of aging and the individual: Psychological and biological aspects*. Chicago, Illinois: Univ. of Chicago Press, 1959.

Bishop, Y. M., Fienberg, S. E., & Holland, P. W. *Discrete multivariate analysis: Theory and practice*. Cambridge, Massachusetts: MIT Press, 1975.

Blalock, H. M. Making causal inferences for unmeasured variables from correlations among indicators. *American Journal of Sociology*, 1963, *69*, 53–62.

Blalock, H. M. (Ed.). *Measurement in the social sciences*. Chicago: Aldine, 1974.

Bock, R. D. Components of variance analysis as a structural and discriminal analysis for psychological tests. *British Journal of Statistical Psychology*, 1960, *13*, 151–163.

Bock, R. D. Multivariate analysis of variance of repeated measurements. In C. W. Harris (Ed.), *Problems in measuring change*. Madison: Univ. of Wisconsin Press, 1963.

Bock, R. D. Estimating item parameters and latent ability when responses are scored in two or more nominal categories. *Psychometrika*, 1972, *37*, 29–51.

Bock, R. D. *Multivariate statistical methods in behavioral research*. New York: McGraw-Hill, 1975.

Bock, R. D. Basic issues in the measurement of change. In D. N. M. de Gruijter and L. J. T. van der Kamp (Eds.), *Advances in psychological and educational measurement*. London: Wiley, 1976.

Bock, R. D., & Jones, L. V. *The measurement and prediction of judgment and choice*. San Francisco, California: Holden-Day, 1968.

Bock, R. D., & Repp, B. H. *MATCAL: Double-precision matrix operations subroutines for the IBM System/360–370 computers.* Chicago, Illinois: Nat. Educational Resources, 1974.

Bock, R. D., & Thissen, D. M. Statistical problems in fitting individual growth curves. In F. Johnston, A. F. Rocher, and C. Susanne (Eds.), *Methodologies for the analysis of human growth and development*. New York: Plenum, 1979.

Bock, R. D., & Thrash, W. Characterizing a latent trait distribution. In P. R. Krishnaiah (Ed.), *Applications of Statistics*. Amsterdam: North Holland Publ., 1977.

Bock, R. D., Wainer, H., Petersen, A., Murray, J., & Roche, A. A parameterization for individual human growth curves. *Human Biology*, 1973, *45*, 63–80.

Bohrnstedt, G. W. Observations on the measurement of change. In E. F. Borgatta (Ed.),. *Sociological methodology: 1969*. San Francisco, California: Jossey-Bass, 1969.

Bolz, C. R. Types of personality. In R. M. Dreger (Ed.), *Multivariate personality research: Contributions to the understanding of personality in honor of Raymond B. Cattell*. Baton Rouge, Louisiana: Claitor, 1972.

Bowker, A. H. A test for symmetry in contingency tables. *Journal of the American Statistical Association*, 1948, *43*, 572–574.

Bowles, S., & Gintis, H. I.Q. in the U.S. class structure. *Social Policy*, 1972, *3*, 63–96.

Box. G. E. P. Problems in the analysis of growth and wear curves. *Biometrics*, 1950, *6*, 362–389.

Box, G. E. P. Bayesian approaches to some bothersome problems in data analysis. In J. C. Stanley (Ed.), *Improving experimental design and statistical analysis*. Chicago, Illinois: Rand McNally, 1967.

Box, G. E. P., & Jenkins, G. M. *Time-series analysis: Forecasting and control*. San Francisco, California: Holden-Day, 1970.

Bradley, R. H., & Caldwell, B. M. Early home environment and changes in mental test performance in children from 6 to 36 months. *Developmental Psychology*, 1976, *12*, 93–97. (a)

Bradley, R. H., & Caldwell, B. M. The relation of infants' home environments to mental test performance at fifty-four months: A follow-up study. *Child Development*, 1976, *47*, 1,172–1,174. (b)

Bronfenbrenner, U. Developmental research, public policy, and the ecology of childhood. *Child Development*, 1974, *45*, 1–5.

Bronfenbrenner, U. *The experimental ecology of education*. Paper presented at the meeting of the American Educational Research Association, San Francisco, California, April 1976.

Bronfenbrenner, U. Toward an experimental ecology of human development. *American Psychologist*, 1977, *32*, 513–531.

Browne, E. T. *Introduction to the theory of determinants and matrices*. Chapel Hill: Univ. of North Carolina Press, 1958.

Bryk, A. S., & Weisberg, H. I. Use of the nonequivalent control group design when subjects are growing. *Psychological Bulletin*, 1977, *84*, 950–962.

Buss, A. R. An extension of developmental models that separate ontogentic change and cohort differences. *Psychology Bulletin*, 1973, *80*, 466–479.

Buss, A. R. A general developmental model for interindividual differences, intraindividual differences and intraindividual changes. *Developmental Psychology*, 1974, *10*, 70–78. (a)

Buss, A. R. Generational analysis: Description, explanation, and theory. *Journal of Social Issues*, 1974, *30*, 55–71. (b)

Buss, A. R. Multivariate model of quantitative, structural, and quantistructural ontogenetic change. *Developmental Psychology*, 1974, *10*, 190–203. (c)

Cahen, L. S., & Linn, R. L. Regions of significant criterion differences in aptitude-treatment-interaction research. *American Educational Research Journal*, 1971, *8*, 521–530.

Calsyn, R. J., & Kenny, D. A. Self-concept of ability and perceived evaluation of others: Cause or effect of academic achievement? *Journal of Educational Psychology*, 1977, *69*, 136–145.

Camerer, W. Gewichts- und Längenwachstum der Kinder. In M. Pfaundler & A. Schlossmann (Eds.), Handbuch der Kinderheilkunde (Vol. I), Berlin: Vogel, 1910.

Campbell, D. T. From description to experimentation: Interpreting trends as quasi-experiments. In C. W. Harris (Ed.), *Problems in measuring change*. Madison: Univ. of Wisconsin Press, 1963.

Campbell, D. T. Reforms as experiments. *American Psychologist*, 1969, *24*, 409–429.

Campbell, D. T. Reforms as experiments. In E. L. Struening & M. Guttentag (Eds.), *Handbook of evaluation research* (Vol. 1). Beverly Hills, California: Sage, 1975.

Campbell, D. T., & Erlebacher, A. How regression artifacts in quasi-experimental evaluations can mistakenly make compensatory education look harmful. In *The disadvantaged child*. Compensatory education: A national debate, edited by J. Hellmuth, vol. 3. New York: Brunner-Mazel, 1970.

Campbell, D. T., & Stanley, J. C. Experimental and quasi-experimental designs for research on teaching. In N. L. Gage (Ed.), *Handbook of research on teaching*. Chicago, Illinois: Rand McNally, 1963.

Campbell, D. T., & Stanley, J. C. *Experimental and quasi-experimental designs for research.* Chicago, Illinois: Rand McNally, 1967.

Campbell, R. T. Longitudinal designs in life course research: A critique. Unpublished manuscript, Duke University, 1978.

Carus, F. A. *Psychologie zweiter Theil: Specialpsychologie.* Leipzig: Barth, 1808.

Cattell, R. B. *Description and measurement of personality.* Yonkers, New York: World Book, 1946.

Cattell, R. B. The three basic factor-analytic research designs: Their interrelations and derivatives. *Psychological Bulletin, 1952, 49,* 499–520.

Cattell, R. B. The structuring of change by P-technique and incremental R-technique. In C. W. Harris (Ed.), *Problems in measuring change.* Madison: University of Wisconsin Press, 1963.

Cattell, R. B. *The High School Personality Questionnaire.* Champaign, Illinois: Inst. for Personality and Ability Testing, 1964.

Cattell, R. B. The data box: Its ordering of total resources in terms of possible relational systems. In R. B. Cattell (Ed.), *Handbook of multivariate experimental psychology.* Chicago, Illinois: Rand McNally, 1966.

Cattell, R. B. Separating endogenous, exogenous, ecogenic, and epogenic component curves in developmental data. *Developmental Psychology, 1970, 3,* 151–162.

Cattell, R. B., Coulter, M. A., & Tsujioka, B. The taxonometric recognition of types and functional emergents. In R. B. Cattell (Ed.), *Handbook of multivariate experimental psychology.* Chicago, Illinois: Rand McNally, 1966.

Chandler, M. J. Social cognition and life-span approaches to the study of child development. In H. W. Reese & L. P. Lipsitt (Eds.), *Advances in child development and behavior* (Vol. 11). New York: Academic Press, 1976.

Cicchetti, D. V. A new measure of agreement between rank-ordered variables. *Proceedings of the 80th Annual Convention of the American Psychological Association, 1972, 7,* 17–18. (Summary)

Clarke, A. D. B., Clarke, A. M., & Brown, R. I. Regression to the mean: A confused concept. *British Journal of Psychology, 1960, 51,* 105–117.

Clarke, A. M., & Clarke, A. D. B. (Eds.). *Early experience: Myth and evidence.* New York: Free Press, 1976.

Clarke-Stewart, K. A. Interactions between mothers and their young children: Characteristics and consequences. *Monographs of the Society for Research in Child Development, 1973, 38* (6–7, Serial No. 153).

Clarke-Stewart, K. A. Dealing with the complexity of mother-child interaction. Paper presented at meeting of the Society for Research in Child Development, Denver, Colorado, April 1975.

Cohen, J. A coefficient of agreement for nominal scales. *Educational and Psychological Measurement, 1960, 20,* 37–46.

Cohen, J. Weighted kappa: Nominal scale agreement with provision for scaled disagreement or partial credit. *Psychological Bulletin, 1968, 70,* 213–220.

Cohen, J., & Cohen, P. *Applied multiple regression/correlation analysis for the behavioral sciences.* Hillsdale, New Jersey: Erlbaum, 1975.

Cole, J. W. L., & Grizzle, J. E. Application of multivariate analysis of variance to repeated measurements experiments. *Biometrics, 1966, 22,* 810–827.

Coleman, J. S. *Introduction to mathematical sociology.* New York: Free Press, 1964.

Coleman, J. S. The mathematical study of change. In H. M. Blalock & A. B. Blalock (Eds.), *Methodology in social research.* New York: McGraw-Hill, 1968.

Coleman, J. S., Katz, E., & Menzel, H. The diffusion of an innovation among physicians. *Sociometry, 1957, 20,* 253–270.

Converse, P. E. Cohort-analyzing party identification. Unpublished manuscript, Univ. of Michigan, 1976.

Cook, T. D., & Campbell, D. T. The design and conduct of quasi-experiments and true experiments in field settings. In M. D. Dunnette (Ed.), *Handbook of industrial and organizational research.* Chicago, Illinois: Rand McNally, 1975.

Corballis, M. C. A factor model for analysing change. *The British Journal of Mathematical & Statistical Psychology,* 1973, *26,* 90–97.

Corballis, M. C., & Traub, R. E. Longitudinal factor analysis. *Psychometrika,* 1970, *35,* 79–98.

Count, E. W. Growth patterns of human physique. *Human Biology,* 1943, *15,* 1–32.

Cox, D. R., & Miller, H. D. *Theory of stochastic processes.* London: Methuen, 1965.

Crano, W. D. Causal analysis of the effects of socioeconomic status and initial intellectual development and academic achievement. In D. Green (Ed.), *The aptitude-achievement distinction.* Monterey, California: CTB/McGraw Hill, 1974.

Crano, W. D. What do infant mental tests test? A cross-lagged panel analysis of selected data from the Berkeley Growth Study. *Child Development,* 1977, *48,* 144–151.

Crano, W. D., Kenny, D. A., & Campbell, D. T. Does intelligence cause achievement?: A cross-lagged panel analysis. *Journal of Educational Psychology,* 1972, *63,* 258–275.

Cronbach, L. J. The two disciplines of scientific psychology. *American Psychologist,* 1957, *12,* 671–684.

Cronbach, L. J. Beyond the two disciplines of scientific psychology. *American Psychologist,* 1975, *30,* 116–127.

Cronbach, L. J., & Furby, L. How should we measure "change"—Or should we? *Psychological Bulletin,* 1970, *74,* 68–80.

Cronbach, L. J., Rogosa, D. R., Floden, R. E., & Price, G. *Analysis of convariance in nonrandomized experiments: Parameters affecting bias.* Stanford, California: Stanford Univ., Stanford Evaluation Consortium, 1977.

Cronbach, L. J., & Webb, N. Between-class and within-class effects in a reported aptitude × treatment interaction: Reanalysis of a study by G. L. Anderson. *Journal of Educational Psychology,* 1975, *67,* 717–727.

Damon, A. Discrepancies between findings of longitudinal and cross-sectional studies in adult life: Physique and physiology. *Human Development,* 1965, *8,* 16–22.

Darwin, C. A biological sketch of an infant. *Mind,* 1877, *2,* 285–294.

Datan, N., & Reese, H. W. (Eds.). *Life-span development psychology: Dialectical perspectives on experimental research.* New York: Academic Press, 1977.

Dayton, C. M. *Design of educational experiments.* New York: McGraw-Hill, 1970.

Deakin, M. A. B. Gompertz curves, allometry and embryogenesis. *Bulletin of Mathematical Biophysics,* 1970, *32,* 445–452.

Dearborn, W. F., & Rothney, J. W. M. *Predicting the child's development.* Cambridge: Sci-Art, 1941.

DeLury, D. B. *Values and integrals of the orthogonal polynomials up to* $n=26$. Toronto: Univ. of Toronto Press, 1950.

Deming, J. Application of the Gompertz curve to the observed pattern of growth in length of 48 individual boys and girls during the adolescent cycle of growth. *Human Biology,* 1957, *29,* 83–122.

Dempster, A. P., Laird, N. M., & Rubin, D. B. Maximum likelihood from incomplete data via the EM algorithm. *Journal of the Royal Statistical Society* (Series B), 1977, *39,* 1–38.

Dohrenwend, B. S., & Dohrenwend, B. P. (Eds.). *Stressful life events.* New York: Wiley, 1974.

Duncan, O. D. Path analysis: Sociological examples. *American Journal of Sociology,* 1966, *72,* 1–16.

Duncan, O. D. Contingencies in constructing causal models. In E. Borgatta (Ed.), *Sociological methodology 1969.* San Francisco, California: Jossey-Bass, 1969. (a)

Duncan, O. D. Some linear models for two wave, two-variable panel analysis. *Psychological Bulletin,* 1969, *72,* 177–182. (b)

Duncan, O. D. Unmeasured variables in linear models for panel analysis. In H. L. Costner (Ed.), *Sociological methodology: 1972,* San Francisco, California: Jossey-Bass, 1972.

Duncan, O. D. *Introduction to structural equation models.* New York: Academic Press, 1975. (a)

Duncan, O. D. Some linear models for two-wave, two-variable panel analysis with one-way causation and measurement errors. In H. M. Blalock (Ed.), *Quantitative sociology: International perspectives on mathematical and statistical modelling.* New York: Academic Press, 1975. (b)

Eckensberger, L. H. Methodological issues of cross-cultural research in developmental psychology. In J. R. Nesselroade & H. W. Reese (Eds.), *Life-span developmental psychology: Methodological issues.* New York: Academic Press, 1973.

Elardo, R. Bradley, R., & Caldwell, B. M. The relation of infants' home environments to mental test performance from six to thirty-six months: A longitudinal analysis. *Child Development,* 1975, *46,* 71–76.

Elder, G. H., Jr. *Children of the Great Depression.* Chicago, Illinois: University of Chicago Press, 1974.

Elder, G. H., Jr. Age differentiation and the life course. *Annual Review of Sociology,* 1975, *1,* 165–190.

Elder, G. H., Jr. Family history and the life course. *Journal of Family History,* 1977, *2,* 279–304.

Elder, G. H., Jr. Historical change in life patterns and personality. In P. B. Baltes & O. G. Brim, Jr., (Eds.), *Life-span development and behavior* (Vol. 2). New York: Academic Press, 1979.

Emmerich, W. Personality development and concepts of structure. *Child Development,* 1968, *39,* 671–690.

Eron, L. D., Huesmann, L. R., Lefkowitz, M. M., & Walder, L. O. Does television violence cause aggression? *American Psychologist,* 1972, *27,* 253–263.

Evans, S. H., & Anastasio, E. J. Misuse of analysis of covariance when treatment effect and covariate are confounded. *Psychological Bulletin,* 1968, *69,* 225–234.

Featherman, D. L. Retrospective longitudinal research: Methodological considerations. *Journal of Economics and Business,* in press.

Federer, W. T. *Experimental design: Theory and application.* New York: Macmillan, 1955.

Feller, W. *An introduction to probability theory and its applications* (2nd ed.). New York: Wiley, 1957.

Feller, W. *An introduction to probability theory and its applications* (Vol. 1). New York: Wiley, 1966.

Feller, W. *Introduction to probability theory and its applications* (Vol. 1). New York: Wiley, 1968.

Feller, W. *Introduction to probability theory and its applications* (Vol. 2). New York: Wiley, 1971.

Ferguson, G. A. *Statistical analysis in psychology and education* (2nd ed.). New York: McGraw-Hill, 1966.

Fienberg, S. E., & Mason, W. M. Identification and estimation of age-period-cohort models in the analysis of discrete archival data. In K. Shuessler (Ed.), *Sociological methodology 1979.* San Francisco, California: Jossey-Bass, 1979.

Finn, J. D. *Multivariance: Univariate and multivariate analysis of variance, covariance, and regression.* Chicago, Illinois: Nat. Educational Resources, 1974.

Finn, J. D. Personal communication, 1976.

Finn, J. D., & Mattsson, I. *Multivariate analysis in educational research: Applications of the MULTIVARIANCE program.* Chicago, Illinois: Nat. Educational Resources, 1977.

Finney, D. J. *Statistical method in biological assay* (2nd ed.) London: Griffin, 1964.

Fisher, R. A. Studies in crop variation. I. An examination of the yield of dressed grain from Broadbalk. *Journal of Agricultural Science*, 1921, *11*, 107–135.

Fisher, R. A., & Yates, F. *Statistical tables for biological, agricultural, and medical research* (6th ed.). New York: Hafner, 1963.

Fiske, D. W., & Rice, L. Intra-individual response variability. *Psychological Bulletin*, 1955, *52*, 217–250.

Fleiss, J. L. Measuring nominal scale agreement among many raters. *Psychological Bulletin*, 1971, *76*, 378–382.

Forthofer, R. N., & Koch, G. G. An analysis for compounded functions of categorical data. *Biometrics*, 1973, *29*, 143–157.

Frederiksen, C. R. Models for the analysis of alternative sources of growth in correlated stochastic variables. *Psychometrika*, 1974, *39*, 223–245.

Freeman, J., & Hannan, M. T. Growth and decline processes in organizations. *American Sociological Review*, 1975, *40*, 215-228.

Furby, L. Interpreting regression toward the mean in developmental research. *Developmental Psychology*, 1973, *8*, 172–179.

Gagné, R. M. Contributions of learning to human development. *Psychological Review*, 1968, *75*, 177–191.

Gaito, J., & Wiley, D. E. Univariate analysis of variance procedures in measurement of change. In C. W. Harris (Ed.), *Problems in measuring change*. Madison: Univ. of Wisconsin Press, 1963.

Games, P. A. Limitations of analysis of covariance on intact group quasi-experimental designs. *Journal of Experimental Education*, 1976, *44*, 51–53.

Games, P. A., & Klare, G. R. *Elementary statistics: Data analysis for the behavioral sciences*. New York: McGraw-Hill, 1967.

Gantmacher, F. R. *Theory of matrices* (Vol. 1). New York: Chelsea, 1960.

Gardner, H. *The quest for mind: Piaget, Levi-Strauss, and the structuralist movement*. New York: Vintage, 1972.

Geisser, S. A Bayes approach for combining correlated estimates. *Journal of the American Statistical Association*, 1965, *60*, 602–607.

Geisser, S., & Kappenman, R. F. A posterior region for parallel profile defferentials. *Psychometrika*, 1971, *36*, 71–78.

Gergen, K. J. Stability, change, and chance in understanding human development. In N. Datan & H. W. Reese (Eds.), *Life-span development psychology: Dialectical perspectives on experimental research*. New York: Academic Press, 1977.

Gesell, A. The ontogenesis of infant behavior. In L. Carmichael (Ed.), *Manual of child psychology*. New York: Wiley, 1954.

Ghosh, M., Grizzle, J. E., & Sen, P. K. Nonparametric methods in longitudinal studies. *Journal of the American Statistical Association*, 1973, *68*, 29–36.

Ginsberg, R. Semi-Markov processes and mobility. *Journal of Mathematical Sociology*, 1971, *1*, 233–263.

Glass, G. V., Willson, V. L., & Gottman, J. M. Design and analysis of time-series experiments (Laboratory of Educational Research Report). Boulder: Univ. of Colorado, 1972.

Glenn, N. D. Cohort analysts' futile quest: Statistical attempts to separate age, period and cohort effects. *American Sociological Review*, 1976, *41*, 900–904.

Goldberger, A. S. Econometrics and psychometrics: A survey of communalities. *Psychometrika*, 1971, *36*, 83–108.

Goldberger, A. S. Structural equation methods in the social sciences. *Econometrica*, 1972, *40*, 979–1,001.

Goldberger, A. S. Structural equation models: An overview. In A. Goldberger & O. D. Duncan (Eds.), *Structural equation models in the social sciences*. New York: Seminar Press, 1973.

Goldberger, A. S., & Duncan, O. D. (Eds.), *Structural equation models in the social sciences*. New York: Seminar Press, 1973.

Gompertz, B. On the nature of the function expressive of the law of human mentality. *Philosophical Transactions of the Royal Society*, 1825, *115*, 513–583.

Goodman, L. A. The analysis of systems of qualitative variables when some of the variables are unobservable. I. A modified latent structure approach. *American Journal of Sociology*, 1974, *79*, 1,179–1,259.

Goodman, L. A., & Kruskal, W. H. Measures of association for cross-classification. *Journal of the American Statistical Association*, 1954, *49*, 732–764.

Gordon, R. A. Issues in multiple regression. *American Journal of Sociology*, 1968, *73*, 592–616.

Gottman, J. M. Detecting cyclicity in social interaction. *Psychological Bulletin*, 1979, *86*, 338–348.

Goulet, L. R. Longitudinal and time-lag designs in educational research: An alternate sampling model. *Review of Educational Research*, 1975, *45*, 505–523.

Goulet, L. R., Hay, C. M., & Barclay, C. R. Sequential analysis and developmental research methods: Descriptions of cyclical phenomena. *Psychological Bulletin*, 1974, *81*, 517–521.

Greenhouse, S. W., & Geisser, S. On methods in the analysis of profile data. *Psychometrika*, 1959, *24*, 95–112.

Grizzle, J. E., & Allen D. M. Analysis of growth and dose response curves. *Biometrics*, 1969, *25*, 307–318.

Grizzle, J. E., Starmer, C. F., & Koch, G. G. Analysis of categorical data by linear models. *Biometrics*, 1969, *25*, 489–504.

Grizzle, J. E., & Williams, O. D. Log linear models and tests of independence for contingency tables. *Biometrics*, 1972, *28*, 137–156.

Groffmann, K. J. Life-span developmental psychology in Europe. In L. R. Goulet & P. B. Baltes (Eds.), *Life-span developmental psychology: Research and theory*. New York: Academic Press, 1970.

Guttman, L. A. A new approach to factor analysis: The radex. In P. F. Lazarsfeld (Ed.), *Mathematical thinking in the social sciences*. New York: Columbia Univ. Press, 1954.

Hald, A. *Statistical tables and formulas*. New York: Wiley, 1952.

Haller, C. A., Scott, E. M., & Hammes, L. M. Height, weight and growth of Alaskan Eskimos. *American Journal of Diseases of Childhood*, 1967, *113*, 338–344.

Hannan, M. T., & Burstein, L. Estimation from grouped observations. *American Sociological Review*, 1974, *39*, 374–392.

Hannan, M. T., Rubinson, R., & Warren, J. T. The causal approach to measurement error in panel analysis: Some further contingencies. In H. M. Blalock (Ed.), *Measurement in the social sciences*. Chicago, Illinois: Aldine, 1974.

Hannan, M. T., & Young, A. A. Estimation in panel models: Results on pooling cross-sections and time-series. In D. R. Heise (Ed.), *Sociological Methodology 1977*. San Francisco, California: Jossey-Bass, 1977.

Härnqvist, K. Relative changes in intelligence from 13 to 18. *Scandinavian Journal of Psychology*, 1968, *9*, 50–82.

Harris, C. W. Canonical factor models for the description of change. In C. W. Harris (Ed.), *Problems in measuring change*. Madison: Univ. of Wisconsin Press, 1963. (a)

Harris, C. W. (Ed.). *Problems in measuring change*. Madison: Univ. of Wisconsin Press, 1963. (b)

Harris, D. B. (Ed.). *The concept of development*. Minneapolis: Univ. of Minnesota Press, 1957. (a)

Harris, D. B. Problems in formulating a scientific concept of development. In D. B. Harris (Ed.), *The concept of development*. Minneapolis: Univ. of Minnesota Press, 1957. (b)

Hartup, W. W. Toward a social psychology of childhood. In *Patterns of child rearing to 1984*.

APA Division 7 Presidential Address, presented at the meeting of the Amer. Psych. Assoc., Washington, D.C., September 1976.

Hartup, W. W., & Lempers, J. A problem in life-span development: The interactional analysis of family attachments. In P. B. Baltes & K. W. Schaie (Eds.), *Life-span developmental psychology: Personality and socialization.* New York: Academic Press, 1973.

Heise, D. R. Separating reliability and stability in test-retest correlations. *American Sociological Review,* 1969, *34,* 93–101.

Heise, D. R. Causal inference from panel data. In E. F. Borgatta and G. W. Bohrnstedt (Eds.), *Sociological methodology: 1970.* San Francisco, California: Jossey-Bass, 1970.

Heise, D. R. *Causal analysis.* New York: Wiley, 1975.

Hersen, M., & Barlow, D. H. *Single case experimental designs: Strategies for studying behavioral change.* New York: Pergamon, 1976.

Hilton, T. L. *Growth study annotated bibliography* (Progress report 69–11). Princeton, New Jersey: Educational Testing Service, 1969.

Hindley, C. B. The place of longitudinal methods in the study of development. In F. J. Monks, W. W. Hartup, & J. de Wit (Eds.), *Determinants of behavioral development.* New York: Academic Press, 1972.

Hoel, P. G., Port, S. C., & Stone, C. J. *Introduction to stochastic processes.* Boston, Massachusetts: Houghton, 1972.

Hoem, J. Inhomogeneous semi-Markov processes, select actuarial tables, and duration dependence in demography. In T. N. E. Greville (Ed.), *Population dynamics.* New York: Academic Press, 1972.

Hofstätter, P. R. Tatsachen und Probleme einer Psychologie der Lebenslaufes. *Zeitschrift für Angewandte Psychologie,* 1938, *53,* 273–333.

Höhn, E. Geschichte der Entwicklungspsychologie und ihrer wesentlichsten Ansätze. In H. Thomae (Ed.), *Entwicklungspsychologie.* Göttingen: Hogrefe, 1959.

Hollingworth, H. L. *Mental growth and decline: A survey of developmental psychology.* New York: Appleton, 1927.

Hoppe, S., Schmid-Schönbein, C., & Seiler, T. B. *Entwicklungssequenzen.* Bern, Switzerland: Huber, 1977.

Horn, J. L. Significance tests for use with r_p and related profile statistics. *Educational and Psychological Development,* 1961, *21,* 363–370.

Horn, J. L., & Donaldson, G. On the myth of intellectual decline in adulthood. *American Psychologist,* 1976, *31,* 701–719.

Hultsch, D. F., & Hickey, T. External validity in the study of human development: Theoretical and methodological perspectives. *Human Development,* 1978, *21,* 86–91.

Hultsch, D. F., & Plemons, J. K. Life events and life-span development. In P. B. Baltes & O. G. Brim, Jr. (Eds.), *Life-span development and behavior* (Vol. 2). New York: Academic Press, 1979.

Hummel-Rossi, B., & Weinburg, S. L. Practical guidelines in applying current theories to the measurement of change. I. Problems in measuring change and recommended procedures. JSAS *Catalog of Selected Documents in Psychology,* 1975, *5,* 226. (Ms. No. 916)

Humphreys, L. G. Investigations of the simplex. *Psychometrika,* 1960, *25,* 313–323.

Humphreys, L. G., & Stubbs, J. A longitudinal analysis of teacher expectation, student expectation, and student achievement. *Journal of Educational Measurement,* 1977, *14,* 261–270.

Huston-Stein, A., & Baltes, P. B. Theory and method in life-span developmental psychology: Implications for child development. In H. W. Reese & L. P. Lipsitt (Eds.), *Advances in child development and behavior* (Vol. 11). New York: Academic Press, 1976.

Huynh, H., & Feldt, L. S. Conditions under which mean square ratios in repeated measurement designs have exact F-distributions. *Journal of the American Statistical Association,* 1970, *65,* 1,582–1,589.

Israelsohn, W. J. Description and modes of analysis of human growth. In J. M. Tanner (Ed.), *Human growth*. New York: Pergamon, 1960.

Jackson, D. J. A reformulation of Schaie's model of developmental change. Paper presented at the meeting of the Gerontological Society, Louisville, Kentucky, October 1975.

Jackson, D. N. *Personality research form*. Goshen, New York: Research Psychologist Press, 1968.

Jamison, P. L. Anthropometric variation. In P. L. Jamison & S. L. Zegura (Eds.), *The Eskimos of north western Alaska: A biological perspective*. Stroudsburg, Pennsylvania: Dowden, 1977.

Jenss, R. M., & Bayley, N. A mathematical method for studying growth in children. *Human Biology*, 1937, *9*, 556–563.

Jones, H. E. Problems of method in longitudinal research. *Vita Humana*, 1958, *1*, 93–99.

Jones, R. H., Crowell, D. H., & Kapuniai, L. E. Change detection model for serially correlated data. *Biometrics*, 1970, *26*, 269–280.

Jöreskog, K. G. Estimation and testing of simplex models. *The British Journal of Mathematical and Statistical Psychology*, 1970, *23*, 121–145. (a)

Jöreskog, K. G. Factoring the multitest-multioccasion correlation matrix. In C. E. Lunneborg (Ed.), *Current problems and techniques in multivariate psychology*. Proceedings of a conference honoring Paul Hors. Univ. of Washington, Seattle, 1970. (b)

Jöreskog, K. G. A general method for analysis of covariance structures. *Biometrika*, 1970, *57*, 239–251. (c)

Jöreskog, K. G. Simultaneous factor analysis in several populations. *Psychometrika*, 1971, *36*, 409–426.

Jöreskog, K. G. Analysis of covariance structures. In P. R. Krishnaiah (Ed.), *Multivariate analysis—III*. New York: Academic Press, 1973. (a)

Jöreskog, K. G. A general method for estimating a linear structural equation system. In A. S. Goldberger & O. D. Duncan (Eds.), *Structural equation models in the social sciences*. New York: Seminar Press, 1973. (b)

Jöreskog, K. G. Structural equation models in the social sciences: Specification, estimation and testing. In P. R. Krishnaiah (Ed.), *Applications of statistics*. Amsterdam: North Holland Publ., 1977.

Jöreskog, K. G., & Sörbom, D. Statistical models and methods for test-retest situations. In D. N. M. de Gruijter & L. J. van der Kamp (Eds.), *Advances in psychological and educational measurement*. London: Wiley, 1976.

Jöreskog, K. G., & Sörbom, D. Statistical models and methods for analysis of longitudinal data. In D. J. Aigner & A. S. Goldberger (Eds.), *Latent variables in socioeconomic models*. Amsterdam: North Holland Publ., 1977.

Jöreskog, K. G., & Sörbom, D. *LISREL IV—A general computer program for estimation of linear structural equation systems by maximum likelihood methods*. Chicago, Illinois: Int. Educational Services, 1978.

Jöreskog, K. G., van Thillo, M., & Gruvaeus, G. T. ACOVSM—A general computer program for analysis of covariance structures including generalized MANOVA. (Res. Bull. 70-01). Princeton, New Jersey: Educational Testing Service, 1970.

Kagan, J. American longitudinal research on psychological development. *Child Development*, 1964, *35*, 1–32.

Kagan, J. Resilience and continuity in psychological development. In A. M. Clarke & A. D. B. Clarke (Eds.), *Early experience: Myth and evidence*. New York: Free Press, 1976.

Kaplan, B. The study of language in psychiatry. In S. Arieti (Ed.), *American handbook of psychiatry* (Vol. 3). New York: Basic Books, 1966.

Karlin, S. *A first course in stochastic processes*. New York: Academic Press, 1966.

Kendall, M. G., & Stuart, A. *Inference and relationship*. The advanced theory of statistics, vol. 2. London: Griffin, 1961.

Kendall, M. G., & Stuart, A. *The advanced theory of statistics* (Vol. 3, 2nd ed.). London: Griffin, 1968.

Keniston, K. Psychological development and historical change. *Journal of Interdisciplinary History*, 1971, *2*, 330–345.

Kenny, D. A. Cross-lagged and synchronous common factors in panel data. In A. S. Goldberger & O. D. Duncan (Eds.), *Structural equation models in the social sciences*. New York: Seminar Press, 1973.

Kenny, D. A. Cross-lagged panel correlation: A test for spuriousness. *Psychological Bulletin*, 1975, *82*, 887–903. (a)

Kenny, D. A. A quasi-experimental approach to assessing treatment effects in the nonequivalent control group design. *Psychological Bulletin*, 1975, *82*, 345–362. (b)

Kerlinger, F. N. *Foundations of behavioral research*. New York: Holt, 1964.

Kessen, W. Research design in the study of developmental problems. In P. H. Mussen (Ed.), *Handbook of research methods in child development*. New York: Wiley, 1960.

Kessen, W. Stage and structure in the study of children. *Monographs of the Society for Research in Child Development*, 1962, *27*, (2, Serial No. 83).

Khatri, C. G. A note on a MANOVA model applied to problems in growth curves. *Annals of the Institute of Statistical Mathematics*, 1966, *18*, 75–86.

Kirk, R. E. *Experimental design: Procedures for the behavioral sciences*. Belmont, California: Brooks/Cole, 1968.

Kleinbaum, D. G. A generalization of the growth curve model which allows missing data. *Journal of Multivariate Analysis*, 1973, *3*, 117–124.

Koch, G. G. Some aspects of the statistical analysis of 'split plot' experiments in completely randomized layouts. *Journal of the American Statistical Association*, 1969, *64*, 485–505.

Koch, G. G. The use of non-parametric methods in the statistical analysis of a complex split plot experiment. *Biometrics*, 1970, *26*, 105–128.

Koch, G. G., Imrey, P. B., Freeman, D. H., Jr., & Tolley, H. D. The asymptotic covariance structure of estimated parameters from contingency table log-linear models. *Proceedings of the 9th International Biometric Conference*, Boston, Massachusetts, August 1976.

Koch, G. G., Imrey, P. B., & Reinfurt, D. W. Linear model analysis of categorical data with incomplete response vectors. *Biometrics*, 1972, *28*, 663–692.

Koch, G. G., Johnson, W. D., & Tolley, H. D. A linear models approach to the analysis of survival and extent of disease in multidimensional contingency tables. *Journal of the American Statistical Association*, 1972, *67*, 783–796.

Koch, G. G., Landis, J. R., Freeman, J. L., Freeman, D. H., Jr., Landis, J. R., & Lehnen, R. G. A general methodology for the analysis of experiments with repeated measurement of categorical data. *Biometrics*, 1977, *33*, 133–158.

Koch, G. G., & Reinfurt, D. W. The analysis of categorical data from mixed models. *Biometrics*, 1971, *27*, 157–173.

Kodlin, D., & Thompson, D. J. An appraisal of the longitudinal approach to studies of growth and development. *Monographs of the Society for Research in Child Development*, 1958, *23*, (1, Whole No. 67).

Kohlberg, L. Early education: A cognitive-developmental view. *Child Development*, 1968, *39*, 1,013–1,061.

Kohlberg, L. Continuities in childhood and adult moral developmental revisited. In P. B. Baltes & K. W. Schaie (Eds.), *Life-span developmental psychology: Personality and socialization*. New York: Academic Press, 1973.

Kowalski, C. J. The performance of some rough tests for bivariate normality before and after coordinate transformations to normality. *Technometrics*, 1970, *12*, 517–544.

Kowalski, C. J. A commentary on the use of multivariate statistical methods in anthropometric research. *American Journal of Physical Anthropology*, 1972, *36*, 119–131.

Kowalski, C. J., & Guire, K. E. Longitudinal data analysis. *Growth*, 1974, *38*, 131–169.

Kratochwill, T. R. (Ed.). *Single subject research: Strategies for evaluating change.* New York: Academic Press, 1978.

Kuhlen, R. G. Social change: A neglected factor in psychological studies of the life span. *School and Society,* 1940, *52,* 14–16.

Kuhlen, R. G. Age and intelligence: The significance of culture change in longitudinal vs. cross-sectional findings. *Vita Humana,* 1963, *6,* 113–124.

Kuhn, D. Inducing development experimentally: Comments on a research paradigm. *Developmental Psychology,* 1974, *10,* 590–600.

Labouvie, E. W. Developmental causal structures of organism–environment interactions. *Human Development,* 1974, *17,* 444–452.

Labouvie, E. W. Descriptive developmental research: Why only time? *Journal of Genetic Psychology,* 1975, *126,* 289–296. (a)

Labouvie, E. W. The dialectical nature of measurement activities in the behavioral sciences. *Human Development,* 1975, *18,* 396–403. (b)

Labouvie, E. W. Longitudinal designs. In P. M. Bentler, D. J. Lettieri, & G. A. Austin (Eds.), *Data analysis strategies and designs for substance abuse research.* Rockville, Maryland: Nat. Inst. on Drug Abuse, 1976.

Labouvie, E. W. Experimental sequential strategies for the exploration of ontogenetic and socio-historical changes. *Human Development,* 1978, *21,* 161–169.

Labouvie, E. W., Bartsch, T. W., Nesselroade, J. R., & Baltes, P. B. On the internal and external validity of simple longitudinal designs. *Child Development,* 1974, *45,* 282–290.

Labouvie-Vief, G. Adult cognitive development: In search of alternative explanations. *Merrill-Palmer Quarterly,* 1977, *23,* 227–263.

Labouvie-Vief, G., & Chandler, M. J. Cognitive development and life-span developmental theories: Idealistic versus contextual perspectives. In P. B. Baltes (Ed.), *Life-span development and behavior* (Vol. 1). New York: Academic Press, 1978.

Lamb, M., Soumi, S., & Stephenson, G. (Eds.). *Methodological problems in the study of social interaction.* Madison: Univ. of Wisconsin Press, in press.

Landis, J. R. *A general methodology for the measurement of observer agreement when the data are categorical.* (Mimeo Series No. 1022, 1–192). Chapel Hill: Univ. of North Carolina, Institute of Statistics, 1975.

Landis, J. R., & Koch, G. G. A review of statistical methods in the analysis of data arising from observer reliability studies. I. *Statistica Neerlandica,* 1975, *29,* 101–123. (a)

Landis, J. R., & Koch, G. G. A review of statistical methods in the analysis of data arising from observer reliability studies. II. *Statistica Neerlandica,* 1975, *29,* 151–161. (b)

Landis, J. R., & Koch, G. G. An application of hierarchical kappa-type statistics in the assessment of majority agreement among multiple observers. *Biometrics,* 1977, *33,* 363–374. (a)

Landis, J. R., & Koch, G. G. The measurement of observer agreement for categorical data. *Biometrics,* 1977, *33,* 159–174. (b)

Landis, J. R., Stanish, W. M., Freeman, J. L., & Koch, G. G. A computer program for the generalized chi-square analysis of categorical data using weighted least squares (GENCAT). *Computer Programs in Biomedicine,* 1976, *6,* 196–231.

Lee, W. *Experimental design and analysis.* San Francisco, California: Freeman, 1975.

Lee, Y. K. A note on Rao's reduction of Pottoff and Roy's generalized linear model. *Biometrika,* 1974, *61,* 349–351.

Lerner, R. M. *Concepts and theories of human development.* Reading, Massachusetts: Addison-Wesley, 1976.

Lerner, R. M., & Ryff, C. D. Implementation of the life-span view of human development: The sample case of attachment. In P. B. Baltes (Ed.), *Life-span development and behavior* (Vol. 1). New York: Academic Press, 1978.

Lewis, M., & Rosenblum, L. (Eds.). *The effect of the infant on its caregivers.* New York: Wiley, 1974.

Light, R. J. Measures of response agreement for qualitative data: Some generalizations and alternatives. *Psychological Bulletin*, 1971, *76*, 365–377.

Lindquist, E. F. *Design and analysis of experiments in psychology and education*. Boston, Massachusetts: Houghton, 1953.

L'Insee (Ed.). *The econometrics of panel data*. Paris: Institut National de la Statistique et des Etudes Economiques, 1978.

Loevinger, J. The meaning and measurement of ego development. *American Psychologist*, 1966, *21*, 195–206. (a)

Loevinger, J. Models and measures of developmental variation. *Annuals of the New York Academy of Sciences*, 1966, *134*, 585–590. (b)

Lord, F. M. Large-sample covariance analysis when the control variable is fallible. *Journal of the American Statistical Association*, 1960, *55*, 307–321.

Lord, F. M. Elementary models for measuring change. In C. W. Harris (Ed.), *Problems in measuring change*. Madison: Univ. of Wisconsin Press, 1963.

Lord, F. M. Estimation of latent ability and item parameters when there are omitted responses. *Psychometrika*, 1974, *39*, 247–264. (a)

Lord, F. M. Significance test for a partial correlation corrected for attenuation. *Educational and Psychological Measurement*, 1974, *34*, 211–220. (b)

Lord, F. M., & Novick, M. N. *Statistical theories of mental test scores*. Reading, Massachusetts: Addison–Wesley, 1968.

Lund, R. D. *Development and plasticity of the brain*. New York: Oxford Univ. Press, 1978.

McCall, R. B. Challenges to a science of developmental psychology. *Child Development*, 1977, *48*, 333–344.

McCall, R. B., & Appelbaum, M. I. Bias in the analysis of repeated measures designs: Some alternative approaches. *Child Development*, 1973, *44*, 401–415.

McFarland, D. D. Intra-generational social mobility as a Markov process: Including a time-stationary Markovian model that explains declines in mobility rates over time. *American Sociological Review*, 1970, *35*, 463–476.

McGinnis, R. A stochastic model of social mobility. *American Sociological Review*, 1968, *33*, 712–722.

McKeon, J. J. F approximations to the distribution of Hotellings T_0^2. *Biometrika*, 1974, *61*, 381–383

McNemar, Q. *Psychological statistics* (4th ed.). New York: Wiley, 1969.

Madaus, G. F., Woods, E. M., & Nuttall, R. L. A causal model analysis of Bloom's taxonomy. *American Educational Research Journal*, 1973, *10*, 253–262.

Mason, K. O., Mason, W. M., Winsborough, H. H., & Poole, W. K. Some methodological issues in cohort analysis of archival data. *American Sociological Review*, 1973, *38*, 242–258.

Meredith, D. Poisson distributions of error in mental test theory. *British Journal of Mathematical and Statistical Psychology*, 1971, *24*, 49–82.

Montada, L., & Filipp, S. H. Implications of life-span developmental psychology for childhood education. In H. W. Reese & L. P. Lipsitt (Ed.), *Advances in child development* (Vol. 11). New York: Academic Press, 1976.

Morrison, D. F. *Multivariate statistical methods*. New York: McGraw-Hill, 1967.

Morrison, D. F. The analysis of a single sample of repeated measurements. *Biometrics*, 1972, *28*, 55–71.

Müller-Lyer, F. C. *The history of social development*. New York: Knopf, 1921.

Myers, J. L. *Fundamentals of experimental design* (2nd ed.). Boston, Massachusetts: Allyn & Bacon, 1972.

National Institute of Child Health and Human Development. *Colloquium on longitudinal studies*. Unpublished manuscript. Washington, D.C., 1965.

Nesselrode, J. R. Application of multivariate strategies to problems of measuring and structuring long-term change. In L. R. Goulet & P. B. Baltes (Eds.), *Life-span developmental psychology: Research and theory*. New York: Academic Press, 1970.

Nesselroade, J. R. Note on the "longitudinal factor analysis" model. *Psychometrika*, 1972, *37*, 187–191.

Nesselroade, J. R. Issues in studying developmental change in adults from a multivariate perspective. In J. E. Birren & K. W. Schaie (Eds.), *Handbook of the psychology of aging*. New York: Van Nostrand-Reinhold, 1977.

Nesselroade, J. R., & Baltes, P. B. Adolescent personality development and historical change: 1970–1972. *Monographs of the Society for Research in Child Development*, 1974, *39* (1, Serial No. 154).

Nesselroade, J. R., & Reese, H. W. *Life-span developmental psychology: Methodological issues*. New York: Academic Press, 1973.

Nesselroade, J. R., Schaie, K. W., & Baltes, P. B. Ontogenetic and generational components of structural and quantitative change in adult behavior. *Journal of Gerontology*, 1972, *27*, 222–228.

Neugarten, B. L. Continuities and discontinuities of psychological issues into adult life. *Human Development*, 1969, *12*, 121–130.

Neugarten, B. L., & Datan, N. Sociological perspectives on the life cycle. In P. B. Baltes & K. W. Schaie (Eds.), *Life-span developmental psychology: Personality and socialization*. New York: Academic Press, 1973.

Neugarten, B. L., & Hagestad, G. O. Age and the life course. In R. H. Binstock & E. Shanas (Ed.), *Handbook of aging and the social sciences*. New York: Van Nostrand-Reinhold, 1976.

Neyman, J. Contribution to the theory of the χ^2 test. In J. Neyman (Ed.), *Proceedings of the Berkeley symposium on mathematical statistics and probability*. Berkeley: Univ. of California Press, 1949.

Olsson, U., & Bergman, L. R. A longitudinal factor model for studying change in ability structure. *Multivariate Behavioral Research*, 1977, *12*, 221–242.

Overton, W. F. On the assumptive base of the nature-nurture controversy: Additive versus interactive conceptions. *Human Development*, 1973, *16*, 74–89.

Overton, W. F. The active organism in structuralism. *Human Development*, 1976, *19*, 71–86.

Overton, W. F., & Reese, H. W. Models of development: Methodological implications. In J. R. Nesselroade & H. W. Reese (Eds.), *Life-span developmental psychology: Methodological issues*. New York: Academic Press, 1973.

Parzen, E. *Stochastic processes*. San Francisco, California: Holden-Day, 1962.

Pearson, E. S., & Hartley, H. O. *Biometrika tables for statisticians* (Vol. 1, 3rd ed.). Cambridge: Cambridge Univ. Press, 1966.

Petermann, F., *Veränderungsmessung*. Stuttgart: Kohlhammer, 1978.

Phillips, D. C., & Kelley, M. E. Hierarchical theories of development in education and psychology. *Harvard Educational Review*, 1975, *45*, 351–375.

Piaget, J. *The construction of reality in the child*. New York: Basic Books, 1954.

Piaget, J. The general problem of the psychobiological development of the child. In J. M. Tanner & B. Inhelder (Eds.), *Discussions on child development* (Vol. 4). New York: Int. Univ. Press, 1960.

Piaget, J. Piaget's theory. In P. H. Mussen (Ed.), *Charmichael's Manual of Child Psychology* (Vol. 1). New York: Wiley, 1970.

Pillai, K. C. S. *Statistical tables for tests of multivariate hypotheses*. Manila: Univ. of the Philippines, Statistical Center, 1960.

Pillai, K. C. S., & Jayachandran, K. On the exact distribution of Pillai's V^s criterion. *Journal of the American Statistical Association*, 1970, *65*, 447–454.

Popper, K. R. *Conjectures and refutations* (4th ed.). London: Routledge, 1972.

Porter, A. C. *The effects of using fallible variables in the analysis of covariance*. Unpublished doctoral dissertation, Univ. of Wisconsin, 1967.

Pottoff, R. F., & Roy, S. N. A generalized multivariate analysis of variance model useful especially for growth curve problems. *Biometrika*, 1964, *51*, 313–326.

Prahl-Anderson, B., & Kowalski, C. J. A mixed longitudinal interdisciplinary study of the growth and development of Dutch children. *Growth,* 1973, *37,* 281–295.

Preece, M. A., & Bains, M. J. A new family of mathematical models describing the human growth curve. *Annals of Human Biology,* 1978, *5,* 1–24.

Preyer, W. *Die Seele des Kindes.* Leipzig: Fernau, 1882.

Price, D. O. *A respecification of variables in cohort analysis.* Unpublished manuscript, Univ. of Texas at Austin, 1976.

Purkey, W. W. *Self-concept and school achievement.* Englewood Cliffs, New Jersey: Prentice-Hall, 1970.

Quetelet, A. *Sur l'homme et le développement de ses facultés.* Paris: Bachelier, 1835.

Quetelet, A. *A treatise on man and the development of his faculties.* Edinburg: William and Robert Chambers, 1842.

Radin, N. Maternal warmth, achievement motivation, and cognitive functioning in lower-class preschool children. *Child Development,* 1971, *42,* 1,560–1,565.

Radin, N. Observed maternal behavior with four-year-old boys and girls in lower-class families. *Child Development,* 1974, *45,* 1,126–1,131.

Rao, C. R. Some statistical methods for the comparison of growth curves. *Biometrics,* 1958, *14,* 1–17.

Rao, C. R. Some problems involving linear hypotheses in multivariate analysis. *Biometrika,* 1959, *46,* 49–58.

Rao, C. R. The theory of least squares when parameters are stochastic and its application to the analysis of growth curves. *Biometrika,* 1965, *52,* 447–458.

Rao, C. R. Covariance adjustment and related problems in multivariate analysis. In P. R. Krishnaiah (Ed.), *Multivariate analysis.* New York: Academic Press, 1966.

Rao, C. R. Least-squares theory using an estimated dispersion matrix and its applications to measurement of signals. *Proceedings of the 5th Berkeley Symposium,* 1967, *1,* 355–372.

Rao, M. N., & Rao, C. R. Linked cross-sectional study for determining norms and growth rates: A pilot survey of Indian school-going boys. *Sankhya B,* 1966, *28,* 237–258.

Rasch, G. *Probabilistic models for some intelligence and attainment tests.* Copenhagen: Univ. of Copenhagen, Inst. of Mathematics and Statistics, 1960.

Reese, H. W. The scope of experimental child psychology. In H. W. Reese & L. P. Lipsitt (Eds.), *Experimental child psychology.* New York: Academic Press, 1970.

Reese, H. W., & Overton, W. F. Models of development and theories of development. In L. R. Goulet & P. B. Baltes (Eds.), *Life-span developmental psychology: Research and theory.* New York: Academic Press, 1970.

Reinert, G. Grundzüge einer Geschichte der Human-Entwicklungspsychologie. In H. Balmer (Ed.), *Die Europäische Tradition: Tendenzen, Schulen, Entwicklungslinien. Die Psychologie des 20 Jahrhunderts,* vol. 1. Zürich: Kindler, 1976.

Reinert, G. Prolegomena to a history of life-span developmental psychology. In P. B. Baltes & O. G. Brim, Jr. (Eds.), *Life-span development and behavior* (Vol. 2). New York: Academic Press, 1979.

Riegel, K. F. Time and change in the development of the individual and society. In H. W. Reese (Ed.), *Advances in child development and behavior* (Vol. 7). New York: Academic Press, 1972.

Riegel, K. F. Developmental psychology and society: Some historical and ethical considerations. In J. R. Nesselroade & H. W. Reese (Eds.), *Life-span developmental psychology: Methodological issues.* New York: Academic Press, 1973.

Riegel, K. F. The dialectics of human development. *American Psychologist,* 1976, *31,* 689–700. (a)

Riegel, K. F. From traits and equilibrium toward developmental dialectics. In W. J. Arnold & J. K. Cole (Eds.), *Nebraska symposium on motivation* (Vol. 24). Lincoln: Univ. of Nebraska Press, 1976. (b)

Riegel, K. F., & Meacham, J. A. (Eds.). *The developing individual in a changing world.* Chicago, Illinois: Aldine, 1976.

Riegel, K. F., & Rosenwald, G. C. (Eds.). *Structure and function: Developmental and historical aspects.* New York: Wiley, 1975.

Riley, M. W. Age strata in social systems. In R. Binstock & E. Shanas (Eds.), *Handbook of aging and the social sciences.* New York: Van Nostrand-Reinhold, 1976.

Riley, M. W. (Ed.). *Aging from birth to death.* Boulder, Colorado: Westview Press, 1979.

Riley, M. W., Johnson, W., & Foner, A. (Eds.). *A sociology of age stratification.* Aging and society, vol. 3. New York: Russell Sage Foundation, 1972.

Rogosa, D. R. *Time and time again: Some analysis problems in longitudinal research.* Chicago, Illinois: Univ. of Chicago Press, 1978.

Rogosa, D. R. & Ambron, S. R. *Analyzing reciprocal effects in child development: Applications to attachment.* Paper presented at the Western Psychological Association Convention, Los Angeles, California, April 1976.

Rogosa, D. R., Webb, N., & Radin, N. *An application of causal models to data on cognitive development in lower-class children.* Unpublished manuscript, Univ. of Chicago, 1978.

Rosow, I. What is a cohort and why? *Human Development,* 1978, *21,* 65-75.

Roy, J. Step-down procedure in multivariate analysis. *Annals of Mathematical Statistics,* 1958, *29,* 1,177-1,187.

Roy, S. N. *Some aspects of multivariate analysis.* New York: Wiley, 1957.

Roy, S. N., & Bargmann, R. E. Tests of mutiple independence and the associated confidence bounds. *Annals of Mathematical Statistics,* 1958, *29,* 491-503.

Rubin, D. B. Characterizing the estimation of parameters in incomplete data problems. *Journal of the American Statistical Association,* 1974, *69,* 467-474.

Rudinger, G. Methoden der Längsschnittforschung. *Zeitschrift für Gerontologie,* 1972, *5,* 397-423.

Rudinger, G. Die Bedeutung von Längsschnitt- und Querschnittsuntersuchungen für die Messung intra- und interindividueller Differenzen. In U. Lehr & F. Weinert (Eds.), *Entwicklung und Persönlichkeit: Festschrift für Hans Thomae.* Stuttgart: Kohlhammer, 1975.

Rychlak, J. R. The multiple meanings of dialectic. In J. R. Rychlak (Ed.), *Dialectic: Humanistic rationale for behavior and development.* New York: Karger, 1976.

Ryder, N. B. The cohort as a concept in the study of social change. *American Sociological Review,* 1965, *30,* 843-861.

Sackett, G. P. The lag sequential analysis of contingency and cyclicity in behavioral interaction research. In J. Osofsky (Ed.), *Handbook of infant development.* New York: Wiley, 1977.

Samejima, F. Estimation of latent ability using a response pattern of graded scores. *Psychometrika, Supplements* Monograph No. 18, 1969.

Scammon, R. E. The first seriation study of human growth. *American Journal of Physical Anthropology,* 1927, *10,* 329-336.

Scarr, S., & Weinberg, R. A. Influence of "family background" on intellectual attainment. *American Sociological Review,* 1978, *5,* 674-692.

Schaie, K. W. *Examiner manual for the Test of Behavioral Rigidity.* Palo Alto, California: Consulting Psychologists Press, 1960.

Schaie, K. W. A general model for the study of development problems. *Psychological Bulletin,* 1965, *64,* 92-107.

Schaie, K. W. A reinterpretation of age-related changes in cognitive structure and functioning. In L. R. Goulet & P. B. Baltes (Eds.), *Life-span developmental psychology: Research and theory.* New York: Academic Press, 1970.

Schaie, K. W. Can the longitudinal method be applied to the study of psychological development? In F. J. Monks, W. W. Hartup, & J. de Wit (Eds.), *Determinants of behavioral development.* New York: Academic Press, 1972.

Schaie, K. W. Methodological problems in descriptive developmental research on adulthood and aging. In J. R. Nesselroade & H. W. Reese (Eds.), *Life-span developmental psychology: Methodological issues.* New York: Academic Press, 1973.

Schaie, K. W. Quasi-experimental research designs in the psychology of aging. In J. E. Birren & K. W. Schaie (Eds.), *Handbook of the psychology of aging.* New York: Van Nostrand-Reinhold, 1977.

Schaie, K. W. The primary mental abilities in adulthood: An exploration in the development of psychometric intelligence. In P. B. Baltes & O. G. Brim, Jr. (Eds.), *Life-span development and behavior* (Vol. 2). New York: Academic Press, 1979.

Schaie, K. W., & Baltes, P. B. On sequential strategies in developmental research: Description or explanation? *Human Development,* 1975, *18,* 384–390.

Schaie, K. W., Labouvie, G. V., & Buech, B. V. Generational and cohort-specific differences in adult cognitive functioning: A fourteen-year study of independent samples. *Developmental Psychology,* 1973, *9,* 151–166.

Schaie, K. W., & Parham, I. A. Cohort-sequential analyses of adult intellectual development. *Developmental Psychology,* 1977, *13,* 649–653.

Schaie, K. W., & Strother, C. R. The effects of time and cohort differences on the interpretation of age changes in cognitive behavior. *Multivariate Behavioral Research,* 1968, *3,* 259–294.

Shirley, M. M. *The first two years: Personality manifestations* (Vol. 1). Minneapolis: Univ. of Minnesota Press, 1933.

Shock, N. W. Growth curves. In S. S. Stevens (Ed.), *Handbook of experimental psychology.* New York: Wiley, 1951.

Shontz, F. C. Single-organism designs. In P. M. Bentler, D. J. Lettieri, & G. A. Austin (Eds.), *Data analysis strategies and designs for substance abuse research* (Nat. Inst. on Drug Abuse, Research Issues Series, Vol. 13). Washington, D.C.: U.S. Government Printing Office. 1976.

Sidman, M. *Tactics of scientific research: Evaluating experimental data in psychology.* New York: Basic Books, 1960.

Silvey, S. D. *Statistical inference.* Middlesex: Penguin Books, 1970.

Simon, H. Spurious correlations: A causal interpretation. *Journal of the American Statistical Association,* 1954, *49,* 467–479.

Singer, B., & Spilerman, S. Social mobility models for heterogeneous populations. In H. Costner (Ed.), *Sociological methodology 1973-74.* San Francisco, California: Jossey-Bass, 1974.

Singer, B., & Spilerman, S. The representation of social processes by Markov models. *American Journal of Sociology,* 1976, *82,* 1–54.

Sörbom, D. A general method for studying differences in factor means and factor structure between groups. *British Journal of Mathematical & Statistical Psychology,* 1974, *27,* 229–239.

Sörbom, D. Detection of correlated errors in longitudinal data. *British Journal of Mathematical & Statistical Psychology,* 1975, *28,* 138–151.

Sörbom, D. An alternative to the methodology for analysis of covariance. *Psychometrika,* 1978, *43,* 381–396.

Sörbom, D., & Jöreskog, K. G. *Confirmatory factory analysis with model modification.* Chicago, Illinois: Int. Educational Services 1976.

Spilerman, S. The analysis of mobility processes by the introduction of independent variables into a Markov chain. *American Sociological Review,* 1972, *37,* 277–294. (a)

Spilerman, S. Extensions of the mover-stayer model. *American Journal of Sociology,* 1972, *78,* 599–626. (b)

Steel, R. G. D., & Torrie, J. H. *Principles and procedures of statistics.* New York: McGraw-Hill, 1960.

Stern, W. Über Aufgabe und Anlage der Psychographie. *Zeitschrift für Angewandte Psychologie und Psychologische Sammelforschung,* 1910, *3,* 166–190.

Summers, G. F., Hough, R. L., Scott, J. T., & Folse, C. L. *Before industrialization: A rural social system base study.* (Bulletin No. 736.) Urbana: Univ. of Illinois, Illinois Agricultural Experiment Station, 1969.

Suppes, P. Facts and fantasies of education. In M. C. Wittrock (Ed.), *Changing education: Alternatives from educational research.* Englewood Cliffs, New Jersey: Prentice-Hall, 1973.

Suppes, P. The place of theory in educational research. *Educational Researcher,* 1974, *3,* 3–10.

Süssmilch, J. P. *Die göttliche Ordnung in den Veränderungen des menschlichen Geschlechtes, aus der Geburt, dem Tod und der Fortpflanzung desselben erwiesen.* Berlin: Realschulbuchhandlung, 1741.

Sutton-Smith, B. Developmental laws and the experimentalist's ontology. *Merrill-Palmer Quarterly,* 1970, *16,* 253–259.

Taine, H. Note sur l'acquisition du langage chez les enfants et dans l'espace humaine. *Revue Philosophique,* 1876, *1,* 3–23. [Translated in *Mind,* 1877, 2, 252–257.]

Tetens, J. N. *Philosophische Versuche über die menschliche Natur und ihre Entwicklung.* Leipzig: Weidmanns Erben und Reich, 1777.

Thissen, D. M. *Incorporating item response latencies in latent trait estimation.* Unpublished doctoral dissertation, Univ. of Chicago, 1976.

Thissen, D. M., Bock, R. D., Wainer, H., & Roche, A. F. Individual growth in stature: A comparison of four growth studies in the U.S.A. *Annals of Human Biology,* 1976, *3,* 529–542.

Thomae, H. (Ed.). *Entwicklungspsychologie.* Göttingen: Hogrefe, 1959. (a)

Thomae, H. Forschungsmethoden der Entwicklungspsychologie. In H. Thomae (Ed.), *Entwicklungspsychologie.* Göttingen: Hogrefe, 1959. (b)

Thomae, H. The concept of development and life-span developmental psychology. In P. B. Baltes & O. G. Brim (Eds.), *Life-span development and behavior* (Vol. 2). New York: Academic Press, 1979.

Thomas, E. A. C., & Martin, J. A. Analyses of parent-infant interaction. *Psychological Review,* 1976, *83,* 141–156.

Thorndike, R. L. Intellectual status and intellectual growth. *Journal of Educational Psychology,* 1966, *57,* 121–127.

Thurstone, L. L., & Thurstone, T. G. *Examiner manual for the SRA Primary Mental Abilities Test.* Chicago, Illinois: Science Research Associates, 1949.

Thurstone, L. L., & Thurstone, T. G. *SRA Primary Mental Abilities.* Chicago, Illinois: Univ. of Chicago Press, 1962.

Tiedemann, D. Beobachtungen über die Entwicklung der Seelenfähigkeit bei Kindern. *Hessische Beiträge zur Gelehrsamkeit und Kunst,* 1787, *2* (2–3, Whole No. 6–7).

Timm, N. H. *Multivariate analysis with applications in education and psychology.* Monterey, California: Brooks/Cole, 1975.

Torgerson, W. S. *Theory and methods of scaling.* New York: Wiley, 1958.

Trawinski, I. M., & Bargmann, R. E. Maximum likelihood estimation with incomplete multivariate data. *Annals of Mathematical Statistics,* 1964, *35,* 647–658.

Tubbs, J. D., Lewis, T. O., & Duran, B. S. A note on the analysis of MANOVA model and its applications to growth curves. *Communications in Statistics,* 1975, *4,* 643–653.

Tuddenham, R. D., & Snyder, M. M. *Physical growth of boys and girls from birth to eighteen years.* Berkeley: Univ. of California Press, 1954.

Tukey, J. Causation, regression, and path analysis. In O. Kempthorne (Ed.), *Statistics and mathematics in biology.* Ames: Iowa State Univ. Press, 1954.

Underwood, B. J. Individual differences as a crucible in theory construction. *American Psychologist,* 1975, *30,* 128–134.

Urban, H. B. The concept of development from a systems perspective. In P. B. Baltes (Ed.), *Life-span development and behavior* (Vol. 1). New York: Academic Press, 1978.

Urban, H. B., & Lago, D. Life history antecedents in psychiatric disorders of the aging. In P. B. Baltes (Ed.), Life-span models of psychological aging: A white elephant? *Gerontologist,* 1973, *13,* 502–508.

Van den Daele, L. D. Qualitative models in developmental analysis. *Developmental Psychology,* 1969, *1,* 303–310.

van't Hof, M. A., Prahl-Andersen, B., & Kowalski, C. J. A model for the study of developmental processes in dental research. *Journal of Dental Research,* 1976, *55,* 359–366.

van't Hof, M. A., Roede, M. J., & Kowalski, C. J. A mixed longitudinal data analysis model. *Human Biology,* 1977, *49,* 165–179.

Wald, A. The fitting of straight lines if both variables are subject to error. *Annals of Mathematical Statistics,* 1940, *11,* 284–300.

Wald, A. Tests of statistical hypotheses concerning general parameters when the number of observations is large. *Transactions of the American Mathematical Society,* 1943, *54,* 426–482.

Walker, H. M., & Lev, J. *Statistical inference.* New York: Holt, 1953.

Wall, W. D., & Williams, H. L. *Longitudinal studies and the social sciences.* London: Heinemann, 1970.

Wallis, W. A., & Roberts, H. V. *Statistics: A new approach.* Glencoe, Illinois: Free Press, 1956.

Wampler, R. H. A report on the accuracy of some widely used least squares computer programs. *Journal of the American Statistical Association,* 1970, *65,* 549–565.

Weinbach, A. P. The human growth curve II: Birth to puberty. *Growth,* 1941, *5,* 235–247.

Weinraub, M., & Lewis, M. The determinants of children's responses to separation. *Monographs of the Society for Research in Child Development,* 1977, *42,* (Serial No. 172).

Weisz, J. R. Transcontextual validity in developmental research. *Child Development,* 1978, *49,* 1–12.

Welford, A. T. Méthode longitudinale et transversale dans les recherches sur le vieillissement. In Colloques Internationaux du Centre de la Recherche Scientifique (Ed.), *Le vieillissement des fonctions psychologiques et psycho-physiologiques.* Paris: Centre National, 1961.

Werner, H. The concept of development from a comparative and organismic point of view. In D. B. Harris (Ed.), *The concept of development.* Minneapolis: Univ. of Minnesota Press, 1957.

Werts, C. E., Jöreskog, K. G., & Linn, R. L. Comment on "The estimation of measurement error in panel data." *American Sociological Review,* 1971, *36,* 110–113.

Werts, C. E., Linn, R. L., & Jöreskog, K. G. A simplex model for analyzing academic growth. *Educational and Psychological Measurement,* 1977, *37,* 745–756.

Wheaton, B., Muthén, B., Alwin, D. F., & Summers, G. F. Assessing reliability and stability in panel models. In D. R. Heise (Ed.), *Sociological methodology, 1977.* San Francisco, California: Jossey-Bass, 1977.

Wiley, D. E., & Harnischfeger, A. *Post hoc, ergo propter hoc. Problems in the attribution of change.* (Report No. 7). Chicago: Univ. of Chicago, 1973.

Wiley, D. E., & Hornik, R. *Measurement error and the analysis of panel data.* (Report No. 5) Chicago, Illinois: Univ. of Chicago, Studies of Educative Processes, 1973.

Wiley, D. E., & Wiley, J. A. The estimation of measurement error in panel data. *American Sociological Review,* 1970, *35,* 112–117.

Willems, E. P. Behavioral ecology and experimental analysis: Courtship is not enough. In J. R. Nesselroade & H. W. Reese (Eds.), *Life-span developmental psychology: Methodological issues.* New York: Academic Press, 1973.

Winer, B. J. *Statistical principles in experimental design.* New York: McGraw-Hill, 1962.

Winer, B. J. *Statistical principles in experimental design* (2nd ed.). New York: McGraw-Hill, 1971.

Wishart, J. Growth rate determinations in nutrition studies with the bacon pig, and their analysis. *Biometrika,* 1938, *30,* 16–28.

Wishart, J. Statistical treatment of animal experiments. *Journal of the Royal Statistical Society* (Suppl. No. 6), 1939, 1–22.

Wohlwill, J. F. The age variable in psychological research. *Psychological Review,* 1970, *77,* 49–64. (a)

Wohlwill, J. F. Methodology and research strategy in the study of developmental change. In L. R. Goulet and P. B. Baltes (Eds.), *Life-span developmental psychology: Research and theory.* New York: Academic Press, 1970. (b)

Wohlwill, J. F. *The study of behavioral development.* New York: Academic Press, 1973.

Wold, H. Causal inference from observational data: A review of ends and means. *Journal of the Royal Statistical Society* (Series A), 1956, *119,* 28–61.

Woodrow, H. Quotidian variability. *Psychological Review,* 1932, *39,* 245–256.

Zazzo, R. Diversité, realité et mirages de la méthode longitudinale. *Enfance,* 1967, *20,* 131–136.

Author Index

Numbers in italics refer to the pages on which the complete references are listed.

Subject Index